JACQUES PÉPIN'S TABLE

JACQUES PÉPIN'S TABLE

THE COMPLETE *TODAY'S GOURMET*

WRITTEN AND ILLUSTRATED BY JACQUES PÉPIN

PHOTOGRAPHS BY PENINA • DESIGNED BY BARBARA MARKS

First paperback edition published 2003 by Bay Books

Bay Books is an imprint of BAY/SOMA Publishing, Inc.,
444 De Haro Street, No. 130, San Francisco, CA 94107.

Publisher: James Connolly
Editorial Director: Pamela Byers
Production Coordinator: Zipporah W. Collins
Art Director and Designer: Barbara Marks
Photographer: Penina
Photography Food and Prop Stylists: Heidi Gintner, Bernie Schimbke
Photography Chefs: Carl Abbott, Brian Miller
Assistants to Jacques Pépin: Norma Galehouse, Tina Salter
Copyeditors: Barbara Fuller, Zipporah W. Collins
Nutritional Consultant: Carol Ceresa
Illustrations by Jacques Pépin

Photography props provided by:
Biordi Art Imports, Botticelli, Bourgeat USA, Crate & Barrel, Domestications Catalog, Sandra Griswold, Limoges, Macy's California, Pier 1 Imports, Pierre Deux, Pottery Barn, Saint-Louis Cristal—Hermès Art de la Table, Sakura, Inc., Signature China, Tag, Williams-Sonoma

Photography food provided by:
Allied SYSCO, BiRite Foodservice Distributors, California Crayfish, Inc., East Coast Exotics, Inc., Greenleaf Produce Company, Marin County Farmers Market, Modesto Food Distributors, C. J. Olson Cherries, Rapelli of California, Royal Hawaiian Seafood, United Meat Company, Inc., The Wine Club.

Library of Congress Cataloging-in-Publication Data
Pépin, Jacques.
Jacques Pépin's table : the complete Today's gourmet / written and illustrated by Jacques Pépin.
p. cm.
Based on author's Public Television series.
Includes index.
ISBN 0-912333-19-7
1. Cookery. 2. Menus. 3. Today's gourmet (Television program).
I. Today's gourmet (Television program). II. Title.
TX714.P459 1995
614.5—dc20 9524062
CIP

ISBN 0-912333-19-7 (Hardcover)
ISBN 1-57959-525-1 (Paperback)
Pinted in China

10 9 8 7 6 5 4 3 2 1

Distributed to the trade by Publishers Group West

to my television friends :

may you enjoy these recipes as
much as I enjoyed cooking them
for you on "today's Gourmet."

Contents

Main Courses 161

Brunch & Lunch Dishes 453

Breads & Basics 465

Health Notes 483

Introduction

Jacques Pépin's Table is the compilation of all the recipes I demonstrated on the three seasons of my PBS-TV series, *Today's Gourmet.* First aired in 1991, the series has been an important part of my life for the past five years, and I am pleased that the contents of the shows are now together in this one volume—seventy-eight menus and 304 recipes! The recipes are organized here into chapters according to the course in which the dish would usually be served.

Jacques Pépin's Table reflects my style of life and the importance I attach to food, which is tightly interwoven into the context of my relationships with both family and friends. Food is the common denominator that brings people together in my house, and this is evidenced in the collection of recipes that follows.

When I recall the food that we used to serve at Le Pavillon in New York when I first came to the United States thirty-five years ago, I realize how much cooking in general has changed and improved since then, especially in the last twenty years or so.

I know that my cooking has changed a great deal over the past two decades. Probably in response to social changes that have made all our lives much busier, my cooking—and that of most other chefs—has become simpler, healthier, and more in tune with nature than it used to be. But, as often occurs in revolutions like the one we've experienced lately in the food world, a good idea can be carried to extremes. Some chefs, cookbook authors, and food editors are so consumed now with the health aspects of food that counting calories and determining fat content have become more important than the taste of the dish.

My objective in *Today's Gourmet* was to introduce a commonsense cuisine, one that demonstrated a rational approach to cooking. The series, and now this book, promote a sensitive and sensible way to cook, a cooking style that exhibits elegance and joy while emphasizing aspects of health in a reasonable way.

Health concerns me greatly, and the recipes in the book illustrate this. My approach to health includes a diverse diet with more fiber and less saturated fat, more fish and shellfish, smaller portions of well-trimmed meat, and vegetables cooked in a manner that preserves their vitamins and nutrients.

Although this book is not intended to be a low-calorie, low-fat, low-sodium, or low-cholesterol manual, its recipes reflect how important I think it is to moderate our intake of these nutritional components. Keep in mind, however, that I am a cook, not a doctor. I am not a guru of macrobiotic food,

ON THE RELATIONSHIP OF GASTRONOMY TO CULTURE

"THERE IS NO ASPECT OF SOCIAL STUDIES, IN MY OPINION, THAT IS NOT TOUCHED BY FOOD. IF YOU ARE STUDYING RELIGION, YOU CAN TALK ABOUT THE FOOD TABOOS IN THE BIBLE. IN LITERATURE, YOU CAN DISCUSS THE WEDDING FEAST IN *MADAME BOVARY* OR PROUST'S MADELEINES. FOOD IS COMMUNICATION. IF YOU DO A BUFFET WITH BELUGA CAVIAR AND DOM PERIGNON, YOU'RE SENDING A DIFFERENT MESSAGE THAN IF YOU OFFER MEATBALLS WITH JUG WINE, YOU KNOW? THEY'RE BOTH GOOD MESSAGES, BUT THEY'RE DIFFERENT. YOU CANNOT DISASSOCIATE FOOD FROM SOCIAL STUDIES."

insisting on the wholesomeness of grains and fiber, nor have I assumed the role of a nutritionist, advising people on what they should or should not eat. Eating, for me, has always meant enjoyment and sharing, never prohibitions.

In a reflection of life, some of the menus are more concerned with health than others. When we join with friends and family on holidays and other special occasions, we sometimes don't count calories—we indulge. At other times we are more careful. I don't banish all butter, cream, and other types of fat from my recipes. Instead, I use small amounts of the best possible quality of these, adding them at just the right moment to maximize the flavor. Essentially this is modern cooking—a blend of substance and sophistication, contemporary food that appeals to everyone.

Some people are terrified of one ingredient or another. If they read something about salt, they go to the extreme and totally eliminate it. When I'm working in the kitchen at the French Culinary Institute, for instance, and I put a little salt on something, students turn to me, very righteously: "You put salt on it? Are you trying to kill us?" I tell them, "If you want to cook, cook well. I think I am careful about fat and salt, but the first thing for me is palatability. If it doesn't taste good, I have no use for it."

The kind of cooking I do here avoids gimmicks and trends; rather, it satisfies the tastes of a discriminating audience while meeting their nutritional needs in a nonrestrictive way. I want a cuisine that appeals to the epicurean and the jogger as well as the busy home cook and the single professional. Some of the recipes are simple, lending themselves to family meals; others, containing costlier ingredients, are more elaborate, better suited to parties.

The concerns of modern, well-educated eaters parallel those of modern, well-educated chefs and go beyond how food tastes and how it is presented. Today's astute food buyer wants produce that is not only fresh but also free of chemicals. The quality of the products in our diet directly affects the quality of our health and the health of our families. We have to look after our environment; if the chickens we eat feed on grass and natural grains in an area free of pesticides and insecticides, their quality and the quality of the eggs they produce will be substantially better. Consequently, I advocate the use of organic products whenever possible.

Each of the recipes in this book was demonstrated as part of a menu on one of the television shows, and I have reproduced all of these menus here. Understand that the dishes were grouped into menus because of considerations that were important at the time the shows were taped—to illustrate a seasonal theme, for example, or to demonstrate a certain cooking style—so use the groupings as only a guide in your meal planning. Feel free to pick one

ON THE IMPORTANCE OF TECHNIQUE

"THERE'S SOMETHING TO BE SAID FOR REPETITION. YOU LEARN IN A DEEPER WAY, IN A DIFFERENT WAY. IT GIVES YOU SPEED AND KNOWLEDGE, AND YOU UNDERSTAND THE FOOD BETTER AND MORE COMPLETELY. THERE ARE YOUNG CHEFS TODAY WHO CAN DO A GREAT MOUSSELINE OF SCALLOPS, BUT DON'T KNOW HOW TO WASH SPINACH OR POACH AN EGG. THIS IS WRONG. YOU HAVE TO MASTER THE TECHNIQUES BEFORE YOU CAN START THINKING AND CREATING WITH YOUR HEAD. YOU HAVE TO FREE YOUR HANDS. IT'S THE SAME IN PAINTING, YOU KNOW? UNLESS YOUR HAND IS DEFT, IT DOESN'T WORK. CRAFTSMANSHIP COMES FIRST."

or two dishes from one menu and combine them with dishes from another menu according to your food preferences, the time of year, the money you wish to spend, and the time you can devote to meal preparation.

Since it is in the French tradition to have a glass of wine with most meals, I have included at least one wine suggestion—sometimes white, sometimes red, sometimes champagne or sweet dessert wine—with each menu. My choices aren't limited to the wines of France and the United States; because there are good wines everywhere, many areas of the world are represented.

Although my selections are specific—including the names of particular vineyards and/or regions where the wines are made—I don't give vintages (specific years of wine production) in this book. In general, it is difficult to obtain older vintages, so listings of them become obsolete very quickly. My wine choices are just suggestions. You can serve other wines instead that you find appealing or, if wine is not compatible with your way of life, eliminate it entirely.

In addition to providing nutritional profiles for individual dishes, I have included the total calorie counts for each menu, because many people have requested this information. Keep in mind, however, that wine and bread are not included in this breakdown.

All in all, I look on nutritional profiles—whether for individual recipes or entire meals—as merely guidelines, not absolutes. Nutritional analyses are compiled from data on the raw ingredients used in a dish and may not take into account preparation techniques employed by the chef that alter the values. So I try to use nutritional data sensibly, not rigidly.

To date, I have written fifteen cookbooks. My early books, *La Méthode* and *La Technique,* were intended as practical guides to the fundamental skills of cooking. These books had some recipes, but they were provided primarily as examples to help readers understand and carry out cooking techniques. *The Art of Cooking* also taught technique but did so within the context of many more recipes and step-by-step color photographs to illustrate their preparation. More recently, in *Cuisine Economique,* I have concentrated on creating recipes that would help people stretch their food dollars, and, in *The Short-Cut Cook,* I have provided streamlined cooking techniques as part of quick, easy recipes for people on the go. The recipes in my latest book, *Jacques Pépin's Simple and Healthy Cooking,* illustrate the importance of healthy eating.

Today's Gourmet has always encapsulated, for me, the themes of all my books. In the television series, and now in *Jacques Pépin's Table: The Complete Today's Gourmet,* I have endeavored to "do it all," so to speak, providing

ON TRAINING A CHILD'S PALATE

"I'M OFTEN INVITED TO DINNER AT THE HOMES OF PEOPLE WHO HAVE CHILDREN, AND MY HOSTS WILL SAY, 'WELL, THE KIDS ARE GOING TO EAT FIRST.' I'M SERVED A ROAST OF VEAL WITH ARTICHOKES, AND THE KIDS HAVE PIZZA OR A HOT DOG. THAT'S ABSOLUTELY WRONG. YOU CANNOT CONDITION A CHILD AROUND FOUR DISHES—PIZZA, HOT DOGS, FRIED CHICKEN, HAMBURGERS—FOR TWELVE TO FOURTEEN YEARS AND THEN, AT AGE FOURTEEN, SAY, 'OH! NOW THE WHOLE THING CHANGES. NOW YOU'VE GOT TO SIT AT THE TABLE AND EAT OUR FOOD.' THEY DON'T LIKE IT. OF COURSE THEY DON'T LIKE IT!"

ON THE POWER OF FOOD MEMORIES

"WHAT ARE MEMORIES MADE OF? OF FAMILY, AND OF DINNERS, AND OF TASTES. I KNOW THE FOOD MY MOTHER PREPARED DURING THE WAR WAS NOTHING THAT WE WOULD EAT NOW. BUT I STILL REMEMBER THE TASTES, AND THEY MEAN SOMETHING TO ME. THE FOOD YOU HAVE AT HOME GROWS ON YOU AND BECOMES MORE IMPORTANT THAN SIMPLY THE FOOD ITSELF. IT BECOMES ASSOCIATED WITH ALL PARTS OF YOUR LIFE IN A VERY DEEP WAY, PART OF YOUR ROOTS, YOUR INNER SELF."

recipes that are delicious and, in large part, quick to prepare, uncomplicated, inexpensive, and healthy. In addition, the medium of television has enabled me to teach the cooking techniques that are used consistently as part of recipes—how to defat a stock, how to trim a piece of meat properly, how to prepare artichoke bottoms, and how to make crêpes, for example. Mastering techniques like these saves time and effort, which helps make cooking more enjoyable.

You should have a good time in the kitchen and then emerge from it with flavorful, wholesome, attractive dishes that you can share and enjoy with family and friends. My cuisine is not a complicated or contrived mix of esoteric ingredients, and it is not intended for an elite group of people. It is for everyone.

Finally, I want to show the importance of togetherness, conviviality, and *joie de vivre* in the kitchen. Cooking should be fun—nothing compares to the enjoyment of sharing food while spending time with family and friends! Most of all, I hope the knowledge readers gain from *Jacques Pépin's Table* will make their lives richer, healthier, and more enjoyable.

Acknowledgments

The production of *Today's Gourmet* was an exciting experience that demanded a great deal of teamwork on the part of many capable people. As we celebrate the success of this PBS-TV series by bringing together in *Jacques Pépin's Table* the 304 recipes I demonstrated on the 78 shows, I want to thank everyone associated with all aspects of this five-year project for their help and support.

Although it is impossible to name everyone involved, I especially want to thank *Peter Stein* and *Marjorie Poore,* executive producers of the series, who provided the vision and drive to make the project a reality; *Peggy Lee Scott* and *Linda Brandt,* my producers, for amiably overseeing every detail of the shows; *Tina Salter* and *Susie Heller,* my associate producers, who created the perfect bond between the back kitchen and the set, and understood me so well that they could perfectly "block" my movements; *June Ouellette,* staff associate producer, who cheerfully and efficiently managed all the nitty-gritty details behind the scenes; *Katherine Russell,* director, and *Linda Giannecchini,* assistant director, for beautiful close-ups of the food and for following all my moves; *Mindy Hall* and *Leslee Newcomb,* makeup artists, who helped me "lose" all those years; *Katherine Zilavy,* assistant to the producer, whose great work on the computer produced clear instructions for us all; *Harry Betancourt, Brad Cochrane, Greg Overton,* and *Mike Ratusz,* the dedicated camera operators for their great collective "eye"; *Greg King,* who ably operated the remote camera and lit the set; *Margaret Clarke, Jean Tuckerman,* and *Jim Summers,* floor managers, for their professionalism and for giving me the proper cues on time; *Greg Swartz,* production manager, for my beautiful counter; *Joanne Sutro,* for her perseverance in marketing; and *Jolee Hoyt,* unit manager, for paying all the bills.

I am most grateful to the back kitchen staff, whose help was indispensable to the success of the three seasons of shows: *Carl Abbott* and *Dan Bowe,* capable and affable back kitchen supervisors, and their incredible teams, among them *Michelle Royston,* who took me marketing and ran countless errands; *Bernice Chuck Fong,* who happily helped where needed; *Mike Pleiss,* always so reliable; *Joseph Strebler,* for his great bread; and *Christine Swett, Dan Trudeau, Christine Wolf, Gwilym Fong, Mary Cramer, Josie Ingber, Travis Brady, Jeff Forman, Robin Margolin, Amy McKenzie,* and *Michael Pollock* for their excellent work and devotion.

I also want to thank *Bernie Schimbke, Ron Haake, Heidi Gintner, Lorraine Battle, Merilee Hague,* and *Ken Short,* food stylists and kitchen set designers extraordinaire; and *Carol Ceresa, Stephanie Turner,* and *Claire*

ON THE IMPORTANCE OF FAMILY MEALS

"I KNOW PEOPLE WHO PROBABLY HAVEN'T HAD A CONVERSATION WITH THEIR CHILDREN FOR YEARS, BECAUSE THE CHILDREN COME HOME, SAY, 'HI, DAD,' AND GO STRAIGHT TO THE REFRIGERATOR FOR A SANDWICH. THE DINNER TABLE SHOULD BE THE STAGE WHERE YOU TALK AT THE END OF THE DAY. THE CONVERSATION MAY NOT ALWAYS BE PLEASANT—MAYBE YOU HAVE AN ARGUMENT ABOUT WHAT HAPPENED IN SCHOOL—BUT IT IS A VERY NECESSARY THING THAT BRINGS THE FAMILY TOGETHER."

ON FOOD AND INTERACTION

"FOOD AND THE SHARING OF FOOD SUSTAIN HUMAN RELATIONSHIPS MORE THAN ANYTHING ELSE, INCLUDING SEX. IT'S AN EXTRAORDINARILY IMPORTANT PART OF THE FAMILY STRUCTURE AND THE COMMON DENOMINATOR THAT BRINGS PEOPLE TOGETHER IN A HOUSE—CERTAINLY IN MINE! MAYBE IT SOUNDS CORNY, BUT FOR ME, FOOD IS AN EXPRESSION OF LOVE, BECAUSE YOU ALWAYS COOK FOR 'THE OTHER'—WIFE, CHILD, LOVERS, FRIENDS. FOOD IS LIFE."

From an interview by Janet Fletcher, author, restaurant reviewer, and editor of American Wine and Food.

Bechtel, nutritional consultants, whose precise notes helped me to provide valuable health information to our audience.

I am most pleased to have had three very special people in my life join me on a few of the shows. Thanks to my daughter, *Claudine,* for cooking with me; my wife, *Gloria,* for finally agreeing to appear with me on camera and for supporting me through the years; and my good friend *Jean-Claude Szurdak,* who not only gave me a hand on one of the shows but helped out with the food behind the scenes as well.

For their fine work on this volume and the books that accompanied the series, I want to thank *Pamela Byers* and *Mark Powelson,* the publisher and the vice president for publishing, respectively, whose professionalism we all appreciated and found beneficial; *Zipporah Collins,* the production coordinator, for her flawless attention to detail; *Barbara Marks,* the book designer and art director, whose beautiful layout and sense of style I truly appreciate; *Penina,* the photographer, who made the food look great and also took complimentary photos of me; and, of course, *Norma Galehouse,* my long-time assistant, for her complete dedication and talent.

—JACQUES PÉPIN

JACQUES PÉPIN'S TABLE

MENUS

Menus

On the following pages I list the menus that were featured on my television series, Today's Gourmet with Jacques Pépin. *Any recipe grouping is arbitrary, influenced by such factors as market availability and personal food preferences.*

Use my menus merely as a point of departure. Reorganize as you wish, taking a recipe from one menu and adding it to another. Although there are only a few salad recipes in the book, you'll note that I have listed salads on most of my menus. We eat salads every day, and I recommend them for taste and balance in a diet. Bread and wine are also part of our daily fare. If you include them with your meals as well, remember to take into account the calories they add.

We don't eat desserts on a regular basis at my house, preferring to end our meals with fresh fruits. I have generally included dessert recipes here, however, to complete the menus and make them special enough for occasions when you entertain.

For readers who are interested, I supply the total calorie count for each menu. These counts do not include generic salads, fresh fruits, and breads for which recipes are not given in the book.

My Mother's Favorites

Garlic Soup 63

Veal Roast with Artichokes 270

Salad

Almond Cake with Mango Coulis 402

SUGGESTED WINE:

Mercurey (red)

This menu has a homey feeling. The garlic soup, containing potatoes and leeks, and the roast of veal, cooked in a dutch oven, with artichokes and lots of garlic, remind me of my youth in France. The almond cake dessert, originally called *pain de Gênes,* or "bread of Genoa," is usually very rich, calling for lots of egg yolks and butter. In my version, I reduce the number of calories in the cake by substituting a flavorful mango *coulis* for the traditional rich custard sauce.

Calories per serving in menu: 1,007

Mediterranean Flavors

Tuna Tartare on Marinated Cucumbers 133

Chicken and Seafood Paella 202

Salad

Calimyrna Figs in Spicy Port Sauce 392

SUGGESTED WINE:

Marques de Riscal (red)

The diverse flavors of the Mediterranean basin are reflected in this menu. I begin with tuna *tartare* served on a bed of marinated cucumbers, which suggests regions of Italy or southern France. Next comes a classic dish—in fact, one might call it the national dish of Spain—paella: saffron-flavored rice combined with pieces of hot sausage, pieces of chicken, an assortment of shellfish, and fresh vegetables. I conclude with figs poached in a spicy port sauce, a dessert that reminds me of Portugal with a touch of Italy thrown in, because, after all, I use Campari in the sauce.

Calories per serving in menu: 1,188

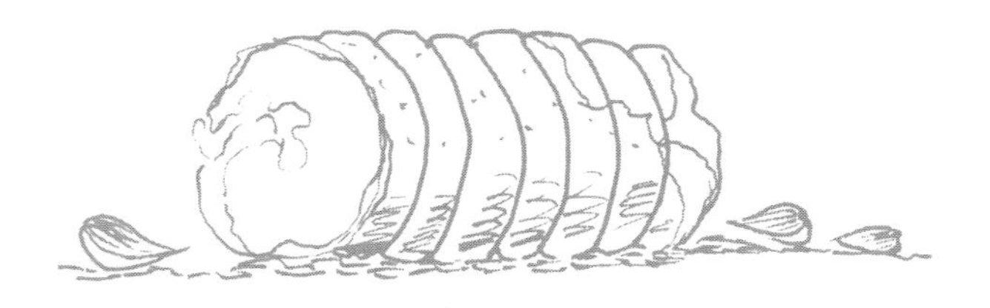

Nouvelle Cuisine

Potato Crêpes with Caviar 98

Grilled Chicken with Cabbage Anchoyade 208

Salad

Chocolate Soufflé Cake with Raspberry-Rum Sauce 440

SUGGESTED WINE:

Sauvignon Blanc, Casa Lapostolle

This menu captures the essence of nouvelle cuisine—fresh ingredients, quickly cooked light sauces, and interesting combinations of food with great visual appeal. As the first course, thick potato crêpes are garnished with sour cream, herbs, and two types of caviar. Grilled boneless, skinless chicken breasts are thinly sliced and served on a bed of shredded cabbage seasoned with anchovies, garlic, and olive oil as a main course. The meal ends with a deliciously light chocolate cake served with a concentrated raspberry-rum sauce.

Calories per serving in menu: 1,344

A Party Menu

Leeks with Tomato and Olive Oil 91

Smoked Pork Roast with Mustard-Honey Glaze 250

Braised Sour Cabbage 305

Salad

Strawberry Buttermilk Shortcakes 425

SUGGESTED WINE:

Zinfandel, Amador County

This menu is ideal for casual entertaining. The braised leeks with tomatoes are best served at room temperature, so they are perfect in a buffet setting. This is true, too, of the smoked pork shoulder roast with mustard-honey glaze; I place it on the buffet table along with a sharp knife and let guests help themselves. A bowl of braised cabbage and a simple salad are set out as side dishes. For dessert, strawberry shortcakes are always a hit. You can assemble the shortcakes in advance, or bring everything to the table and let guests serve themselves.

Calories per serving in menu: 940

Cooking Against the Clock

Hot Shrimp on Spinach 155

Grilled Savory Lamb Chops 256

Curried Bulgur with Currants 339

Tomatoes and Onion with Parsley Vinaigrette 297

Salpicon of Pineapple (Diced Pineapple) 411

Suggested Wine:

Merlot, St. Francis

If you cook in the following sequence, this interesting menu can be ready in half an hour. Begin by making the bulgur. While it cooks, prepare the pineapple, and let it macerate in the liqueur. Then grill the lamb chops, and as they cook, begin the first course by sautéing the damp greens. Arrange the greens on plates while the cooked chops rest in a warm oven. Prepare the tomato salad, then sauté the shrimp, and arrange it over the greens. Finally, arrange the lamb chops on individual plates, and serve with the bulgur and salad. Spoon the pineapple dessert into bowls for serving.

Calories per serving in menu: 760

Earthy Country Cooking

Gratin of Scallions 101

Ragout of Rabbit 239

Cornmeal au Gruyère 341

Salad

Fresh Fruit with Minted Apricot Fondue 435

Suggested Wine:

Fitou (red) from Corbières

This hearty menu begins with a gratin of scallions. Although made with half-and-half, it is still relatively low in fat. The delicious ragout of rabbit is typical of the country cooking of France, where rabbit sautéed dry, as I prepare it here, is a popular main dish. Another grain to give variety to your repertoire of complex carbohydrates is cornmeal, flavored in this version with Gruyère. A salad is next, followed by fresh fruit with a delightful apricot dipping sauce.

Calories per serving in menu: 1,123

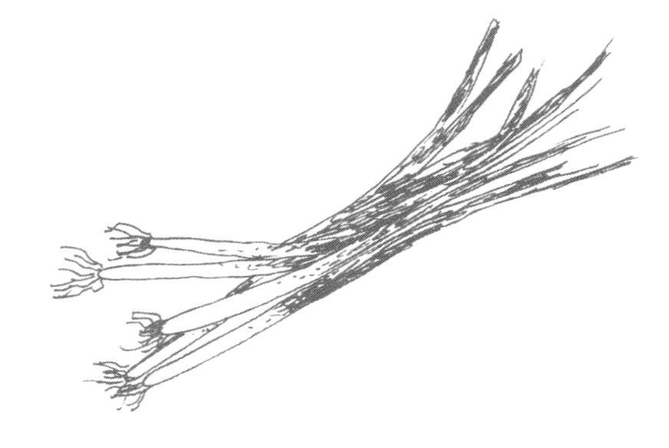

Bistro Cooking of New York

Sautéed Eggplant Rolls 86

Red Snapper in Potato Jackets 184

Salad

Baked Apple Tart 357

SUGGESTED WINE:

Chardonnay, Simi

Although a bit more trendy than most French bistro food, New York bistro food is similar. Young chefs everywhere—and especially in New York—are interested in a lighter, more imaginative cuisine than in the past, one that will satisfy not only the epicurean but also the average person who wants to eat flavorful food without feeling guilty. The eggplant rolls, served as a first course, contain an assortment of vegetables combined with cheese, raisins, and seasonings, and served atop vinaigrette tomatoes. As a main course, red snapper is cooked between layers of sliced potato. The potatoes become crisp while the fish remains moist. Following a salad, I serve my interpretation of a classic bistro dish, apple tart.

Calories per serving in menu: 1,105

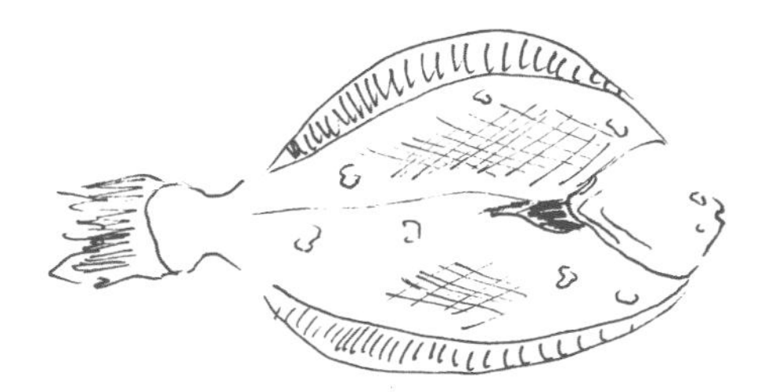

A Hearty Supper

Clam Croquettes 140

Braised Pork Cocotte 249

Pasta and Zucchini 336

Salad

Caramelized Apple Timbales 351

SUGGESTED WINE:

Ruffino (red) Reserve Ducale Gold

This is a meal to come home to on a cold night! Delicious clam croquettes are followed by a favorite of mine, meat and vegetables braised together until all their juices blend. Dried tomatoes, onions, garlic, and carrots add flavor to the cooking juices of the well-trimmed pork, and are good served with it. Pasta with zucchini sauce complements the main course. Next comes a salad, followed by the perfect dessert, caramelized apple timbales.

Calories per serving in menu: 1,021

The Healthy Gourmet

Braised Endive in Lemon Juice 88

Poule au Pot (Chicken Stew) 221

Salad

Grapes and Raisins in Lime Cookie Cones 395

Suggested Wine:

Beaujolais, Moulin-à-Vent

Here is a menu designed to be low in calories. In fact, total calories for this meal (not counting a salad) are about 700 per person, with less than 22 percent of these coming from fat. Braised with lemon juice, steamed endive makes a refreshing first course. Poached chicken is served as a main course, with an assortment of vegetables, concentrated broth, and baguette slices. After a salad, I offer dessert—a large, cone-shaped cookie filled with grapes and the little raisins known as dried currants.

Calories per serving in menu: 586

Potpourri Dinner

Beef Carpaccio 159

Catfish on Ratatouille 171

Salad

Hazelnut Parfait with Candied Violets 448

Suggested Wine:

Abymes (white) from Savoie

This menu is interesting because it combines dishes of a new style that has become popular in the last few years. Beef *carpaccio,* a reinterpretation of steak *tartare,* is great for supper or for an after-the-theater party. You can make it ahead, and it is always well received. Thick, fleshy catfish, served on a bed of fiber-rich ratatouille, is a very satisfying main course. A simple salad of mixed greens follows, and then comes dessert—a wonderful hazelnut parfait.

Calories per serving in menu: 1,130

Holiday Traditions

Sautéed Scallops with Snow Peas 151

Roasted Turkey with Mushroom Stuffing 228

Puree of Carrot with Ginger 307

Salad

Chocolate Mint Truffles 438

Candied Orange Rind 450

SUGGESTED WINE:

Red Côtes du Roussillon

In my home, we splurge a little over the holidays and expand our menu. Even so, at 889 calories per serving, this festive meal is conservative compared to most holiday fare. Garnished with snow peas and red pepper, the first course scallop dish is colorful and original. Next, I serve oven-roasted turkey with a dried-mushroom stuffing containing whole wheat bread, and a ginger-flavored carrot puree, which makes a delightful side dish. For dessert, two holiday treats—chocolate mint truffles and candied orange rind—provide a festive finish to this holiday menu.

Calories per serving in menu: 889

Big Taste on a Small Budget

Potage de Légumes au Vermicelle (Vegetable and Vermicelli Soup) 47

Saucisses au Chou (Sausages with Savoy Cabbage) on Lentils 244

Salad

Baked Pears with Figs 405

SUGGESTED WINE

Ruffino Labaio (white)

This menu emphasizes economy in the kitchen. I love to make vegetable soup; it takes only a few minutes and is a great vehicle for using leftover vegetables—something that I always have in my refrigerator. Here I finish the soup with pasta such as vermicelli. The main course consists of lean sausage wrapped in cabbage leaves, grilled, and served on a bed of lentils. For the finale, try this delicious fruit dessert that combines baked pears and figs.

Calories per serving in menu: 732

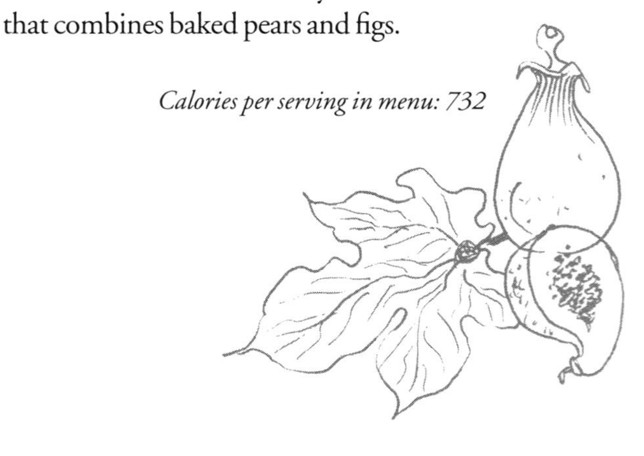

Cooking for the Family

Mushroom-Stuffed Potato Pancakes 97

Veal Chops with Mushrooms 267

Corn and Pepper Sauté 312

Salad

Chocolate and Fruit Nut Cups 437

Suggested Wine:

Goldstream Hills (white)

Because much of this meal can be prepared ahead, it is a great menu for the family to cook together on weekends. Older kids can help form the potato pancakes and fill them with the flavorful mushroom-olive mixture. Younger children can help with the dessert by pressing pieces of fresh and dried fruits, nuts, and seeds into small cups of melted chocolate. The quick and easy main course, lightly cooked veal chops, served here with a simple corn and red pepper sauté, is always a hit.

Calories per serving in menu: 760

Spring Elegance

Asparagus in Mustard Sauce 78

Spicy Beef Shell Roast 279

Carottes à la Ciboulette (Carrots with Chives) 306

Peas à la Française 318

Pistachio Floating Island
with Black Currant Sauce 383

Suggested Wine:

St. Joseph (red)

Celebrate spring with this elegant, well-balanced menu. The vegetables—peas, carrots, and asparagus—and the fresh strawberries, served in a deliciously light "floating island" dessert, provide fiber, complex carbohydrates, and vitamins. The well-trimmed beef roast, coated here with a mixture of dried herbs and black and cayenne peppers, is a good source of iron.

Calories per serving in menu: 826

Cooking for Friends

Steamed Cod on Tapenade 116

Poulet au Vin Rouge (Chicken with Red Wine) 218

Turnips and Mashed Potatoes 323

Salad

Blueberries with Brown Sugar 415

Suggested Wine:

Zinfandel Caymus

Cooking for friends is a great pleasure for me. One of my favorite menus begins with steamed cod on *tapenade,* the Provençal puree traditionally made with olives, capers, and anchovies. This is followed by *poulet au vin rouge.* A classic chicken dish, it is garnished with mushrooms, glazed shallots, and croutons, and is served with a garlic-flavored potato-and-turnip mixture. To conclude, I serve fresh blueberries topped with plain yogurt and a sprinkling of brown sugar. The sugar melts through the yogurt, sweetening it slightly and creating an attractive design.

Calories per serving in menu: 1,081

Country French/Belgian Menu

Braised Stuffed Artichokes 75

Moules Maison (Mussels Home-Style) 193

French Fries 327

Salad

Coffee Crème Caramel 444

Suggested Wine:

White Orvieto

The idea of combining mussels and fried potatoes actually comes from Belgium, but my "French" family really enjoys this combination, too. In Connecticut, where I live, mussels are plentiful and inexpensive in the summertime. When temperatures soar, we prefer to cook both the mussels and the French fries outdoors. Another family favorite, braised stuffed artichokes, is a nice side dish. For dessert, we enjoy a light version of traditional coffee crème caramel.

Calories per serving in menu: 1,067

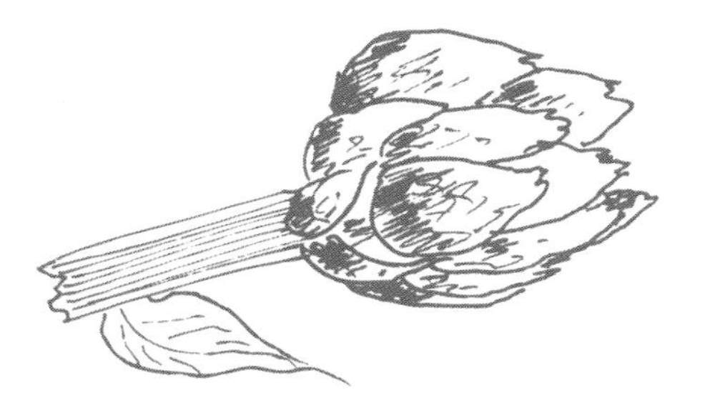

Pasta with Fresh Vegetable Sauce 111
Grilled Leg of Lamb 261
Cauliflower in Scallion Sauce 309
Salad
Cherry Bread Pudding 369

Suggested Wine:

Bordeaux St. Emilion

This flavorful menu combines various tastes, textures, and colors in an interesting way. For starters, fresh vegetable sauce over pasta is a healthy, high-fiber alternative to more common pasta sauces made with butter and cream. Next, a well-trimmed leg of lamb is marinated in a pungent sauce, then grilled and served with a scallion and cauliflower dish. For dessert, a cherry bread pudding flavored with almonds is baked in a gratin dish.

Calories per serving in menu: 1,136

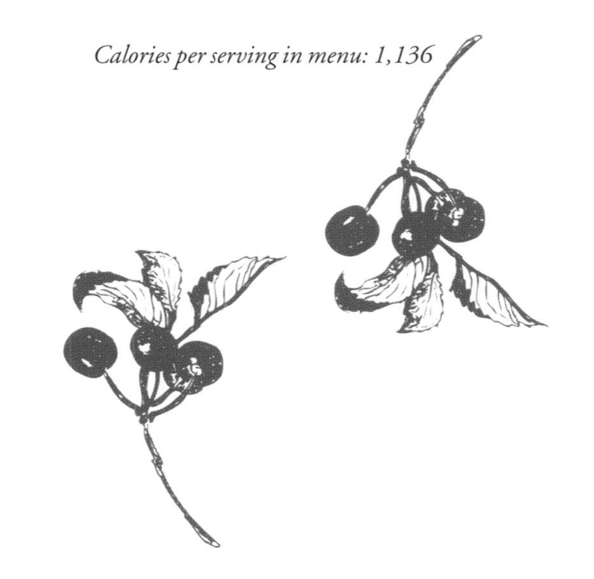

Oeufs Cocotte (Eggs in Ramekins) 456
Smoked Whitefish Molds 134
Oatmeal Leek Soup 49
Mushroom Omelet 454
Buttermilk Bread 474
Orange and Grapefruit Segments 399

Suggested Beverage:

Fruit Juice or Champagne, Moët et Chandon

In this menu, you will find many different recipes, some with variations. I have provided more types of dishes than you would actually want to serve for any one breakfast or brunch. Any of these recipes, though, will make a savory breakfast, a good alternative to one containing an abundance of sweets. Choose from three variations of the basic *oeufs cocotte,* a smoked whitefish mold, flavorful oatmeal leek soup, a classic mushroom omelet, hearty buttermilk bread, and a fruit dish combining grapefruit and orange segments.

Calories per serving in menu: 1,057
(not all dishes would be served in one menu)

Light and Leisurely

Sautéed Salmon on Greens 123

Chicken Legs with Wine and Yams 210

Salad

Baked Bananas in Lemon-Rum Sauce 368

Suggested Wine:

Dry Riesling Amity

Much of this elegant menu can be prepared ahead. The last-minute work—sautéing the salmon steaks, finishing the chicken dish, and cooking the bananas—can be done in an unhurried manner if you study the recipes carefully in advance and have an orderly plan for completing their final steps. The beautiful first course pairs salmon and spinach flavored with onion and tomatoes. The main dish, made with chicken legs, includes an assortment of vegetables, among them mushrooms, garlic, shallots, and yams. A salad follows, and this well-balanced meal ends with a dessert of baked bananas served with a zesty lemon sauce.

Calories per serving in menu: 1,004

Great Sandwiches

Breads 472—81

Roasted Eggplant Sandwiches 460

Olive and Tomato Toasts 457

James Beard's Onion Sandwiches 458

Pan Bagna 463

Smoked Salmon and Cucumber Sandwiches 461

Jam Sandwiches 426

Suggested Wine:

Pouilly Fuissé (white)

There is an endless variety of great-tasting sandwiches. With fillings that range from cold cuts to leftover meats, fish, or even vegetables, sandwiches can be as complex as the Provençal specialty, *pan bagna*—containing many vegetables, fish, and olives—or as simple as James Beard's onion sandwiches. They are also versatile, appropriate for serving at any meal, for snacks, at picnics, or on buffet tables. Good cooks know that the most important component of any sandwich is the bread. High-gluten bread doughs are easy to make in a food processor, and, depending on the grain and flour you use, adaptable enough to be formed into loaves of various sizes and shapes.

Calories per serving in menu: 1,939
(not all dishes would be served in one menu)

Classic and Chic

Trout Sauté Terry 132

Grilled Quail on Quinoa with Sunflower Seeds 237

Salad

Raspberry Granité 419

SUGGESTED WINE:

Chateau Simone (red) from Provence

In this menu, some classic recipes are updated—made chic—with the help of some unusual ingredients. Sautéed trout, a standard restaurant offering, is served here with a colorful sauce made from the pan drippings, to which are added mushrooms, tomato, oil-cured olives, and diced lemon. Another longtime favorite, grilled boneless quail, is served here with quinoa, a high-protein grain that is rapidly gaining in popularity. Sunflower seeds lend crunch to the quinoa, and dried currants give it some chewiness. Following a salad, the perfect finish to this meal is raspberry *granité,* a concentrated sherbet made with raspberry puree.

Calories per serving in menu: 1,185

Bistro Cooking of Lyon

Beans and Broccoli Rabe 80

Wine Merchant Steak 283

Pommes Persillades

(Potatoes with Parsley and Garlic) 322

Salad

Baked Apricots with Almonds 365

SUGGESTED WINE:

Barolo (red)

Bistro cooking is casual and sophisticated at the same time. The bistro setting is usually simple, while the food—although recognizable and familiar—is a bit more complex than meals you would prepare at home. I think that those little unpretentious restaurants called *bistrots* in Lyon serve the most authentic French cooking you can find in France. For the first course, I combine beans with broccoli rabe, a bitter-tasting member of the mustard green family. With the main steak dish, I serve sautéed potatoes, followed by a salad. I finish with a refreshing baked apricot dessert.

Calories per serving in menu: 873

Around-the-World Menu

Crab Cakes with Avocado Garnish 140

Irish Lamb Stew 254

Salad

Figs Vilamoura 391

Suggested Wine:

Merlot, Magaña Bodegas

This menu is diverse, composed of dishes from around the world that work well together. The crabmeat cakes come from the southern United States, although I've added an avocado sauce to give them an unusual twist. Irish lamb stew is a classic. I make it from either lamb shoulder or leg of lamb, and thicken the cooking juices with the trimmings of the vegetables I use as garnishes. Following a salad, I complete the meal with an interesting dessert of dried figs studded with fresh almonds, similar to those found in the markets of southern Portugal.

Calories per serving in menu: 882

Low-Cal Steamed Dinner

Salmon Pojarski 178

Pommes à l'Anglaise (Steamed Potatoes) 321

Broccoli Piquant 302

Salad

Oranges in Grand Marnier 400

Suggested Wine:

Trebbiano White

Weight watchers will like this special menu. Salmon is high in omega-3 fatty acids, which help to reduce blood cholesterol. Potatoes, containing complex carbohydrates high in potassium, have only 20 calories per ounce, while broccoli is loaded with vitamins C and A, potassium, and iron. The refreshing poached orange dessert contains vitamin C. I cook the salmon, potatoes, and broccoli in a three-tiered bamboo steamer in about half an hour, staggering the additions based on the cooking time required for each dish. I begin with the potatoes, steaming them in one tier for 15 minutes. Then I add a second tier, containing the broccoli, and steam for 5 more minutes. Finally, I add the salmon patties in the third tier, and steam for 6 to 7 minutes longer. Total steaming time is 26 to 27 minutes.

Calories per serving in menu: 582

The Frugal Kitchen

Split Pea Soup with Cracklings 50

Brown Rice Chicken Fricassee 217

Chicken in Tarragon Sauce 216

Salad

Fruit Medley

SUGGESTED WINE:

Rosso di Montalcino

The dishes featured here would not be served together. Instead, this "menu" exemplifies the concept of economy in the kitchen, demonstrating what can be done with different parts of a chicken. Three of the recipes are made with chicken parts that you might ordinarily discard—the skin, the carcass, and the gizzard. Perhaps the most sophisticated dish on the menu, chicken served in a tarragon-flavored sauce is made with the breast and leg meat, which are poached in white wine and finished with a tarragon cream. Interestingly enough, this dish has fewer calories than any of the others because it is poached in wine rather than sautéed in fat. The amount of cream added is negligible: only 1 tablespoon, or 45 calories, per person.

Calories per serving in menu: 851
(both chicken dishes would not be served in one menu)

New England Summer Supper

Chicken and Spinach Velouté 65

Couscous of Lobster 200

Salad

Crêpe Soufflés in Grapefruit Sauce 388

SUGGESTED WINE:

Sauvignon Blanc, Chinook

I eat a lot of lobster in the summer, living as I do on the coast of Connecticut. I usually steam it and serve it with corn on the cob and potatoes, but sometimes I like to incorporate it into a more elegant menu. In this recipe, lobster is made with couscous, a quick-cooking granulated wheat that is fluffy and tender when cooked. Instead of using a caloric butter sauce, I serve a delicate chive sauce made from the reduced cooking stock, a little olive oil, and minced chives. The smooth chicken and spinach velouté makes a satisfying first course. For dessert, we have individual crêpe soufflés served with a tangy grapefruit sauce.

Calories per serving in menu: 925

From Garden and Grill

Spinach, Ham, and Parmesan Soufflé 104

Grilled Salmon Fillets 177

Ragout of Asparagus 298

Grilled Portobello Mushrooms 315

Salad

Strawberries in the Sun 427

SUGGESTED WINE:

Muscadet, Domaine de la Saulzaie

Our menu begins with a soufflé that is baked in a gratin dish, making it easy to serve and giving it a beautifully crusty top. This is followed by salmon fillets, cooked just long enough to take on a grilled flavor, and finished in a warm oven. The salmon is served with two side dishes: asparagus, flavored simply with a little butter and salt; and Portobello mushroom caps, which I grill alongside the salmon. For dessert, we have a sun-dried strawberry jam—for me the best jam in the world—that can be served either as a spread or as a dessert topping. The berries are "cooked" either in the full sun of early summer or in a low-temperature oven, until they become soft and plump and the liquid surrounding them thickens into a syrup.

Calories per serving in menu: 994

A Make-Ahead Menu

Skate with Beets and Flavored Oil 128

Breast of Veal Cocotte 274

Salad

Blueberry Crumble 418

SUGGESTED WINE:

Gigondas, Domaine du Cayron

I love slowly braised casserole dishes, not only because the long cooking makes the meat in them tender and delicious, but also because they can be prepared almost entirely ahead and served family-style from the pot at the table. This is the case with our breast of veal main course; the meat is braised until fork-tender and then garnished with carrots, onions, and garlic. Preceding the *cocotte* is a dish featuring poached skate, which I serve on top of a fresh beet salad. Some of the beet juice is spooned around the skate, and then it is sprinkled with curry- and cilantro-flavored oils for a stunning presentation and enticing taste. Finally, for dessert, a cobbler makes good use of berries in season. I use blueberries, lightly sweetened with apricot preserves and covered with crumbled pound cake, sponge cake, or cookies before baking.

Calories per serving in menu: 798

A Budget Feast

Grilled Squid on Watercress 137

Slow-Cooked Pork Roast 242

Darphin Potatoes 324

Salad

Frozen Black Velvet 443

SUGGESTED WINE:

Cabernet Sauvignon President's Selection, Wolf Blass

Squid, one of the least expensive seafoods and almost waste-free, is our first course. Impaled on skewers and briefly grilled, it is served on watercress. The stems from the watercress can be used for a thrifty soup to be served at another meal. Following the squid we have a small pork roast flavored with honey, ginger, and cayenne pepper, cooked slowly, and served with a dish common to the Lyon area of France where I grew up, julienned potatoes pressed into a compact "cake" and sautéed in a nonstick skillet. A flavorful dessert completes this menu. Frozen vanilla yogurt (or ice cream, as a richer substitute) is topped with Kahlua, dried figs, and chocolate-coated coffee beans.

Calories per serving in menu: 825

Thrifty Kitchen

Pea Pod Soup 60

Steak Maître d'Hôtel

(Steak with Parsley Butter) 284

Stew of Peas and Ham 319

Salad

Potted Plums with Phyllo Dough 412

SUGGESTED WINE:

Pinot Noir, Robert Stemmler

Economy in the kitchen is always a concern for me, and a good chef should know how to create beautiful menus with leftover food. I begin this meal with an appealing soup made with pods reserved from peas I shell for the pea and ham stew that I serve later in the meal. Onions, leeks, and potatoes round out the flavor of the soup. I use a relatively inexpensive, lesser-known, but tender and juicy cut of beef from the hip—the triangle, which is part of the top sirloin—for the grilled steak main dish, but any other so-called butcher steak, such as hanging tenderloin or oyster steak, can be substituted. The steak is flavored with a *beurre maître d'hôtel*, consisting of a blend of unsalted butter, parsley, lemon juice, and cracked pepper. I end the meal with plums served in individual ramekins, each with a crushed "hat" of crisp, brown phyllo pastry on top.

Calories per serving in menu: 869

Midweek Dinner— A Family Meal

Sausage, Potato, and Cabbage Soup 51

Turkey Fricadelles with Vegetable Sauce 234

Salad

Grapefruit and Kiwi Ambrosia 397

Suggested Wine:

Pinot Blanc, Trimbach (White Alsace)

In this menu, I combine a hearty, nourishing soup starter with a lighter entrée. The turkey *fricadelles* are made with lean turkey meat, spinach, and other seasonings and served with a light mushroom and tomato sauce. To add a touch of elegance in the middle of the week, for dessert I serve a mixture of grapefruit and kiwi flavored with a little Sauternes-type sweet wine from the Bordeaux region of France.

Calories per serving in menu: 604

Foods of the Forest

Wild Mushroom Toast 89

Red Pepper Pasta with Walnuts 162

Salad

Country Apple Tart 358

Suggested Wine:

Napa Valley Chardonnay, Girard

This would be a typical summer menu at my house. I often go foraging in the woods for wild mushrooms and prefer them cooked quickly and served simply, spooned over toast. I follow this with pasta, another summer staple. I sometimes serve it with pesto made with basil from my garden, but here I top it with a fresh red bell pepper sauce flavored with walnuts and parmesan cheese. This makes a nutritious main course, rich in vitamins, minerals, and complex carbohydrates. I finish this great menu with a country-style apple tart, a free-form concoction of thinly rolled dough covered with thinly sliced apples. Baked until the pastry is dark brown and crusty, the tart is best served while lukewarm or at room temperature.

Calories per serving in menu: 1,001

Vegetable Feast

Tomatoes Stuffed with Yellow Grits 106

Risotto with Vegetables 165

Salad

Cheese, Apple, and Nut Mélange 352

Suggested Wine:

Vernaccia di San Gimignano-Falchini

Meat will not be missed in this healthful menu. To start, large, firm summer tomatoes are hollowed out, stuffed with a mixture containing mushrooms, garlic, onion, scallions, and cooked yellow grits, and then baked. Another grain—round *arborio*-type rice—is used in the risotto main dish. Cooked in the conventional way with chicken stock, the rice is extended and flavored with an assortment of vegetables. The meal ends with a mélange of blue cheese and apple sprinkled with black pepper and served with pecans and sprigs of basil or arugula leaves.

Calories per serving in menu: 914

Personal Favorites

Salad with Saucisson 70

Fines Herbes Omelets 455

Potato Sauté à Cru 326

Pain au Chocolat et Noisettes
(Bread with Chocolate and Hazelnuts) 441

Suggested Wine:

Brouilly, Château de la Chaize

Even though in classic French cooking the salad is served after the meat course, at home in Lyon years ago and now in Connecticut I often start my meal with a salad. That good French-style hard salami called *saucisson* is available now in most parts of the United States, and it is wonderful with salad greens. I cut it into thin slices—about 1 ounce per person—and arrange it around a helping of escarole (as white as possible) that has been tossed with a Dijon-style mustard dressing. I follow this with thinly sliced potatoes that are sautéed raw (*à cru*), rather than after they are cooked. This gives them a distinctive flavor that is ideal with a *fines herbes* omelet—my personal favorite. I especially enjoy this type of omelet in the spring and summer, when I can readily find its traditional fresh herb components: parsley, tarragon, chives, and chervil. As a finish for this nostalgic meal, I expand a little on an after-school treat that I enjoyed as a child: a piece of *ficelle* ("string" bread) and dark, bittersweet chocolate, to which I add some seedless grapes and toasted hazelnuts. I roast the nuts ahead and store them still in their shells until serving time, so that they retain the freshly roasted taste.

Calories per serving in menu: 1,166

Cold-Weather Comfort

Composed Salad 66

Braised Beef in Red Wine 286

Glazed Strawberries 428

Suggested Wine:

Cahors, Château du Cèdre

The intensely flavored daube of beef is a comforting, hearty winter entrée. Lean, gelatinous beef from the shoulder or shank is braised slowly with red wine, herbs, and seasonings and then garnished with carrots, onions, potatoes, and mushrooms. To begin the menu, a green salad featuring caramelized pecans and apples lends sophistication and interest. The simple but elegant dessert consists of whole strawberries dipped in melted currant jelly to subtly sweeten and intensify their flavor and give them a beautiful sheen.

Calories per serving in menu: 790

Summer Elegance

Scallops in Scallion Nests 152

Roasted Leg of Lamb 262

Potatoes Boulangère 325

Salad

Apricot and Fig Soufflé 374

Suggested Wine:

Château Fourcas Hosten

This makes a good Sunday menu for family and friends who want to eat elegant food in a relaxed atmosphere. The meal begins with scallops cooked briefly over intense heat until their exterior is crusty brown. We serve these in a "nest" of cooked scallions and garnish them with a mustard sauce. A classic leg of lamb roast follows. Well defatted, the leg is partially roasted, then patted with a seasoned bread crumb mixture, and returned to the oven until the coating is beautifully crusty. I serve the lamb with its classic companion, potatoes and thinly sliced onions cooked in chicken stock and white wine until most of the liquid is absorbed. To finish, there is an apricot and fig soufflé, made with dried apricots that have been transformed into an intensely flavored puree. Small pieces of fig provide color contrast in the soufflé, which can be served on its own or with yogurt or sour cream.

Calories per serving in menu: 949

Autumn Fare

Cauliflower Gribiche 81

Lamb Shanks and Beans Mulligan 257

Salad

Grapes in Red Wine Sauce 394

SUGGESTED WINE:

Château Greysac Grand Cru Bourgeois

I spend a few weekends each fall and winter skiing and cooking with friends—many of whom are chefs—at Hunter Mountain in New York. This easy menu, featuring a lamb shank entrée, is typical of the hearty meals we prepare together. The lamb is braised here with Great Northern beans, onions, garlic, and thyme leaves to create a kind of mulligan stew that is served with a salad. Our first course features cauliflower flavored with an interesting sauce containing red onion, parsley, gherkins, anchovy fillets, red wine vinegar, and hard-cooked egg. We finish with seedless Red Flame grapes, cooked in a little fruity red wine, flavored with cinnamon, and served with plain yogurt.

Calories per serving in menu: 953

City Fish and Country Fowl

Salmon in Nori 121

Stuffed and Roasted Cornish Hens 227

Salad

Fruits

SUGGESTED WINE:

Chardonnay, Buena Vista "Carneros"

For the first course, we begin with salmon in seaweed. Fresh salmon is available almost everywhere now. I cut completely cleaned pieces of it into strips and then roll each strip in *nori,* which is a Japanese seaweed that has been compressed into sheets. This attractive concoction is then cut into slices, steamed, and served with a light sauce made of lemon juice and rind, balsamic vinegar, and seasonings. The salmon skin, usually discarded, is transformed into a crackling used to garnish the salmon slices. After this esoteric first course, we continue with a classic main dish, boned and stuffed Cornish hens. Bulgur wheat provides the base for a stuffing that includes garlic, onion, jalapeño pepper, and unpeeled pieces of Granny Smith apple. This combination goes particularly well with these little birds, but it is good as a stuffing for chicken and duck, too. A salad and fresh fruit round out this filling menu.

Calories per serving in menu: 662

Elegant and Modern

Grilled Eggplant on Greens 85

Seafood with "Handkerchiefs" 189

Salad

Prickly Meringues with Fruit Sauce 384

SUGGESTED WINE:

Chardonnay, Mâcon-Lugny les Charmes

Our seafood main dish is both elegant and modern: each serving is topped with a casually dropped pasta "handkerchief" made of two egg roll wrappers sealed around watercress leaves, which are visible through the cooked wrappers. The dessert, also elegant, consists of pointy-topped meringues served with a pungent, slightly acidic raspberry-orange sauce. The light first course features eggplant prepared in a modern way—grilled—and served with a light sauce on a bed of greens. There is a flavorful assortment of vegetables in this healthful, meatless menu.

Calories per serving in menu: 825

Today's Approach to Old Classics

Christmas Oysters 146

Chicken Supreme Kiev-Style 212

Bulgur Wheat Pilaf 342

Salad

Prunes and Grapefruit in Red Wine Sauce 413

SUGGESTED CHAMPAGNES:

Dom Ruinart Blanc de Blancs; Bollinger Grande Année Brut; Veuve Clicquot Ponsardin

This menu exemplifies one aspect of my philosophy: reinterpret old recipes in a modern style to produce lighter, lower-calorie dishes. Chicken Kiev is traditionally made with unskinned, boneless chicken breasts that are wrapped around large quantities of herb-seasoned butter, then dipped in beaten eggs—often mixed with cream—coated with bread crumbs, and deep-fried. My version is a world away from the calorie-laden original: the breasts are skinless, they are filled with a mushroom puree containing garlic and herbs, they are coated lightly with milk and a mixture of oiled, seasoned bread crumbs, and they are baked. The "Christmas" oysters first course can, of course, be served at any time of the year when fresh oysters are available, although their presentation—in or out of their shells—on a bed of bright green spinach surrounded by a vivid red bell pepper sauce makes them a perfect holiday dish. A refreshing dessert of prunes cooked in a red wine sauce and served with grapefruit segments finishes the meal.

Calories per serving in menu: 994

Classic and Modern Mix

Eggs in Aspic with Tarragon 72

Tuna Steaks with Peppercorns 187

Gratin of Tomato and Bread 332

Salad

Pineapple Délice 409

Suggested Wine:

Napa Valley Chardonnay, Hess Collection

This is a great summer menu. I adore aspic, especially this classic preparation that includes another favorite food of mine, eggs, which I can eat sensibly here. One egg per person is sufficient in this dish, since each egg is surrounded by an intensely flavored, totally fat-free *gelée* made from a stock flavored with tarragon and containing a little lean ham for color. Contrast is provided by a modern-style entrée of tuna steaks with pepper, a dish that is somewhat like the standard pepper steak made with beef, although for variety I use an assortment of peppercorns here. With a fresh piece of tuna, this preparation is absolutely delicious, especially if the tuna is served slightly rare. I accompany the tuna with a tasty gratin containing cubes of leftover bread, cherry tomatoes, garlic, parsley, olive oil, and parmesan cheese. A fruit dessert is always a welcome finale, and I conclude this meal with fresh, ripe pineapple pieces flavored with lime, honey, and kirsch.

Calories per serving in menu: 715

Russian Flavors

Codfish in Olive and Horseradish Sauce 115

Chicken in Cilantro Sauce 205

Julienne of Zucchini 335

Salad

Russian Cranberry Kissel 372

Suggested Wine:

Gewürztraminer, Trimbach (Alsace)

Codfish in an interesting and flavorful olive and horseradish sauce begins this Russian-inspired menu. It is followed by chicken thighs prepared with onion, garlic, a little white wine, and cilantro leaves and stems. The thighs are served with a julienne of zucchini, briefly sautéed. For dessert, we have a classic *kissel,* a fruit puree made here with astringently flavored cranberries. This is served with plain yogurt or sour cream and decorated with pomegranate seeds and mint.

Calories per serving in menu: 786

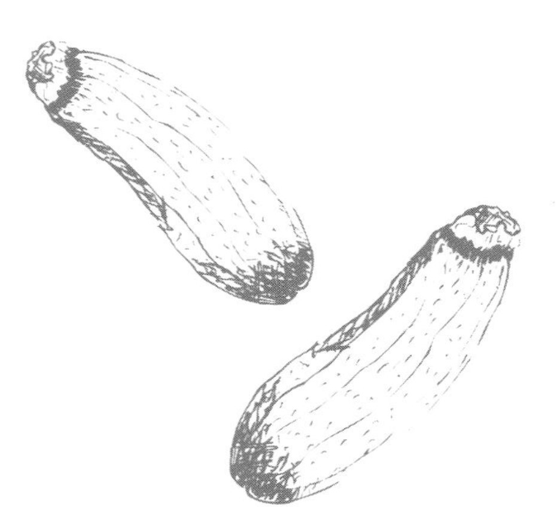

From the North Sea to North Africa

Cured Salmon in Molasses 118

Couscous of Lamb 252

Salad

Fresh and Dried Fruits

Suggested Wine:

Chianti Classico Riserva

This menu features couscous, the national stew of Morocco, Algeria, and Tunisia, which takes its name from the wheat grain traditionally served with it. Here, the couscous grain is cooked until light and fluffy and served with its classic stew companion. My version uses a minimum of lamb in combination with kohlrabi, squash, eggplant, carrot, zucchini, and the like, in a broth flavored with a hot sauce called *harissa.* The sauce contains a spicy red pepper paste often used as a seasoning in North Africa. The first course, more European than African, consists of salmon cured in a molasses mixture containing an assortment of spices, among them cumin, nutmeg, and paprika. Fresh and dried fruits are suggested as a light finish to this copious menu.

Calories per serving in menu: 1,070

Provençal Tastes

Eggplant and Red Pepper Terrine 83

Red Snapper in Brunoise Sauce 186

Cucumber with Tarragon 313

Salad

Jam Omelet Soufflé 373

Suggested Wine:

Bandol, Domaine Tempier

This menu from the south of France begins with a terrine of eggplant and red bell pepper layered with cheese. Unmolded, it is served with a raw tomato sauce, consisting of ripe tomato chunks, a touch of garlic, olive oil, and vinegar. After this fresh-tasting starter, we have red snapper, a fish common to the Mediterranean, cooked and served with an array of sliced vegetables. As a side dish, cucumbers are stewed and flavored with tarragon. To finish, we offer a "surprise omelet," made mostly of egg whites lightly flavored with egg yolk and vanilla. Shaped like a conventional omelet, it is really a soufflé that is baked on slices of pound cake spread with black currant preserves.

Calories per serving in menu: 847

Vietnamese Flavors

Hanoi Soup 52

Asian Savoy Salad 296

Banana Tartlets 360

SUGGESTED BEERS:

Tsing Tao; Anchor Steam;

La Belle Strasbourgeoise

This is one of my wife's favorite menus. She loves to cook Asian food—Chinese, Japanese, and particularly Vietnamese—since we have so many friends of these nationalities. Her interpretation of Hanoi soup, which begins our menu, is a meal in itself. The most important element in this soup is an intensely flavored stock, made here with oxtail, beef shank, and beef bones. After it is totally defatted, the stock is returned to the stove, and garnishes of napa cabbage, bean sprouts, and rice sticks are cooked in it. Additional garnishes—among them red onion, scallions, hot pepper, and cilantro—are added to the bowls at the table. With the soup we serve a cabbage salad flavored with rice wine vinegar, soy sauce, and oyster sauce to give it an Asian flavor. We finish with banana tartlets, made from a sweet dough that is covered with a light pastry cream, garnished with banana slices, and glazed with apricot preserves.

Calories per serving in menu: 713

French Atlantic Cooking

Endive with Olives 87

Lobster in Artichoke Bottoms 197

Broccoli with Butter 304

Salad

Pears au Gratin 408

SUGGESTED WINE:

Chablis, Domaine de la Maladiere

Two of my favorite foods—lobster and artichokes—are served together here. The lobsters are quickly steamed, and their meat is removed. Then the shells are returned to the pot and boiled to create an extra dish not in our menu, a full-flavored broth thickened with pasta. The lobster meat is served in artichoke bottoms accompanied by broccoli cooked simply and enhanced with a dash of butter. Endive, braised and garnished with olives, soy sauce, and chives, provides a light and interesting start to the meal. For dessert, ripe pear slices are baked with a crumb topping made of bread, butter, sugar, and pecans. This easy dish makes good use of leftover fruit and bread.

Calories per serving in menu: 660

Menu for a Sunday Gathering

Dried and Fresh Mushroom Soup 61

Poulet Rôti (Roasted Chicken) 222

Coquillettes au Gruyère

(Pasta Shells with Swiss Cheese) 338

Salad

Crêpes à la Confiture 386

Suggested Wine:

Côtes du Rhône, Saint-Joseph

This meal brings back memories of my childhood. Along with fresh mushrooms, which were the main ingredient in my mother's mushroom soup, I use dried mushrooms, because they bring a great intensity of flavor to this simple first course soup. I also flavor it with a leek, thicken it with a potato, and finish it with milk instead of cream, the more traditional but richer choice of most fancy restaurants. The soup is followed by what is for me the ultimate chicken dish: a whole chicken roasted in a very hot oven until the skin is crisp and brown and the flesh moist and succulent. In this menu, the natural juices and a little of the fat that emerge from the chicken as it cooks are combined with pasta shells flavored with swiss cheese. After a salad, I offer a dessert recipe from my youth: crêpes, hot from the pan, spread with a good-quality jam (or sprinkled with a little granulated sugar or grated chocolate), folded, and eaten immediately.

Calories per serving in menu: 1,298

Special Guest Menu

Nage Courte of Striped Bass 112

Grilled Veal Chops with Caper Sauce 268

Vegetable Burgers 334

Salad

Pears in Espresso 404

Suggested Wine:

Chardonnay, Merryvale Napa Valley

This is a special menu not only because the recipes are a bit more elegant than those for every day but also because they contain more costly ingredients. Veal chops, for example, are expensive, but for a special occasion they are delicate and delicious grilled and served with a caper sauce. Vegetable burgers, composed of an assortment of vegetables bound together with cooked grits, make an interesting and succulent side dish. As a first course, striped bass—either whole or in fillets—are cooked in a flavorful vegetable and wine mixture. We conclude with a light dessert of pears cooked in espresso and flavored with lemon rind and Kahlua.

Calories per serving in menu: 1,010

A Romantic Dinner

Gratin of Breaded Oysters 148

Pan-Seared or Grilled Marinated Flank Steak 285

Caramelized Mushrooms with Shallots 317

Salad

Raspberry Velvet 422

Suggested Wines:

Brut Champagne, Mumm Cordon Rouge;

Vino Rosso Reserva, Siglo Rioja

The first course in this menu demonstrates a delicious and different way of preparing oysters. They are first blanched in their own juices, then arranged in a gratin dish with seasoned bread crumbs on top, and finished under a hot broiler. I follow this with a flank steak, trimmed of all surrounding fat and marinated in a piquant mixture of honey, soy sauce, garlic, coriander, and cayenne pepper before it is grilled or pan-seared at serving time. While not too many years ago it was thought that a steak weighing 1¼ pounds would feed only one person, my flank steak of that weight is sufficient for four when it is cut on the bias into thin slices. Tender and flavorful, the steak is served with whole caramelized mushrooms. I like to use older, darker mushrooms with somewhat open gills for this dish, finding they acquire the concentrated taste I want when they are cooked a long time. I conclude with a refreshing berry velvet. Made from a puree of raspberries frozen to a slushlike consistency, this dessert is served in stemmed glasses that are rimmed—margarita-style—with lime juice and sugar.

Calories per serving in menu: 584

A Midsummer Night's Tête-à-Tête

Gazpacho with Black Olives 55

Grilled Lamb Chops Riviera 258

Salad

Ice-Cream Phyllo Napoleons 449

Suggested Wines:

Fleur de Champagne, Perrier-Jouet;

Gevrey-Chambertin, Pierre Ponnelle

For me, gazpacho is the ideal summer menu starter and, served in larger quantities with an earthy country bread, can almost stand as a meal on its own. A liquid salad, it contains a host of vegetables—among them tomatoes, cucumbers, red bell pepper, and red onion—some of which are cut into chunks for serving as a garnish, while the rest are pureed with garlic, bread, and seasonings to create this tasty, colorful soup. Grilled lamb chops are the centerpiece of this menu. I limit the quantity to one per person and prepare them in the style of the south of France, serving them on a bed of spinach with garnishes of eggplant, tomato, and black olives. After a salad, I finish with ice cream layered napoleon-style between squares of crisp and delicate baked phyllo dough.

Calories per serving in menu: 832

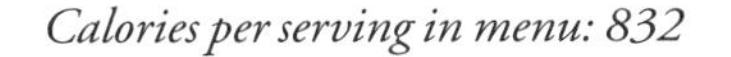

Leisurely Sunday Dinner

Spaghetti Squash in Fresh Tomato Sauce 109

Long-Roasted Lamb 264

Flageolets in Mirepoix 300

Salad

Tartelettes aux Fruits Panachés 362

Suggested Wine:

Saint-Emilion Grand Cru, Château Lapelletrie

Even though leg of lamb is generally served rare or medium these days, I occasionally like it slow-cooked until well done, as it is in this menu. Trimmed of fat and sinews, the boneless leg is spread with a mixture of garlic, anchovies, and *herbes de Provence,* tightly rolled, and tied for cooking in a dutch oven. I serve the lamb with a traditional French side dish, flageolets, which are long, narrow beans picked while still light green. They are available—dried, primarily—at specialty food stores in the United States. I cook the flageolets with leek, onion, carrot, celery, and herbs in this recipe and stir a little fresh tomato and olive oil into the mixture just before serving. This summer menu begins with spaghetti squash, much lower in calories than spaghetti and quite good served in the same manner. My recipe features strands of baked squash tossed and served in a garlicky fresh tomato sauce. For dessert, ripe apricot and dark plum wedges are arranged on very thin pastry rounds and cooked in a hot oven until the dough is crisp and the fruit juicy and tender.

Calories per serving in menu: 1,106

The New-Fashioned Cook

Instant Smoked Scallops
with Orange-and-Onion Sauce 150

Vegetable Bouquet on Fettucine 168

Salad

Grapefruit in Nectar 398

Suggested Wine:

Gavi di Gavi, Villa Merrigi

I present a quick smoking technique in this menu, heating a few wood chips to impart a light, delicate, smoky flavor to scallops. The scallops are then served as a first course with a wonderfully complementary orange-and-onion sauce. I continue with a vegetable and pasta dish that is decidedly more "vegetable" than "pasta." Light and colorful, it consists of a host of lightly sautéed vegetables—among them broccoli, mushrooms, zucchini, tomatoes, and corn—served with a modest amount of fettucine. A salad follows, and the meal is concluded with a grapefruit dessert. For this dish, I prepare a caramel, flavor it with grapefruit juice, and pour it over grapefruit segments and a julienne of blanched grapefruit peel.

Calories per serving in menu: 839

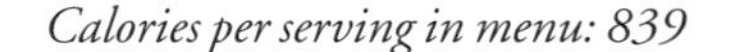

Fresh and Imaginative

Pizza of Cured Salmon and Sour Cream 124

Grilled Chicken with Tarragon Butter 215

Sautéed Haricots Verts and Shallots 299

Arugula and Olive Salad 294

Fresh Fruits

SUGGESTED WINE:

Syrah, Cambria, Tepusquet Vineyard

Beginning with an elegant cold pizza, this menu reflects modern—even trendy—cuisine. The crunchy, delicious pizza crust is made ahead from a dough prepared in a food processor and pressed into round shapes for baking. Just before serving, the rounds are layered with sour cream, thinly sliced red onion, cured salmon (my type of instant gravlax), basil leaves, and black olive pieces. The main course consists of grilled chicken, served with either tarragon butter or tarragon-flavored olive oil, both of which impart the flavor of tarragon but don't have the richness of a standard béarnaise sauce. The chicken is served with two classic French side dishes: For the first, *haricots verts*—very thin French green beans—are cooked until tender but still firm and served with sautéed shallots; for the second, arugula, or *roquette,* is combined with croutons and black olive flakes and tossed in a lemon dressing. A bowl of fresh fruits provides the perfect ending.

Calories per serving in menu: 1,077 (chicken with skin); 950 (chicken without skin)

Light and Tasty Supper

Cold Cream of Pea Soup with Mint 59

Crab Ravioli with Red Pepper Sauce 190

Skillet Spinach with Nutmeg 331

Salad

Apricot Délice 366

SUGGESTED WINE:

Pinot Gris, Trimbach Reserve

This delightful dinner begins with a refreshing, bright green, cold soup made with very thin-skinned frozen or fresh peas and regular or nonfat yogurt. I use wonton wrappers for the crab ravioli main dish, sealing two around a mixture of crabmeat and chopped herbs. Boiled gently in water just before serving, the ravioli are topped with a red pepper sauce. Spinach with nutmeg—a classic pairing in French cooking—serves as a side dish, and we finish with an apricot dessert. Deep orange, full summer apricots (with sticky juice—the best indicator of ripeness) are poached in a sweet wine that is flavored with basil; then the tender fruit is served in the cooking juices with diced kiwi and basil leaves for decoration.

Calories per serving in menu: 795

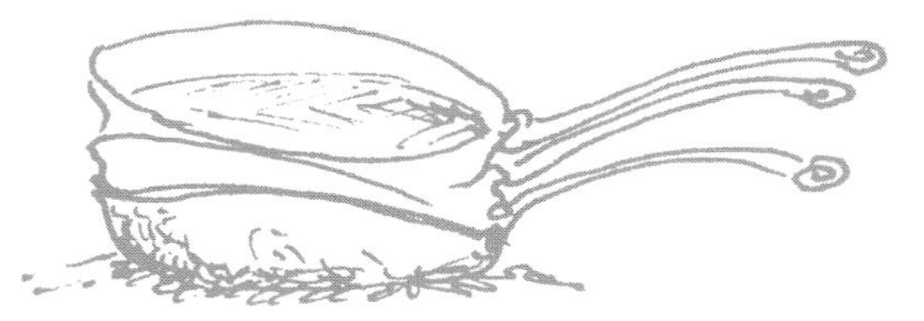

Feast from the Sea

Mussels Marinière 144

Monkfish Roulade with Broccoli Rabe Stuffing 181

Steamed Cauliflower with Chives 308

Salad

Cranberry Soufflés with Cranberry—Red Wine Sauce 375

Suggested Wine:

Chardonnay, Louisvale

Drawing heavily from the sea, this meal begins with a classic French bistro dish—mussels cooked and served simply in a savory, wine-flavored broth. A monkfish roulade is the centerpiece of the menu. For this dish, a fillet of firm-fleshed, meaty monkfish is wrapped around a mixture of seasoned *broccoli di rape* and mushrooms, and cooked on top of the stove. The roulade is served in slices with a sauce created from the monkfish cooking juices, to which are added white wine, tomatoes, and tarragon. Steamed cauliflower makes a delicious side dish. Individual cranberry soufflés complete the meal. Lightly sweetened fresh cranberries are cooked until tender, then half the fruit mixture is used as the soufflé base, with the remainder processed with red wine and served as a companion sauce.

Calories per serving in menu: 738

Seafood Lovers' Delight

Timbales of Shrimp and Spinach 157

Salmon in Savory Broth 180

Celeriac and Potato Puree 310

Salad

Soufflé of Mango with Mango Sauce 378

Suggested Wine:

Pouilly-Fumé, Domaine de Saint-Laurent-l'Abbaye

For a first course with a touch of elegance, sautéed spinach and shrimp are layered in small timbales or molds, and then the compacted mixture is unmolded onto individual plates for serving. The main dish features salmon fillets poached in a fragrant broth containing lemon peel, lemon juice, fennel, leek, and white wine. The salmon is served with a puree of celeriac and potato, one of my family's favorite side dishes, and this is followed by a salad. A mango soufflé provides an exotic finish to the meal. For this dessert, the flesh of two mangoes is pureed; half the puree is combined with beaten egg whites to create the soufflé, and the remainder is flavored with grenadine and Grand Marnier to serve as a sauce for the dish.

Calories per serving in menu: 936

A Touch of the Exotic

Cured Salmon on
Fennel-and-Mustard-Seed Salad 117
Haddock Steaks in Rice Paper
with Shallot-and-Soy Sauce 173
Gratin of Eggplant and Tomato 314
Salad
Blackberries in Creamy Honey Sauce 414

Suggested Wine:
Royale White Meritage, Kendall-Jackson

Cured salmon is served on a salad of paper-thin slices of seasoned fennel as a first course in this menu. Cut into ½-inch slices, the salmon takes only about an hour to cure and is deliciously complemented by the mustard seed flavoring on the fennel. As a main course, haddock steaks are wrapped in softened rice paper, sautéed, and served with a shallot-soy sauce. An eggplant and tomato gratin is a light, flavorful side dish for the haddock. The healthy new twist in this recipe is that the eggplant slices—requiring a lot of oil when sautéed in a skillet on top of the stove—need only a light coating of oil when baked until tender in a single layer on a cookie sheet. The softened slices are then layered with tomatoes in a gratin dish, coated with seasoned bread crumbs, and finished in the oven. After a salad, the meal ends with blackberries served in a smooth honey sauce with a nonfat yogurt base.

Calories per serving in menu: 719

The Unconventional Cook

Walnut Sausage 158
Lentil and Potato Salad 71
Stuffed Zucchini "Boats"
with Red Pepper—Tomato Sauce 166
Salad
Meringue Chocolate Mousse 442

Suggested Wine:
Moulin-à-Vent, Domaine Diochon

This menu, composed of dishes that all can be brought to the table at one time, goes to the core of what we are attempting to do in *Today's Gourmet.* I love sausage but limit my consumption of commercially made varieties, since most of them contain at least 30 percent fat. Here, using very lean pork from the loin, fillet, or well-trimmed shoulder, I create a light homemade sausage that contains no more fat than chicken meat. I pair the sausage with its classic companion, potato salad, my rendition of which contains lentils and is seasoned with herbs. As a main course, I hollow out zucchini halves and stuff the resulting "boats" with a mixture of the reserved zucchini flesh, dried mushrooms, onion, garlic, and seasoned bread crumbs. Topped with cheese, the "boats" are baked, then broiled briefly, and served with a colorful sauce redolent of tomato and red pepper. A fat-free chocolate mousse—made of cocoa powder, espresso coffee, and a boiled-frosting-type meringue containing beaten egg whites—completes the meal.

Calories per serving in menu: 891

JACQUES PÉPIN'S TABLE

Cooking with a Special Friend

SUGGESTED WINE:

Merlot, Fortant de France

In the part of France where I grew up, near Lyon, a meal commonly begins with a gratin. I create one here with a small amount of pasta and a large variety of vegetables, including eggplant, corn, pattypan squash, tomatoes, and string beans. I specifically select a large, tubular pasta for this dish, because it swells as it cooks, giving me the volume I need with much less pasta (and so, fewer calories) than would be required if a string pasta, such as spaghetti or fettucine, were used. This is followed by my version of a French classic, chicken *chasseur.* Although I season the *chasseur* in the conventional "hunting-style" manner, with onion, tomatoes, garlic, mushrooms, and white wine, I use skinless chicken—a break with tradition that makes my *chasseur* leaner than its namesake. A delightful lima bean puree absorbs the sauce of the chicken well, making it an ideal accompaniment. The perfect ending to this relaxed family meal: a sumptuous white peach tart.

Calories per serving in menu: 1,092

A Tasty Potpourri

SUGGESTED WINE:

Rosé de Syrah, Réserve St. Martin

An amalgam of different styles of cooking, this menu is interesting and flavorful. It begins with a refreshing French summer classic, melon with port wine, which opens the appetite well to a south-of-the-border specialty, chili con carne, served here with plain boiled rice. The conventional chili ingredient ratio—lots of fatty beef to very few, if any, beans—is reversed here. Essentially just flavored with very lean ground beef, my chili features a substantial quantity of red kidney beans along with a host of seasoning ingredients. I follow this hot, spicy dish with crisp romaine lettuce in a refreshing low-fat dressing. The meal concludes with an apple flake confection, consisting of thin slices of apple dried in a convection oven until crisp and served with frozen yogurt.

Calories per serving in menu: 769

Vegetable Elegance

Mushroom-Stuffed Wontons
in Red Wine Sauce 92

Potato and Spinach Galette 163

Salad

Caramel Cups with Coffee Frozen Yogurt 446

Crystallized Mint Leaves and Rose Petals 451

Suggested Wine:

Red Burgundy, Fixin

This light menu begins with an elegant pasta dish featuring large wonton wrappers enclosed around a reduction of shallots, leeks, and mushrooms, and served with an assertively flavored red wine sauce. This is followed by one of my family's favorites, a thick pancakelike "sandwich" of potato with a seasoned spinach filling. The caramel cup dessert is a real showstopper. I fill the cups with frozen yogurt and decorate them with crystallized mint leaves and rose petals, a nice do-ahead enhancement for this and other desserts.

Calories per serving in menu: 752

Good Foods from the Earth

Corn Polenta with Mushroom Ragout 100

Grilled Pork Paillards with Rosemary 248

Potato Gaufrettes or Chips 328

Salad

Spicy Apple Charlotte 354

Suggested Wine:

Pinot Noir, Cambria, Julia's Vineyard

What is more "down to earth" than a flavorful corn polenta? Here, I serve this cornmeal dish with a fragrant mushroom ragout or stew as a first course, although it could be served as a meatless main course or as a side dish for meat or poultry. Lean pork fillets are butterflied and pounded into thin steaks, or *paillards,* for the menu main course. Seasoned with rosemary, the *paillards* are grilled and served with thin potato wafers (*gaufrettes*) or potato chips, prepared unconventionally in the oven so they don't absorb much fat. We finish with a comforting and always welcome apple charlotte, flavored here with cinnamon, allspice, and cloves.

Calories per serving in menu: 757

Rustic Breads and Soup

Garbure Soup Farmer-Style 240

Large Country Bread 477

Farmer Bread 478

Farmer Bread with Mixed Leavening 479

Gros Pain 480

Long-Proofed Baguettes 481

Salad

Pineapple in Cantaloupe Sauce 410

SUGGESTED WINE:

Madiran, Château d'Aydie

In this menu, I particularly want to demonstrate the making of bread—from the big, round farmer bread to the large country bread, which I used to eat as a child. For me, bread is truly the staff of life; it appears on my table at every meal. If properly made, large bread loaves will keep for days, and I make use of some leftover bread here, slicing it for a garnish with cheese atop *garbure* soup, a French meat and vegetable concoction that is a meal in itself. My version of this classic soup—made with well-trimmed pork shoulder—is delicious but much lighter than the original, which often contained poultry, sausages, and other meats. The menu ends with refreshing pineapple and plum slices served in a sauce made of pureed cantaloupe, honey, and a little Grand Marnier.

Calories per serving in menu: 764 (without breads)

Joys of Cooking

Asparagus en Fête 79

Barley-Stuffed Cabbage Rolls 276

Salad

Lemon Bananas in Crisp Shells 367

SUGGESTED WINE:

Gewürztraminer, Stonestreet

Much of this menu, including the stuffed cabbage main course, can be prepared in advance. The cabbage dish, consisting of cooked cabbage leaves wrapped around a mixture of seasoned barley and a little lean beef, can even be baked ahead in the sweet-sour sauce, then reheated in the sauce at serving time. Asparagus begins the meal. It is served *en fête,* meaning "in a holiday style," which is a reference to the dish's colorful garnishes of black olives, tomatoes, and capers. For the dessert that completes the menu, packaged wonton squares are poached, then baked until crisp, and filled with bananas flavored with lemon juice, lemon rind, peach preserves, and rum.

Calories per serving in menu: 862

Zucchini and Tomato Fans 107

Daube of Beef Arlésienne 280

Salad

Red Wine and Cassis Strawberries 423

Suggested Wines:

Fendant du Valais, Gilliard;

Châteauneuf-du-Pape, Domaine du Vieux Télégraphe

Whenever I think of the artist Vincent van Gogh, I am reminded of the south of France and the town he made famous—Arles—which is also the birthplace of the daube of beef main dish in this menu. We begin the meal with another favorite Provençal combination, zucchini and tomatoes, arranged here in fan-shaped configurations and baked with herbs until cooked through and brown on top. I continue with the beef and vegetable dish, cooking the meat in a wine-flavored broth that I season and thicken at the end in the authentic *Arlésienne* manner with a powder made from bread, toasted hazelnuts, garlic, and parsley. A green salad makes a great side dish for the daube. This menu ends with a refreshing fruit dish, this one composed of strawberries flavored with both red wine and black currant or blackberry liqueur.

Calories per serving in menu: 626

Sautéed Soft-Shell Crabs on Asparagus 142

Chicken Ballottine Stuffed with Red Rice 224

Salad

Pears in Grenadine 406

Suggested Wine:

Chardonnay, Cambria Reserve

This blend of French and American cuisines represents the best of both worlds. I start with soft-shell crabs, a great American delicacy. They are sautéed briefly here and served on lightly cooked asparagus strips with a garnish of tomato flavored with garlic and tarragon. I continue with a classic French chicken *ballottine,* stuffed here unconventionally with a mixture of chewy, red, California-grown wehani rice, dried mushrooms, leek, and chicken stock. The dish is served with a red wine sauce that includes the accumulated drippings from cooking the chicken. The skin of the chicken is left on to protect the meat as it cooks but may be removed after the *ballottine* is sliced, if you want to eliminate a few calories. The meal concludes with Bosc pears cooked in white wine, lime juice, sugar, and grenadine, and served in a syrupy reduction of the cooking liquid.

Calories per serving in menu: 725

A Savory Mélange

Squid and Posole Hodgepodge 138

Veal Chops with Olive Shavings 269

Sautéed Lettuce Packages 330

Farina Bavarian Cream Cake
with Apricot Sauce 433

SUGGESTED WINES:

Côte de Beaune les Pierres Blanches, Pierre Ponnelle;
Muscat de Rivesaltes, Château de Jau

We begin with an unusual hodgepodge of squid and *posole.* A Native American food made of treated corn kernels that swell to the size of chickpeas when cooked, *posole* has a flavor I find irresistible. It appears frequently in the cooking of the southwestern United States and Mexico, and can be found—dried and canned—in most specialty food stores and some supermarkets. The *posole* is combined with blanched squid, onion, garlic, tomato, white wine, a dash of Tabasco, and tarragon. For our main course, veal chops are sautéed briefly, then transferred to a warm oven while a sauce is made from their pan drippings, onion, a little butter, and shavings of several olive varieties. As a side dish, Boston lettuce heads are cooked, drained, and then folded into neat packages that are sautéed at serving time. We finish with an egg-free pudding. Made with gelatin, a small amount of farina, and a little cream, this light dessert is unmolded for serving with a lemon- and cognac-flavored apricot sauce.

Calories per serving in menu: 977

A Chic Townhouse Meal

Artichokes with Ravigote Sauce 76

Seared Calves' Liver
with Tarragon-Lemon Sauce 275

Red Swiss Chard with Ginger 311

Salad

Oeufs à la Neige in Peach Sauce 380

SUGGESTED WINE:

Pinot Noir, La Crema

This elegant winter menu is ideal for entertaining. *Ravigote* sauce replaces the classic accompaniments for artichokes in France, melted butter or hollandaise sauce. *Ravigote,* which means "invigorate," is a much lighter sauce, consisting of wine vinegar, a variety of herbs, capers, and red onion. Seared calves' liver, our main course, is finished with lemon juice, tarragon, and capers for this elegant meal. Cooked at the last moment, it is ideal for a small party. I accompany this with young red Swiss chard, seasoning it here with ginger and jalapeño pepper. The meal concludes with a classic French dessert, *oeufs à la neige,* or "snow eggs," which are conventionally served with a rich custard sauce but are presented here in a delightful, low-calorie, custard cream look-alike, made of peaches pureed with yogurt.

Calories per serving in menu: 882

Classic Fall Feast

Codfish Flakes in Vegetable Brunoise 113

Venison Steaks in Sweet-Sour Sauce 289

Raw Relish of Grapefruit and Peach 347

Skillet Sweet Potatoes 329

Salad

Mango Symphony 403

SUGGESTED WINES:

Château Bouscaut, Pessac-Leognan;

Pinot Noir, Cambria Reserve

The pièce de résistance in this menu is venison steaks served in a sweet-sour sauce. Venison, available now through specialty or fancy food stores, is usually very lean, flavorful, and rich enough so that you don't need large portions. The base of the standard companion sauce is generally a *demi-glace*—a rich brown sauce reduction that restaurants always have on hand—but my lighter substitute is essentially made from the venison pan drippings, vinegar, and currant jelly. With the steaks I serve a spicy raw grapefruit and peach relish, and my vegetable side dish consists of sweet potato slices that are boiled and then sautéed in a nonstick skillet until tender and lightly browned. The menu begins with one of my favorites, thick codfish fillets, which tend to break into flakes as they cook. I serve the flakes with onion, tomatoes, and black olives seasoned with tarragon. We finish this feast with slices of ripe mango and pieces of plum that have been marinated in a delightful honey-rum sauce.

Calories per serving in menu: 821

Great Food for Special Guests

Red Onion and Orange Salad 69

Osso Buco 272

Brown Saffron Rice 345

Salad

Raspberry Trifle with Nectarine Sauce 420

SUGGESTED WINE:

Barolo, Bricco Castelletto

This menu is inspired by Italian cuisine, often featured at our house. We begin with an onion and orange salad, ideally featuring long, narrow, red Torpedo onions and blood oranges when either or both are available, along with flat-leaf parsley, plum tomatoes, olive oil, and cider vinegar. I continue with a staple of Italian cuisine, osso buco, which is made with slices of veal shank with the bones attached. The meat is browned lightly and cooked for a long time with seasonings that include onion, leek, carrot, garlic, *herbes de Provence,* and white wine. Finished with grated rind of orange and lemon, the osso buco is served with chewy brown rice flavored with saffron. The meal concludes with a raspberry trifle. Instead of using heavy cream or mascarpone cheese—traditional trifle ingredients—I use homemade yogurt cheese, layering it with rounds of pound cake and fresh raspberries in individual soufflé molds. The trifle is served with a refreshing nectarine sauce flavored with orange juice and cognac.

Calories per serving in menu: 974

FIRST COURSES

ONION SOUP WITH VERMICELLI

This is one of those easy, quickly prepared soups that we often make at home when we feel like eating soup and have no time to cook. I like it when the onions are cooked for long enough over high heat to become a rich, dark brown color.

To make a standard onion soup, a gratinée, *omit the pasta and chives, top each bowl of soup with two or three toasted baguette slices and some grated Gruyère cheese, and place the bowls in a 400-degree oven until the cheese on top is crusty and brown. This is very good, certainly, although much more caloric than the rendition that follows.*

- 1 tablespoon corn oil
- 4 medium onions (1 pound total), peeled and thinly sliced
- 6 cups light stock, consisting of 4 cups homemade unsalted and defatted chicken stock (see page 466) or beef stock, or a mixture of both, or lower-salt canned broth, mixed with 2 cups water (see Light Stock)
- ¾ teaspoon salt
- ¼ teaspoon freshly ground black pepper
- ⅔ cup (2 ounces) vermicelli (angel hair pasta)
- 2 tablespoons minced fresh chives

1. Heat the oil until it is hot but not smoking. Add the onions, and sauté them over medium to high heat for 10 to 12 minutes, until they are soft and a rich, dark brown color.
2. Add the stock, salt, and pepper. Bring the mixture to a boil, cover, and boil for 5 minutes.
3. Add the pasta, bring back to a boil, cover, and boil gently for 5 minutes.
4. Divide among four bowls, sprinkle with the chives, and serve.

LIGHT STOCK

I LIKE THE FLAVOR OF THE ONIONS—RATHER THAN THE STOCK—TO DOMINATE IN THIS PARTICULAR SOUP, SO I COOK THEM IN WHAT I CALL A LIGHT STOCK: TWO PARTS STOCK AND ONE PART WATER. ANOTHER POSSIBILITY: IF THE ONIONS ARE PROPERLY CARAMELIZED BEFOREHAND, THEY CAN BE COOKED IN SEASONED WATER ONLY. THE WATER WILL TAKE ON ENOUGH RICH TASTE AND COLOR FROM THE BROWNED ONIONS TO CREATE A FLAVORFUL VEGETARIAN BROTH.

YIELD: 4 SERVINGS (6 CUPS)

NUTRITIONAL ANALYSIS PER SERVING:

Calories 168
Protein 6 gm.
Carbohydrates 22 gm.
Fat 6.1 gm.
Saturated fat 1.1 gm.
Cholesterol 0 mg.
Sodium 496 mg.

Potage de Légumes au Vermicelle (Vegetable and Vermicelli Soup)

I serve this hearty soup as a first course, but it would also make a satisfying light supper with the addition of a crunchy bread, a salad, and a piece of cheese. *(See photograph, page 62.)*

SOUP INGREDIENTS

I CHOOSE THE VEGETABLES FOR THIS SOUP BASED ON WHAT IS IN MY REFRIGERATOR. WHILE I THICKEN THE SOUP HERE WITH VERMICELLI, YOU COULD USE ANOTHER TYPE OF STARCH—FROM OATMEAL TO COUSCOUS, TAPIOCA, OR CREAM OF WHEAT.

- 1 tablespoon virgin olive oil
- ½ tablespoon unsalted butter
- 1 leek (about 3 ounces), trimmed of damaged leaves, cleaned, and cut into ½-inch pieces
- 1 medium onion (about 4 ounces), peeled and coarsely chopped (1 cup)
- 2 carrots (about 4 ounces), peeled and cut into ½-inch pieces
- 1 zucchini (about 4 ounces), trimmed and cut into ¾-inch pieces
- 4 mushrooms (4 ounces), coarsely chopped (1 cup)
- 1 yam (about 6 ounces), peeled and cut into ½-inch pieces
- 7 cups water
- 1 teaspoon salt
- ¼ teaspoon freshly ground black pepper
- 1 cup vermicelli (angel hair pasta) or very thin noodles (about ¾ ounce)

1. Heat the oil and butter in a saucepan. When hot, add the leek and onion, and sauté for 2 minutes. Then add the carrots, zucchini, mushrooms, and yam, and mix well. Add the water, salt, and pepper.
2. Bring to a boil, cover, reduce the heat, and boil gently for about 12 minutes.
3. Add the pasta. Bring back to a boil, and cook, covered, for about 4 minutes. Serve.

YIELD: 6 SERVINGS (8 CUPS)

NUTRITIONAL ANALYSIS PER SERVING:

Calories 105
Protein 2 gm.
Carbohydrates 15 gm.
Fat 4.6 gm.
Saturated fat 1.1 gm.
Cholesterol 3 mg.
Sodium 378 mg.

Carrots are rich in beta-carotene. Pasta has no fat and provides quick energy.

Lobster Broth with Pasta

This is one way of extending a recipe. When preparing Lobster in Artichoke Bottoms, page 197, I reserve the lobster-cooking liquid. This broth can be frozen and used as needed. Reduced, it makes a simple and delicious soup with the addition of pastina or, if you prefer, angel hair pasta or rice.

6 cups lobster broth (from Lobster in Artichoke Bottoms, page 197)
½ cup pastina
½ teaspoon freshly ground black pepper
Salt to taste (amount depending on saltiness of broth)
2 tablespoons chopped chives

1. Bring the broth to a boil in a stainless steel saucepan.
2. Add the pastina, and stir well. Bring the broth back to a boil, cover, and boil gently for about 10 minutes, until the pastina is very tender. Add the pepper and salt.
3. Ladle the soup into four soup bowls, and sprinkle with the chives. Serve immediately.

YIELD: 4 SERVINGS

NUTRITIONAL ANALYSIS PER SERVING:

Calories 77
Protein 3 gm.
Carbohydrates 15 gm.
Fat 0.3 gm.
Saturated fat 0.04 gm.
Cholesterol 0 mg.
Sodium 195 mg.

This soup is rich in potassium.

Oatmeal Leek Soup

This soup can be prepared in a few minutes. I use whole milk, but you can use nonfat or lower-fat milk if it better meets your caloric needs. You can substitute scallions for the leeks, too, and use cornmeal or farina instead of oats to thicken the soup.

- **1 small leek**
- **3½ cups whole milk**
- **¼ teaspoon freshly ground black pepper**
- **½ teaspoon salt**
- **1 cup quick-cooking oats**

1. Trim the leek, wash it well, and mince it to make about 1 cup.
2. In a saucepan, bring the leek, milk, pepper, and salt to a boil. Simmer for 2 minutes, and then stir in the oats.
3. Cook for about 2 minutes. Serve immediately, or keep warm, covered, in a double boiler over warm water. (If the soup thickens, thin it to the desired consistency with milk or water.)

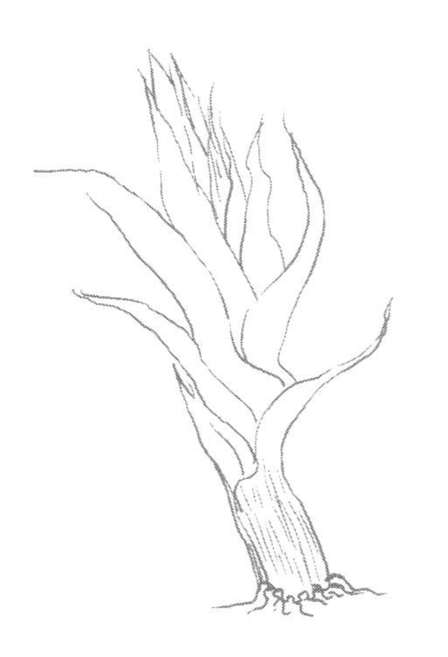

Yield: 4 Servings

NUTRITIONAL ANALYSIS PER SERVING:

Calories 217
Protein 10 gm.
Carbohydrates 26 gm.
Fat 8.4 gm.
Saturated fat 4.7 gm.
Cholesterol 30 mg.
Sodium 382 mg.

One serving of milk supplies 40 percent of an adult's calcium requirements. Oats supply soluble fiber and essential vitamins and minerals.

Split Pea Soup with Cracklings

This makes a great winter meal when served with crusty bread and a simple first course salad. The soup can be frozen, although it might require additional water when reheated, since it tends to thicken when refrigerated or frozen. (See photograph, page 62.)

6 ounces chicken skin, cut into 1-inch pieces
2 medium onions (8 ounces), peeled and cut into 1-inch pieces
2 to 3 cloves garlic, peeled, crushed, and coarsely chopped
8 cups water
2 teaspoons *herbes de Provence* (see page 467)
2 teaspoons salt
½ teaspoon freshly ground black pepper
¼ teaspoon Tabasco hot pepper sauce
1 pound dried split peas
Additional Tabasco hot pepper sauce (optional)

1. Place the chicken skin pieces in a skillet, and sauté over high heat for 8 to 10 minutes, until the fat is rendered and the skin is crisp. Transfer the cracklings and 3 tablespoons of the fat to a large saucepan. Discard the remainder of the fat.
2. Add the onions to the saucepan, and sauté for 5 minutes. Then add the garlic, mix well, and stir in the water, *herbes de Provence,* salt, pepper, ¼ teaspoon Tabasco sauce, and split peas.
3. Bring to a boil, cover, reduce the heat, and boil gently for 1 hour. Stir the soup well. It should be fairly thick, but if you prefer to thin it a little, add some water.
4. To serve, divide the soup among six bowls, and offer extra Tabasco sauce, if desired.

Making Cracklings

For cracklings, I cook chicken skin until it renders its fat and becomes crisp. I discard most of the cooking fat, retaining only 3 tablespoons, which I use to brown the onions for the soup. To reduce your calorie intake further, eliminate the cracklings altogether, and start your soup in the chicken fat or 3 tablespoons of peanut oil.

Yield: 6 Servings

NUTRITIONAL ANALYSIS PER SERVING:

Calories 354
Protein 20 gm.
Carbohydrates 49 gm.
Fat 9.3 gm.
Saturated fat 2.6 gm.
Cholesterol 9 mg.
Sodium 755 mg.

Split peas are rich in protein, high in soluble fiber, and a good source of B vitamins.

Sausage, Potato, and Cabbage Soup

It's worthwhile to make a large batch of this soup and freeze the remainder for another meal. Followed by a salad, it makes an ideal lunch on a cold winter day. If you are concerned about your calorie intake, use only half the amount of sausage called for here, or eliminate the sausage entirely for a different but still delicious result. Leftovers can be reheated again and again, and they taste better every time.

- **8 ounces coarsely ground sausage meat**
- **½ pound onions, peeled and cut into 1-inch slices (1½ cups)**
- **6 scallions, cut into ½-inch pieces (1¼ cups)**
- **6 cups water**
- **1 pound potatoes, peeled and cut into ½-inch slices**
- **8 ounces savoy cabbage, cut into 1½-inch pieces (4 cups)**
- **1¼ teaspoons salt**
- **French bread**

1. Break the sausage meat into pieces, and place it in a saucepan over high heat. Sauté for 10 minutes, stirring and scraping the bottom of the pan with a spoon to keep the meat from sticking, until the sausage is well browned.
2. Add the onions and scallions, and cook for 1 minute. Stir in the water, potatoes, cabbage, and salt. Bring to a boil, cover, reduce the heat to low, and cook for 45 minutes.
3. Serve the soup in bowls with chunks of crusty French bread.

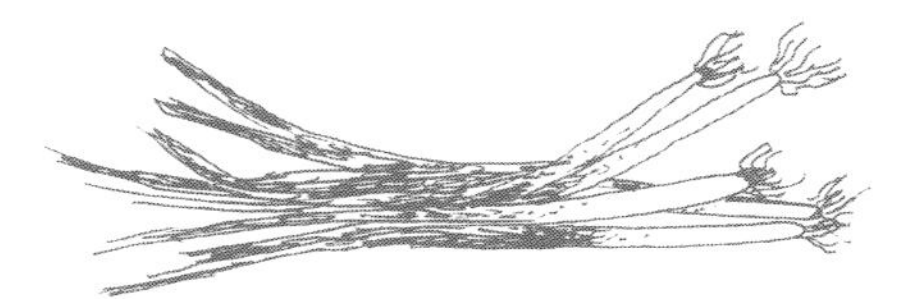

Yield: 8 Servings (About 10 Cups)

NUTRITIONAL ANALYSIS PER SERVING:

Calories 174
Protein 5 gm.
Carbohydrates 13 gm.
Fat 11.5 gm.
Saturated fat 4.1 gm.
Cholesterol 19 mg.
Sodium 545 mg.

This soup is high in vitamin C and potassium.

Hanoi Soup

This is my wife's rendition of a classic Vietnamese soup. One of my favorites, it is a meal in itself, quite satisfying on a cold winter night. The esoteric ingredients—star anise, rice sticks, and nuoc nam*—are available in Asian markets and can also be found in the Asian section of many supermarkets. (See About Southeast Asian Ingredients.)*

This colorful soup should be served in large bowls (2- to 3-cup capacity) to accommodate all the garnishes. There is enough here for four generous or six smaller servings.

- 1½ pounds oxtail, cut into 2- or 3-inch pieces
- 1½ pounds beef shank (about 2 slices, each 1 inch thick, with bones)
- 1 pound beef bones, cut into 3-inch pieces
- 6 quarts cold water
- 3 whole shallots, peeled (about 3 ounces)
- 1 piece ginger (about 2 inches), unpeeled
- 3 pieces star anise
- 1 thin cinnamon stick (about 3 inches long)
- 1 teaspoon salt

GARNISHES

- 9 cups water
- 1½ cups bean sprouts (6 ounces)
- 5 ounces rice sticks (rice vermicelli)
- 1½ cups freshly shredded napa cabbage
- Fish sauce (*nuoc nam*) to taste
- 1 cup (loosely packed) cilantro (coriander or Chinese parsley)
- 1 cup very finely sliced red onion
- 2 tablespoons hot pepper, seeded and sliced
- 4 scallions, cleaned and minced (½ cup)
- 1 lime, cut into 4 wedges

1. Place the oxtail, shank, beef bones, and cold water in a stainless steel stockpot. Bring to a boil over high heat. (This will take 25 to 30 minutes.) Skim off and discard any impurities that rise to the surface, and continue to cook at a fairly high boil for 5 minutes, removing surface scum as it collects. Reduce the heat to low.
2. Impale the shallots and ginger on a skewer, and hold them over the flames of a gas stove or directly above the heated burner of an electric stove for about 5 minutes, turning them often, until they are charred on all sides.

(continued)

ABOUT SOUTHEAST ASIAN INGREDIENTS

Nuoc nam is the Vietnamese name for the thin, salty, brownish fermented fish sauce that is as popular throughout Southeast Asia as soy sauce is in China and Japan. Some cooks consider *nam pla*, the Thai version of this odiferous sauce, to be the finest. Related to the magnolia family, star anise is an eight-pointed, star-shaped cluster of brown pods, each containing a pea-size seed that has a similar—though more bitter—flavor than regular anise seeds. Two or three points of this aromatic spice are usually sufficient to add fragrance and subtle spiciness to dishes like Hanoi Soup.

BEEF STOCK

THE BASE OF THIS SOUP IS A VERY GOOD STOCK MADE WITH OXTAIL, BEEF SHANK, AND BEEF BONES. IT IS FLAVORED WITH STAR ANISE, GINGER, AND SHALLOTS THAT HAVE BEEN HELD OVER A GAS FLAME OR HOT ELECTRIC BURNER UNTIL WELL CHARRED ON ALL SIDES. IN ADDITION TO GIVING THE STOCK A RICH COLOR, THE BURNED SHALLOTS IMPART A VERY SPECIFIC TASTE.

3. Add the shallots, ginger, star anise, and cinnamon to the stock. Boil the mixture very gently for 4 hours.
4. Transfer the bones and meat to a bowl, and strain the liquid twice through a paper towel–lined strainer to eliminate the fat. (You will have 8 to 9 cups.)
5. Wash the stockpot, return the stock to it, and add the salt. Pick the meat from the bones, eliminating any fat and sinew, and break it into pieces. (You will have about 3 cups.) Set aside.

FOR THE GARNISHES

6. Bring 3 cups of the water to a boil, and add the bean sprouts. Cook for 3½ to 4 minutes, until the mixture comes back to a strong boil. Drain.
7. Bring the remaining 6 cups of water to a boil. Add the rice sticks, and bring back to a boil. Boil for about 2½ minutes, until tender. Drain in a colander, and run briefly under cold water to cool.
8. At serving time, bring the stock to a boil. Heat the meat in a microwave oven or with a little stock in a saucepan on top of the stove. Place some of the rice sticks, shredded cabbage, bean sprouts, and meat in each of four large bowls (2- to 3-cup capacity), and fill the bowls with the boiling stock. Bring to the table, and pass around the fish sauce, cilantro, red onion, hot pepper, and scallions. Each diner can add as much of these ingredients as desired. Squeeze the juice of a lime wedge over each bowl, and eat the soup immediately.

YIELD: 4 SERVINGS

NUTRITIONAL ANALYSIS PER SERVING:

Calories 252
Protein 37 gm.
Carbohydrates 6 gm.
Fat 8.2 gm.
Saturated fat 2.4 gm.
Cholesterol 83 mg.
Sodium 628 mg.

Gazpacho with Black Olives

This classic Spanish soup is ideal for summer. Low in calories, it is like a raw vegetable salad. The idea is to create a smooth liquid with the vegetables, which is why I push the mixture through a food mill to strain it after it is processed. If you don't object to small pieces of vegetable or tomato skin in your soup, you can serve it unstrained. A little of each vegetable is reserved and diced as a colorful soup garnish along with olive pieces and toasted bread cubes. *(See photograph on page 56.)*

3 ripe tomatoes (about 1 pound)
3 cucumbers (about 1¾ pounds)
1 red bell pepper (about 7 ounces)
1 red onion (about 6 ounces)
3 cloves garlic
3 ounces bread (preferably from a dense sourdough loaf), cut into ½-inch cubes (1¾ cups)
1 tablespoon corn oil
12 to 15 black olives (preferably oil-cured)
1½ cups cold water
1½ teaspoons salt
1 teaspoon paprika
⅛ teaspoon cayenne pepper
2 tablespoons virgin olive oil
2 tablespoons red wine vinegar

1. Preheat the oven to 400 degrees.
2. Cut one of the tomatoes in half, and press the halves over a large bowl to remove the seeds and juice. Cut the flesh into ½-inch pieces (you will have about 1 cup), and set them aside for use as a garnish. Cut the two remaining tomatoes into 1-inch pieces, and add them, seeds and all, to the bowl.
3. Peel the cucumbers, halve one of them lengthwise, and scrape it with a spoon to remove the seeds. Add these seeds to the tomatoes in the bowl. Cut the flesh of the seeded cucumber into ½-inch pieces (you will have about 1 cup), and set them aside for garnish. Cut the two remaining cucumbers into 1-inch pieces, and add them to the bowl.

(continued)

GAZPACHO WITH BLACK OLIVES (*continued*)

4. Using a vegetable peeler, peel the skin from about half of the red pepper, and then cut the pepper so that you have one peeled half and one unpeeled half. Seed the pepper, and cut the peeled half into ¼-inch pieces (you will have about ½ cup). Set these aside for garnish. Cut the remainder of the pepper into 1-inch pieces, and add them to the bowl.
5. Peel the onion, and finely mince half (½ cup) of it. Place the minced onion in a small strainer and rinse it thoroughly under cold tap water. Drain well, and set aside for garnish. Cut the remainder of the onion coarsely, and add it to the bowl.
6. Peel the garlic cloves, crush them, and add them to the bowl. (You should have about 6 cups of vegetable pieces.)
7. Place the bread cubes in a small bowl, and mix them with the corn oil. Spread the cubes on a cookie sheet, and bake them at 400 degrees for 8 to 10 minutes, until nicely browned. Remove them, and set them aside for garnish.
8. Pit the olives, cut them into ¼-inch pieces (you should have about ¼ cup), and set them aside for garnish.
9. Place the 6 cups of vegetable pieces in the bowl of a food processor. Add the water, salt, paprika, and cayenne, and process until pureed. (If you have a small food processor, do this in two batches.) Then push the mixture through a food mill fitted with a fine screen. Mix in the olive oil and vinegar, and refrigerate the gazpacho until cold. (You will have 5 cups.)
10. At serving time, ladle the gazpacho into four soup bowls, and let guests sprinkle spoonfuls of the reserved garnishes on top.

YIELD: 4 SERVINGS

NUTRITIONAL ANALYSIS PER SERVING:

Calories 253
Protein 5 gm.
Carbohydrates 29 gm.
Fat 14.4 gm.
Saturated fat 1.8 gm.
Cholesterol 0 mg.
Sodium 1,244 mg.

Tomatoes and red bell peppers are rich in vitamin C. Tomatoes are also a good source of carotene, and red peppers have nine times the vitamin A of green peppers.

COLD MUSSEL AND BEAN SOUP

This is a bonus recipe using the liquid resulting from cooking the Stew of Lima Beans and Mussels with Spinach (see page 195). I serve the soup cold here, but the ingredients can be heated and served hot as well. If you decide not to make this soup when you prepare the stew, freeze the cooking liquid in small plastic containers. Then, when you want to make the soup, defrost the juices slowly under refrigeration for 24 hours before proceeding with the recipe.

2 cups liquid from cooking the beans for the Stew of Lima Beans and Mussels (see page 195), cooled
2 cups liquid from cooking the mussels for the Stew of Lima Beans and Mussels, cooled
½ cup sour cream
3 tablespoons chopped fresh chives
¼ teaspoon Tabasco hot pepper sauce

1. Place all the ingredients in a large bowl, and mix them together with a whisk until combined. Refrigerate until cool.
2. At serving time, spoon the cold soup into soup bowls, and serve immediately.

YIELD:
4 SERVINGS

NUTRITIONAL ANALYSIS PER SERVING:

Calories 72
Protein 2 gm.
Carbohydrates 3 gm.
Fat 6.1 gm.
Saturated fat 3.8 gm.
Cholesterol 13 mg.
Sodium 332 mg.

Cold Cream of Pea Soup with Mint

This soup is bright green when freshly made. If you are preparing it more than a few hours ahead, do not add the yogurt until just before serving, because the acid in it will tend to discolor the peas, making the soup a darker, less appealing shade. It is important that you use thin-skinned fresh peas or frozen petite peas here for a smooth result.

1 tablespoon virgin olive oil
1 medium onion (about 5 ounces), peeled and thinly sliced (1¼ cups)
3 cups chicken stock, preferably homemade unsalted and defatted (see page 466), or lower-salt canned chicken broth
¾ teaspoon salt (less if canned broth is used)
1 cup (loose) fresh mint leaves
1 package (10 ounces) frozen petite peas, unthawed, or equivalent amount of fresh peas
1½ cups plain yogurt, regular or nonfat
1 tablespoon unsalted butter
1 teaspoon sugar
¼ teaspoon Tabasco hot pepper sauce

1. Heat the oil until hot in a large stainless steel saucepan. Add the onion, and sauté for 2 minutes. Stir in the stock and salt, and bring the mixture to a boil over high heat.
2. After reserving a few of the mint leaves to decorate the finished soup, add the remainder along with the peas to the boiling stock. Bring the mixture back to a boil (this will take 3 or 4 minutes), and continue to boil it vigorously over high heat for 3 minutes.
3. Immediately place half the pea mixture in the bowl of a food processor, and process it until very smooth. Transfer the puree to a bowl, and process the remaining pea mixture along with 1 cup of the yogurt and the butter. Strain both batches of the puree through a fine strainer for a smooth soup. (If not strained, the soup will have a slightly granular texture.) Mix in the sugar and Tabasco, cover with plastic wrap, and refrigerate until serving time.
4. At serving time, process the remaining yogurt for a few seconds, until it is liquefied (it should have the consistency of a salad dressing). Divide the soup among four bowls, and swirl 1 to 2 tablespoons of the liquefied yogurt over each serving. Decorate with reserved mint leaves, and serve.

Yield: 4 Servings

NUTRITIONAL ANALYSIS PER SERVING:

Calories 200
Protein 9 gm.
Carbohydrates 18 gm.
Fat 10.5 gm.
Saturated fat 4.3 gm.
Cholesterol 19 mg.
Sodium 655 mg.

Peas are a good source of soluble fiber. Yogurt is rich in calcium and a good source of potassium.

ABOUT THE FOOD MILL

AN INVALUABLE (AND MODESTLY PRICED) KITCHEN UTENSIL, THE FOOD MILL IS ESSENTIALLY A MECHANIZED SIEVE. TURNING A HANDLE ON TOP PROPELS PADDLE-BLADES SET OVER A STRAINER PLATE IN THE BASE OF THE DEVICE. AS THE BLADES ROTATE, THEY PUSH THE FOOD THROUGH THE STRAINER, LEAVING BEHIND SKIN, SEEDS, AND—IN THE CASE OF THE PEA PODS, FOR EXAMPLE—FIBER.

Pea Pod Soup

This is a bonus recipe, made with the pods from the fresh peas shelled for the Stew of Peas and Ham, page 319. Be sure to sort through the pods and discard any that are damaged before proceeding.

It is absolutely essential that you strain this soup through a food mill before serving it. (See About the Food Mill.) Pea pods are, of course, full of inedible fiber, but they also contain soft flesh, which is extruded when the pods are pushed through the food mill. Using a food processor and then straining the mixture through a conventional strainer is not a good alternative.

For a richer soup, add some light or heavy cream to the completed recipe, and serve with croutons, if desired.

YIELD: 4 SERVINGS (ABOUT 5½ CUPS)

NUTRITIONAL ANALYSIS PER SERVING:

Calories 148
Protein 4 gm.
Carbohydrates 23 gm.
Fat 4.9 gm.
Saturated fat 2.0 gm.
Cholesterol 8 mg.
Sodium 425 mg.

1½ teaspoons corn oil
1 onion (about 4 ounces), cut into 1-inch pieces
1 leek (about 5 ounces), green and white portions cleaned and cut into 1-inch pieces
3 cups water
¾ teaspoon salt
4 or 5 potatoes (12 ounces total), peeled and cut into 2-inch pieces
10 ounces fresh pea pods, reserved from peas shelled for Stew of Peas and Ham, page 319
1 tablespoon unsalted butter
Croutons, for garnish (optional)

1. Heat the oil in a saucepan, and add the onion and leek. Cook for 2 to 3 minutes over medium to high heat. Add the water, salt, and potatoes, and bring to a boil.
2. Meanwhile, wash the pods, and discard any damaged ones. Add the pods to the saucepan, bring the mixture to a boil again, and boil, covered, for 30 minutes.
3. Push the mixture through a food mill. (You should have about 5½ cups.) Add the butter, and mix until it has melted.
4. Serve the soup as is or with croutons, if desired.

Dried and Fresh Mushroom Soup

Dried mushrooms are responsible for the great intensity of flavor in this soup, although fresh mushrooms—primarily stem pieces—help create the base for the soup, and their caps are used as a garnish. The soup can be made richer with the addition of cream at the end, and it can be served cold as well as hot.

½ ounce dried cèpe mushrooms (½ cup)
1 cup milk
4 ounces fresh mushrooms, cleaned
1½ teaspoons virgin olive oil
1 medium onion (about 3 ounces), peeled and cut into ½-inch cubes
1 small leek (about 3 ounces), cleaned and thinly sliced
1 medium to large potato (about 6 ounces), peeled and cut into ½-inch cubes
1 teaspoon salt
2½ cups water

1. Soak the dried mushrooms in the milk for at least 1 hour. Drain, reserving the milk.
2. Cut enough of the fresh mushroom caps into julienne strips to measure ¾ cup. Set aside.
3. Heat the oil in a large saucepan. When it is hot, add the onion and leek, and sauté for 2 minutes over low heat. Add the cèpe mushrooms, potato, salt, remaining fresh mushroom pieces, and water. Bring to a boil, cover, reduce the heat to low, and simmer gently for 25 minutes.
4. Puree the soup in the saucepan using a hand blender, or puree it in a food processor and return it to the saucepan. Add the julienned mushroom caps, and bring to a boil.
5. At serving time, stir in the reserved milk, bring to a boil, and serve immediately.

Yield: 4 Servings (5 cups)

NUTRITIONAL ANALYSIS PER SERVING:

Calories 115
Protein 4 gm.
Carbohydrates 17 gm.
Fat 4.0 gm.
Saturated fat 1.5 gm.
Cholesterol 9 mg.
Sodium 589 mg.

Potatoes and mushrooms contribute potassium, and milk is high in calcium.

Garlic Soup

Leek, onion, and a lot of garlic flavor this soup. Cooked as they are here in liquid, however, these potent ingredients are quite subtle, even mild. Although I use potato as a thickening agent, you can thicken the same soup with leftover bread, couscous, or cornmeal instead. My mother used to finish this soup with cream, but I use milk; the result is wonderfully satisfying.

- **1 leek (about 4 ounces)**
- **1 onion (about 4 ounces)**
- **2 tablespoons peanut oil**
- **8 to 10 cloves garlic, peeled and crushed (2 tablespoons)**
- **2 cups homemade unsalted and defatted chicken stock (see page 466), or lower-salt canned chicken broth**
- **2 cups water**
- **1 pound potatoes, peeled and cut into 2-inch pieces**
- **1 teaspoon salt (less if using canned broth)**
- **½ teaspoon freshly ground black pepper**
- **2 slices white bread**
- **1 tablespoon canola oil**
- **1 cup milk**

1. Preheat the oven to 400 degrees.
2. Trim the leek, wash it well, and cut it into 1-inch pieces. (You should have about 1 cup.) Peel and coarsely chop the onion.
3. Heat the peanut oil in a saucepan. When hot, add the leek, onion, and garlic, and sauté for 2 minutes. Then add the stock, water, potatoes, salt, and pepper. Bring to a boil. Cover, reduce the heat to low, and boil gently for 25 minutes.
4. Meanwhile, remove the crusts from the bread, and cut it into ½-inch croutons. (You should have 1¼ cups.) Moisten the croutons with the canola oil, and spread them on a cookie sheet. Bake at 400 degrees for 8 to 10 minutes, until nicely browned.
5. When the soup is cooked, strain it through a sieve, retaining the liquid. Place the solids in the bowl of a food processor, and process until smooth. Return to the saucepan with the reserved liquid, and add the milk. Bring to a boil. Serve with the croutons.

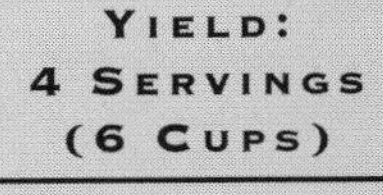

YIELD: 4 SERVINGS (6 CUPS)

NUTRITIONAL ANALYSIS PER SERVING:

Calories 268
Protein 7 gm.
Carbohydrates 32 gm.
Fat 14.1 gm.
Saturated fat 3.2 gm.
Cholesterol 9 mg.
Sodium 757 mg.

Garlic has been associated with lower cholesterol and triglyceride levels, less clotting of red blood cells, and lowered blood pressure.

CLOCKWISE FROM TOP:
POTAGE DE LÉGUMES AU VERMICELLE (VEGETABLE AND VERMICELLI SOUP) (SEE PAGE 47);
SPLIT PEA SOUP WITH CRACKLINGS (SEE PAGE 50); GARLIC SOUP (ABOVE).

A COLD VERSION

THIS SOUP FREEZES WELL AND CAN BE SERVED COLD AS WELL AS HOT. WITH THE ADDITION OF CREAM OR MILK, THE COLD SOUP CAN BE TRANSFORMED INTO A TYPE OF VICHYSSOISE.

Watercress Soup

This thrifty recipe makes use of the stems of the watercress leaves I used in Grilled Squid on Watercress, page 137. Sometimes tough and often strong-flavored, the stems are ideal for soup. Since the soup will be pureed, the vegetables need only be coarsely cut before they are added to the pot. The mixture can be transferred to a food processor or food mill for pureeing, but, to save time and labor, a hand blender immersed directly into the cooking pot works well here.

- 1 tablespoon canola oil
- 4 ounces watercress stems (reserved from Grilled Squid on Watercress, page 137), washed
- 1 stalk celery (2 ounces), coarsely diced (about 1 cup)
- 1 onion (6 ounces), coarsely diced (about 2 cups)
- 2 cloves garlic, peeled
- 2½ cups homemade unsalted and defatted stock (chicken—see page 466—beef, veal, or a mixture of these), or lower-salt canned broth
- ¾ teaspoon salt (more or less, depending on the saltiness of the stock)
- ¾ pound potatoes, peeled and cut into 2-inch pieces
- Croutons, for garnish (optional)

1. Heat the oil in a saucepan. When it is hot, add the watercress stems, celery, onion, and garlic, and cook for 2 minutes. Add the stock, salt, and potatoes, and bring the mixture to a boil. Cover, reduce the heat to low, and boil gently for 30 minutes.
2. Puree the mixture, either with a hand-held blender in the pot or by pushing it through a food mill or processing it in a food processor.
3. Serve the soup hot, garnished, if desired, with croutons.

YIELD: 4 SERVINGS

NUTRITIONAL ANALYSIS PER SERVING:

Calories 127
Protein 4 gm.
Carbohydrates 18 gm.
Fat 4.5 gm.
Saturated fat 0.5 gm.
Cholesterol 0 mg.
Sodium 544 mg.

Watercress is a great source of vitamin A.

Chicken and Spinach Velouté

The quality of this soup depends on the quality of the chicken stock used. Homemade chicken stock should be completely defatted and highly concentrated. I thicken the velouté with Cream of Wheat, which cooks quite quickly, but cornmeal, tapioca, and semolina work equally well.

- **4 cups homemade unsalted and defatted chicken stock (see page 466), or lower-salt canned chicken broth**
- **1 cup water**
- **¾ teaspoon salt (less if using canned broth)**
- **¼ teaspoon freshly ground black pepper**
- **6 tablespoons instant Cream of Wheat**
- **6 ounces spinach, stems removed**
- **⅓ cup heavy cream**

1. Bring the stock, water, salt, and pepper to a boil in a stainless steel saucepan. Add the Cream of Wheat. Mix well. Bring back to a boil, reduce the heat to low, and cook gently for 3 minutes.
2. Wash the spinach, cut it very coarsely, and add it to the pan. Bring back to a boil, and boil for 2 minutes. Stir in the cream, and serve immediately.

Yield: 4 Servings

Nutritional Analysis per Serving:

Calories 167
Protein 7 gm.
Carbohydrates 17 gm.
Fat 10.1 gm.
Saturated fat 5.3 gm.
Cholesterol 27 mg.
Sodium 646 mg.

Spinach is a rich source of vitamins A and C and is a good vegetable source of iron.

ABOUT COMPOSED SALAD

A composed salad consists of greens and any of an almost endless variety of other ingredients, from cooked vegetables to fruits, nuts, poultry, lamb, beef, fish, and shellfish. Depending on the contents, the salad can be served cold, lukewarm, or at room temperature, as either a first or a main course.

Composed Salad

In this composed salad, I add cheese, apple, and caramelized pecans to curly endive or escarole. The combination makes the salad an ideal summer supper or lunch main course or elegant dinner first course.

Spicy Caramelized Pecans

- ¼ cup pecan halves
- ½ teaspoon canola oil
- 1 tablespoon sugar
- Dash of salt
- Dash of cayenne pepper

- 1 medium apple (about 4 ounces), preferably russet or Golden Delicious
- 1½ teaspoons lemon juice

Vinaigrette

- 1½ tablespoons oil (a mixture of walnut, hazelnut, and/or canola)
- 1½ teaspoons sherry vinegar
- ⅛ teaspoon salt
- ¼ teaspoon freshly ground black pepper

- 4 cups salad greens (preferably the white center of curly endive or escarole), cut into 1½- to 2-inch pieces, washed and thoroughly dried in a salad spinner
- 1 ounce semi-dry or hard goat cheese, crumbled into pieces about ½ inch in size

1. Place the pecans in a skillet, and cover (barely) with water. Bring to a simmer over high heat, and drain immediately.
2. Place the pecans back in the pan with the oil, sugar, salt, and cayenne. Cook over medium to high heat, stirring until the nuts brown and the mixture caramelizes.
3. Transfer the pecans to a plate to cool.
4. Wash the apple, halve it, and remove the core. Cut it into ½-inch slices. Stack the slices, and cut them into ½-inch strips. Mix the apple strips with the lemon juice, and set them aside.
5. Mix the sherry vinaigrette ingredients together in a salad bowl.
6. At serving time, toss the greens with the vinaigrette, and arrange on individual plates. Sprinkle with the apple strips, crumbled cheese, and pecans. Serve immediately.

Yield: 4 Servings

NUTRITIONAL ANALYSIS PER SERVING:

Calories 164
Protein 3 gm.
Carbohydrates 10 gm.
Fat 12.9 gm.
Saturated fat 2.6 gm.
Cholesterol 7 mg.
Sodium 138 mg.

Pecans and apples are sources of fiber.

Tomato and Avocado Salad

Flesh of a ripe avocado, combined here with a little lemon juice and olive oil, is piled on top of thick tomato slices and presented on a bed of mesclun salad greens that have been tossed with a lemon-flavored dressing. Available now in many supermarkets, mesclun is a mixture of young greens and herbs that are common to the south of France. If you can't find mesclun in your area, substitute Boston lettuce or other greens to your liking.

- 1 ripe avocado (about 8 ounces)
- 2 teaspoons lemon juice
- 1 tablespoon virgin olive oil
- ¼ teaspoon salt
- ¼ teaspoon freshly ground black pepper
- 1 large ripe tomato (12 to 16 ounces)

Lemon Dressing

- 1½ tablespoons lemon juice
- 3 tablespoons virgin olive oil
- ¼ teaspoon salt
- ¼ teaspoon freshly ground black pepper

- 4 cups (loose) mesclun salad greens (a mixture of different young, tender greens and herbs), rinsed and thoroughly dried
- ¼ cup coarsely chopped fresh cilantro

1. No more than 2 hours before serving the salad, cut the avocado in half, remove the pit, and cut the flesh into ½-inch pieces. In a small bowl, toss the avocado pieces with the 2 teaspoons of lemon juice, 1 tablespoon olive oil, and ⅛ teaspoon each of the salt and pepper. Set aside.
2. At serving time, cut the tomato into four thick slices, and sprinkle with the remaining ⅛ teaspoon each of salt and pepper.
3. Combine the dressing ingredients in a bowl large enough to hold the salad greens. Add the greens, and toss thoroughly.
4. Divide the greens among four salad plates. Place a slice of tomato in the center of each plate of greens, and top with the avocado. Sprinkle with the cilantro, and serve immediately.

Yield: 4 Servings

Nutritional Analysis per Serving:

Calories 220
Protein 2 gm.
Carbohydrates 10 gm.
Fat 20.4 gm.
Saturated fat 2.9 gm.
Cholesterol 0 mg.
Sodium 290 mg.

Although high in calories and fat, avocado is an excellent source of vitamins A and E and potassium.

USING EGG ROLL WRAPPERS

Egg roll wrappers are available packaged in the produce section of most supermarkets. Here, these thin, low-calorie pastry sheets are brushed with oil, baked until crisp, and sandwiched around my salad. The crisp wrappers can also be served with cheese in place of toast or bread.

√ Fennel and Pear Salad

This salad has diverse ingredients—reconstituted dried tomatoes, fennel, pumpkin seeds, and pears—but the distinctive flavor of each is delightful in combination with the others.

- 1 teaspoon corn, peanut, or canola oil
- 8 egg roll wrappers, each cut to form an oval 4½ by 3 inches
- ¼ cup pumpkin seeds
- 6 cups water
- ½ cup dried tomatoes (about 1 ounce)
- 1 small fennel bulb (about 10 ounces), thinly sliced (about 2½ cups), with stem removed and feathery leaves (about ¼ cup) set aside for decoration
- 1 Bosc pear (about 5 ounces), peeled, cored, and cut into ½-inch pieces

SHERRY VINAIGRETTE

- 2 tablespoons virgin olive oil
- 1 tablespoon sherry vinegar
- ¼ teaspoon salt
- ¼ teaspoon freshly ground black pepper

1. Preheat the oven to 400 degrees.
2. Brush a cookie sheet lightly with ½ teaspoon of the oil. Arrange the egg roll ovals on the sheet, and brush the tops of them with another ½ teaspoon of oil.
3. Bake at 400 degrees until brown and crisp, about 6 to 7 minutes. Transfer to a plate, and set aside until serving time.
4. Spread the pumpkin seeds on a cookie sheet, and toast them lightly in a 400-degree oven for about 4 or 5 minutes. Set aside.
5. Bring 2 cups of the water to a boil in a saucepan, drop in the dried tomatoes, and bring back to a boil. Cover the pan, and set it off the heat for 10 minutes. Drain, reserving the cooking liquid in the refrigerator or freezer for use in soups or stews. Cut the tomatoes into 1-inch pieces.
6. Bring the remaining 4 cups of water to a boil. Add the fennel, and cook it over high heat for about 3 minutes, or just until the water returns to a boil. Drain and cool for a few minutes.
7. In a bowl, gently mix together the fennel, pear, and tomato pieces with the pumpkin seeds and all the vinaigrette ingredients.
8. To serve, place an egg roll crisp on each of four plates. Spoon the fennel mixture on top of the crisps, and top each serving with another egg roll crisp to create a salad "sandwich." Garnish with the reserved fennel leaves, and serve immediately.

YIELD: 4 SERVINGS

NUTRITIONAL ANALYSIS PER SERVING:

Calories 294
Protein 9 gm.
Carbohydrates 43 gm.
Fat 10.3 gm.
Saturated fat 1.4 gm.
Cholesterol 39 mg.
Sodium 217 mg.

Red Onion and Orange Salad

This colorful salad is a standard at our house in summer, when tomatoes are at their flavor peak. I like it made with a Torpedo onion, a flavorful, long, narrow, red variety. Although I use regular seedless oranges here to lend acidity to the dish, if you happen to live in an area where blood oranges are available, substitute them instead for color and taste. *(See photograph, page 94.)*

- **1 red onion, preferably Torpedo (about 6 ounces), peeled**
- **2 seedless oranges (10 to 12 ounces each)**
- **6 ripe plum tomatoes (12 ounces)**
- **½ cup (lightly packed) fresh flat-leaf parsley leaves**

Cider Vinegar Dressing

- **2 tablespoons cider vinegar**
- **3 tablespoons virgin olive oil**
- **1 teaspoon Worcestershire sauce**
- **½ teaspoon freshly ground black pepper**
- **½ teaspoon salt**

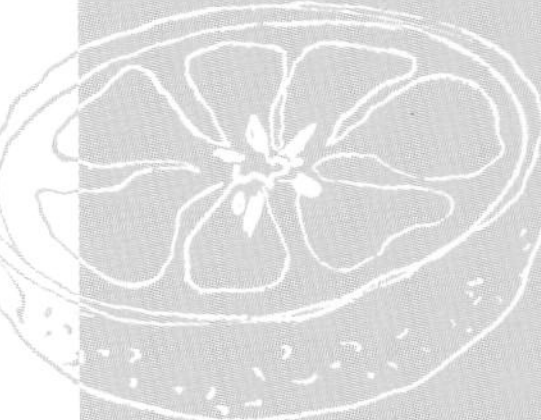

1. Cut the onion crosswise into ⅛-inch-thick slices. Separate the slices into rings, and place them in a serving bowl large enough to hold the finished salad.
2. Peel the oranges, removing all the white pith surrounding the flesh. Cut the oranges crosswise into ¼-inch slices, and add them to the onion rings in the bowl.
3. Cut the tomatoes in half crosswise, and squeeze them gently to remove the seeds (which can be reserved for stock). Cut the tomato halves into 1-inch pieces, and add them to the oranges and onions. Add the parsley leaves.

For the Cider Vinegar Dressing

4. Mix the vinegar, olive oil, Worcestershire sauce, pepper, and salt in a small bowl.
5. At serving time, add the dressing to the bowl of onions, oranges, and tomatoes, toss the salad, and serve.

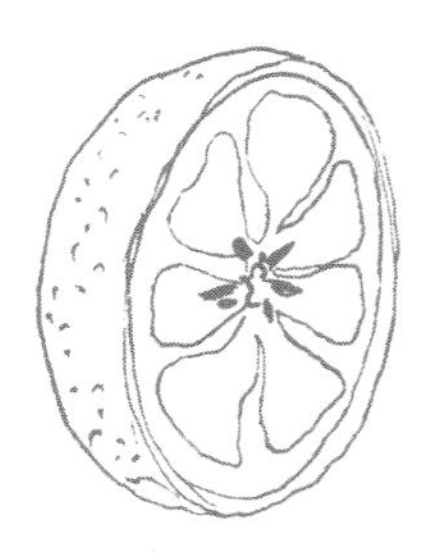

Yield: 4 Servings

Nutritional Analysis per Serving:

Calories 180
Protein 2 gm.
Carbohydrates 22 gm.
Fat 10.7 gm.
Saturated fat 1.4 gm.
Cholesterol 0 mg.
Sodium 302 mg.

Oranges are high in potassium and soluble fiber.

Salad with *Saucisson*

This salad with a garlicky mustard vinaigrette is classic in French bistros, where it is enjoyed as a light lunch or a snack, either during the day or after the theater. It is traditionally served with slices of pâté or a good hard salami, called saucisson *in French. A crusty baguette is the perfect accompaniment.*

4 ounces good-quality, hard French *saucisson* salami
1 large head escarole, as white as possible, cut into 1½-inch pieces (about 8 cups)

GARLIC-DIJON VINAIGRETTE

2 cloves garlic, cut into very small dice (about 2 teaspoons)
¼ teaspoon freshly ground black pepper
¼ teaspoon salt
2 teaspoons Dijon-style mustard
1 tablespoon red wine vinegar
2 tablespoons peanut oil

Crusty bread

1. Remove the "skin," or casing, from the *saucisson,* and cut it into about twenty very thin slices (about five slices per person).
2. Wash the escarole thoroughly, dipping it up and down in a sink filled with cold water, and dry it in a salad spinner to remove moisture that would otherwise dilute the vinaigrette.

FOR THE GARLIC-DIJON VINAIGRETTE

3. In the bowl you will use for serving the salad, mix together all the vinaigrette ingredients. The mixture should not be homogenized; the ingredients should separate somewhat.
4. At serving time, add the escarole to the bowl, and toss it thoroughly with the vinaigrette. Divide it among four plates, and arrange the *saucisson* slices around the periphery of each plate. Serve with crusty bread.

YIELD:
4 SERVINGS

NUTRITIONAL ANALYSIS PER SERVING:

Calories 201
Protein 8 gm.
Carbohydrates 5 gm.
Fat 16.9 gm.
Saturated fat 4.6 gm.
Cholesterol 22 mg.
Sodium 760 mg.

Allicin, a natural component of garlic, has antibiotic properties and helps reduce cholesterol and triglyceride levels.

LENTIL AND POTATO SALAD

Sausage is a classic accompaniment for potato salad and is often served with lentils, so it seems appropriate to serve this herb-flavored salad containing both vegetables with Walnut Sausage (see page 158). In my salad, I use lentilles du Puy. *If you can't find them, substitute another dried lentil in this dish.*

LENTILLES DU PUY

LENTILLES DU PUY ARE TINY GREEN LENTILS, NAMED AFTER THEIR PLACE OF ORIGIN IN THE CENTER OF FRANCE. OBTAINABLE AT SPECIALTY FOOD STORES AND SOME SUPERMARKETS, THIS VARIETY HOLDS ITS SHAPE VERY WELL AS IT COOKS.

- **¾ cup dried lentils (about 4½ ounces), preferably imported *lentilles du Puy* (green lentils)**
- **1 teaspoon salt**
- **2¾ cups cold water**
- **4 small to medium potatoes (¾ pound), washed**
- **¾ cup finely chopped onion**
- **3 cloves garlic, peeled, crushed, and finely chopped (2 teaspoons)**
- **¼ cup chopped fresh herb mixture (parsley, basil, savory, and tarragon)**
- **3 or 4 scallions, finely minced (3 tablespoons)**
- **¼ cup virgin olive oil**
- **2 tablespoons red wine vinegar**
- **½ teaspoon freshly ground black pepper**

1. Place the lentils and ¼ teaspoon of the salt in a large saucepan with the cold water. Bring to a boil, cover, and boil gently for 45 minutes, until the lentils are tender. Set the pan off the heat, and let the lentils cool for 15 minutes at room temperature. (Most of the liquid should have evaporated.)
2. Meanwhile, place the potatoes in a saucepan with enough cold water to cover them. Bring to a boil over high heat, reduce the heat to low, and cook the potatoes gently, uncovered, for about 35 minutes (replacing water as needed to keep the potatoes covered) or until tender when pierced with the point of a knife. Drain the water, and let the potatoes cool to lukewarm.
3. When the potatoes are cool enough to handle, cut them crosswise into ⅜-inch-thick slices, and place them in a bowl. Add the lentils, and combine them gently with the potatoes. Add the onion, garlic, herbs, scallions, olive oil, vinegar, pepper, and remaining ¾ teaspoon salt, and mix just enough to combine well.
4. Transfer the salad to a large platter. Serve it immediately, while still lukewarm, with ¾-inch-thick slices of Walnut Sausage (see page 158) arranged on top, if desired.

YIELD: 4 SERVINGS

NUTRITIONAL ANALYSIS PER SERVING:

Calories 315
Protein 11 gm.
Carbohydrates 39 gm.
Fat 13.9 gm.
Saturated fat 1.8 gm.
Cholesterol 0 mg.
Sodium 562 mg.

Lentils offer complex carbohydrate high in fiber, iron, and B vitamins.

Eggs in Aspic with Tarragon

Eggs in aspic—oeufs en gelée—*is a classic dish in French bourgeois cooking. In the summer, my family adores a good aspic, which means one made with a good stock. There is nothing more refreshing than eggs or fish, for example, served in a cold, flavorful* gelée. *Even though you may have avoided aspic dishes in the past, thinking them too sophisticated, try this one; it is stunningly beautiful and delicious.*

Clarifying Stock for Aspic

The clarification of the stock to make the aspic is a time-honored process and doesn't take long. Egg white is used as a coagulant to meld together all extraneous materials in the stock, making them easy to strain off. The result is a crystal-clear stock—free of fat and beautiful in color. The greens and peppercorns are used here the way you use tea: steeping them in the boiling stock for a few minutes imparts flavor to the stock and lends substance to the clarification. Unflavored gelatin provides the texture needed to hold the stock together in an aspic.

- 4 small eggs
- 2 cups water

Clarified Aspic

- 1 teaspoon salt (less if using canned chicken broth)
- 1 egg white
- 2 cups mixed leaves of celery, green parts of leeks, and available fresh herbs, like parsley and tarragon
- ½ teaspoon black peppercorns, coarsely crushed (*mignonnette*) (see Making a *Mignonnette,* page 352)
- 2 envelopes (½ ounce each) unflavored gelatin (1½ tablespoons)
- 2½ cups homemade unsalted and defatted chicken stock (see page 466), or lower-salt canned chicken broth

- 1 tablespoon coarsely chopped fresh tarragon leaves
- ⅓ cup julienned lean boiled ham (about 1½ ounces)

- 4 cups mixed salad greens, washed and dried

Toast

1. Prick the rounded end of each egg with a thumbtack to relieve pressure and keep the eggs from cracking when they are cooked.
2. Bring the water to a boil in a saucepan, and gently lower the eggs into the water. Bring the water back to a boil, and boil the eggs very gently for 4½ minutes. Then drain them, and place them in a bowl of ice water.
3. When the eggs are completely cool, shell them carefully (preferably under cool running water, which makes the peeling easier and so helps protect the soft yolks inside), and return them to the cold water. Refrigerate until ready to use. (The recipe can be prepared to this point a few hours ahead.)
4. Mix all the clarification ingredients except the stock in a large stainless steel saucepan.

5. In another saucepan, bring the stock to a boil.
6. Add about ⅓ cup of the boiling stock to the clarification mixture, and mix well. Then add the rest of the stock, mix well, and place over high heat. Bring to a boil, mixing often to prevent the ingredients from sticking to the bottom of the pan and scorching. As soon as the mixture comes to a strong boil, reduce the heat to low, and boil very gently for 4 minutes. *Do not disturb the mixture by stirring or shaking the pan.*
7. Remove the pan from the heat, and let the mixture stand, undisturbed, for 10 minutes. Then strain it carefully through a strainer or colander lined with a paper or cloth towel. (You should have about 2½ cups of very clean and clear liquid.)
8. Place about 2 tablespoons of the liquid aspic in each of four round or oval ramekins (¾-cup capacity). When the aspic has set, sprinkle the tarragon and ham strips on top, dividing them among the four ramekins.
9. Remove the eggs from the cold water, and pat them dry with paper towels. Place an egg in each of the ramekins.
10. Cool the remainder of the aspic, and when it is cool but not yet set, spoon it around the eggs, filling up the ramekins. Refrigerate until set firm, about 2 hours.
11. To serve, arrange the mixed greens on a platter. Run a sharp knife around the edge of the ramekins to loosen the aspic, and invert the molded eggs onto the greens. (*Note:* If unmolding is difficult, dip the bottoms of the ramekins into hot water for 4 to 5 seconds before unmolding.) Serve with toast.

OEUFS MOLLETS

FOR THIS RECIPE, I PREPARE WHAT ARE KNOWN IN FRENCH CUISINE AS *OEUFS MOLLETS*. I FOLLOW THE SAME PROCEDURE THAT I USE FOR HARD-COOKING EGGS EXCEPT THAT I REMOVE THEM FROM THE BOILING WATER AFTER ONLY 4½ MINUTES. THIS BRINGS THE INTERIOR TEMPERATURE OF THE EGGS TO BETWEEN 140 AND 150 DEGREES. BOILING EGGS FOR 4 MINUTES KILLS ANY SALMONELLA BACTERIA THAT MAY BE LURKING THERE BUT LEAVES THE YOLKS SOFT, LIKE THOSE OF POACHED EGGS.

YIELD: 4 SERVINGS

NUTRITIONAL ANALYSIS PER SERVING:

Calories 137
Protein 16 gm.
Carbohydrates 5 gm.
Fat 6.2 gm.
Saturated fat 1.8 gm.
Cholesterol 218 mg.
Sodium 757 mg.

Melon in Port Wine

This dish is often served in France as a first course. The melon of choice there is the small, flavorful cavaillon*—named for the town in the south of France where it was first grown—and one melon is traditionally served per person. I substitute a ripe cantaloupe, which will serve four people, in my rendition of this classic dish. After first scooping as many balls from the fruit as possible, I scrape out the remaining flesh and create a sauce from these trimmings. The melon balls are marinated in this sauce and some port wine, and served, if desired, with a sprinkling of pepper.*

ALTERNATIVE SERVING SUGGESTION

DISCARD THE MELON SHELLS. SERVE THE MELON BALLS AND MARINADE IN GLASS GOBLETS, GARNISHING EACH WITH A SPRIG OF SAGE AND SEVERAL GRINDINGS OF BLACK PEPPER, IF DESIRED.

- 1 **ripe cantaloupe (2¾ to 3 pounds)**
- ¼ **cup good-quality port wine**
- 2 **sprigs sage**
- **Freshly ground black pepper (optional)**

1. Cut the cantaloupe in half crosswise. Spoon out and discard the seeds. Using a melon baller, scoop out a layer of balls from the flesh of one of the halves, and place them in a bowl. Then, still using the melon baller, scrape out the flesh trimmings from between the holes, and set them aside in another bowl. Repeat this procedure, working layer by layer, until all the flesh has been removed from both melon halves. You should have about 2½ cups of melon balls and 1 cup of trimmings. Reserve the empty melon shells.
2. Add the port to the bowl containing the melon balls, and mix thoroughly. Place the melon trimmings in the bowl of a food processor or blender, and liquefy them. Add this mixture to the melon balls, mix well, cover, and refrigerate for at least 1 or 2 hours.
3. Meanwhile, using a sharp paring knife, cut the edge of each reserved melon shell into decorative pointed "teeth."
4. At serving time, fill the shells with the melon balls and marinade, and decorate each with a sprig of sage. At the table, spoon the melon balls onto individual dessert plates, and serve cold with freshly ground pepper sprinkled on top, if desired.

YIELD: 4 SERVINGS

NUTRITIONAL ANALYSIS PER SERVING:

Calories 80
Protein 1 gm.
Carbohydrates 15 gm.
Fat 0.5 gm.
Saturated fat 0 gm.
Cholesterol 0 mg.
Sodium 16 mg.

Cantaloupe is rich in vitamins A and C and is a good source of potassium.

Braised Stuffed Artichokes

Instead of stuffing these artichokes, you can serve them simply with a little olive oil and lemon juice. If you do this, however, increase the initial cooking time from 20 to 30 minutes, since you won't cook them again as you do the stuffed ones. (See photograph, page 337.)

- **4 large artichokes (about 8 ounces each), preferably with stems**
- **6 tablespoons virgin olive oil**
- **1 medium onion (about 6 ounces), peeled and coarsely chopped (about 1½ cups)**
- **3 cloves garlic, peeled, crushed, and finely chopped (1½ teaspoons)**
- **6 ounces mushrooms, rinsed and coarsely chopped (1¾ cups)**
- **3 slices white bread (3 ounces)**
- **¾ teaspoon salt**
- **¾ teaspoon freshly ground black pepper**
- **1 cup water**

1. Prepare the artichokes. (See Perfect Artichokes.)

For the Stuffing

2. Heat 4 tablespoons of the oil in a skillet, and sauté the onion for about 1 minute. Add the garlic and mushrooms, and continue sautéing for about 2 minutes.
3. Tear the bread slices into the bowl of a food processor, and process for a few seconds, until crumbed. (You should have about 1½ cups of crumbs.) Add the bread crumbs to the mixture in the skillet, and sauté for about 3 to 4 minutes, until nicely browned. Stir in ½ teaspoon each of the salt and pepper, and set aside.

For the Artichokes

4. When the artichokes are cool enough to handle, hold them upside down over the sink, and squeeze out as much water as possible. Remove the thin center leaves to expose the chokes, and discard. Cut off the stems, and if they are tender, chop them coarsely. Add them to the stuffing. Fill the center of the artichokes with the stuffing, and insert the remaining stuffing between the leaves.
5. Place the stuffed artichokes upright in a saucepan, and pour in the water, the remaining 2 tablespoons of oil, and the remaining ¼ teaspoon each of salt and pepper. Bring to a boil, and boil gently, covered, for 15 minutes. If the pan becomes dry and the artichokes begin to fry, add 2 to 3 tablespoons of water. Arrange the artichokes on a serving plate, and serve with any remaining natural juices.

PERFECT ARTICHOKES

WITH A LARGE, SHARP KNIFE, TRIM ABOUT 1½ INCHES FROM THE TOPS OF THE ARTICHOKES. USING SCISSORS, CUT OFF THE THORNY TOP THIRD OF THE REMAINING LEAVES. BRING ABOUT 6 CUPS OF WATER TO A BOIL IN A SAUCEPAN. ADD THE ARTICHOKES, AND BRING THE WATER BACK TO A BOIL. BOIL OVER HIGH HEAT, COVERED, FOR 20 MINUTES. COOL UNDER COLD RUNNING WATER.

YIELD: 4 SERVINGS

NUTRITIONAL ANALYSIS PER SERVING:

Calories 308
Protein 6 gm.
Carbohydrates 26 gm.
Fat 21.4 gm.
Saturated fat 3.0 gm.
Cholesterol 0 mg.
Sodium 615 mg.

Artichokes contain fiber, calcium, and potassium.

Artichokes with *Ravigote* Sauce

You can cook the artichokes for this dish a day ahead, refrigerate them, then halve them and remove the chokes shortly before serving. A quick reheating in a microwave oven, a regular oven, or boiling water takes the chill off the artichokes, which are best served slightly cool or at room temperature.

RAVIGOTE SAUCE

THIS VERSATILE SAUCE—A MIXTURE OF RED ONION, CAPERS, VINEGAR, OIL, AND HERBS—IS ALSO GOOD WITH POACHED OR GRILLED FISH.

- 2 quarts water
- 4 firm, dark green artichokes (about 2 pounds)

Ravigote Sauce

- ¼ cup coarsely chopped red onion
- 1 tablespoon drained capers
- ¼ teaspoon salt
- ½ teaspoon freshly ground black pepper
- 2 tablespoons red wine vinegar or sherry vinegar
- 4 tablespoons virgin olive oil
- 3 tablespoons chopped fresh herbs (a mixture of parsley, chives, and tarragon), plus 1 tablespoon for garnish

1. Bring the water to a boil in a large saucepan.
2. Meanwhile, place the artichokes on their sides on a cutting board, and, using a sharp knife, trim about 1½ inches from the top of each. Then, using scissors, trim an additional 1 inch from the tops of all the leaves. Trim the artichoke stems, and peel off their fibrous outer surface. Wash the artichokes thoroughly.
3. Add the artichokes to the boiling water, and place a sieve on top to hold them under the water. Bring the water back to a boil, and boil the artichokes, uncovered, for 25 minutes, or until an outer leaf can be pulled easily from the base and the base of the leaf is tender.
4. Pour the hot water out of the pot, and add enough ice to cover the artichokes and cool them quickly. When they are cool, gently press them between your palms to extract as much water from them as possible without breaking them. Remove the center leaves from each artichoke, pulling them out together in one clump (and

(continued)

YIELD: 4 SERVINGS

NUTRITIONAL ANALYSIS PER SERVING:

Calories 169
Protein 3 gm.
Carbohydrates 11 gm.
Fat 13.6 gm.
Saturated fat 1.9 gm.
Cholesterol 0 mg.
Sodium 277 mg.

Low in calories, artichokes are a good source of potassium. Olive oil is rich in vitamin E and monounsaturated fat, which helps to lower blood cholesterol.

CLOCKWISE FROM LEFT: ASPARAGUS *EN FÊTE* (SEE PAGE 79);
ARTICHOKES WITH *RAVIGOTE* SAUCE (ABOVE);
ZUCCHINI AND TOMATO FANS (SEE PAGE 107).

reserving the clumps) to expose the chokes. Quarter the artichokes lengthwise, and remove and discard the chokes.

FOR THE *RAVIGOTE* SAUCE

5. Combine the onion, capers, salt, pepper, vinegar, olive oil, and 3 tablespoons of herbs in a small bowl.
6. To serve, arrange four artichoke pieces (the equivalent of one whole artichoke) attractively on each of four plates, with the stems extending outward. Arrange a reserved clump of center artichoke leaves in the middle of each plate, and spoon some of the *ravigote* sauce over the artichoke pieces. Garnish with the 1 tablespoon of herbs, and serve.

Asparagus in Mustard Sauce

I peel the asparagus stalks for this recipe (so they are completely edible) and cook them in just enough water so that most of it has evaporated by the time the asparagus is cooked, thus preserving the vitamins and nutrients in the vegetable. The pungent mustard dressing should be served at room temperature.

Yield: 4 Servings

NUTRITIONAL ANALYSIS PER SERVING:

Calories 93
Protein 4 gm.
Carbohydrates 5 gm.
Fat 7.1 gm.
Saturated fat 0.5 gm.
Cholesterol 0 mg.
Sodium 366 mg.

Asparagus is a good source of folacin, a B-complex vitamin.

- **1¼ pounds asparagus (about 15 stalks)**
- **¾ cup water**
- **1 tablespoon Dijon-style mustard**
- **2 tablespoons canola oil**
- **¼ teaspoon freshly ground black pepper**
- **½ teaspoon salt**

1. Using a vegetable peeler, peel the bottom third of the asparagus stalks to remove the fibrous skin. Cut the asparagus diagonally into 2- to 3-inch pieces. (You should have about 3 cups.)
2. Place the asparagus in a stainless steel saucepan, and add the water. Cover, bring to a boil, and boil for 3 minutes, until the asparagus is just tender and most of the liquid has evaporated.
3. Drain off any remaining water, and place the asparagus in a bowl. Add the mustard, oil, pepper, and salt, and mix well. Serve at room temperature.

Asparagus en Fête

En fête *means "holiday-style" in French, and I use the term here to underscore the festive appearance of this dish. Cooked, trimmed asparagus spears are split in half lengthwise up to the tip and the stems spread apart and arranged in a "frame" design on the plates. Colorful olives, capers, and tomatoes are then tossed with the trimmed asparagus stem ends and piled in the center of the "frames." The dish is served with a lemony mustard sauce.* *(See photograph, page 77.)*

1½ pounds asparagus (about 20 stalks), peeled and trimmed (about 18 ounces, peeled and trimmed)
1 cup hot tap water

LEMON-MUSTARD SAUCE
1 tablespoon Dijon-style mustard
½ teaspoon salt
¼ teaspoon freshly ground black pepper
2 teaspoons lemon juice
4 tablespoons virgin olive oil

24 oil-cured black olives
2 tablespoons drained capers
1 ripe tomato (5 ounces), seeded and cut into ½-inch pieces (1 cup)
¼ cup (loosely packed) fresh flat-leaf parsley leaves

1. Place the asparagus in no more than two layers in the bottom of a saucepan, preferably stainless steel. Add the hot tap water, and bring it to a boil over high heat. Cover the pan, and continue to boil the asparagus over high heat for 4 to 5 minutes, until it is tender but still firm. Most of the water will have evaporated.
2. Remove the asparagus from the pan, and spread it out on a platter to speed cooling. When it is cool enough to handle, measure down 5 inches from the tip of each spear, and cut off and reserve the remainder of the stem ends. Then, starting at the bottom of the spears, split the stems in half lengthwise, stopping when you get to the tips and leaving the heads intact. Cut the reserved stem ends into 1-inch pieces.
3. Combine the sauce ingredients in a small bowl.
4. At serving time, mix the 1-inch pieces of asparagus with the olives, capers, and tomato in a bowl. Arrange four asparagus spears on each plate so the tips extend to the edge of the plate and the stalks, spread open where they are cut, connect to create a "frame" around an open area in the center. Arrange some of the tomato-olive mixture in the center of each plate, and spoon some sauce over both the spears and the mixture. Sprinkle with the parsley leaves, and serve.

YIELD:
4 SERVINGS

NUTRITIONAL ANALYSIS PER SERVING:

Calories 209
Protein 5 gm.
Carbohydrates 8 gm.
Fat 19.3 gm.
Saturated fat 2.5 gm.
Cholesterol 0 mg.
Sodium 977 mg.

Asparagus provides soluble fiber. Olives contain oil that is rich in vitamin E.

COOKING DRIED BEANS

THE COMMON BELIEF THAT COOKING DRIED BEANS TAKES A LONG TIME IS FALSE. AT THE OUTSET, YOU DO NOT NEED TO SOAK THE BEANS BEFORE YOU COOK THEM, ALTHOUGH YOU CAN DO SO FOR 1 TO 2 HOURS IF YOU LIKE. LONGER SOAKING CAUSES THE BEANS TO FERMENT, WHICH MAKES THEM DIFFICULT TO DIGEST. I SIMPLY WASH THEM, PLACE THEM IN A POT WITH ENOUGH COLD WATER TO COVER THEM, AND COOK THEM UNTIL TENDER (1 TO 1½ HOURS, DEPENDING ON THE BEANS).

YIELD:
4 SERVINGS

NUTRITIONAL ANALYSIS PER SERVING:

Calories 325
Protein 19 gm.
Carbohydrates 43 gm.
Fat 10.0 gm.
Saturated fat 1.8 gm.
Cholesterol 12 mg.
Sodium 732 mg.

Beans and Broccoli Rabe

Cooked beans can be served warm with a little olive oil. Any type of little white bean—navy, Great Northern, pea, or Boston—will work well here. I combine greens with the beans to enhance the flavor, lend color, and make them more nutritious. The beans contain fiber, and the broccoli rabe (broccoli di rape*) contains vitamin A, which is present in all leafy green vegetables.* *(See photograph, page 90.)*

½ pound navy or Great Northern dried beans
4 cups cold water
¾ teaspoon salt
2 sprigs fresh thyme (or ½ teaspoon dried thyme leaves)
3 ounces ham, cut into ½-inch dice
1 medium onion, peeled and cut into ¾-inch dice (1¼ cups)
½ pound broccoli rabe, or Chinese broccoli
2 tablespoons virgin olive oil
2 cloves garlic, peeled, crushed, and finely chopped
¼ teaspoon red pepper flakes
Additional olive oil (optional)

1. Wash the beans in cool water, and remove and discard any pebbles or damaged beans.
2. In a pot, combine the beans with the cold water, salt, thyme, ham, and onion. Bring to a boil, cover, reduce the heat to low, and cook at a gentle boil for about 1½ hours, until the beans are tender and most of the water has been absorbed. Just enough water should remain to make the beans look moist and juicy.
3. Meanwhile, wash the broccoli rabe, and cut into 2-inch pieces.
4. Heat the oil in a skillet, add the garlic and pepper flakes, and sauté for about 10 seconds. Then add the broccoli rabe (still wet from washing), and sauté for about 1 minute. Cover, and cook over medium heat for 5 to 6 minutes, until the greens soften, become tender, and render some of their juices.
5. At serving time, combine the beans and broccoli, rewarming them if necessary. If desired, sprinkle a little extra olive oil on each serving.

Cauliflower *Gribiche*

I enjoy eating this dish with a chunk of bread for lunch, but it also makes a great dinner first course or salad course and can even be served as a snack. I love cauliflower and find it particularly appealing garnished with red onion and anchovy fillets.

SERVING THE *GRIBICHE*

The *gribiche* should be served at room temperature. If you make it ahead and refrigerate it, take the chill off by heating it momentarily in a microwave oven.

- **1 head cauliflower (1¼ to 1½ pounds), without greens**
- **3 cups water**
- **1 large egg**
- **¼ cup sour gherkins, coarsely chopped**
- **⅓ cup coarsely chopped fresh parsley**
- **⅓ cup diced (¼-inch dice) red onion**
- **1 can (2 ounces) undrained flat anchovy fillets in oil, cut into ¼-inch pieces**
- **1 tablespoon red wine vinegar**
- **2 tablespoons virgin olive oil**
- **½ teaspoon salt**
- **½ teaspoon freshly ground black pepper**

1. Separate the cauliflower into florets, and cut each floret into pieces about 1 inch across at the flower. (You should have about 6 cups.)
2. Place the cauliflower in a large saucepan, and add 1 cup of the water. Bring the water to a strong boil, cover, and cook over high heat for 3 to 4 minutes, until the water has evaporated. Transfer the cauliflower to a bowl.
3. Bring the remaining 2 cups of water to a boil in a small saucepan. Carefully lower the egg into the water, cover, reduce the heat, and boil gently for 9 minutes. Immediately pour out the hot water, and replace it with ice water. Cool the egg completely. Then peel it, and cut it into ¼-inch pieces.
4. Add all the remaining ingredients except the egg to the cauliflower in the bowl. Mix. Transfer the mixture to a serving platter, sprinkle the egg on top, and serve immediately.

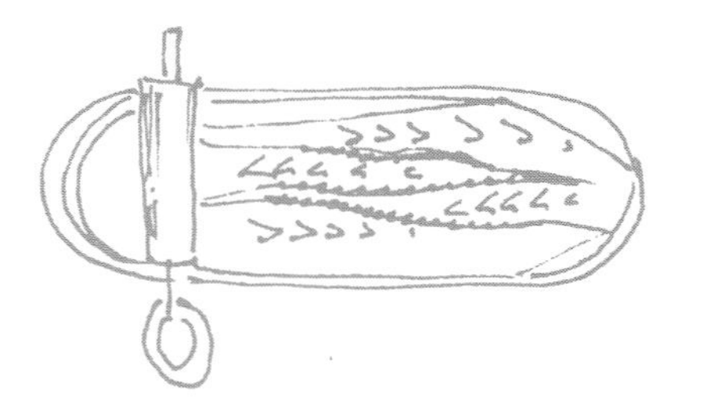

YIELD: 4 SERVINGS

NUTRITIONAL ANALYSIS PER SERVING:

Calories 149
Protein 8 gm.
Carbohydrates 10 gm.
Fat 9.5 gm.
Saturated fat 1.6 gm.
Cholesterol 59 mg.
Sodium 931 mg.

Cauliflower has natural substances that prevent cancer-causing chemicals from damaging cells.

Eggplant and Red Pepper Terrine

Serving eight people, this is an ideal dish for a summer party. I like to use narrow eggplants that are about as long as my mold, which is 11 inches long, 4 inches wide, and 3 inches high, so I can make nice layers with lengthwise strips of the eggplant. The paler Japanese eggplants work well here, but if you don't have access to them, just select regular eggplants that are somewhat long and thin. The peppers and eggplants can be cooked and the dish assembled a day ahead. The terrine should not be unmolded, however, until just before serving.

The raw tomato sauce is easy to make and could also be served on its own as a cold tomato gazpacho soup.

- **3 large red bell peppers (about 1½ pounds)**
- **2 large, long (11-inch), firm eggplants (about 2½ pounds)**
- **2 tablespoons peanut oil**
- **¾ teaspoon salt**
- **1½ cups (loose) fresh flat-leaf parsley leaves**
- **½ teaspoon freshly ground black pepper**
- **8 ounces firm Brie cheese, cut into ⅛-inch slices (about 14 slices)**

Raw Tomato Sauce

- **3 cloves garlic, peeled**
- **2 to 3 ripe tomatoes (1¼ pounds), each cut into 6 to 8 pieces**
- **⅓ cup water**
- **¼ cup virgin olive oil**
- **2 tablespoons red wine vinegar**
- **½ teaspoon salt**
- **¼ teaspoon freshly ground black pepper**
- **¼ teaspoon Tabasco hot pepper sauce**

1. Arrange the red peppers on a tray, and place them under a hot broiler so that their upper surfaces are about ½ inch from the heat. Broil for 15 minutes, turning occasionally, until the peppers are blistered and black on all sides. Immediately transfer them to a large plastic bag, and seal or tie the bag shut. Let the peppers "steam" in their own residual heat inside the bag for 10 minutes. Then peel them (the skin will slide off), split them, and seed them under cool running water. Dry the flesh with paper towels.

(continued)

Baking Eggplant

I grill rather than fry the eggplant slices for this dish because much less oil is required—and because I especially like the flavor of grilled eggplant. If you don't have access to an indoor or outdoor grill, however, you can get a low-fat result by baking the slices. Preheat the oven to 400 degrees. Cut the eggplant, then oil and salt the slices as indicated in the recipe, and arrange them in one layer on a jelly roll pan. Bake for 15 minutes, turn carefully with a spatula, and bake for another 15 minutes. Cool the slices, and complete the terrine according to the recipe.

CHEESE ALTERNATIVES

I USE BRIE WITH THE EGGPLANT; IT IS FLAVORFUL AND EASY TO CUT INTO THE THIN STRIPS I NEED IN THE TERRINE. ANOTHER CHEESE—MOZZARELLA, FOR EXAMPLE—CAN BE SUBSTITUTED, ALTHOUGH IT MAY BE HARDER TO SLICE THINLY. OR, IF YOU WANT TO REDUCE THE CALORIE COUNT OF THIS DISH FURTHER, ELIMINATE THE CHEESE ALTOGETHER.

YIELD: 8 SERVINGS

NUTRITIONAL ANALYSIS PER SERVING:

Calories 261
Protein 9 gm.
Carbohydrates 18 gm.
Fat 18.5 gm.
Saturated fat 1.5 gm.
Cholesterol 28 mg.
Sodium 540 mg.

2. Heat a grill until very hot. Cut the eggplants lengthwise into ½-inch slices (ten to twelve total), brush the slices on both sides with the peanut oil, and sprinkle with half the salt. Cook the eggplant slices on the grill, covered, for 4 minutes on each side, until they are nicely browned and soft. (If your grill does not have a lid, make a tentlike lid of aluminum foil, and place it over the eggplant as it cooks.)
3. While the eggplant is grilling, soften the parsley by blanching it in boiling water for 5 to 10 seconds. Remove, cool under cold water, and drain.
4. Line a terrine mold (loaf or pâté pan) with plastic wrap. Arrange a layer of eggplant in the bottom of the mold, and top it with about a third each of the red pepper pieces, parsley, remaining salt, black pepper, and cheese. Repeat, beginning and ending with a layer of eggplant, until all the ingredients are used. Cover with plastic wrap, and press on the wrap to compact the mixture. Refrigerate.

FOR THE RAW TOMATO SAUCE

5. Place the garlic in the bowl of a food processor, and process for 10 seconds. Add the tomatoes, and process until pureed. Push the mixture through a food mill (fitted with a fine screen) set over a bowl. Add the remainder of the sauce ingredients. Mix well.
6. To serve, pour some of the sauce on a large platter, and unmold the terrine in the center. Cut it into slices, and serve with the remainder of the sauce.

GRILLED EGGPLANT ON GREENS

The smaller, sweeter Japanese eggplants are ideal for this dish, but if they are not available use the standard American variety. My family loves the unique taste that grilling gives eggplant, and this simple recipe makes an ideal first course for a summer meal. I especially like the eggplant served on young home-grown greens such as radicchio and arugula. Their slightly bitter flavor offsets the natural sweetness of the eggplant. (See also Baking Eggplant on page 83.)

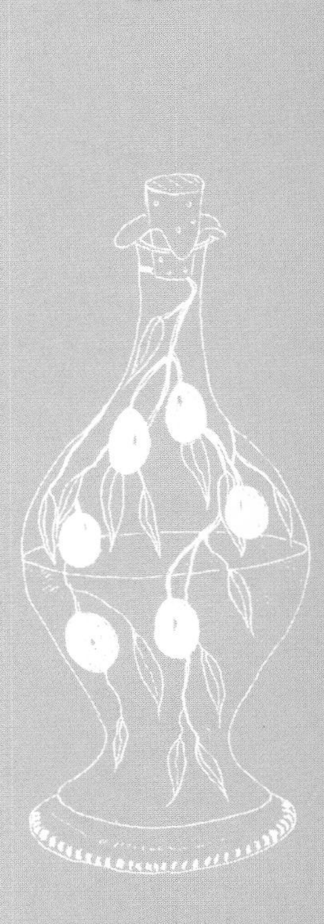

2 small, firm eggplants, preferably the long, narrow Japanese variety (about 1 pound total)
1 tablespoon canola oil
½ teaspoon salt
2 tablespoons virgin olive oil
1 tablespoon soy sauce
1 tablespoon rice vinegar
3 cups (loose) mixed salad greens, thoroughly washed and dried

1. Cut off and discard the top and bottom ends of the eggplants, and cut them lengthwise into ½-inch slices. (You should have about eight slices.) Rub the slices on both sides with the canola oil, and sprinkle them with the salt.
2. Heat a grill until very hot. Place the eggplant slices on the grill, and cook for 3 minutes on each side.
3. Meanwhile, combine the olive oil, soy sauce, and vinegar in a small bowl.
4. Arrange the salad greens on a platter, and place the grilled eggplant slices on top. Pour the sauce over both. Serve immediately.

YIELD: 4 SERVINGS

NUTRITIONAL ANALYSIS PER SERVING:

Calories 129
Protein 2 gm.
Carbohydrates 9 gm.
Fat 10.4 gm.
Saturated fat 1.2 gm.
Cholesterol 0 mg.
Sodium 539 mg.

Eggplant is high in soluble fiber, which can reduce the risk of heart disease and diabetes by controlling blood sugar and blood fat levels.

Sautéed Eggplant Rolls

This is a great party dish, perfect on a buffet table. You can sauté and stuff the eggplant ahead of time and change the filling mixture at will to accommodate leftover meat or fish. The vinaigrette tomatoes, delicious with the eggplant, are also good with poached fish or mixed with a green salad.

- ¼ cup canola oil
- 1 eggplant (1 pound), cut into 16 slices, each about ⅜-inch thick
- Salt and freshly ground black pepper to taste
- 3 tablespoons olive oil
- 1 small onion (3 ounces), finely chopped (about ½ cup)
- 3 ounces mushrooms, coarsely chopped (about 1¼ cups)
- 2 to 3 large cloves garlic, peeled, crushed, and finely chopped (1½ teaspoons)
- 4 ounces Monterey Jack or another soft cheese, coarsely chopped or grated
- 3 tablespoons golden raisins
- 1 tablespoon Worcestershire sauce
- ½ teaspoon salt
- ½ teaspoon freshly ground black pepper
- 4 tablespoons chopped fresh chives

Vinaigrette Tomatoes

- 2 large ripe tomatoes (1 pound)
- 1 small onion (about 3 ounces), chopped (about ½ cup)
- 2 teaspoons red wine vinegar
- 2 tablespoons virgin olive oil
- ½ teaspoon salt
- ¼ teaspoon freshly ground black pepper

1. Heat 2 tablespoons of the canola oil in a nonstick skillet. When hot, add eight slices of the eggplant. Sprinkle lightly with salt and pepper, and cook 5 minutes on each side over medium heat. Remove to a dish, and repeat with the remaining eggplant and canola oil. Set aside.
2. Heat 2 tablespoons of the olive oil in a skillet, and sauté the onion in the hot oil for 1 minute. Add the mushrooms, and sauté for another minute. Stir in the garlic, and remove from the heat.
3. In a bowl, combine the cheese with the onion-mushroom mixture, and mix in the raisins, the Worcestershire sauce, the ½ teaspoon of salt, the ½ teaspoon of pepper, 3 tablespoons of the chives, and the remaining tablespoon of olive oil. Divide the mixture among the sixteen slices of eggplant, mounding it in the centers of the slices.

Yield: 4 Servings

Nutritional Analysis per Serving:

Calories 476
Protein 11 gm.
Carbohydrates 24 gm.
Fat 39.7 gm.
Saturated fat 8.3 gm.
Cholesterol 30 mg.
Sodium 757 mg.

Monterey Jack is rich in calcium.

4. Cut the tomatoes in half horizontally, and gently squeeze out the seeds. Chop into ¼-inch pieces.
5. Combine the chopped tomatoes, onion, vinegar, oil, salt, and pepper in a bowl.
6. Spread the tomato mixture on a large serving plate. Wrap the eggplant slices around the filling to create rolls, and arrange the rolls, seam side down, on top of the tomato mixture. Sprinkle with the remaining tablespoon of chives, and serve at room temperature.

Endive with Olives

This easy recipe is attractive and delicious as a light first course or as an accompaniment to grilled meat or grilled or broiled fish. It is ready in a few minutes, and the combination of flavors—bitter endive with garlic, olives, and soy sauce—makes it an interesting and unusual dish.

- ½ cup water
- 2 large heads Belgian endive (about 8 ounces total), thoroughly washed, drained, and quartered lengthwise
- 2 cloves garlic, peeled, crushed, and chopped (1 teaspoon)
- 1½ tablespoons virgin olive oil
- 1 tablespoon red wine vinegar
- ¼ teaspoon salt
- ¼ teaspoon freshly ground black pepper
- 2 tablespoons coarsely chopped oil-cured black olives
- 1 teaspoon light soy sauce
- 1 tablespoon chopped chives

1. Place all the ingredients except the olives, soy sauce, and chives in a stainless steel saucepan. Bring the mixture to a boil, cover, reduce the heat to low, and boil gently for 10 minutes.
2. Stir in the olives and soy sauce, and divide among six plates, allowing two pieces of endive per plate. Sprinkle with the chives. Serve.

Yield: 6 Servings

Nutritional Analysis per Serving:

Calories 43
Protein 0.7 gm.
Carbohydrates 3 gm.
Fat 3.7 gm.
Saturated fat 0.5 gm.
Cholesterol 0 mg.
Sodium 152 mg.

Olive oil, a monounsaturated fat, is widely used in Mediterranean countries, where the incidence of heart disease is low.

Braised Endive in Lemon Juice

Cooked with lemon juice, braised endive is a refreshing vegetable and makes a wonderful first course. Served lukewarm with this seasoned juice, it makes a great accompaniment to meat and fish.

BRAISING ENDIVE

IN THIS RECIPE, I COOK THE ENDIVE WITH A LITTLE LEMON JUICE, LEMON PEEL, BUTTER, WATER, SUGAR, AND SALT. YOU WILL NOTICE THAT ONLY A LITTLE LIQUID IS IN THE BOTTOM OF THE PAN WHEN YOU BEGIN THE COOKING PROCESS. IF YOU PLACE A PLATE ON TOP OF THE ENDIVE TO PRESS IT DOWN AS IT COOKS, HOWEVER, IT WILL RENDER A LOT OF JUICE AND, IN FACT, EVENTUALLY FINISH COOKING ALMOST IMMERSED IN ITS OWN COOKING LIQUID.

4 large or 8 small heads Belgian endive (about 1 pound total)
1 tablespoon fresh lemon juice
3 1-inch strips of lemon peel, removed with a vegetable peeler and each cut into 4 pieces
1 tablespoon unsalted butter
¼ cup water
½ teaspoon sugar
¼ teaspoon salt

1. Rinse the endive thoroughly. If the heads are large, cut them in half lengthwise; if they are small, leave them whole.
2. Place the endive (preferably in one layer) in a stainless steel saucepan. Add the rest of the ingredients.
3. Bring to a boil. Place an inverted plate slightly smaller than the pan over the endive. Reduce the heat to low, and cook the endive, covered, for 20 minutes, until just tender. Serve lukewarm.

YIELD: 4 SERVINGS

NUTRITIONAL ANALYSIS PER SERVING:

Calories 46
Protein 1 gm.
Carbohydrates 5 gm.
Fat 3.0 gm.
Saturated fat 1.8 gm.
Cholesterol 8 mg.
Sodium 143 mg.

Wild Mushroom Toast

This is one of my favorite first courses in summer, when I often go mushrooming in the woods with my wife and daughter, my friends, or sometimes just my dog.

I use a mixture of domestic and wild mushrooms here. I spoon them over toast, but this recipe would also be good as a garnish for steak or grilled veal or lamb chops.

2 tablespoons unsalted butter
1 tablespoon virgin olive oil
1 pound mixed domestic and wild mushrooms (King Boletus, chanterelle, and oyster), cleaned and cut into large pieces or left whole
4 shallots, finely sliced (½ cup)
½ cup chopped fresh herbs (mixture of oregano, chives, and parsley)
½ teaspoon salt
½ teaspoon freshly ground black pepper
4 slices fine-textured white bread, each about 4 inches in diameter and ½ inch thick, crusts removed
Additional virgin olive oil, for garnish (optional)

1. Heat the butter and 1 tablespoon oil until very hot and hazelnut in color. Add the mushrooms, and sauté over high heat for 10 seconds. Cover, and continue cooking over high heat for 3 minutes. Uncover, and cook over high heat for 2 to 3 minutes, until dry. Add the shallots, herbs, salt, and pepper, and cook for 1 minute longer.
2. Lightly toast the slices of bread, and arrange them on a plate. Spoon the mushroom mixture on top of the toast, sprinkle a little oil on top, if desired, and serve immediately.

MUSHROOM HUNTING

If you don't know wild mushrooms, I strongly advise against picking them on your own, since some are toxic. Mycological societies throughout the country organize tours, however. If this activity appeals to you, contact the society nearest to you, and go on a hunt with people who are knowledgeable about wild mushrooms. It's great fun, and the wild mushrooms you find yourself are free.

Yield: 4 Servings

NUTRITIONAL ANALYSIS PER SERVING:

Calories 195
Protein 5 gm.
Carbohydrates 22 gm.
Fat 10.4 gm.
Saturated fat 4.3 gm.
Cholesterol 16 mg.
Sodium 412 mg.

Mushrooms are a good source of potassium.

Leeks with Tomato and Olive Oil

Fresh leeks, trimmed and cooked until just tender, are served with a tangy sauce flavored with diced tomatoes, olive oil, and Dijon-style mustard.

- 2 cups water
- 4 medium to large leeks (about 1¼ pounds), trimmed and washed
- 1 ripe tomato (about 7 ounces), peeled, seeded, and cut into ¼-inch pieces
- 3 tablespoons virgin olive oil
- 1 tablespoon red wine vinegar
- 1 tablespoon Dijon-style mustard
- 1 teaspoon Worcestershire sauce
- ½ teaspoon salt
- ¼ teaspoon freshly ground black pepper

1. Bring the water to a boil in a stainless steel saucepan. Add the leeks, bring back to a boil, and boil gently, covered, for 10 minutes or until tender.
2. Drain, reserving the liquid for soup. When cool enough to handle, squeeze the leeks to extract most of the remaining liquid, and reserve this with the other liquid.
3. Cut the leeks into 2-inch pieces, and arrange them in a gratin dish, mixing the white and green parts.
4. Mix together the tomato, oil, vinegar, mustard, Worcestershire sauce, salt, and pepper. Spoon the mixture over the leeks. Serve lukewarm or at room temperature.

Trimming and Cooking Leeks

Use most of the green from the leeks, trimming off and discarding only the tips of the leaves and the wilted or damaged outer leaves. Cut the leeks open, leaving them attached at the root end, and wash them thoroughly. Cook leeks in unsalted water. The resulting leek stock has a wonderfully intense flavor, making it ideal to keep, refrigerated or frozen, for use in soups.

Yield: 4 Servings

Nutritional Analysis per Serving:

Calories 143
Protein 1 gm.
Carbohydrates 11 gm.
Fat 10.4 gm.
Saturated fat 1.4 gm.
Cholesterol 0 mg.
Sodium 394 mg.

Left: Leeks with Tomato and Olive Oil (above).
Right: Beans and Broccoli Rabe (see page 80).

Mushroom-Stuffed Wontons in Red Wine Sauce

For this recipe, I use the square wonton wrappers that are available now in packages in the refrigerator or produce sections of most supermarkets. (See About Wonton Wrappers or Skins, page 190.)

The large mushroom ravioli are dropped into boiling water just before serving, and they cook in 4 to 5 minutes. I serve them in a red wine sauce made with a reduction of wine that is flavored with onion, garlic, a little tomato juice, and thyme, but another sauce can be substituted, or the ravioli can be served with just a little melted butter or olive oil drizzled on top.

- 1 tablespoon peanut oil
- 1 tablespoon unsalted butter
- ¼ cup chopped shallots (about 3 large shallots)
- ⅓ cup chopped leek, half white and half green (about half a small leek, thoroughly washed)
- 8 ounces mushrooms (all domestic or a mixture of domestic and wild), cleaned and coarsely chopped
- ½ teaspoon salt
- ¼ teaspoon freshly ground black pepper
- 24 wonton wrappers, each 3 inches square (6 ounces total)

Red Wine Sauce

- 1 tablespoon peanut oil
- 1 medium onion (4 ounces), peeled and chopped (1 cup)
- 3 cloves garlic, peeled, crushed, and finely chopped (2 teaspoons)
- ½ teapoon fresh or ¼ teaspoon dried thyme leaves
- 1 cup robust, fruity red wine (anything from a Rhône wine to a cabernet)
- ½ cup tomato juice
- 1 tablespoon soy sauce

- 3 to 4 quarts water
- 1 tablespoon chopped fresh chives

1. Heat the oil and butter until hot in a saucepan. Add the shallots and leek, and sauté them over medium to high heat for 2 minutes. Add the mushrooms, salt, and pepper, and cook, uncovered, over high heat, for about 7 minutes, until the liquid that emerges from the mushrooms evaporates and the mushrooms begin to brown. Transfer the mixture to a dish, and let cool.
2. Lay twelve of the wonton wrappers out on a flat work surface, and brush them lightly with some water around the edges. Divide the mushroom mixture among the wrappers, mounding approximately 1½ tablespoons in the center of each. Cover with the remaining wrappers, and press gently around the edges with the base of a glass or cup to seal well. Trim the edges, if desired. Arrange the wontons in one layer with no overlap on a tray. Set aside, uncovered (to prevent them from becoming wet and sticky), in the refrigerator until cooking time (no longer than 12 hours).

For the Red Wine Sauce

3. Heat the peanut oil until hot in a skillet. Add the onion, and sauté over medium to high heat for about 2 minutes. Add the garlic and thyme, and sauté for an additional 30 seconds. Stir in the wine, and boil until it is reduced by half. Add the tomato juice and soy sauce, and bring the mixture back to a boil. Boil vigorously over high heat for 30 seconds. Using a blender, food processor, or hand blender, puree the mixture until fairly smooth. Set aside in the skillet. (You will have 1⅓ cups.)
4. At serving time, bring the water to a boil in a large saucepan while reheating the sauce in the skillet. Drop the stuffed wontons into the boiling water, bring the water back to a boil, and boil the wontons very gently for 2 to 3 minutes. Using a skimmer, remove the wontons from the water, draining as much water from them as possible, and arrange them on a serving plate. Top with the sauce, garnish with the chives, and serve immediately.

Yield: 4 Servings

NUTRITIONAL ANALYSIS PER SERVING:

Calories 260
Protein 7 gm.
Carbohydrates 36 gm.
Fat 10.6 gm.
Saturated fat 3.1 gm.
Cholesterol 12 mg.
Sodium 894 mg.

Mushrooms are low in calories and high in chromium. Leeks are low in calories and high in dietary fiber.

Braised Shiitake Mushrooms on Bitter Salad

My taste preference in shiitake mushrooms is for the dried, which I find much more flavorful than the fresh—although either could be used here. If you shop for your dried mushrooms in Asian markets, you will notice that the quality of dried shiitakes varies widely. I tend to buy the costlier specimens; usually their caps are cracked with white lines and are thicker, meatier, and more flavorful than the caps of other dried shiitakes.

In combination with the mushrooms, bitter-tasting radicchio and Belgium endive give distinction to this first course.

16 dried shiitake mushrooms, preferably high-quality, imported specimens
3 cups hot water
1 small, tight head radicchio (about 5 ounces)
1 large, tight head Belgian endive (4 to 5 ounces)

GARLIC DRESSING
1 to 2 cloves garlic, peeled, crushed, and finely chopped (1 teaspoon)
¼ teaspoon salt
¼ teaspoon freshly ground black pepper
4 teaspoons red wine vinegar
3 tablespoons virgin olive oil

¼ teaspoon salt
¼ teaspoon freshly ground black pepper
1½ tablespoons virgin olive oil
2 to 3 tablespoons water, as needed
12 fresh basil leaves, coarsely shredded

1. Place the mushrooms in a bowl, and cover them with the hot water. Let soak for 1 to 2 hours, stirring them occasionally.
2. Drain the mushrooms (reserving the soaking liquid), and remove the stems. Reserve 1½ cups of the liquid for use in cooking the mushrooms.
3. No more than 1 hour before serving time, rinse and dry the radicchio and endive

(continued)

CLOCKWISE FROM TOP: ARUGULA AND OLIVE SALAD (SEE PAGE 294);
RED ONION AND ORANGE SALAD (SEE PAGE 69);
BRAISED SHIITAKE MUSHROOMS ON BITTER SALAD (ABOVE).

WASTE NOT, WANT NOT

WHEN YOU ARE RECONSTITUTING DRIED MUSHROOMS IN WATER, SAVE THE FLAVORFUL SOAKING LIQUID THAT IS CREATED IN THE PROCESS. I COOK THE MUSHROOMS IN SOME OF THIS LIQUID HERE, AND THEN RESERVE THE REMAINDER (COVERED AND REFRIGERATED OR FROZEN) FOR LATER USE IN SOUPS, STOCKS, OR SAUCES. SAVE THE MUSHROOM STEMS AS WELL; ALTHOUGH THEY ARE TOO FIBROUS AND TOUGH FOR THIS DISH, THEY LEND FLAVOR TO STOCKS AND, FINELY CHOPPED, ARE GOOD IN STUFFINGS.

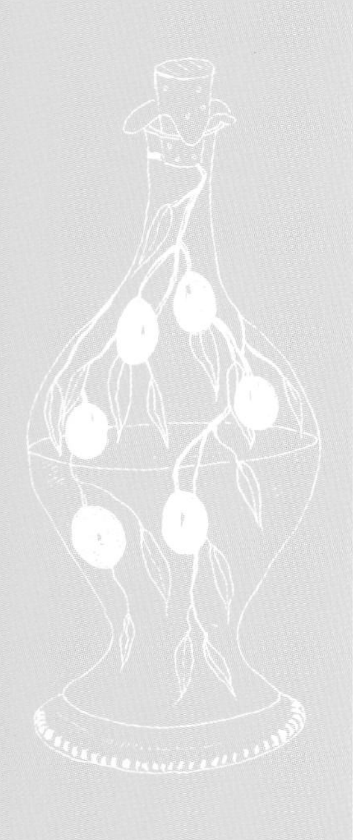

heads. Cut the radicchio in half lengthwise (through the stem) and then into 1-inch pieces; place in a bowl. Cut the endive in half lengthwise and then into ¼-inch-wide lengthwise sticks or strips; place in another bowl.

For the Garlic Dressing

4. Combine all the dressing ingredients in a bowl, then divide the dressing between the radicchio and the endive, and toss well.
5. Place the shiitake caps flat in one layer in a large skillet, and add the 1½ cups reserved mushroom-soaking liquid, ¼ teaspoon salt, ¼ teaspoon pepper, and 1½ tablespoons oil. Bring the mixture to a boil, reduce the heat to medium, cover, and boil gently for about 12 minutes, removing the lid occasionally and adding a few tablespoons of water as needed, until the caps are cooked and most of the liquid has evaporated. Uncover, and continue cooking the mushrooms until all the liquid is gone, 3 or 4 minutes. Then cook 3 to 4 minutes longer, turning the caps occasionally, until they are lightly browned on both sides.
6. To serve, make a border of endive around the edge of each of four plates, and pile the radicchio in the center. Sprinkle the shredded basil over the endive and radicchio, and arrange the mushroom caps on top of the radicchio so that about half are cap side up and half gill side up. Serve immediately.

Yield: 4 Servings

Nutritional Analysis per Serving:

Calories 180
Protein 2 gm.
Carbohydrates 11 gm.
Fat 15.4 gm.
Saturated fat 2.1 gm.
Cholesterol 0 mg.
Sodium 277 mg.

Shiitake mushrooms contain potassium and are low in calories. Also low in calories are radicchio and endive. All provide fiber.

Mushroom-Stuffed Potato Pancakes

Depending on how they are cooked, potato pancakes can have as many as 500 calories per pancake. Sautéed simply in a little oil in a nonstick skillet, as they are in this recipe, they have about 200 calories in each serving of three pancakes. I serve them as a first course here, but they make a delightful main course, too.

4 to 5 potatoes (about 1½ pounds), cleaned
¾ teaspoon salt
½ teaspoon freshly ground black pepper
5 tablespoons canola oil
4 shallots, peeled and thinly sliced (⅓ cup)
2 cloves garlic, peeled, crushed, and finely chopped (1 teaspoon)
4 ounces mushrooms, chopped (¼ cup)
12 oil-cured black olives, pitted and cut into ½-inch dice

1. Place the potatoes in a saucepan, and cover with cool water. Bring to a boil, reduce the heat to low, and boil gently for 30 minutes or until tender. Remove the potatoes, and let them cool. Then peel them, and push them through a food mill. Season with ½ teaspoon of the salt and ¼ teaspoon of the pepper.
2. Meanwhile, in a large skillet or saucepan, heat 1 tablespoon of the oil, add the shallots, and sauté for 1 minute. Add the garlic and mushrooms, and cook for about 3 minutes, until the moisture is almost gone. Remove from the heat, and add the olives and the remaining salt and pepper. Cool.
3. Divide the cold potato puree into twenty-four balls of equal size. Arrange the balls about 6 inches apart on a large sheet of plastic wrap. Cover with a second piece of plastic, and press on each ball to create a pancake about 3 inches in diameter and ¼-inch thick. Spoon 1 tablespoon of the olive mixture onto each of twelve pancakes; cover with the remaining pancakes.
4. Heat 2 tablespoons of oil in each of two large nonstick skillets over medium to high heat. When hot, add the filled pancakes in a single layer, and cook them for about 3 minutes. Turn carefully with a large spatula, and cook for about 3 minutes on the other side. Remove to a serving platter, and serve immediately, or set aside and reheat in the oven or under the broiler just before serving.

Yield: 6 Servings

NUTRITIONAL ANALYSIS PER SERVING:

Calories 218
Protein 3 gm.
Carbohydrates 24 gm.
Fat 13.2 gm.
Saturated fat 1.0 gm.
Cholesterol 0 mg.
Sodium 438 mg.

Potatoes contain a nutritious carbohydrate and are high in fiber and potassium.

ABOUT SALMON CAVIAR

THE TWO BEST TYPES OF SALMON CAVIAR ARE "NATURAL" AND "RED." I USUALLY USE A GOOD, MODERATELY EXPENSIVE NATURAL CAVIAR.

Potato Crêpes with Caviar

These crêpes, made from a batter that contains just two whole eggs and one egg white, are served covered with red caviar, the amount adjusted to suit your pocketbook. Then, to make the dish superlative, I use a little of the expensive black caviar from sturgeon—beluga, osetra, or sevruga—as a garnish.

Crêpes

- 1 large potato (about 9 ounces)
- 2 tablespoons flour
- 2 large whole eggs
- 1 additional egg white
- ⅓ cup milk
- ¼ teaspoon salt
- ⅛ teaspoon Tabasco hot pepper sauce
- 4 tablespoons canola oil

Garnishes

- About 8 ounces natural red salmon caviar (about 12 tablespoons)
- About 1 cup sour cream
- 1 tablespoon finely chopped fresh chives
- About 2 ounces (3 tablespoons) beluga, osetra, or sevruga caviar (preferably *malossol,* or lightly salted)

For the Crêpes

1. Place the potato in a saucepan with water to cover, and bring to a boil. Cover, reduce the heat, and boil gently for 30 minutes, until the potato is tender. Drain, peel, and press the potato through a food mill into a bowl.
2. Add the flour, whole eggs, and egg white, and mix well with a whisk. Then mix in the milk, salt, and Tabasco.
3. In a skillet, heat 2 teaspoons of the oil. When hot, add about ¼ cup of the crêpe mixture, which should spread to create a circle about 4½ to 5 inches in diameter. Cook over medium heat for about 2 minutes on each side.
4. Transfer to a cookie sheet, and set aside in a warm oven while you make five more crêpes with the remaining batter and oil.

For the Garnishes

5. To serve, spread the entire top surface of the lukewarm crêpes with red caviar (about 2 tablespoons on each), extending the caviar clear to the edge of each crêpe. Mound 2 rounded tablespoons of sour cream in the center of each crêpe, and sprinkle with the chives. Finally, place about 1½ teaspoons of black caviar in the center of each sour cream mound. Serve immediately. (Some people will eat more than one crêpe.)

YIELD: 4 SERVINGS

NUTRITIONAL ANALYSIS PER SERVING:

Calories 541
Protein 25 gm.
Carbohydrates 21 gm.
Fat 41.6 gm.
Saturated fat 9.7 gm.
Cholesterol 551 mg.
Sodium 1,287 mg.

Caviar is rich in riboflavin, a water-soluble B vitamin essential for growth and repair of tissue.

Corn Polenta with Mushroom Ragout

This is a satisfying dish that also can be served in larger portions as a meatless main course. Served on soup plates and eaten with soup spoons, it combines soft polenta with a ragout or stew of mushrooms that is particularly delicious when it incorporates some wild mushroom varieties. *(See photograph, page 108.)*

Yield: 4 Servings

Nutritional Analysis per Serving:

Calories 187
Protein 5 gm.
Carbohydrates 28 gm.
Fat 7.5 gm.
Saturated fat 2.5 gm.
Cholesterol 8 mg.
Sodium 302 mg.

Low in calories, mushrooms are a good source of chromium, which helps maintain normal blood-sugar levels.

Polenta

- 2 cups water
- ½ cup yellow cornmeal
- ¼ teaspoon salt
- ¼ teaspoon freshly ground black pepper

Mushroom Ragout

- 1 tablespoon unsalted butter
- 1 tablespoon peanut oil
- 1 small onion (3 ounces), peeled and chopped (½ cup)
- 5 ounces mushrooms (domestic, wild, or a combination), washed and cut into ½-inch pieces (2 cups)
- 3 cloves garlic, peeled, crushed, and finely chopped (2 teaspoons)
- 4 plum tomatoes (8 ounces), halved, seeded, and cut into ½-inch pieces (1¼ cups)
- 2 small ears sweet corn (8 ounces), husked and kernels cut off (1 cup)
- ½ cup homemade unsalted and defatted chicken stock (see page 466), or lower-salt canned chicken broth
- ¼ teaspoon salt (less if using canned chicken broth)
- ⅛ teaspoon freshly ground black pepper

- 2 tablespoons chopped fresh chives

For the Polenta

1. Bring the water to a boil in a medium saucepan. Sprinkle the cornmeal on top while you mix it in with a whisk, and stir in the ¼ teaspoon each of salt and pepper. Bring the mixture to a boil, reduce the heat to low, cover with a lid to prevent splattering, and cook gently for 6 to 8 minutes, stirring occasionally, until the polenta is the consistency of a creamy puree. Set aside, covered.

For the Mushroom Ragout

2. Heat the butter and oil in a large saucepan. When they are hot, add the onion and sauté for 30 seconds. Add the mushrooms, and sauté over high heat for about 2

minutes, until the liquid emerges from them and evaporates. Add the garlic, tomatoes, corn, chicken stock, salt, and pepper, and bring the mixture to a strong boil. Then reduce the heat to medium, and cook for 2 to 3 minutes.

3. To serve, ladle the polenta into the center of four soup plates, and pour the mushroom stew on top of and around it, dividing the stew among the plates. Sprinkle with the chives, and serve.

Gratin of Scallions

These scallions can be cooked and coated ahead with the finishing half-and-half and bread crumbs and then reheated at the last minute. If you prepare them early and allow them to cool, however, increase the baking time by 5 minutes to ensure that they are hot.

4 bunches of scallions, about 6 scallions to the bunch (1¼ pounds total)
1 cup water
½ cup half-and-half
½ slice fresh bread (½ ounce)
2 tablespoons grated parmesan cheese
¼ teaspoon salt
¼ teaspoon freshly ground black pepper

1. Preheat the oven to 450 degrees.
2. Remove and discard the top 2 inches and any damaged or wilted leaves from the scallions. Rinse them thoroughly.
3. Place the scallions and water in a stainless steel saucepan. Bring to a boil, cover, and cook over high heat for 5 minutes. Most of the liquid will evaporate.
4. Arrange the scallions in a gratin dish, and pour the half-and-half over them.
5. Break the bread into pieces, place in the bowl of a food processor, and process momentarily, just until crumbed. (You should have ¼ cup.)
6. Mix the bread crumbs, cheese, salt, and pepper in a small bowl. Sprinkle the mixture over the scallions. Bake at 450 degrees for 10 minutes.

YIELD: 4 SERVINGS

NUTRITIONAL ANALYSIS PER SERVING:

Calories 104
Protein 5 gm.
Carbohydrates 13 gm.
Fat 4.6 gm.
Saturated fat 2.7 gm.
Cholesterol 13 mg.
Sodium 235 mg.

Parmesan cheese has nearly twice as much calcium per ounce as soft cheeses.

Gratin of Ziti and Vegetables

Only 4 ounces of dried pasta—1 ounce per person—are used in this gratin. Although this is a small amount, remember that ziti, penne, elbow macaroni, and other pastas of that general shape swell dramatically as they cook. Also, since the pasta is mixed with a great many vegetables—onion, string beans, eggplant, squash, tomatoes, corn—the quantity called for is sufficient. The vegetable selection can be altered based on seasonal considerations and market availability.

The ziti and vegetables can be cooked and the dish assembled up to 8 hours in advance, so that at serving time it need only be heated through and browned on top in a hot oven.

- 2 quarts water
- 4 ounces ziti or penne
- 3 tablespoons virgin olive oil
- 1 onion (about 8 ounces), peeled and coarsely chopped
- 4 ounces string beans, trimmed and cut into ½-inch pieces (1 cup)
- 1 small eggplant (about 8 ounces), cut into ½-inch pieces (2½ cups)
- 1 teaspoon *herbes de Provence* (see page 467)
- 1 pattypan (or another variety) squash (8 ounces), cut into ½-inch pieces (2 cups)
- 1½ teaspoons salt
- ¼ teaspoon freshly ground black pepper
- 2 ripe tomatoes (about 10 ounces), cut into ½-inch pieces (2 cups)
- 2 ears sweet corn (about 1 pound), husked and kernels cut off (1½ cups)
- ½ cup black olive shavings, preferably from Nyons olives (about 2 dozen olives)

Crumb Topping

- 1 slice fine-textured white bread, processed into crumbs in a food processor (⅔ cup)
- ⅓ cup grated parmesan cheese
- 1 tablespoon virgin olive oil
- ½ cup minced chives

1. If you will bake the gratin immediately after it is prepared, preheat the oven to 400 degrees.
2. Bring the water to a boil in a large pot or saucepan. Add the ziti, stir well, and bring the water back to a boil. Boil the ziti, uncovered, for about 12 minutes, or until they are tender yet still somewhat firm to the bite (al dente). Drain and refresh the ziti briefly under cold water to stop the cooking. Cover, and set aside. (You should have 2 cups of cooked pasta.)
3. Heat the 3 tablespoons of oil in a large skillet. Add the onion and string beans, and cook, covered, over medium heat for about 2 minutes. Add the eggplant and *herbes de Provence,* and cook, covered, over medium heat for 8 minutes, stirring occasionally. Then add the squash, salt, and pepper, and cook, covered, another 2 minutes.
4. Remove the skillet from the heat, and mix in the tomatoes, corn, and olive shavings. Cool the mixture to lukewarm, mix in the cooked pasta, and arrange the mixture in an 8-cup gratin dish.
5. Mix the topping ingredients well in a small bowl, and sprinkle them over the mixture in the gratin dish. (*Note:* The dish can be prepared to this point, covered, and refrigerated for up to 8 hours.)
6. Bake the gratin at 400 degrees for 20 to 30 minutes, until it is heated through and nicely browned on top. Serve immediately.

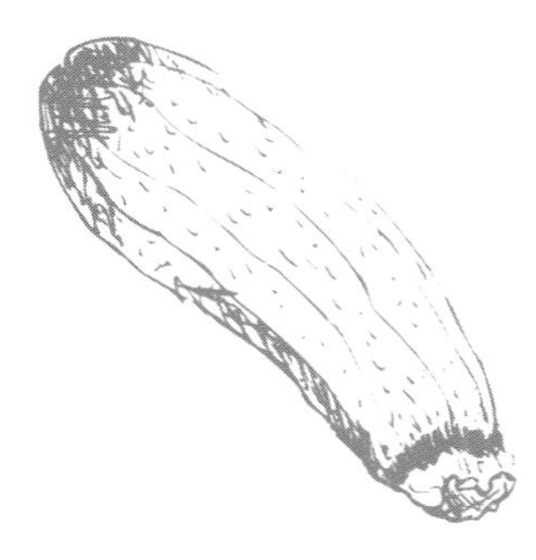

YIELD: 4 SERVINGS

NUTRITIONAL ANALYSIS PER SERVING:

Calories 415
Protein 12 gm.
Carbohydrates 53 gm.
Fat 19.2 gm.
Saturated fat 3.6 gm.
Cholesterol 6 mg.
Sodium 1,155 mg.

This dish contains a medley of high-fiber, low-calorie vegetables, plus olive oil, rich in vitamin E.

SOUFFLÉ IN A GRATIN DISH

ALTHOUGH THIS SOUFFLÉ CAN BE PREPARED IN A CONVENTIONAL SOUFFLÉ MOLD, I LIKE IT BEST MADE IN A GRATIN DISH. THE CRUST AND TOPPING, MADE OF PARMESAN CHEESE AND BREAD CRUMBS, WILL BE BROWNER AND CRUNCHIER AS A RESULT, IMPROVING THE LOOK AND TASTE OF THE DISH AND MAKING IT EASIER TO SERVE AT THE TABLE. *NOTE:* LEFTOVER SOUFFLÉ WILL REINFLATE IF REHEATED IN A CONVENTIONAL OVEN (PREHEATED TO 375 DEGREES) INSTEAD OF A MICROWAVE OVEN.

YIELD:
8 SERVINGS

NUTRITIONAL ANALYSIS PER SERVING:

Calories 203
Protein 15 gm.
Carbohydrates 10 gm.
Fat 11.2 gm.
Saturated fat 4.5 gm.
Cholesterol 130 mg.
Sodium 641 mg.

SPINACH, HAM, AND PARMESAN SOUFFLÉ

A soufflé is always an impressive addition to a meal. As a first course, this recipe will serve six to eight, but it also makes a great luncheon main dish for four people. You can eliminate the ham if you are cutting down on calories. Another green, or even mushrooms, can be substituted for the spinach.

10 ounces spinach, fibrous stems removed (8 ounces trimmed)
1 slice bread, processed in a food processor to make crumbs (½ cup)
½ cup freshly grated parmesan cheese
4 teaspoons unsalted butter
1 tablespoon canola oil
3 tablespoons all-purpose flour
1½ cups cold nonfat milk
¼ teaspoon salt
¼ teaspoon freshly ground black pepper
3 egg yolks
4 ounces lean ham, julienned (1 cup)
5 egg whites

1. Preheat the oven to 375 degrees.
2. Wash the spinach, and place it, still wet, in a skillet. Cook over medium to high heat for 2 minutes, until the spinach is wilted. Remove from the heat, and cool. When it is cool, drain it, chop it coarsely, and set it aside.
3. Mix the bread crumbs and 3 tablespoons of the parmesan cheese together in a small bowl. Using 1 teaspoon of the butter, grease the sides and bottom of a 6-cup gratin dish that is about 1½ inches deep. Add half of the bread crumb and parmesan cheese mixture, and shake the dish until the crumbs coat the sides and bottom. Set aside.
4. Melt the remaining 3 teaspoons of butter in a saucepan, and add the oil and flour. Mix with a whisk, and cook over medium to high heat for about 30 seconds. Whisk in the milk, salt, and pepper, and bring to a boil, whisking continuously until the mixture boils and thickens. Remove from the heat, and whisk in the egg yolks. Add the reserved spinach and the ham, and mix well.
5. In a mixing bowl, beat the egg whites until they are firm but still soft. Fold them into the spinach mixture along with the remaining cheese.
6. Pour the soufflé mixture into the prepared gratin dish, sprinkle the remaining bread crumb and cheese mixture on top, place the dish on a tray, and bake it at 375 degrees for about 35 minutes, until the soufflé is set inside and the top is puffy and brown.
7. Spoon the soufflé directly from the gratin dish onto plates, and serve immediately. (The soufflé can be unmolded from the dish by inverting it onto a plate, if you prefer to present it in this way.)

OTHER USES FOR GRITS

THE GRITS MIXTURE IN THIS RECIPE CAN BE SERVED ON ITS OWN AS A GARNISH OR AS A CUSHION UNDER A PIECE OF POACHED OR GRILLED FISH OR SAUTÉED MEAT.

Tomatoes Stuffed with Yellow Grits

I prefer to use quick yellow grits, which have a coarser texture and are brighter yellow than cornmeal, in this lean recipe that is best made in full summer, when tomatoes are ripe, flavorful, and inexpensive. Although I use almost any leftovers—fish and meat, for example—to stuff tomatoes, this combination of grits, scallions, and mushrooms is perfect for a meatless lunch or dinner.

- 2½ cups water
- 1¼ teaspoons salt
- ½ cup quick yellow grits or yellow cornmeal
- 4 large, firm tomatoes (about 2 pounds)
- 3 tablespoons virgin olive oil
- 6 scallions, cleaned and cut into ½-inch pieces (1 cup)
- 1 medium onion (4 ounces), peeled and chopped (1 cup)
- 2 cloves garlic, chopped (1½ teaspoons)
- ½ pound mushrooms, coarsely chopped (2 cups)

1. Preheat the oven to 375 degrees.
2. Bring the water to a boil in a saucepan. Stir in ½ teaspoon of the salt and the grits, and return the mixture to a boil. Boil, covered, removing the lid and stirring with a whisk occasionally, for 5 minutes, until most of the water has been absorbed and the grits are tender. Spread the grits on a plate, and cool them to lukewarm.
3. Meanwhile, cut a ½-inch-thick crosswise slice from the stem end of each tomato. Reserve these "caps." Using a sharp-edged metal measuring tablespoon, remove the interior of the tomatoes, leaving a shell ½ inch thick. Chop the tomato insides in a food processor. (You should have 1½ to 2 cups.) Add ¼ teaspoon of the salt and 1 tablespoon of the oil, process briefly to mix, and set aside. This will be the sauce.
4. Heat the remaining 2 tablespoons of oil in a skillet. Add the scallions and onion, and sauté over medium to high heat for 2 minutes. Stir in the garlic, mushrooms, and remaining ½ teaspoon of salt. Cook for about 4 minutes, until most of the juices have evaporated. Transfer the mixture to a bowl, and stir in the grits.
5. Fill the tomato shells with the grits mixture, and top each with a "cap." Arrange the stuffed tomatoes in a gratin dish, and pour the processed tomato sauce around them.
6. Bake at 375 degrees for 40 minutes. Cool to lukewarm. Serve.

YIELD: 4 SERVINGS

NUTRITIONAL ANALYSIS PER SERVING:

Calories 243
Protein 6 gm.
Carbohydrates 33 gm.
Fat 11.4 gm.
Saturated fat 1.5 gm.
Cholesterol 0 mg.
Sodium 713 mg.

Tomatoes are a good source of vitamin A and potassium.

Zucchini and Tomato Fans

This is a great dish in summer, when small, firm zucchini are most plentiful. The idea is first to make zucchini "fans" by cutting the zucchini lengthwise into slices that remain attached at the stem end. Then, with the zucchini fanned out in a roasting pan, long narrow slices of plum tomatoes and thin slices of garlic are inserted between the zucchini slices, and the dish is baked. Leftovers are good served cold with a little vinaigrette on top. *(See photograph, page 77.)*

- **4 long, narrow plum tomatoes (about 12 ounces)**
- **4 small, firm zucchini, about 1½ inches in diameter and 6 inches long (1¼ pounds)**
- **4 large cloves garlic, peeled**
- **2 tablespoons virgin olive oil**
- **¼ teaspoon salt**
- **¼ teaspoon freshly ground black pepper**
- **½ teaspoon *herbes de Provence* (see page 467)**

1. Preheat the oven to 400 degrees.
2. Wash the tomatoes, and cut each of them lengthwise into four slices. Wash the zucchini and trim off the stem end of each. Then, starting at the flower end, cut each zucchini lengthwise into ¼-inch slices, leaving the slices attached at the stem end so they can be opened like a fan. Each zucchini should have four slits.
3. Arrange the zucchini side by side in a roasting pan or large gratin dish with enough space between so each one can be fanned out. Slide a slice of tomato into each slit and press down firmly on the zucchini to create a fan with alternating segments of zucchini and tomato.
4. Cut each garlic clove lengthwise into eight thin slices, and slide the slices into the fans alongside the tomato slices. Brush the entire surface of the fans with the oil and sprinkle the salt, pepper, and *herbes de Provence* on top.
5. Bake at 400 degrees for 30 minutes, until the vegetables are soft and the fans are nicely browned on top. Using a large spatula, transfer the fans to four plates, and serve immediately.

Yield: 4 Servings

NUTRITIONAL ANALYSIS PER SERVING:

Calories 104
Protein 3 gm.
Carbohydrates 10 gm.
Fat 7.3 gm.
Saturated fat 1.0 gm.
Cholesterol 0 mg.
Sodium 148 mg.

Zucchini are a good source of fiber, tomatoes are rich in vitamins A and C, and garlic contains natural substances that protect the heart.

Herbs

Spaghetti Squash in Fresh Tomato Sauce

We often enjoy spaghetti squash at our house and occasionally serve it as a low-calorie substitute for pasta. It doesn't taste like pasta, obviously, but its fresh flavor and crisp texture are complemented by pasta sauces. There are different ways of cooking spaghetti squash, but I think roasting it, as we do here, produces a great result and is especially easy.

For the delicious fresh tomato sauce served here with the squash, two heads of garlic are halved crosswise, wrapped in foil, and roasted alongside the squash. Then, when the cloves are soft and nicely browned on their cut edges, their tender flesh is squeezed out and added to a sauce composed of onion, fresh tomato pieces, and seasonings. Mild and tender, roasted garlic can also be served on its own or with other dishes.

- 1 spaghetti squash (2½ to 3 pounds)
- 2 teaspoons canola oil
- 2 heads garlic (about 6 ounces total)
- 3 tablespoons virgin olive oil
- 1 onion (about 4 ounces), peeled and chopped (1 cup)
- 3 or 4 ripe tomatoes (1 pound), cut into 2-inch pieces
- 1 teaspoon *herbes de Provence* (see page 467)
- 1½ teaspoons salt
- ¾ teaspoon freshly ground black pepper
- ⅓ cup water
- 1 tablespoon chopped fresh chives
- 2 or 3 tablespoons grated parmesan cheese (optional)

1. Preheat the oven to 400 degrees.
2. Cut the squash in half crosswise, and scoop out the seeds with a spoon. Brush the cut side of the squash halves with 1 teaspoon of the canola oil, and place them cut side down on a cookie sheet or in a roasting pan.
3. Cut a rectangle of aluminum foil about 6 by 12 inches, and spread the remaining

(continued)

TOP: CORN POLENTA WITH MUSHROOM RAGOUT (SEE PAGE 100).
BOTTOM: SPAGHETTI SQUASH IN FRESH TOMATO SAUCE (ABOVE).

teaspoon of canola oil over half its surface. Cut the heads of garlic in half crosswise, and place them cut side down next to one another on the oiled half of the foil. Fold the unoiled half over the garlic, and fold the edges of the foil together tightly.

4. Place the foil package containing the garlic next to the squash halves on the cookie sheet or in the roasting pan, and bake at 400 degrees for 40 to 45 minutes. The squash should be tender when pierced with a knife, and its cut sides should be nicely browned; the garlic cloves should be soft throughout, and their cut surfaces should be nicely browned.
5. Heat 2 tablespoons of the olive oil until hot but not smoking in a medium saucepan. Add the onion, and sauté for 2 or 3 minutes. Add the tomatoes, *herbes de Provence,* 1 teaspoon of the salt, and the pepper. Squeeze the soft garlic cloves out of their skins, and add them to the saucepan. Mix well, add the water, and bring the mixture to a strong boil. Cover, and boil over high heat for 10 minutes. Then push the mixture through a food mill set over a saucepan. Set aside.
6. Using a fork, loosen and release the "spaghetti" strands from the squash halves, and mix them gently but thoroughly in a bowl with the remaining ½ teaspoon of salt and 1 tablespoon of olive oil.
7. At serving time, reheat the "spaghetti" until it is hot in a microwave oven for 1½ to 2 minutes, or in a conventional oven set at 400 degrees for 10 to 12 minutes. Reheat the sauce in the saucepan until it is hot, and then ladle a large spoonful of it onto each of four dinner plates. Divide the "spaghetti" among the plates and drizzle about 1 tablespoon of the remaining sauce on top of each serving. Sprinkle with the chives, and serve immediately, with the cheese, if desired.

**YIELD:
4 SERVINGS**

NUTRITIONAL ANALYSIS PER SERVING:

Calories 271
Protein 5 gm.
Carbohydrates 35 gm.
Fat 14.2 gm.
Saturated fat 1.9 gm.
Cholesterol 0 mg.
Sodium 878 mg.

Spaghetti squash is a wonderful low-calorie alternative to pasta. Canola oil is the oil lowest in saturated fat. Parmesan cheese is rich in calcium.

Pasta with Fresh Vegetable Sauce

Here's a low-calorie pasta dish that can be made in less than 20 minutes. Remember to put the pasta-cooking water on to boil before you begin this recipe; it takes only about 7 minutes to make the sauce and 8 minutes to cook the pasta, so bringing the water to a boil is the most time-consuming part of the preparation.

PREVENTING STICKY PASTA

NOTICE THAT I DON'T SALT THE PASTA-COOKING WATER. I SEE NO DIFFERENCE IN THE COOKING PROCESS, AND I'D RATHER SAVE THE SALT FOR USE IN THE SAUCE. TO PREVENT THE COOKED PASTA FROM STICKING TOGETHER OR BEING TOO DENSE, I RESERVE A LITTLE OF THE PASTA-COOKING WATER AND ADD IT TO THE VEGETABLES BEFORE TOSSING THEM WITH THE PASTA.

- 3 quarts water
- ½ pound spaghetti (number 4)
- ¼ cup virgin olive oil
- 1 large red onion, peeled and thinly sliced (1½ cups)
- 1 small eggplant (6 ounces), cut into ½-inch pieces
- 3 to 4 cloves garlic, peeled, crushed, and finely chopped (about 2 teaspoons)
- 2 ripe tomatoes (12 ounces), seeded and cut into ½-inch pieces
- 1 teaspoon salt
- ½ teaspoon freshly ground black pepper
- 2 tablespoons coarsely chopped fresh parsley
- About 2 tablespoons grated parmesan cheese

1. Bring the water to a boil. Add the pasta, return the water to a boil, and cook for about 8 minutes, until the pasta is just tender to the bite.
2. Meanwhile, heat the oil in a large saucepan, and sauté the onion and eggplant until soft and lightly browned, 6 to 7 minutes. Remove the pan from the heat, and mix in the garlic. Add the tomatoes, salt, and pepper; mix thoroughly, and set aside.
3. Remove ⅓ cup of the pasta-cooking liquid, and add it to the eggplant mixture. Drain the pasta, add it to the saucepan, and toss to coat it with the vegetables.
4. Divide the pasta and vegetables among four plates, sprinkle with the parsley, and serve with cheese to taste.

YIELD: 4 SERVINGS

NUTRITIONAL ANALYSIS PER SERVING:

Calories 397
Protein 11 gm.
Carbohydrates 55 gm.
Fat 15.5 gm.
Saturated fat 2.5 gm.
Cholesterol 2 mg.
Sodium 617 mg.

Nage Courte of Striped Bass

I like to cook whole fish occasionally; the flesh slides off the bones easily and tends to have more flavor than when cooked as fillets. If you decide to prepare this recipe with fillets instead of whole fish, however, adjust the cooking time as indicated in the note following the recipe.

ABOUT STRIPED BASS

STRIPED BASS USED TO BE ALMOST IMPOSSIBLE TO FIND. ORIGINALLY A SPORT FISH, IT BECAME SO SCARCE FOR A TIME THAT FISHING FOR IT WAS PROHIBITED. NOW STRIPED BASS OF EXCELLENT QUALITY ARE RAISED, OR "FARMED," AND AVAILABLE COMMERCIALLY IN MOST PARTS OF THE COUNTRY. IF YOU CAN'T FIND STRIPED BASS WHERE YOU LIVE, HOWEVER, REPLACE IT WITH A FISH OF APPROXIMATELY THE SAME SIZE—ANYTHING FROM RED SNAPPER TO PORGY TO BLACK BASS.

YIELD: 4 SERVINGS

NUTRITIONAL ANALYSIS PER SERVING:

Calories 330
Protein 32 gm.
Carbohydrates 15 gm.
Fat 12.1 gm.
Saturated fat 3.3 gm.
Cholesterol 144 mg.
Sodium 694 mg.

¾ cup water
1 leek (about 5 ounces), thoroughly cleaned and cut into julienne strips (about 2 cups)
1 large carrot (about 4 ounces), peeled and cut into julienne strips (about 1 cup)
4 strips lemon peel, removed with a vegetable peeler, stacked together, and cut into fine julienne strips (about 1½ tablespoons)
5 cloves garlic, peeled and thinly sliced (1½ tablespoons)
1 small red onion, peeled and thinly sliced (1 cup)
¾ cup dry white wine, such as a chardonnay
1½ tablespoons virgin olive oil
1 tablespoon unsalted butter
1 teaspoon salt
2 whole striped bass, gutted, with heads removed (1¼ pounds each, ready to cook) or 4 fillets striped bass (about 6 ounces each) (if using fillets, see note following step 3)
¼ teaspoon freshly ground black pepper

1. Place all the ingredients except the fish and pepper in a large stainless steel saucepan, and bring to a boil over high heat. Cover, reduce the heat to medium, and boil gently for 2 minutes.
2. Add the fish, bring to a boil, cover, reduce the heat to low, and cook for 5 minutes. Let the fish rest, covered, in the broth for 10 minutes before serving.
3. To serve, carefully remove the fish from the broth with a slotted spoon, and place them on a clean work surface. Lift off the fillets, and remove and discard the skin. Transfer the fillets to four individual plates. Add the pepper to the stock, and bring the mixture to a boil. Spoon the stock over the fish. Serve immediately.

Note: If you are using fillets instead of whole fish, boil the vegetables for about 4 minutes before adding the fish. Place the fillets on top of the vegetables, and bring the mixture to a boil. Cover, and simmer for 1 minute. Then set aside for 5 minutes. Serve the fillets with or without the skin, as desired.

Codfish Flakes in Vegetable *Brunoise*

I like scrod, haddock, and pollock, but my first preference in this fish family is cod—especially when it is presented, as it is here, in thick, heavy, white fillets. Cod fillets tend to separate into beautiful flakes as they cook, and the idea in this recipe is to combine those natural flakes with sautéed onions, zucchini, tomatoes, and black olives, all of which are scented with tarragon.

2 tablespoons peanut oil
1 tablespoon unsalted butter
1 medium onion (6 ounces), peeled and finely chopped (1 cup)
4 pieces codfish fillet, each about 1¼ inches thick (1¼ pounds total)
2 small, firm zucchini (10 ounces), washed and cut into ½-inch dice (2 cups)
1 teaspoon salt
½ teaspoon freshly ground black pepper
⅔ cup dry, fruity white wine (such as Semillon, Lakewood)
6 plum tomatoes (13 ounces), seeded and cut into ½-inch dice (2 cups)
¼ cup diced oil-cured black olives (½-inch dice)
2 teaspoons chopped fresh tarragon

1. In a large saucepan, heat the oil and butter until they are hot. Add the onion, and sauté for 1 minute. Add the cod in one layer along with the zucchini, salt, pepper, and wine. Bring the mixture to a boil, cover, reduce the heat, and cook for about 3 minutes, until the fish flakes but is still slightly underdone in the center.
2. Transfer the fish to a platter, and cover it with a pan lid so it stays warm and continues to cook in its own residual heat.
3. Add the tomatoes and olives to the skillet, and sauté them, uncovered, for 1 minute. Add the tarragon, and mix it in.
4. To serve, arrange the codfish, which will flake into pieces, on four dinner plates. Divide the vegetable mixture, juice and all, among the plates, and mix it gently into the fish flakes. Serve immediately.

Yield: 4 Servings

NUTRITIONAL ANALYSIS PER SERVING:

Calories 281
Protein 27 gm.
Carbohydrates 10 gm.
Fat 11.9 gm.
Saturated fat 3.3 gm.
Cholesterol 69 mg.
Sodium 14 mg.

Codfish is an excellent low-fat source of protein.

Codfish in Olive and Horseradish Sauce

The pungent flavors of horseradish, capers, cilantro, and black olives dominate the codfish sauce. Even though the recipe contains sour cream, the dish is low-calorie because it uses no oil or butter, the cod is a low-fat fish, and the sour cream amounts to only a tablespoon per person. If cod is not available, use fillets from another fleshy, white fish.

4 cod fillets, about 1½ inches thick (5 to 6 ounces each)
½ cup chopped onion
1 cup dry, fruity white wine (an Alsace wine would be good)
½ teaspoon salt
½ teaspoon freshly ground black pepper
About 12 oil-cured black olives
2 tablespoons small capers, drained
2 tablespoons horseradish, freshly grated or bottled
¼ cup sour cream
4 tablespoons coarsely chopped fresh cilantro (coriander or Chinese parsley)

1. Place the cod, onion, wine, salt, and pepper in a stainless steel saucepan. Bring to a boil over high heat, cover, reduce the heat to low, and boil gently for 2 minutes. (The cod will be undercooked at this point.) With a slotted spoon, carefully transfer the cod to a platter, cover it, and set it aside to continue cooking in its own residual heat.
2. Meanwhile, add the olives, capers, horseradish, and sour cream to the saucepan, and bring to a boil.
3. Arrange a cod fillet on each of four plates, and top with the sauce. Sprinkle with the cilantro. Serve immediately.

Yield: 4 Servings

Nutritional Analysis per Serving:

Calories 234
Protein 29 gm.
Carbohydrates 4 gm.
Fat 6.7 gm.
Saturated fat 2.4 gm.
Cholesterol 73 mg.
Sodium 723 mg.

Cod fillets are high in niacin and protein and are low in fat.

Top: Seafood with "Handkerchiefs" (see page 189).
Bottom: Codfish in Olive and Horseradish Sauce (above).

TIME TO CURE

THIS RECIPE IS EASY TO DO, BUT IT TAKES TIME—THE SALMON IS CURED IN THE SUGAR, SALT, AND SPICES FOR 12 HOURS, THEN MARINATED IN THE MOLASSES AND SAUCE FOR ANOTHER 24 HOURS, AND FINALLY SET ASIDE TO DRY FOR AT LEAST ANOTHER 24 HOURS BEFORE IT IS SLICED AND SERVED. WHEN THIS MUCH TIME IS SPENT ON A RECIPE, IT MAKES SENSE TO CURE A LARGE ENOUGH FILLET SO YOU HAVE SOME ON HAND FOR ENTERTAINING. THIS RECIPE WILL SERVE EIGHT. ANY LEFTOVER SALMON WILL KEEP FOR A WEEK UNDER REFRIGERATION. YOU MIGHT ENJOY SERVING IT ON SALAD GREENS, AS SUGGESTED IN THE VARIATION ON PAGE 120.

Cured Salmon in Molasses

This cured salmon recipe is interesting because the sweet molasses in combination with the dark soy sauce not only gives the salmon a very intense flavor but also colors the salmon flesh, making it almost black on the outside. When you slice it, the inside is a beautifully transparent gold and pink, contrasting dramatically with the black exterior and looking more like a smoked salmon, although no smoking is involved.

- **1 large salmon fillet (about 1½ pounds), preferably center cut, of even thickness throughout, with the skin left on but all bones removed**
- **¼ cup coarse (kosher-style) salt**
- **1 tablespoon sugar**
- **1 teaspoon ground cumin**
- **½ teaspoon ground allspice**
- **½ teaspoon paprika**
- **¼ teaspoon ground nutmeg**
- **¼ teaspoon cayenne pepper**
- **¼ cup dark molasses**
- **2 tablespoons dark soy sauce**
- **Buttered bread**

OPTIONAL GARNISHES

- **Chopped onion**
- **Capers, drained**
- **Olive oil**

1. Lightly score the skin of the salmon in a lattice pattern so the salt, sugar, and spices will penetrate through it to cure the flesh. (It is easier to cut through the skin if you hold the blade of the knife perpendicular to the fillet and run the entire length of the blade across the skin, instead of attempting to score it with just the tip of the blade.) Place the salmon in the center of a large piece of plastic wrap.

2. In a small bowl, mix together the salt, sugar, cumin, allspice, paprika, nutmeg, and cayenne. Spread the mixture evenly on both sides of the salmon, and wrap the salmon tightly in the plastic wrap. Place it on a tray, and refrigerate overnight, or for at least 12 hours, to cure.

3. When ready to proceed, mix the molasses and soy sauce together in a small bowl. Unwrap the salmon, but don't remove it from the plastic wrap. Pour half of the molasses mixture over the top of the salmon, and spread it evenly over the surface.

(continued)

TOP: CURED SALMON IN MOLASSES (ABOVE).
BOTTOM: SALMON IN *NORI* (SEE PAGE 121).

Then turn the salmon over, and coat the other side with the remainder of the molasses mixture. Rewrap the salmon in the plastic wrap, place it on the tray, and return it to the refrigerator for 24 hours.

4. Unwrap the salmon, and remove it from the marinade. (It will have absorbed most of the marinade.) Discard any remaining marinade, pat the fish lightly with paper towels, and arrange it on a wire rack over a tray. Refrigerate it for another 24 hours to dry out.
5. At serving time, slice the salmon thinly on a slant, and serve two or three slices per person with buttered bread. Garnish the salmon, if desired, with chopped onion, capers, and a drizzle of olive oil.

YIELD: 8 SERVINGS

NUTRITIONAL ANALYSIS PER SERVING:

Calories 146
Protein 17 gm.
Carbohydrates 6 gm.
Fat 5.5 gm.
Saturated fat 0.8 gm.
Cholesterol 47 mg.
Sodium 1,948 mg.

VARIATION: CURED SALMON ON SALAD GREENS

Here is another way to serve the salmon.

YIELD: 4 SERVINGS

NUTRITIONAL ANALYSIS PER SERVING:

Calories 138
Protein 12 gm.
Carbohydrates 6 gm.
Fat 7.2 gm.
Saturated fat 1.0 gm.
Cholesterol 31 mg.
Sodium 1,374 mg.

SALAD BASE FOR SALMON SLICES

4 cups radicchio and Boston lettuce, mixed
1 tablespoon virgin olive oil
1½ teaspoons balsamic vinegar
⅛ teaspoon salt
¼ teaspoon freshly ground black pepper

8 to 12 thin slices Cured Salmon in Molasses (see page 118)
Toast

1. Wash the salad greens, and dry them well.
2. Combine the oil, vinegar, salt, and pepper in a bowl, add the greens, and toss gently to coat them with the dressing.
3. Divide the greens among four plates, top each serving with two or three slices of salmon, and serve with toast.

SALMON IN *NORI*

My wife, Gloria, often makes sushi with the dried seaweed sheets called nori. *(See About* Nori.*) For sushi, the seaweed sheets are conventionally covered with cooked rice, which moistens them and thus makes them easy to roll. Here, I dampen one side of the* nori *with water before arranging pieces of salmon on top. The sheets soften immediately, and the salmon can easily be rolled up in them and cut into pieces. These pieces are then steamed (I use a bamboo steamer) just before serving.* *(See photograph, page 119.)*

1 pound completely cleaned salmon, with a 4-by-8-inch piece of skin removed and reserved for crackling
Dash of salt
3 dried *nori* sheets

LEMON SAUCE
2 tablespoons canola oil
1½ teaspoons lemon juice
1 teaspoon julienned lemon rind
1½ teaspoons balsamic vinegar
¼ teaspoon freshly ground black pepper
¼ teaspoon salt

1. Preheat the oven to 375 degrees.
2. Spread the salmon skin on a cookie sheet, salt it lightly, and bake it at 375 degrees for 30 minutes, until crisp.
3. Meanwhile, cut the salmon into three strips, each about 1¼ inches wide and 7 inches long.
4. Wet the *nori* sheets on one side with water, and place them, dampened side up, on a flat work surface. Place a strip of salmon at one end of each sheet, and roll it tightly, enclosing the salmon. Cut each roll in half, and then cut each half into thirds. You should have six slices per roll, or eighteen slices in all, enough for four slices per person with a couple left over to pass around.
5. Arrange the *nori*-wrapped salmon pieces on a plate, and place in a steamer over boiling water. Cover and steam for about 5 minutes, until the salmon is barely cooked, even slightly rare in the center.
6. Meanwhile, combine all the lemon sauce ingredients in a small bowl.
7. Remove the salmon from the steamer, and arrange it on a serving plate. Spoon some sauce over the salmon, and sprinkle some salmon skin crackling on top. Serve.

ABOUT *NORI*

MADE OF DARK GREEN OR PURPLISH DRIED SEAWEED (*PORPHYRA TENERA*), *NORI* SHEETS MEASURE ABOUT 7 BY 8 INCHES AND COME SEALED IN PLASTIC PACKAGES. THEY ARE AVAILABLE AT SOME SUPERMARKETS AND HEALTH FOOD STORES AND AT MOST ASIAN SPECIALTY SHOPS. *NORI* SHEETS ARE FLAVORFUL AND ATTRACTIVE, AND GLORIA'S SUCCESS USING THEM FOR SUSHI SPURRED ME TO CREATE THIS SIMPLE DISH FEATURING SALMON.

YIELD: 4 SERVINGS

NUTRITIONAL ANALYSIS PER SERVING:

Calories 227
Protein 23 gm.
Carbohydrates 1 gm.
Fat 14.0 gm.
Saturated fat 1.6 gm.
Cholesterol 62 mg.
Sodium 243 mg.

Sautéed Salmon on Greens

Salmon is a great seafood choice because it is available practically year-round from your fishmonger. It is especially versatile, accommodating itself to poaching, braising, sautéing, and grilling.

- **4 skinless, boneless salmon fillet steaks (about 5 ounces each)**
- **4 tablespoons virgin olive oil**
- **½ pound spinach, tough stems removed, washed and drained in a colander**
- **¾ teaspoon salt**
- **¼ teaspoon freshly ground black pepper**
- **½ cup finely chopped onion**
- **3 ripe tomatoes (about 1¼ pounds), peeled, seeded, and cut into ½-inch pieces**
- **1 tablespoon coarsely chopped fresh flat-leaf parsley**

1. Arrange the salmon steaks on a plate, spoon 1 tablespoon of the oil over them, cover with plastic wrap, and refrigerate.
2. In a skillet, heat 1 tablespoon of the remaining oil. When hot, sauté the spinach for 1½ minutes. Mix in ¼ teaspoon of the salt and ⅛ teaspoon of the pepper, and divide the spinach among four plates.
3. Heat the remaining 2 tablespoons of oil in the skillet, and sauté the onion for 1 minute. Add the tomatoes, ¼ teaspoon of the salt, and the remaining pepper, and cook for about 30 seconds. Set aside.
4. Remove the salmon from the refrigerator, and sprinkle it with the remaining salt. Heat a nonstick skillet until very hot, add the salmon steaks, and sauté for 1½ minutes on each side. Let rest in the pan a few minutes before serving.
5. Spoon some of the onion-tomato mixture over the spinach, and top with the salmon. Sprinkle with the parsley, and serve immediately.

LIGHT COOKING TECHNIQUES

THE STEAKS ARE MACERATED IN A LITTLE OLIVE OIL; THAT IS ALL THE FAT NEEDED TO COOK THEM, WHICH TAKES ONLY A COUPLE OF MINUTES IN A VERY HOT SKILLET. THE SPINACH IS COOKED "DRY," THE ONLY MOISTURE BEING THE SMALL AMOUNT OF WATER CLINGING TO THE LEAVES AFTER THEY ARE WASHED; THIS HELPS RETAIN NUTRIENTS, COLOR, AND VITAMINS. THE TOMATOES ARE ALSO LIGHTLY SAUTÉED, SO THEY KEEP THEIR FRESH, SWEET TASTE.

**YIELD:
4 SERVINGS**

NUTRITIONAL ANALYSIS PER SERVING:

Calories 365
Protein 31 gm.
Carbohydrates 9 gm.
Fat 23.1 gm.
Saturated fat 3.3 gm.
Cholesterol 78 mg.
Sodium 519 mg.

Salmon is high in omega-3 fatty acids.

Pizza of Cured Salmon and Sour Cream

Although presented as a first course here, this makes an ideal snack and also can be served with aperitifs at a cocktail party. The pizza dough, made with olive oil, is prepared in a food processor. You can either let the dough rise at room temperature for 2 hours or, for a more flavorful result, let it proof in the refrigerator overnight. After the dough is cooked, it is layered with sour cream, cured salmon (instant gravlax), onion, basil leaves, and black olives. The cured salmon is also good on its own.

Pizza Dough

- **1 cup warm (not hot) water**
- **½ teaspoon honey**
- **1 teaspoon granulated yeast**
- **¼ teaspoon canola oil**
- **2¼ cups (about 12 ounces) all-purpose flour**
- **¾ teaspoon salt**
- **1 tablespoon virgin olive oil**

Cured Salmon

- **1 teaspoon salt**
- **1 teaspoon freshly ground black pepper, plus more to taste (optional)**
- **1 1-pound salmon fillet, skinned (14 ounces skinned)**

- **2 tablespoons cornmeal**
- **1 teaspoon virgin olive oil (for moistening your fingers)**
- **1 cup sour cream**
- **1 red onion (about 7 ounces), peeled and very thinly sliced**
- **½ cup (loose) fresh basil leaves**
- **8 oil-cured black olives, pitted and coarsely chopped**

For the Dough

1. Place the warm water and honey in the bowl of a food processor, sprinkle the yeast on top, and let the yeast proof until bubbly, 8 to 10 minutes. Meanwhile, oil the inside of a medium to large bowl with the canola oil, and set it aside.
2. Add the remainder of the dough ingredients to the processor bowl, and process on medium speed for about 30 seconds. The dough will be soft. Transfer it to the oiled bowl, cover it with plastic wrap, and set it aside for about 2 hours at room tempera-

(continued)

ture or, for a more sour, flavorful dough, overnight in the refrigerator. (You will have enough for two 10-inch pizzas.)

FOR THE CURED SALMON

3. Combine the 1 teaspoon salt and 1 teaspoon pepper in a small bowl, then spread half of the mixture out on a large platter. Cut the salmon into about twelve thin slices (about the thickness of sliced smoked salmon), and arrange the slices in one layer on the seasoned platter. Sprinkle the remaining combined salt and pepper on top. Cover with plastic wrap and refrigerate until you are ready to assemble the pizza. (The salmon will be cured (gravlax) and ready to use in about ½ hour but can be refrigerated for up to 48 hours.)
4. When you are ready to cook the pizza dough, preheat the oven to 425 degrees.
5. Break the dough down gently by folding its edges in toward the center and pressing down to release the air. Divide the dough in half, and roll each piece into a ball. Spread half the cornmeal on a cookie sheet, and place one ball of dough on top. Moisten your fingers with a little of the olive oil (to keep them from sticking to the dough), and press the dough into a disk about 10 inches in diameter. Repeat this procedure, shaping the second ball on another cookie sheet. Let the dough disks rise for about 20 minutes, then bake them at 425 degrees for 15 minutes, until they are nicely browned. Remove to a rack, and cool to room temperature.
6. When ready to serve the pizza, spread half the sour cream on the flatter side of each dough disk, and arrange half the onion slices on top. Divide the gravlax between the pizzas, laying the slices side by side over the onions. Top with the basil leaves and black olive pieces, and sprinkle with extra pepper, if desired. Cut each pizza into twelve wedges, and serve.

YIELD: 4 SERVINGS

NUTRITIONAL ANALYSIS PER SERVING:

Calories 383
Protein 18 gm.
Carbohydrates 45 gm.
Fat 14.3 gm.
Saturated fat 5.3 gm.
Cholesterol 46 mg.
Sodium 635 mg.

Salmon is naturally rich in niacin, omega-3 fatty acids, and vitamin D.

Grilled Swordfish with Spicy Yogurt Sauce

Thick, white swordfish steaks are a delicacy. Before grilling 1-inch-thick steaks for this recipe, rub them very lightly with oil, and coat them with herbes de Provence, *a dried herb mixture that you can find in the spice section of many supermarkets or make yourself (see page 467). The steaks are served here with a piquant yogurt sauce that can also accompany other grilled or poached fish, as well as grilled poultry.*

4 swordfish steaks (5 to 6 ounces each), preferably center-cut, each about 1 inch thick
½ teaspoon canola oil
1 teaspoon *herbes de Provence* (see page 467)

Spicy Yogurt Sauce
⅓ cup (loose) fresh cilantro leaves
¼ cup (loose) fresh mint leaves
2 cloves garlic, peeled
1 piece ginger, peeled, about the size of the 2 garlic cloves
1 small jalapeño pepper (optional)
½ teaspoon salt
1 cup nonfat plain yogurt

1. Rub the steaks on both sides with the oil, and sprinkle them with the *herbes de Provence.* Arrange the steaks on a plate, cover them with plastic wrap, and refrigerate them until ready to cook. (The recipe can be prepared to this point a few hours ahead.)
2. Place all the spicy yogurt sauce ingredients except the yogurt in the bowl of a blender or mini-chop, and process until chopped. Add the yogurt, and process until smooth. Set aside, covered.
3. When you are ready to cook the swordfish steaks, preheat a grill until very hot. Preheat the oven to 180 to 200 degrees.
4. Place the steaks on the rack of the grill, and cook them for about 2½ minutes on each side, until well browned. Transfer the steaks to a tray, and place them in the warm oven for 15 or 20 minutes.
5. Spoon enough sauce onto four plates to coat the bottom of each. Place a steak in the center of each plate, and serve immediately. Alternatively, serve the sauce on the side, if you prefer.

COOKING SWORDFISH

GRILLING THE SWORDFISH STEAKS FOR 5 MINUTES GIVES THEM THE DISTINCTIVE SURFACE MARKINGS AND TASTE OF GRILLED MEAT WITHOUT DRYING THEM OUT. WHEN FINISHED IN A WARM OVEN, THEY EMERGE TENDER, JUICY, AND FLAVORFUL.

YIELD: 4 SERVINGS

NUTRITIONAL ANALYSIS PER SERVING:

Calories 251
Protein 38 gm.
Carbohydrates 5 gm.
Fat 7.8 gm.
Saturated fat 2.1 gm.
Cholesterol 70 mg.
Sodium 476 mg.

Swordfish contains omega-3s and selenium, a trace mineral that may reduce the risk of heart disease and cancer.

Skate with Beets and Flavored Oil

Skate, a relatively unknown fish in the United States, is quite common in Europe. Soft-fleshed, tender, moist, and mild-flavored, it is delicious. Conventionally, skate is poached, as it is here, in vinegar and water. Instead of serving it with butter, as is traditional, I coat it with a lower-calorie sauce featuring capers, and garnish it with a julienne of beets seasoned with a fairly acidic dressing. In addition, for flavor and eye appeal, I surround the fish on each plate with some brilliant red beet-cooking liquid that I sprinkle with a little bright yellow Curried Oil (page 470) and vivid green Cilantro Oil (page 469).

- 2 red beets (about 10 ounces total)
- 4 tablespoons red wine vinegar
- ¾ teaspoon salt
- ¼ teaspoon freshly ground black pepper
- ½ teaspoon sugar
- 6 cups water
- 1 large wing of skinned skate (about 1½ pounds)

Caper Sauce

- 3 tablespoons chopped red onion
- 2 tablespoons coarsely chopped scallions
- 1 tablespoon capers, drained
- 2 tablespoons Curried Oil (see page 470)
- 1 tablespoon red wine vinegar
- ¼ teaspoon salt
- ¼ teaspoon freshly ground black pepper

Decorative Oils

- 4 teaspoons Curried Oil (see page 470)
- 4 teaspoons Cilantro Oil (see page 469)

1. Place the beets in a saucepan, cover them with cold water, and bring the water to a boil. Reduce the heat to low, and boil gently, covered, for about 1 hour, until tender. Drain, reserving ⅓ cup of the cooking liquid. (Alternatively, place the beets in a bowl with 2 tablespoons of water. Cover with a glass lid, and cook in a microwave oven until the beets are tender, about 30 minutes. There will be enough juice remaining around the beets for use around the fish.)

2. When the beets are cool enough to handle, peel them, and cut them into thin (¼-inch) julienne strips. Place the strips in the reserved cooking liquid, and set aside.
3. Just before serving time, drain and reserve the beet liquid. To the beets add 1 tablespoon of the vinegar, ¼ teaspoon of the salt, the pepper, and the sugar. Mix well.
4. Bring the water to a boil in a large saucepan. Stir in the remaining 3 tablespoons of vinegar and ½ teaspoon of salt. Add the skate, bring the mixture back to a boil, cover, reduce the heat to low, and boil gently for 15 minutes.
5. Meanwhile, combine all the caper sauce ingredients in a bowl. Mix well, and set aside.
6. To serve, arrange the beets on four plates. Remove the fish from the water, separate the flesh from the bones, and arrange equal amounts of fish on top of the beets. Cover with the caper sauce. Spoon about 1½ tablespoons of the reserved beet juice around the fish on each plate, and sprinkle 1 teaspoon of Curried Oil and then 1 teaspoon of Cilantro Oil on top of the beet juice. The blending of these liquids will create a beautiful design. Serve immediately.

**YIELD:
4 SERVINGS**

NUTRITIONAL ANALYSIS PER SERVING:

Calories 339
Protein 38 gm.
Carbohydrates 7 gm.
Fat 17.2 gm.
Saturated fat 2.0 gm.
Cholesterol 94 mg.
Sodium 759 mg.

Eating seafood often helps protect against heart disease.

SMOKED TROUT WITH SCRAMBLED EGGS ON TOAST

Scrambled eggs and omelets are commonly served as a first course in France, but rarely so in the United States. I cook the eggs here in the traditional French manner—over low heat while stirring constantly—to achieve the smallest possible curds and creamiest texture, but my ingredients produce a dish much lower in cholesterol and calories than its classic counterpart. For example, I use only one egg per person, and I replace the traditional cream and butter enrichment at the end with nonfat plain yogurt.

1 smoked trout (about 8 ounces)
4 large eggs
¼ teaspoon salt
¼ teaspoon freshly ground black pepper
2 tablespoons chopped fresh chives
4 slices whole grain or whole wheat bread (about 4 ounces total)
1 tablespoon unsalted butter
2 tablespoons nonfat plain yogurt

1. Remove the skin and head of the trout, and separate the fillets from the bones. Break each fillet into pieces or flakes, following the natural lines of the fish. Set aside in a lukewarm place. (The trout should be served at room temperature or slightly tepid.)
2. Using a fork or whisk, beat the eggs in a bowl. Add the salt, pepper, and chives, and beat well. Set aside.
3. At serving time, toast the bread, and trim off the crusts. Place one piece of toast on each of four plates, and arrange the trout flakes around the toast.
4. Heat the butter in a sturdy skillet or saucepan. When it is hot, add the egg mixture. Cook over medium to low heat, mixing continuously with a whisk to create the smallest possible curds. Continue cooking for 1½ to 2 minutes, until the mixture is creamy but still slightly runny.
5. Remove the pan from the heat, and continue mixing. (The eggs will keep cooking because of the residual heat in the pan.) Add the yogurt, and mix well. The mixture still should be moist, soft, and slightly runny. Spoon onto the toast, dividing the eggs among the four plates. Serve immediately.

YIELD: 4 SERVINGS

NUTRITIONAL ANALYSIS PER SERVING:

Calories 20
Protein 15 gm.
Carbohydrates 14 gm.
Fat 9.6 gm.
Saturated fat 3.7 gm.
Cholesterol 233 mg.
Sodium 534 mg.

Trout is a good source of heart-protecting omega-3 fatty acids. Whole-grain bread provides complex carbohydrates, B vitamins, chromium, selenium, and zinc.

Trout Sauté Terry

Fresh farm-raised trout are now available all over the country. Delicately flavored, they can often be purchased live from a tank at the local supermarket, so their freshness is guaranteed. I create a sauce by adding mushrooms, tomatoes, olive pieces, and diced lemon to the pan drippings. The result is not only delicious, but beautiful to look at.

- 2 tablespoons unsalted butter
- 2 tablespoons canola oil
- 4 fresh eviscerated trout (about 12 ounces each)
- ½ teaspoon salt
- ½ teaspoon freshly ground black pepper
- 3 or 4 large mushrooms, cut into ½-inch dice (1½ cups)
- 1 large tomato (8 ounces), halved, seeded, and cut into ½-inch dice
- 24 oil-cured olives, pitted and cut into ⅜-inch dice
- 1 small lemon, peeled and cut into ⅜-inch dice (¼ cup)
- 2 tablespoons chopped fresh chives, for garnish

1. Heat the butter and oil in one very large or two 9-inch nonstick skillets. Pat the trout dry, and place them in the hot butter. Sprinkle with the salt and pepper, and cook over medium to high heat, covered, for 4 minutes. Then turn, and cook on the other side for 4 minutes.
2. Leave the bones in the trout and the heads on, or bone the fish. Transfer the trout to a platter, and set them aside in a warm place.
3. To the drippings in the pan, add the mushrooms. Sauté for 1 minute, add the tomatoes, and sauté for 1 minute longer. Add the olive and lemon dice, and toss well. Spoon the contents of the pan over the trout, garnish with the chives, and serve.

Yield: 4 Servings

NUTRITIONAL ANALYSIS PER SERVING:

Calories 426
Protein 36 gm.
Carbohydrates 6 gm.
Fat 29.0 gm.
Saturated fat 6.6 gm.
Cholesterol 112 mg.
Sodium 840 mg.

Trout provide healthful omega-3 fatty acids.

Tuna *Tartare* on Marinated Cucumbers

The tartare *is served on a fresh-tasting garnish composed of sliced cucumber, vinegar, minced chives, peanut oil, and salt. Delicious and attractive, this simple but sophisticated dish makes a great first course. The tuna should be chopped by hand rather than in a food processor.* *(See photograph, page 141.)*

- 1 pound completely cleaned raw tuna
- Salt to taste for tuna slices
- 1 large shallot, peeled and finely chopped (2 tablespoons)
- 2 cloves garlic, peeled, crushed, and finely chopped (1 teaspoon)
- 1 teaspoon salt
- ½ teaspoon freshly ground black pepper
- 2 tablespoons virgin olive oil
- 1½ teaspoons white vinegar
- ¼ teaspoon Tabasco hot pepper sauce

Cucumber Garnish

- 1 cucumber (about 12 ounces)
- 1 teaspoon vinegar
- 1 teaspoon peanut oil
- ¼ teaspoon salt

- 3 tablespoons minced fresh chives
- 1½ teaspoons drained capers

1. Reserve four small slices (1 ounce each) of the tuna, and chop the remainder by hand into ¼-inch dice. Place one of the reserved slices of tuna between two sheets of plastic wrap, and pound it into a thin round about 4 inches in diameter. Repeat with the other three slices.
2. Remove the top sheet of plastic wrap from the slices, and season them lightly with salt. Set aside.
3. In a bowl, mix the chopped tuna with the shallot, garlic, salt, pepper, oil, vinegar, and Tabasco. (Mixed with vinegar, the chopped tuna will "whiten" somewhat, becoming opaque. This is because the acetic acid in the vinegar coagulates, thus "cooking," the protein in the tuna.)

For the Cucumber Garnish

4. Peel the cucumber, and cut long, thin strips from it with a vegetable peeler on all sides until you come to the seeds. Discard the seeds, and mix the strips with the vinegar, oil, and salt.
5. To serve, divide the garnish among four plates. Form the chopped tuna mixture into four balls, and place one ball on top of the cucumbers on each plate. Wrap a slice of tuna around each tuna ball, sprinkle with the chives and capers, and serve.

About Tuna *Tartare*

Tuna *tartare* is a modern recipe inspired by Japanese sashimi. Use only super-fresh fish purchased from a reputable fishmonger, and if you are afraid of parasites, request that your fishmonger freeze the fish you buy for 5 to 7 days at 0 degrees or less, a bit colder than most home freezers can be set.

Yield: 4 Servings

Nutritional analysis per serving:

Calories 250
Protein 27 gm.
Carbohydrates 4 gm.
Fat 13.5 gm.
Saturated fat 2.5 gm.
Cholesterol 43 mg.
Sodium 770 mg.

Tuna is a good source of vitamin B_6 and protein.

Smoked Whitefish Molds

This is an ideal party dish, because it can and should be made ahead. After lining the molds with plastic wrap, add the layers of filling. The compacted mixture can be removed immediately from the molds and stored in the plastic wrap until serving time. You'll need to buy about 10 ounces of whole fish to get 5 ounces of flesh.

4 teaspoons chopped fresh chives
16 teaspoons cream cheese
8 to 10 ounces smoked whitefish or chub
4 large radishes, thinly sliced
⅛ teaspoon freshly ground black pepper
4 slices bread (4 ounces), toasted and cut into triangles

1. Line four ½-cup molds with plastic wrap. Place 1 teaspoon of chives and 2 teaspoons of cream cheese in the bottom of each mold, pressing on the cheese to imbed the chives.
2. Remove the skin and bones from the fish, and divide the flesh into eight pieces.
3. Arrange about three slices of radish on top of the cheese in each cup, and press down again to make the mixture more compact. Place one piece of the fish on top of each, and add another 2 teaspoons of cream cheese. Sprinkle with the pepper, and add another layer of fish and a layer of radish.
4. Cover with plastic wrap, and press on the mixture to make it more compact. Refrigerate until serving time.
5. Unmold, remove the plastic wrap, and serve with toast triangles.

VARIATIONS

In this recipe, I use smoked whitefish, but smoked salmon or another type of smoked fish can be substituted. In place of the radishes, you can layer cucumbers or other vegetables in the molds; caviar, arranged between layers of cream cheese, is even a possibility here. If you're counting calories, replace the cream cheese with cottage cheese.

Yield: 4 Servings

Nutritional Analysis per Serving:

Calories 213
Protein 19 gm.
Carbohydrates 15 gm.
Fat 8.3 gm.
Saturated fat 4.5 gm.
Cholesterol 42 mg.
Sodium 861 mg.

Whitefish and chub are good sources of healthful omega-3 fatty acids.

Squid Salad à la Binh

My wife, Gloria, is addicted to this spicy squid salad inspired by a friend, Vietnamese chef and restaurateur Binh Duong, who prepares a version of it frequently. There is no fat in the salad, and the only salt is in the nuoc nam, *the traditional Vietnamese fish sauce, which is similar to sauces used in Thailand and the Philippines.*

I like hot peppers and use them generously here, but if you prefer your food less spicy, cut back on them. The salad is best made 24 hours ahead and will keep in the refrigerator for 4 or 5 days.

6 cups water
1 pound squid (body and tentacles), thoroughly cleaned
4 cloves garlic, peeled, crushed, and finely chopped (1 tablespoon)
2 to 3 small Thai hot peppers, seeded and chopped (about ½ teaspoon)
1 cup very thinly sliced onion
3 tablespoons lime juice
¼ cup shredded fresh mint
¼ cup shredded fresh cilantro (coriander or Chinese parsley) leaves
2 tablespoons *nuoc nam* (see About Southeast Asian Ingredients, page 52)
½ teaspoon sugar
¼ teaspoon salt
4 large lettuce leaves

1. Bring the water to a boil in a large saucepan. Cut the body pieces of the squid crosswise into 1-inch slices and the tentacles into ½-inch pieces. Add the squid to the pot, and cook for about 3 minutes, stirring occasionally, just until the water comes back to a boil. Drain immediately.
2. Meanwhile, combine the remaining ingredients except the lettuce in a serving bowl large enough to hold the squid. Add the hot, drained squid, and toss until well mixed. Set aside for at least 10 minutes, stirring occasionally, so the dish can develop flavor.
3. Serve on the lettuce leaves.

Yield: 4 Servings

Nutritional Analysis per Serving:

Calories 127
Protein 16 gm.
Carbohydrates 10 gm.
Fat 2.2 gm.
Saturated fat 0.5 gm.
Cholesterol 206 mg.
Sodium 179 mg.

Squid provide omega-3 fatty acids, which help protect the heart from disease.

Grilled Squid on Watercress

Squid is available almost everywhere now and usually comes cleaned in both fish stores and supermarkets. This makes it very easy to use.

Make certain that the watercress is well washed and thoroughly dried so there is no water to dilute the dressing. Toss the salad just before serving, since watercress greens wilt quickly.

- **6 cups water**
- **1½ pounds cleaned, medium-size squid (about 16 pieces plus tentacles)**
- **¼ teaspoon salt**
- **¼ teaspoon freshly ground black pepper**
- **2 tablespoons virgin olive oil**
- **1 teaspoon dried Italian seasoning**
- **1 large bunch watercress, stems removed and reserved for Watercress Soup (page 64), leaves thoroughly washed and dried**
- **1 tablespoon peanut oil**
- **1 teaspoon sherry vinegar**
- **Dash of salt**

1. Bring the water to a boil in a large saucepan. Drop the squid and tentacles into the boiling water, and cook for 1 minute. (The water will not even return to the boil.) Drain the squid in a colander; their residual heat will help them dry.
2. After emptying out any water remaining in the bodies of the squid, arrange them in a dish, and sprinkle them with the ¼ teaspoon salt, the pepper, the olive oil, and the Italian seasoning.
3. Just before serving time, heat a grill until very hot. Toss the watercress with the peanut oil, sherry vinegar, and dash of salt. Arrange the salad on four plates.
4. Skewer the squid and tentacles, dividing them among three or four skewers, and cook them on the clean rack of the hot grill for 1½ minutes on each side.
5. Remove the squid and tentacles from the skewers, and arrange about four squid per person with some of the tentacles on top of the watercress on each plate. Serve immediately.

Top: Grilled Squid on Watercress (above).
Bottom: Scallop Seviche (see page 149).

Cooking Squid

I like the chewy, rubbery texture of squid. It should not be overcooked or undercooked. To make it more flavorful when grilled, I blanch it briefly in boiling water (which tightens the skin and hardens the squid, so it can easily be impaled on skewers), and I season it lightly with olive oil and Italian seasoning. It is imperative that the grill be very hot and the rack clean so the squid is nicely marked but does not stick to the rack.

Yield: 4 Servings

Nutritional Analysis per Serving:

Calories 253
Protein 28 gm.
Carbohydrates 6 gm.
Fat 12.5 gm.
Saturated fat 2.1 gm.
Cholesterol 397 mg.
Sodium 265 mg.

SQUID AND *POSOLE* HODGEPODGE

This interesting dish can also be served as a main course. Although you can buy dried posole *in most health food stores and some supermarkets, it requires at least 2½ hours to cook. To simplify and speed the preparation of this stew, you can use cooked canned hominy instead, available in both white and yellow varieties. Squid makes a delicious addition to the dish.*

POSOLE

- **1 can (14½ ounces) yellow or white hominy or ¾ cup dried *posole* (about 4½ ounces)**
- **4 cups cold water (if using dried *posole*)**
- **¼ teaspoon salt (if using dried posole)**

SQUID

- **3 cups water**
- **1 pound cleaned squid, tentacles left whole and bodies cut into ½-inch rings (3 cups)**
- **¼ cup extra virgin olive oil**
- **½ cup chopped onion**
- **5 to 6 cloves garlic, peeled, crushed, and chopped (1 tablespoon)**
- **1 ripe medium tomato (4 ounces), cut into ½-inch dice (1 cup)**
- **¼ cup dry white wine**
- **1 teaspoon salt**
- **½ teaspoon Tabasco hot pepper sauce**
- **1 tablespoon chopped fresh tarragon**

1. If you are using dried *posole,* place the *posole* in a saucepan with the 4 cups of water, and bring the mixture to a boil. Boil for 2 minutes, uncovered, and set off the heat for 1 hour. Add the ¼ teaspoon salt, and bring the mixture to a boil again. Reduce the heat, cover, and boil gently for 2½ hours. Let cool to lukewarm, and drain. If you are using canned hominy, drain the hominy, rinse under cold water, and drain again. (You will have 2 cups.)
2. Bring the 3 cups of water to a boil in a large saucepan. Add the squid, and cook over high heat for 2 minutes. (The water will not even come back to a boil.) Drain.
3. Heat the oil until hot in a saucepan. Add the onion, and sauté for 2 minutes. Add the garlic and tomato, and mix well. Add the squid, white wine, 1 teaspoon salt, and Tabasco, and cook over high heat for 1 minute, stirring constantly. Add the 2 cups of drained *posole,* mix, and cook for 2 minutes over high heat, until the entire mixture is heated through.
4. Stir in the tarragon, and serve immediately.

ABOUT *POSOLE*

***POSOLE*, OR HOMINY, IS A NATIVE AMERICAN FOOD CONSISTING OF WHOLE KERNELS OF DRIED CORN THAT HAVE BEEN TREATED WITH ASHES. THE DISTINCTIVELY FLAVORED KERNELS PUFF UP TO ABOUT THE SIZE OF CHICKPEAS (GARBANZO BEANS) AS THEY COOK.**

YIELD: 4 SERVINGS

NUTRITIONAL ANALYSIS PER SERVING:

Calories 327
Protein 20 gm.
Carbohydrates 22 gm.
Fat 16.6 gm.
Saturated fat 2.5 gm.
Cholesterol 264 mg.
Sodium 825 mg.

Posole *is high in soluble fiber. The yellow kernels provide more vitamin A than the white kernels.*

Clam Croquettes

I serve these clam croquettes on salad greens, which absorb some of their richness and help balance the dish. You can substitute pieces of oyster or raw shrimp for the clams in this recipe. There are just enough bread crumbs and mayonnaise to bind the mixture together so that it can be formed into patties and sautéed. Use a low-calorie mayonnaise to eliminate a few additional calories.

1 tablespoon virgin olive oil
1 small onion (about 2 ounces), finely chopped (¼ cup)
2 scallions, minced (about ¼ cup)
8 ounces shelled fresh clams, drained and cut into ¼-inch pieces
½ teaspoon finely chopped jalapeño pepper
2 tablespoons mayonnaise
¼ teaspoon Tabasco hot pepper sauce
¼ teaspoon salt
3 slices white bread (3 ounces)
3 tablespoons safflower oil

SEASONED SALAD

1½ cups mixed salad greens, washed and thoroughly dried
1 tablespoon peanut oil
1 teaspoon red wine vinegar
⅛ teaspoon salt
⅛ teaspoon freshly ground black pepper

1. Heat the olive oil in a skillet. When hot, add the onion and scallions, and sauté for 1 minute.
2. Remove from the heat, and place in a bowl. Stir in the clams, jalapeño, mayonnaise, Tabasco, and salt, and mix well.
3. Break the bread slices into pieces, and place them in the bowl of a food processor. Process briefly, just until crumbed. (You should have about 1½ cups of fresh bread crumbs.) Add the crumbs to the mixture in the bowl, and toss them in lightly. Form the mixture into twelve patties.
4. Heat 1½ tablespoons of the safflower oil in a skillet. When hot, add six patties, and sauté for 2½ minutes on each side. Repeat with the remaining oil and patties.
5. In a bowl, toss the salad greens with the oil, vinegar, salt, and pepper.
6. Arrange the greens on four individual plates, and top each serving with three croquettes. Serve.

YIELD:
4 SERVINGS

NUTRITIONAL ANALYSIS PER SERVING:

Calories 309
Protein 10 gm.
Carbohydrates 15 gm.
Fat 23.8 gm.
Saturated fat 3.0 gm.
Cholesterol 24 mg.
Sodium 401 mg.

Clams are very rich in vitamin B_{12}, which is essential for cell reproduction, blood formation, and healthy nerve tissue. They are also a good source of iron.

Crab Cakes with Avocado Garnish

Although I use real crabmeat in my crab cakes, you can substitute surimi, *the imitation crabmeat made with protein and less exotic fish, such as pollack and cod. The product of an old Japanese procedure,* surimi *is widely available in markets, and would be good prepared like this.*

Crab Cakes

- **8 ounces crabmeat**
- **¼ teaspoon freshly ground black pepper**
- **¼ teaspoon dried thyme**
- **1 tablespoon chopped fresh chives**
- **⅛ teaspoon Tabasco hot pepper sauce**
- **¼ teaspoon salt**
- **3 tablespoons mayonnaise**
- **1½ slices bread (1½ ounces), processed to make crumbs (¾ cup)**
- **2 tablespoons peanut oil**

Avocado Garnish

- **1 ripe tomato (5 ounces)**
- **1 small ripe avocado (6 ounces)**
- **1 tablespoon red wine vinegar**
- **2 tablespoons peanut oil**
- **¼ teaspoon freshly ground black pepper**
- **¼ teaspoon salt**
- **3 tablespoons water**

- **1 tablespoon chopped fresh chives**

1. Cut the crabmeat into ¼-inch pieces. (You should have 1½ lightly packed cups.)
2. In a bowl, mix the crabmeat with the pepper, thyme, chives, Tabasco, salt, and mayonnaise. Add the bread crumbs, and toss them lightly into the mixture.
3. Divide the mixture, and form it into four patties, each about 1-inch thick and weighing about ½ ounce. Handle the mixture gently; it should barely hold together.
4. In a large skillet, heat the oil. When it is hot, place the patties carefully in the skillet, and sauté them gently over medium heat for 3 to 4 minutes on each side.
5. While the crabmeat cakes are cooking, skin, seed, and coarsely chop the tomato. Peel and pit the avocado, and coarsely chop it. Place the chopped tomato and avocado in a bowl, and add the vinegar, oil, pepper, salt, and water.
6. To serve, spoon some of the mixture onto four individual plates, sprinkle with the chives, and place a patty on top. Serve immediately.

Yield: 4 Servings

Nutritional Analysis per Serving:

Calories 339
Protein 13 gm.
Carbohydrates 10 gm.
Fat 28.0 gm.
Saturated fat 4.5 gm.
Cholesterol 63 mg.
Sodium 554 mg.

Crabmeat is rich in protein and contains only one-third the cholesterol of shrimp. An avocado has more than twice the potassium of a banana.

Top: Crab Cakes with Avocado Garnish (above).
Bottom: Tuna *Tartare* on Marinated Cucumbers (see page 133).

CLEANING SOFT-SHELL CRABS

TO PREPARE THE CRABS FOR COOKING, LIFT UP THE SKIRT OR APRON OF EACH CRAB, AND TWIST OR CUT IT OFF. CUT OFF AND DISCARD A STRIP FROM THE FRONT PART OF THE SHELL THAT INCLUDES THE EYES AND ANTENNAE. LIFT UP THE TOP SHELL AT BOTH ENDS TO EXPOSE THE SPONGELIKE LUNGS ON EITHER SIDE; PULL THEM OFF, AND DISCARD THEM.

Sautéed Soft-Shell Crabs on Asparagus

Soft-shell crabs are, for me, one of America's greatest delicacies. I particularly enjoy serving them to European visitors, most of whom appreciate the introduction to this delightful treat, which is not available where they live. Be sure to buy your soft-shell crabs from a reliable fishmonger. The crabs are good for only 2 to 3 days after they have shed their hard shell, and the closer you consume them to the moment of their shedding, the softer and more flavorful they are.

In this dish, the crabs are lightly sautéed, which makes them tastier and much lower in calories than if deep-fried, which is how they are often prepared in restaurants. I serve them with a mixture of asparagus, tomato, tarragon, and red onion.

- **8 asparagus stalks with tight, firm heads (about 6 ounces)**
- **1 large ripe tomato (about 12 ounces)**
- **2 tablespoons unsalted butter**
- **¾ cup chopped red onion**
- **1 teaspoon salt**
- **½ teaspoon freshly ground black pepper**
- **2 tablespoons water**
- **2 tablespoons peanut oil**
- **1 teaspoon finely chopped garlic**
- **1 teaspoon chopped fresh tarragon**
- **4 large soft-shell crabs (about 1½ pounds)**

1. Peel the lower third of the asparagus stalks, and cut each stalk in half crosswise. (Each half will be about 3 inches long.) Then cut each half lengthwise into four to six strips.
2. Using a sharp vegetable peeler, peel the tomato, cut it in half, and seed it. Cut the tomato flesh into ½-inch pieces. (You should have about 1½ cups.)

3. Heat 1 tablespoon of the butter until hot in a skillet. Add the onion, and sauté for 1 minute over high heat. Add the asparagus, ¾ teaspoon of the salt, ¼ teaspoon of the pepper, and the water. Bring the mixture to a strong boil, and cook it, covered, for 1 minute. (Most of the water will have evaporated at this point.) Transfer to a bowl, and set aside.
4. Heat 1 tablespoon of the oil in the unwashed skillet. When it is hot, add the tomato pieces, the remaining ¼ teaspoon salt, the garlic, and the tarragon. Sauté over high heat for about 45 seconds, just long enough to warm and slightly soften the tomato. Transfer to a bowl, and set aside.
5. Clean the crabs (see Cleaning Soft-Shell Crabs, page 142), and pat them dry with paper towels.
6. Heat the remaining tablespoon each of butter and oil in the skillet. When they are hot, add the crabs in one layer, and cook them over high heat for about 2 minutes on each side.
7. To serve, divide the asparagus among four plates, and arrange one crab on top of the asparagus in the middle of each plate. Spoon the tomatoes on top of and around the crabs. Pour any juices that may have accumulated in the skillet on top of the crabs. Serve immediately.

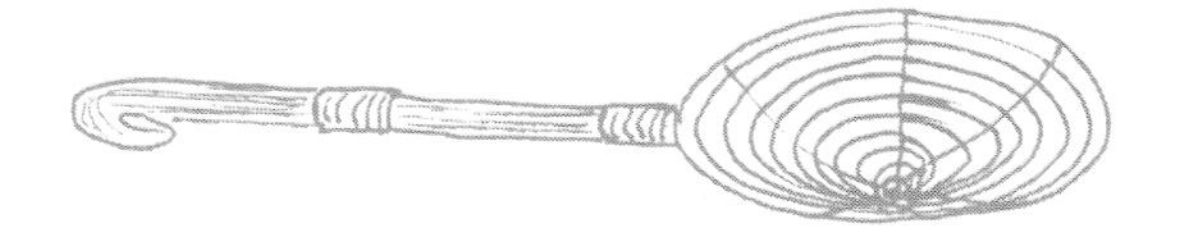

YIELD: 4 SERVINGS

NUTRITIONAL ANALYSIS PER SERVING:

Calories 290
Protein 30 gm.
Carbohydrates 10 gm.
Fat 14.6 gm.
Saturated fat 5.1 gm.
Cholesterol 151 mg.
Sodium 940 mg.

Soft-shell crabs have only half the total fat of shrimp and are a good source of vitamin B_{12}. Asparagus provides soluble fiber.

Mussels Marinière

This is the classic mussels dish you find at bistros in France. Prepared in the style of a marinière, *the wife of a* marin, *a French sailor, the mussels are conventionally cooked with just onion, garlic, herbs, and white wine. My version also includes fennel, which lends a mild anise flavor that complements the other ingredients. The mussels cook quickly and are traditionally served as is, with surrounding juices and vegetables. For a fancier presentation, serve the mussels on the half shell.*

About Mussels

Choose small or medium-size mussels that are heavy, indicating plumpness and freshness. Since they are usually grown on lines or nets now, mussels are fairly clean, although you should still rub them against one another under cool water to remove any residual dirt and sand.

- 4 pounds small to medium mussels
- 1 piece fennel bulb (about 4 ounces), cut into ½-inch pieces (1 cup)
- About 6 scallions (4 ounces), cleaned and cut into ½-inch pieces (1 cup)
- 1 medium onion (4 ounces), peeled and coarsely chopped (1 cup)
- 5 to 6 large cloves garlic, peeled and thinly sliced (3 tablespoons)
- 1 cup dry, fruity white wine (such as a chablis)
- ½ teaspoon freshly ground black pepper

1. Remove any beards or incrustations from the mussels, and wash them in cool water several times, rubbing them against one another under the water to clean the sand from the shells.
2. Place the mussels, fennel, scallions, onion, garlic, wine, and pepper in a large stainless steel saucepan. Cover the pan, and begin timing the cooking as you bring the mixture to a boil over high heat. Shake the pan occasionally to mix the ingredients, and cook the mussels for 7 to 8 minutes from start to finish. Discard any mussels that have not opened at this point.
3. Divide the mussels, vegetables, and juice among four soup plates, and serve. Or, for a fancier presentation, remove and discard the empty top shells, and serve the mussels on the half shell on soup plates along with the vegetables and cooking juices.

Yield: 4 Servings

NUTRITIONAL ANALYSIS PER SERVING:

Calories 188
Protein 17 gm.
Carbohydrates 13 gm.
Fat 3.1 gm.
Saturated fat 0.6 gm.
Cholesterol 37 mg.
Sodium 411 mg.

Mussels are a good source of protein, iron, and zinc.

Mussels Gratiné

This dish makes an excellent first course. The mussels can be opened up to 1 day ahead, the seasonings arranged on top, and the dish refrigerated until ready to place under the broiler. The juices released by the mussels can be frozen for use in soups or sauces.

About 2 pounds mussels (about 24)
3 cloves garlic, peeled
½ cup (loose) fresh flat-leaf parsley
2 slices white bread (2 ounces)
⅛ teaspoon salt
¼ teaspoon freshly ground black pepper
2 tablespoons virgin olive oil
A few drops Tabasco hot pepper sauce (optional)

1. To open the mussels, place them in a pot without any liquid or seasonings and cook over high heat, covered, for 6 to 8 minutes, just until they have opened and released their juice. (Do not overcook, because they will be recooked under the broiler at serving time.)
2. Remove and discard the empty shell of each cooked mussel, and arrange the mussels in the half shells on a cookie sheet.
3. Place the garlic and parsley in the bowl of a food processor, and process until coarsely chopped. Add the bread, and process until the mixture is finely chopped and fluffy.
4. Transfer the parsley-bread mixture to a mixing bowl, and add the salt, pepper, oil, and, if desired, Tabasco. Mix the ingredients lightly with your fingers or a fork, tossing them gently so they are moistened with the oil but still fluffy. Sprinkle the mixture over the mussels.
5. At serving time, place the mussels under the broiler for 2 to 3 minutes, until nicely browned on top and warm inside.

Yield: 4 Servings

NUTRITIONAL ANALYSIS PER SERVING:

Calories 160
Protein 9 gm.
Carbohydrates 11 gm.
Fat 8.8 gm.
Saturated fat 1.3 gm.
Cholesterol 19 mg.
Sodium 337 mg.

Mussels are low in fat and cholesterol.

ABOUT
HIJIKI

HIJIKI SEAWEED IS ALREADY SHREDDED AND STEAMED, SO IT REQUIRES ONLY SOAKING. MY WIFE OFTEN MAKES AN ASIAN SALAD WITH *HIJIKI*, SEASONING IT WITH RICE VINEGAR AND A DASH OF SESAME OIL. IF YOU CAN'T FIND *HIJIKI* WHERE YOU LIVE, OMIT IT AS A GARNISH.

Christmas Oysters

*I call these Christmas oysters (*huîtres de Noël*) because we like to serve oysters during the Christmas holidays and generally eat them as part of our Christmas dinner. We love oysters on the half shell, but at holiday time we like them served in this festive dish featuring a bright red pepper sauce and dark green spinach.*

- **24 oysters, shucked, with juices and the deeper shell of each reserved (if desired for serving)**
- **3 red bell peppers (1 pound), seeded and cut into 1-inch pieces**
- **½ cup water**
- **2 tablespoons unsalted butter**
- **¾ teaspoon salt**
- **3 tablespoons virgin olive oil**
- **3 to 4 cloves garlic, chopped (about 2 teaspoons)**
- **1 pound spinach, washed, with tough stems removed and discarded (about 12 ounces)**
- **¼ teaspoon freshly ground black pepper**
- **⅓ cup dried *hijiki* seaweed (available in Asian markets and many health food stores), soaked for 30 minutes in cold water and drained**

1. Wash the shucked oysters in their own juices, lift them out, and place them in a stainless steel saucepan. Strain the oyster juices over the oysters. Set the pan aside.
2. Place the red peppers in a saucepan with the water. Bring to a boil, cover, and boil for 10 minutes. Remove the lid, and continue cooking until the water has evaporated (about 5 minutes). Push the peppers through a food mill fitted with a fine screen. (You should have 1¼ cups.) Return the peppers to the saucepan, and stir in 1 tablespoon of the butter and half of the salt. Set aside until serving time.
3. Heat 1 tablespoon of the oil in a skillet, add the garlic, and sauté for 10 seconds. Mix in the spinach and the remainder of the salt, and cook for 2 minutes, until the spinach is wilted and softened. Set aside off the heat.
4. At serving time, heat the oysters in their juices until barely boiling. (The oysters are cooked when the mantle, or frill—the lacy collar all around the body—just begins to curl.) With a slotted spoon, transfer the oysters to a bowl, and keep them warm.
5. Bring the oyster juices to a strong boil. (You should have ⅔ cup. If you have more, boil until the juices are reduced to ⅔ cup; if less, add water to reach this amount.)

Add the remaining tablespoon of butter, 2 tablespoons of oil, and the pepper. Bring back to a strong boil. Set aside momentarily while you prepare the plates.

6. To serve the oysters in their shells, arrange six of the reserved shells on each of four plates. Divide about 2 tablespoons of the red pepper sauce evenly among the shells on each plate. Place a rounded teaspoon of spinach on top of the sauce in each shell. Arrange an oyster on top of the spinach in each shell, and spoon about 1 teaspoon of the oyster sauce on top of each oyster. Sprinkle with the *hijiki,* and serve immediately.
7. To serve the oysters on plates, divide the red pepper sauce evenly among four plates, and place a fourth of the spinach in the center of each plate. Arrange six oysters on top of the spinach on each plate, and spoon 2 to 3 tablespoons of the oyster sauce over them. Sprinkle with the *hijiki,* and serve immediately.

Yield: 4 Servings

NUTRITIONAL ANALYSIS PER SERVING:

Calories 251
Protein 10 gm.
Carbohydrates 14 gm.
Fat 18.4 gm.
Saturated fat 5.5 gm.
Cholesterol 62 mg.
Sodium 632 mg.

Oysters are the best food source of zinc, a trace mineral essential for health.

Gratin of Breaded Oysters

This recipe is best made with freshly shucked oysters. Either shuck them yourself, or ask your fishmonger to shuck them at the time of purchase (saving the juice for you in a small container). After the oysters are poached, they are flavored with bottled oyster sauce and chili paste, arranged in individual gratin dishes with seasoned bread crumbs on top, and placed under a hot broiler at the last moment.

YIELD: 4 SERVINGS

NUTRITIONAL ANALYSIS PER SERVING:

Calories 100
Protein 7 gm.
Carbohydrates 7 gm.
Fat 4.7 gm.
Saturated fat 0.9 gm.
Cholesterol 47 mg.
Sodium 197 mg.

Oysters are especially rich in zinc, a trace mineral needed by the immune system, vital to the sense of taste, and used in wound healing.

- 2 **dozen oysters (bluepoints, Chincoteagues, Malpeques, etc.)**
- 1 **slice firm-textured white bread**
- 1 **tablespoon chopped fresh chives**
- 1½ **teaspoons chopped fresh tarragon leaves**
- 2 **teaspoons virgin olive oil**
- ½ **teaspoon freshly ground black pepper**
- 1 **teaspoon Chinese oyster sauce**
- ½ **teaspoon Chinese chili paste with garlic (available in Asian markets and the ethnic food sections of some supermarkets)**

1. Rinse the oysters under cold water, and shuck them over a bowl to catch their juices. Place the shucked oysters in a stainless steel saucepan. Allow the oyster juices to sit for a few minutes in the bowl, and then carefully pour them into the pan with the oysters, leaving behind any sandy residue.
2. Bring the oysters and their juice just to a simmer. When the mantles or frills curl on the oysters, set the pan aside off the heat. The oysters will have firmed somewhat at this point but are still slightly undercooked.
3. Break the bread into the bowl of a food processor, and process it into crumbs. (You should have ½ cup of crumbs.) Toss them lightly with the chives, tarragon, oil, and pepper. (The mixture should be fluffy, not gooey or pasty.)
4. Drain the partially cooked oysters (reserving and freezing the juice for use in soups or sauces). Combine the drained oysters in a bowl with the oyster sauce and chili paste.
5. Preheat an oven broiler. Divide the oyster mixture among four small gratin dishes, and sprinkle the seasoned crumbs evenly on top. Arrange the dishes on a tray, and place the tray on the middle rack of the oven, about 10 inches from the heat. Cook for 5 to 6 minutes, until the crumbs are well browned and the oysters are hot. Serve immediately.

Scallop Seviche

This interpretation of a South American dish is very flavorful and, since I make it without oil, quite lean. A mixture of hot pepper, cilantro, and mint gives it a piquant, fresh taste that makes it a perfect entrée for a muggy summer day. The hotness of the dish can be increased or decreased depending on your tolerance for hot pepper. (See photograph, page 136.)

- 1 pound sea scallops
- 1 small red onion, peeled and cut into ¼-inch pieces (1 cup)
- 1 ripe tomato (about 10 ounces), seeded and cut into ½-inch pieces (1½ cups)
- 3 tablespoons coarsely chopped fresh cilantro (coriander or Chinese parsley)
- 2 tablespoons coarsely chopped fresh mint
- 1 tablespoon finely julienned lime skin
- Juice of 2 limes (about ¼ cup)
- 1 jalapeño pepper, seeded and chopped into fine dice (about 1 tablespoon; more or less can be used, depending on your tolerance for hotness)
- 1 teaspoon salt
- ½ teaspoon freshly ground black pepper
- 2 teaspoons sugar
- 2 tablespoons rice vinegar
- 1 small cucumber (8 ounces), trimmed and peeled

1. Remove and discard any tough muscles from the scallops, rinse them thoroughly, and cut them into ½-inch pieces or slices.
2. Combine all the ingredients except the cucumber in a plastic bag, and refrigerate for at least 3 hours, turning the bag occasionally so the mixture is well combined.
3. Cut the cucumber in half lengthwise, and scrape out the seeds with a sharp-edged metal measuring spoon. Then cut the cucumber halves lengthwise into about twenty-four strips, and set them aside.
4. At serving time, make a decorative arrangement of six cucumber strips on each of four plates. Drain the seviche, and spoon it on top of the cucumber strips. Serve.

**Yield:
4 Servings**

NUTRITIONAL ANALYSIS PER SERVING:

Calories 145
Protein 21 gm.
Carbohydrates 13 gm.
Fat 1.2 gm.
Saturated fat 0.1 gm.
Cholesterol 37 mg.
Sodium 609 mg.

Scallops are a low-fat source of protein.

HOW TO MAKE A HOMEMADE SMOKER

IF YOU DON'T OWN A SMALL COMMERCIAL SMOKER THAT FITS ON YOUR STOVE, MAKE A SMOKER FROM AN OLD POT OR ROASTING PAN: SIMPLY PLACE A LAYER OF WOOD CHIPS OR SAWDUST IN THE BOTTOM OF THE POT, AND ARRANGE A PIECE OF MESH SCREENING SO IT SITS ABOUT 1 INCH ABOVE THE WOOD. THEN PLACE THE SCALLOPS ON TOP OF THE SCREEN, AND COVER THE POT WITH A LID OR PIECE OF ALUMINUM FOIL. COOK AS INDICATED IN THE RECIPE.

YIELD: 4 SERVINGS

NUTRITIONAL ANALYSIS PER SERVING:

Calories 182
Protein 20 gm.
Carbohydrates 9 gm.
Fat 7.2 gm.
Saturated fat 0.9 gm.
Cholesterol 37 mg.
Sodium 460 mg.

Instant Smoked Scallops with Orange-and-Onion Sauce

This recipe illustrates a special technique of smoking scallops, although the same process can be used to smoke other fish and shellfish. When the smoker is placed on a hot burner of an electric or gas stove, the chips or sawdust in the bottom will emit enough smoke and generate enough heat to flavor and cook the fish in a few minutes.

Since the amount of wood and the length of cooking time determine the amount of smoke created, you can make adjustments. The scallops here are smoked lightly, as I prefer them, but you can smoke them longer for a heavier taste of smoke, if that is more to your liking.

Orange-and-Onion Sauce

- 1 seedless orange
- 1 tomato (about 5 ounces), peeled, seeded, and cut into ½-inch pieces (½ cup)
- 2 tablespoons chopped red onion
- 2 tablespoons chopped fresh cilantro
- 1½ teaspoons red wine vinegar
- 1½ tablespoons virgin olive oil
- ½ teaspoon salt
- ¼ teaspoon freshly ground black pepper

Smoked Scallops

- 12 large sea scallops (about 1 pound)
- 1 teaspoon corn oil
- ⅓ cup hickory, cherry, or maple wood chips or sawdust

For the Orange-and-Onion Sauce

1. Peel the orange down to the flesh, and cut enough of the flesh into ½-inch pieces to make ½ cup. Squeeze enough juice from the remaining flesh to measure 2 tablespoons. Place the orange flesh and juice in a small bowl, and add the remaining sauce ingredients. Mix well, and set aside at room temperature.

For the Smoked Scallops

2. Wash the scallops under cool water, removing and discarding any white sinews attached to them. Dry the scallops well, and place them in a bowl with the corn oil.
3. Arrange the wood chips or sawdust in the bottom of a smoker, place a screen 1 inch above the chips, and scatter the scallops in one layer over the screen. Cover the

smoker, and cook the scallops over high heat for about 1 minute, then reduce the heat to low, and cook 4 minutes longer. (The smoker will be full of smoke, and some of the smoke will escape, but the scallops should not burn.)

4. Set the smoker aside off the heat, and let the scallops cool, still covered, for 10 minutes. Remove the scallops from the smoker. (They will be lightly cooked and have a golden yellow exterior.)
5. Divide the sauce among four plates. Cut the scallops in half, and arrange six halves on top of the sauce in the center of each plate. Serve immediately.

Sautéed Scallops with Snow Peas

This red, green, and white dish is perfect for the Christmas holidays. The snow peas are cooked in a minimum of water, and the scallops require only brief sautéing at the last moment; the dish is ready to serve in a few minutes.

SAVING THE NUTRIENTS

I COOK THE SNOW PEAS VERY QUICKLY—JUST UNTIL THE COOKING WATER EVAPORATES—SO THAT THEY RETAIN MOST OF THEIR NUTRIENTS. THE PEAS ARE LOW IN CALORIES AND HIGH IN FIBER AND VITAMIN A, AND THE RED PEPPER, ALSO LOW IN CALORIES, IS HIGH IN VITAMIN C.

½ pound snow peas, trimmed
¼ cup water
½ red bell pepper (4 ounces)
1 tablespoon unsalted butter
2 tablespoons virgin olive oil
12 ounces small sea scallops
¼ teaspoon salt
¼ teaspoon freshly ground black pepper
½ teaspoon Tabasco hot pepper sauce

1. Place the snow peas in one very large or two smaller skillets with the water. Cook, covered, for 2 minutes, and then uncover and cook until dry.
2. Meanwhile, remove the skin from the bell pepper with a vegetable peeler, and cut the flesh into ¼-inch dice. Add the red pepper to the snow peas, and add ½ tablespoon of the butter and 1 tablespoon of the oil. Sauté over high heat for 2 minutes. Arrange on four individual plates.
3. Remove and discard any tough muscles from the scallops. Sprinkle the scallops with the salt and pepper, and heat the remaining butter and oil in a skillet. When very hot, add the scallops and the Tabasco, and sauté over very high heat for 2 to 3 minutes.
4. Arrange the scallops on the snow peas, and serve immediately.

YIELD: 4 SERVINGS

NUTRITIONAL ANALYSIS PER SERVING:

Calories 191
Protein 16 gm.
Carbohydrates 8 gm.
Fat 10.4 gm.
Saturated fat 2.8 gm.
Cholesterol 36 mg.
Sodium 279 mg.

Scallops in Scallion Nests

This is an attractive, flavorful dish, ideal as the first course for an elegant dinner. The scallions, which are cooked briefly in boiling water and served with a mustard sauce, are good on their own—without the scallops—as a first course or salad. This same recipe is often made with leeks, but scallions work well, are less expensive, and can be found all year.

I like this recipe made with large scallops. Cooked in a very hot skillet, they form a sweet brown crust on both sides. If you are using smaller scallops, cut the cooking time a little. The scallops should not be cooked until dry, but they shouldn't be flabby and soft inside either.

4 bunches small scallions (6 to 8 scallions per bunch)
1 cup water

Mustard Sauce
1 tablespoon Dijon-style mustard
1 tablespoon red wine vinegar
¼ cup virgin olive oil
¼ teaspoon salt
2 teaspoons cooking juices from scallions

1 pound large scallops (about 12), washed
2 teaspoons virgin olive oil
⅛ teaspoon paprika

For the Scallions

1. Cut off and discard the root ends of the scallions and about 2 inches of the green ends, along with any damaged leaves. Wash the scallions thoroughly.
2. Bring the water to a boil in a large stainless steel saucepan. Add the scallions, cover, and boil over high heat for 4 to 5 minutes, until tender. Remove the scallions with a slotted spoon (reserving any remaining cooking juices), and place them on a tray to cool. When they are cool, cover them with plastic wrap, and refrigerate them until serving time.

(continued)

Top: Scallops in Scallion Nests (above).
Bottom: Red Snapper in *Brunoise* Sauce (see page 186)
and Cucumber with Tarragon (see page 313).

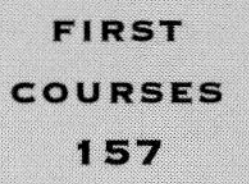

Timbales of Shrimp and Spinach

Although this easy dish takes only minutes to prepare, it is quite tasty and makes an impressive dinner party opener. If you prefer, you can simply arrange the sautéed spinach on individual plates and spoon the sautéed shrimp on top for serving. For a fancier presentation, I take the dish a step further here, layering the ingredients in small receptacles and then unmolding the compacted mixture onto plates. Tomato strips, sprinkled on top, make an attractive garnish.

- **10 unshelled shrimp (about 14 ounces)**
- **¾ pound spinach**
- **2½ tablespoons peanut oil**
- **3 cloves garlic, peeled, crushed, and chopped (2 teaspoons)**
- **½ teaspoon salt**
- **½ teaspoon freshly ground black pepper**
- **2 plum or pear tomatoes (about 8 ounces total), peeled, seeded, and cut into thin strips (julienned)**

1. Shell and devein the shrimp, and cut each into three pieces (about 1⅔ cup). Clean the spinach, and discard any large, tough stems.
2. Heat 1½ tablespoons of the oil in a large skillet. When the oil is hot, add the garlic, and sauté it for 10 seconds. Add the spinach, stir well, and add ¼ teaspoon each of the salt and pepper. Cook over high heat for about 2 minutes, stirring occasionally, until the spinach is wilted. Transfer to a bowl.
3. Heat the remaining tablespoon of oil in the skillet. When it is hot, add the shrimp and the remaining salt and pepper. Cook over high heat, shaking the pan occasionally, for about 1 minute, just until the shrimp become firm. Transfer the shrimp to a bowl, and place the tomato strips in the skillet. Sauté for about 10 seconds, just long enough to take the chill off the tomatoes and soften them slightly. Set aside.
4. Line the bottom and sides of four round-bottomed coffee cups or small timbale molds with about half of the spinach, pressing it into place. Divide the shrimp among the cups, and arrange the leftover spinach on top, so that the shrimp are completely covered. Serve immediately (or keep warm for up to 20 minutes in a 200-degree oven). To serve, unmold the timbales onto individual plates, and garnish them with the tomato strips.

YIELD: 4 SERVINGS

NUTRITIONAL ANALYSIS PER SERVING:

Calories 187
Protein 19 gm.
Carbohydrates 6 gm.
Fat 10.2 gm.
Saturated fat 1.7 gm.
Cholesterol 122 mg.
Sodium 446 mg.

Spinach is a good source of soluble fiber, folacin, iron, and vitamin B_6.

Walnut Sausage

I am very fond of sausages and especially like this light version served with Lentil and Potato Salad (see page 71). Whereas commercial sausages contain a minimum of 30 percent fat, these are made with very lean pork and a little crushed ice to replace some of the moisture lost with the elimination of most of the fat. I use a small amount of saltpeter, available at drugstores, to preserve the pink color of the pork in the sausages (which will otherwise turn gray), but its use is optional. I advocate refrigerating the sausages to cure for at least 3 days before cooking, although they can cure there for up to a week.

- **1 pound very lean pork (chops, shoulder, or fillet), trimmed to remove all fat and sinews**
- **3 tablespoons crushed ice**
- **2 tablespoons dry red wine**
- **2 cloves garlic, peeled, crushed, and chopped (1½ teaspoons)**
- **1½ teaspoons salt**
- **½ teaspoon freshly crushed black peppercorns (see Making a *Mignonnette,* page 352)**
- **3 tablespoons walnut pieces**
- **⅛ teaspoon potassium nitrate (saltpeter or pink salt) (optional)**

1. Cut about two-thirds of the meat (10 ounces) into ¼-inch pieces, and place them in a bowl. Cut the rest of the meat (6 ounces) into 1-inch pieces, and place them in the bowl of a food processor with the ice. Process for 20 to 30 seconds, until the mixture is emulsified. Add this mixture to the pork pieces in the bowl along with the remainder of the ingredients. Mix well.
2. Using plastic wrap, shape the mixture into a sausage about 8 inches long and 1½ inches thick. Enclose it tightly in the plastic wrap, and then roll it and seal it as tightly as possible in aluminum foil. Refrigerate for 3 days to cure before cooking.
3. When you are ready to cook the sausage, place it, still wrapped, in a saucepan. Cover with cold tap water. Bring the water to a boil (this will take about 15 minutes), cover, reduce the heat to low, and cook the sausage at a simmer (about 190 degrees) for 10 minutes. Remove the pan from the heat, and let the sausage rest in the hot water for at least 10 minutes and as long as 1 hour. Unwrap, cut into ¾-inch-thick slices, and serve warm, with Lentil and Potato Salad (see page 71).

YIELD: 4 SERVINGS

NUTRITIONAL ANALYSIS PER SERVING:

Calories 203
Protein 26 gm.
Carbohydrates 2 gm.
Fat 9.2 gm.
Saturated fat 2.3 gm.
Cholesterol 72 mg.
Sodium 900 mg.

Lean pork provides low-fat protein that is rich in thiamine, which is important in the nervous system and the metabolism of carbohydrates.

Beef Carpaccio

In my version of carpaccio, I eliminate the traditional mayonnaise accompaniment and serve the beef with a little olive oil, black pepper, red onion, basil, and parmesan cheese. Quick and easy to prepare, this attractive dish is delicious.

- **1 12-ounce piece beef shell (also called New York strip)**
- **½ teaspoon salt**
- **½ teaspoon freshly ground black pepper**
- **1 small red onion or piece of red onion (2 ounces), very thinly sliced**
- **10 large basil leaves, shredded into thin strips**
- **1½ ounces parmesan cheese (in a chunk)**
- **4 tablespoons extra virgin olive oil**

1. Clean the fat and sinew from the exterior of the beef (leaving 8 to 9 ounces), and cut it into four pieces, each about 2 ounces.
2. Butterfly each piece (see Butterflying Chicken Breasts, page 212), and pound it between two pieces of plastic wrap until it is quite thin and 7 to 8 inches in diameter. Arrange one piece on each of four plates, and sprinkle with the salt and pepper.
3. Place the onion slices in a strainer, and rinse under cold water. Pat dry, and distribute over the meat. Sprinkle the shredded basil on top.
4. Using a vegetable peeler, cut shavings of the cheese, and let them drop directly on top of the meat. Sprinkle 1 tablespoon of the oil on each portion, and serve immediately.

ABOUT CARPACCIO

VITTORE CARPACCIO WAS A FIFTEENTH-CENTURY VENETIAN PAINTER WHO FAVORED RED AND WHITE ON CANVASES. WHEN THE CREATORS OF THIS DISH, FEATURING BRIGHT RED, THINLY POUNDED RAW BEEF, DECIDED TO SERVE IT WITH A STRIP OF MAYONNAISE, IT SEEMED APPROPRIATE TO NAME IT AFTER THE PAINTER MOST ASSOCIATED WITH THESE TWO COLORS.

YIELD: 4 SERVINGS

NUTRITIONAL ANALYSIS PER SERVING:

Calories 280
Protein 22 gm.
Carbohydrates 2 gm.
Fat 20.0 gm.
Saturated fat 4.9 gm.
Cholesterol 59 mg.
Sodium 495 mg.

Beef is rich in iron.

Main Courses

WHY USE A FOOD MILL?

IT IS IMPORTANT TO USE A FOOD MILL IN MAKING THE RED PEPPER SAUCE. IF PUREED IN A FOOD PROCESSOR, THE COOKED PEPPER MUST BE STRAINED AFTERWARD TO REMOVE THE SKIN. THE FOOD MILL DOES THE PUREEING AND STRAINING IN ONE EASY STEP. (SEE ALSO ABOUT THE FOOD MILL, PAGE 60.)

YIELD: 4 SERVINGS

NUTRITIONAL ANALYSIS PER SERVING:

Calories 591
Protein 15 gm.
Carbohydrates 80 gm.
Fat 24.4 gm.
Saturated fat 2.9 gm.
Cholesterol 0 mg.
Sodium 698 mg.

Pasta is a good food choice from the bottom of the food guide pyramid. Red peppers are an excellent source of vitamin C.

Red Pepper Pasta with Walnuts

With its brilliant red color, this red pepper sauce has eye appeal as well as taste appeal. The pasta is seasoned after cooking with chopped onion, olive oil, parmesan cheese (optional), and parsley and is flavorful enough like this to be served as is. The red pepper sauce enhances it greatly, however, making it an ideal meatless main dish for a summer dinner.

8 cups water

RED PEPPER SAUCE

2 to 3 large red bell peppers (1½ pounds), seeded and cut into 1-inch pieces
½ cup water
5 cloves garlic, peeled
¾ teaspoon salt
¼ teaspoon freshly ground black pepper
3 tablespoons virgin olive oil

¾ pound linguine
1 tablespoon virgin olive oil
1 medium onion, peeled and chopped (1 cup)
½ cup walnut pieces
½ teaspoon salt
¼ teaspoon freshly ground black pepper
2 tablespoons coarsely chopped fresh parsley
2 to 3 tablespoons grated parmesan cheese (optional)

1. Bring the 8 cups of water to a boil in a large saucepan. Meanwhile, prepare the sauce.
2. Place the red pepper pieces in a saucepan with the ½ cup of water. Bring to a boil, cover, and boil gently for 10 minutes. Push the peppers and their cooking liquid through a food mill fitted with a fine screen. (You should have 1¾ cups.)
3. Crush the garlic with the flat side of a knife, chop it into a fine puree, and add it to the red pepper mixture with the ¾ teaspoon salt, ¼ teaspoon black pepper, and 3 tablespoons oil. Stir well with a whisk, and set aside in the pan.
4. Add the linguine to the boiling water, and cook it for about 8 minutes, until tender but still firm.
5. Meanwhile, heat the 1 tablespoon of olive oil in a skillet. When it is hot, add the onion and walnut pieces, and sauté over medium heat for about 2 minutes, until the onion begins to brown.
6. Transfer the mixture to the bowl in which you will serve the linguine, and stir in the ½ teaspoon salt, ¼ teaspoon black pepper, and parsley.

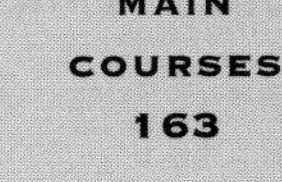

7. Add ½ cup of the pasta-cooking liquid to the onions and walnuts in the bowl. Then drain the linguine in a colander.
8. Place the drained linguine in the serving bowl, and mix well. Bring the red pepper sauce to a boil, and divide it among four large plates. Mound the linguine in the center of each plate, sprinkle with the cheese, if desired, and serve immediately.

Potato and Spinach *Galette*

This main course vegetable dish is prepared in a nonstick skillet or omelet pan so it will release easily when inverted onto a plate for serving. The word galette *denotes a flattish, disk-shaped pancake here; this one is really a "sandwich" of potatoes panfried in a skillet with a filling of garlic-flavored spinach. This* galette *is especially good in summer with a green salad side dish. (See photograph, page 206.)*

1 pound spinach
1½ pounds potatoes (3 or 4), preferably Yukon Gold
3 tablespoons virgin olive oil
1 tablespoon unsalted butter
½ teaspoon salt
3 to 4 large cloves garlic, peeled and very thinly sliced (1½ tablespoons)
¼ teaspoon freshly ground black pepper

1. If you will bake the *galette* immediately after preparing it, preheat the oven to 400 degrees. Remove and discard the tough stems and damaged leaves of the spinach, and wash the remaining leaves.
2. Wash the potatoes, peel them, and cut them into very thin slices by hand or in a food processor fitted with a slicing disk. Wash the slices, drain them, and pat them dry with paper towels.
3. In a 10-inch nonstick ovenproof skillet (preferably an omelet pan), heat 1 tablespoon of the oil and the butter until they are hot. Add the potato slices, and season them with ¼ teaspoon of the salt. Sauté over high heat for 2 or 3 minutes, gently stirring the potatoes, until all the slices are coated with oil and butter and are just starting to soften and become transparent. Transfer the potatoes to a plate, and set them aside.

(continued)

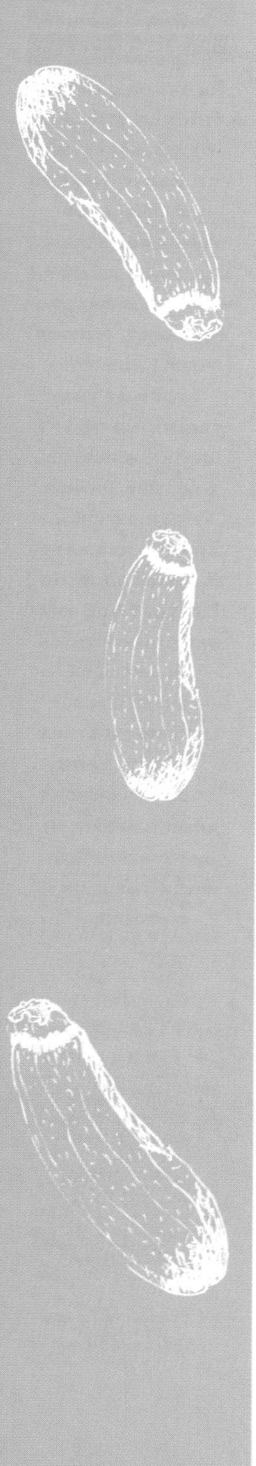

Stuffed Zucchini "Boats" with Red Pepper–Tomato Sauce

Although served hot here, this vegetable main dish is good lukewarm in the summer. Stuffed eggplant and zucchini are traditional in both Middle Eastern and southern French cooking. My stuffing includes not only onion, garlic, and bread but also the insides or flesh of the zucchini. The "boats" are served with a colorful sauce made of red bell pepper and tomato.

Stuffed Zucchini "Boats"

- 6 to 8 dried shiitake mushroom caps (1 ounce)
- 2 cups hot tap water
- 4 small, firm zucchini, each about 2 inches in diameter and 5 inches long (1¼ pounds total)
- 2 tablespoons virgin olive oil
- 1 large onion (8 ounces), peeled and finely chopped (2 cups)
- 5 to 6 cloves garlic, peeled, crushed, and coarsely chopped (1 tablespoon)
- 2 ounces stale bread, preferably from a baguette, processed into crumbs in a food processor (1¼ cups)
- ¼ cup grated parmesan cheese
- 2 tablespoons chopped fresh parsley
- 2 tablespoons chopped fresh chives
- ¾ teaspoon salt
- ½ teaspoon freshly ground black pepper

Red Pepper–Tomato Sauce

- 1 ripe tomato (about 8 ounces)
- 1 red bell pepper (about 8 ounces)
- ¼ cup water
- 1 tablespoon virgin olive oil
- ¼ teaspoon salt
- ¼ teaspoon freshly ground black pepper

For the Stuffed Zucchini "Boats"

1. Place the mushroom caps in a bowl, cover them with the water, and set them aside for at least 30 minutes.
2. Preheat the oven to 350 degrees.
3. Wash the zucchini, trim the stem ends, and split the zucchini in half lengthwise. Using a melon baller or a metal measuring teaspoon, remove and reserve the seeds and flesh, leaving eight oblong "boats" of zucchini with bases and sides about ¼ inch thick. You should have about 12 ounces (2½ cups) of flesh and seeds; chop this mixture coarsely, and set it aside.

4. Remove the mushroom caps from the soaking liquid (reserving the liquid), press them lightly to remove excess liquid, and chop them coarsely. (You should have about ½ cup chopped mushrooms.)
5. Heat the 2 tablespoons of oil in a large skillet. When it is hot, add the onion and mushrooms. Slowly pour in the reserved mushroom-soaking liquid, leaving behind and discarding any sandy residue from the bottom of the bowl. Bring the mixture to a boil, cover, and boil for 6 to 8 minutes, or until all the liquid has evaporated. Then uncover and cook for another 2 to 3 minutes to brown the onion and mushrooms lightly.
6. Add the reserved zucchini flesh and garlic, and cook, covered, for 3 to 4 minutes, until soft. Transfer the mixture to a bowl, and let it cool to room temperature.
7. When the zucchini mixture is cool, add the bread crumbs, 3 tablespoons of the cheese, the parsley, the chives, ½ teaspoon of the salt, and the pepper. Toss the mixture gently but thoroughly.
8. Sprinkle the remaining ¼ teaspoon of salt on the zucchini "boats," and stuff them with the mixture, dividing it evenly and packing it firmly but lightly in place. Sprinkle the remaining tablespoon of cheese on top of the "boats," and arrange them on a baking tray. Bake at 350 degrees for 30 minutes, then place under a hot broiler for 2 to 3 minutes to brown the tops lightly.

For the Red Pepper–Tomato Sauce

9. While the "boats" are baking, cut the tomato into chunks, and place it in the bowl of a food processor. Seed the red pepper, cut it into chunks, and add it to the food processor bowl with the water, oil, salt, and pepper. Process until the mixture is liquefied, and then transfer it to a small saucepan. (You will have 2 cups.)
10. Bring the mixture to a boil, reduce the heat to low, and simmer gently for 5 to 8 minutes. Use as is or, for a smoother sauce, emulsify the mixture further with a hand-held blender.
11. To serve, place two zucchini "boats" on each plate, and surround them with the tomato–red pepper sauce. Serve immediately.

Yield: 4 Servings

NUTRITIONAL ANALYSIS PER SERVING:

Calories 242
Protein 7 gm.
Carbohydrates 28 gm.
Fat 12.7 gm.
Saturated fat 2.5 gm.
Cholesterol 4 mg.
Sodium 744 mg.

Zucchini have twice the fiber of lettuce. Tomatoes and red bell peppers are high in vitamins A and C.

Vegetable Bouquet on Fettucine

Although I use fettucine in this recipe, any pasta of that general shape—from linguine to spaghetti—would be good served this way. The pasta is cooked at the last moment, then tossed with a puree of garlic, basil, tarragon, and a little of the pasta-cooking water. Finally, it is served with a large assortment of sautéed vegetables. Beautiful and fresh-tasting, it makes a wonderful light entrée for summer.

4 tablespoons virgin olive oil
1 tablespoon unsalted butter
½ cup water, plus 4 quarts for cooking the pasta
About 6 scallions, trimmed, washed, and cut into ½-inch pieces (1¼ cups)
About 6 ounces broccoli, stems peeled and both stems and florets cut into 1-inch pieces (2 cups)
4 mushrooms (4 ounces), washed and cut into ½-inch pieces (1¾ cups)
1 small zucchini (4 ounces), washed and cut into ½-inch pieces (1 cup)
1 ear sweet corn, husked and kernels cut from the cob (¾ cup)
2 plum tomatoes (6 ounces), washed and cut into ½-inch pieces (1 cup)
1¼ teaspoons salt
½ teaspoon freshly ground black pepper
5 cloves garlic, peeled and crushed
1 cup lightly packed fresh basil leaves
2 tablespoons lightly packed fresh tarragon leaves
¾ pound dried fettucine or other flat noodles
Grated parmesan cheese to taste

1. Place 1 tablespoon of the olive oil, the butter, and the ½ cup water in a skillet. Bring the mixture to a boil over high heat. Add the scallions and broccoli, bring the mixture back to a boil, and cook over high heat for 3 minutes. Add the mushrooms and zucchini, and cook over high heat for another 2 minutes. Add the corn, tomatoes, ¾ teaspoon of the salt, and ¼ teaspoon of the pepper, and toss the mixture over high heat for about 30 seconds. Set aside.
2. Place the garlic and remaining ½ teaspoon of salt in a mortar, and crush with a pestle until partially pureed. Add the basil and tarragon leaves, and continue pounding with the pestle until you have a coarse puree. Add the remaining 3 tablespoons of oil

(continued)

Haddock Steaks in Rice Paper with Shallot-and-Soy Sauce

My wife, who enjoys and frequently cooks Asian food, always has a supply of transparent rice paper disks on hand. Here, I enclose seasoned haddock steaks in them, then sauté the steaks, and serve them in their lightly browned wrappers.

- 4 Vietnamese rice paper disks (each 8½ inches in diameter)
- ½ teaspoon salt
- ½ teaspoon freshly ground black pepper
- 1 teaspoon finely chopped fresh tarragon
- 4 haddock steaks, each 3 to 4 inches across and 1 inch thick (about 7 ounces each)

Shallot-and-Soy Sauce

- 2 large shallots, peeled and finely chopped (3 tablespoons)
- 2 tablespoons chopped fresh chives
- 1 large clove garlic, peeled, crushed, and finely chopped (1 teaspoon)
- 3 tablespoons rice vinegar
- 4 tablespoons soy sauce
- 1 teaspoon sugar
- ¼ teaspoon Tabasco hot pepper sauce

- 1 tablespoon canola or corn oil

1. Brush the rice paper disks generously on both sides with water, and set them aside to soften for about 5 minutes. In a small bowl, mix the salt, pepper, and tarragon, and sprinkle this mixture on both sides of the haddock steaks.
2. Place each of the seasoned steaks in the center of a softened rice paper disk, then fold the paper around the fish to enclose it securely inside. Place the fish packages in a single layer seam side down on a plate, cover, and refrigerate until cooking time. (The fish can be wrapped up to 4 hours ahead.)
3. Mix all the sauce ingredients in a small bowl, cover, and set aside until serving time.
4. At cooking time, heat the canola oil in a nonstick skillet. When the oil is hot, place the haddock packages seam side down in the skillet, and cook them, uncovered, over medium heat for about 2 minutes. Turn, cover, and cook for an additional 2 minutes. Remove the skillet from the heat, and set aside, covered, for 3 to 4 mintues.
5. Serve one package per person, with some of the sauce drizzled over and around the fish packages.

Top: Gratin of Eggplant and Tomato (see page 314).

Bottom: Haddock Steaks in Rice Paper with Shallot-and-Soy Sauce (above).

About Rice Paper Disks

Available at most Asian markets, Vietnamese rice paper disks soften when dampened with cold water and make ideal edible wrappers.

Yield: 4 Servings

Nutritional Analysis per Serving:

Calories 205
Protein 34 gm.
Carbohydrates 51 gm.
Fat 4.6 gm.
Saturated fat 0.5 gm.
Cholesterol 100 mg.
Sodium 1,426 mg.

Haddock is rich in protein, niacin, and selenium.

Salmon in Aspic with Horseradish Flakes

This is an ideal summer main course. I poach a fillet of salmon in water flavored with wine, herbes de Provence, *mushrooms, and onions, then clarify the poaching liquid, and make an aspic with it while the salmon is cooling. The salmon in aspic is served in slices, with flakes of fresh horseradish root—often available at supermarkets in summer. Its hot flavor goes well with the salmon.*

- **1 center-cut piece salmon fillet (1 pound, 6 ounces), bones, skin, and dark underlying flesh removed (1 pound, 2 ounces trimmed)**
- **4 cups water**
- **1 medium onion (6 ounces), peeled and sliced (1¼ cups)**
- **½ cup dry, fruity white wine (such as sauvignon blanc or chardonnay)**
- **1 teaspoon *herbes de Provence* (see page 467)**
- **1½ teaspoons salt**
- **¼ teaspoon freshly ground black pepper**
- **4 ounces mushrooms, washed and cut into ½-inch dice (2 cups)**
- **½ cup coarsely chopped leek greens, washed in a sieve**
- **½ cup (loose) coarsely chopped fresh parsley**
- **2 tablespoons coarsely chopped fresh tarragon leaves and stems**
- **3 tablespoons coarsely chopped carrot**
- **½ teaspoon black peppercorns, crushed with the base of a heavy pan (*mignonnette*) (see Making a *Mignonnette,* page 352)**
- **2 teaspoons soy sauce**
- **1 egg white**
- **3 envelopes (2 tablespoons) plain gelatin**
- **1 piece fresh horseradish root (3 to 4 ounces)**

1. Cut the salmon in half lengthwise, following the center line of the fillet, to make 2 strips about 3 inches wide and 7 to 8 inches long.
2. Place 3 cups of the water in a 10-inch stainless steel saucepan, add the onion, wine, *herbes de Provence,* 1 teaspoon of the salt, and the pepper, and bring the mixture to a boil. Reduce the heat to low, cover, and boil gently for 5 minutes.
3. Place the salmon strips in the hot liquid (it should barely cover them), and bring back to a light boil. Remove the pan from the heat, cover, and let the salmon sit in the stock for 10 minutes. Then lift out the salmon pieces, place them one on top of

(continued)

the other on a large sheet of plastic wrap, and roll them tightly in the wrap. Cool for at least 2 to 3 hours under refrigeration. Pour the stock through a strainer set over another saucepan, and reserve it. Discard the solids in the strainer.

4. Place the mushrooms in a small saucepan with the remaining cup of water and ½ teaspoon salt. Bring the mixture to a boil, and boil it for 1 minute. Strain through a sieve, adding the liquid to the reserved fish stock and reserving the mushrooms separately. (You will have 3½ cups stock.)
5. Combine the leek greens, parsley, tarragon, carrot, pepper *mignonnette,* soy sauce, egg white, and gelatin in a bowl. Add ½ cup of the reserved stock, and mix well. Set aside.
6. Bring the remaining 3 cups of reserved stock to a boil. Add the leek mixture, and bring back to a full boil, stirring constantly, over high heat. Then reduce the heat to low, and boil the stock very gently for 1 minute *without disturbing it.* Set it aside to rest off the heat for 10 minutes, then strain it (still not stirring, so the aspic will be crystal clear) through a paper towel–lined strainer into another container. Add the reserved mushrooms to the strained stock, and set the pan in a bowl of ice to cool until the stock is syrupy.
7. Place about 1 cup of the syrupy stock in the bottom of a 6- to 8-cup terrine, and refrigerate until set (about 1 hour). Unwrap the salmon, and pat it dry with paper towels to remove any seeping liquid. Place the salmon on top of the hardened aspic in the terrine, and pour the remaining stock syrup over and around it. (The salmon should be covered.) Refrigerate until the aspic is set, cover with plastic wrap, and refrigerate again until ready to serve. (The salmon will keep, covered and refrigerated, for 2 to 3 days.)
8. Within a few hours of serving, wash and peel the skin from the horseradish root with a sharp knife. Then, using a vegetable peeler, remove small flakes from the root, and arrange in a small serving dish.
9. To serve, cut the salmon crosswise into 1-inch slices with a sharp knife. Arrange a slice on each of four plates, and spoon some aspic alongside. Pass the dish of horseradish flakes. (*Note:* The flakes are very pungent and peppery; use as desired.)

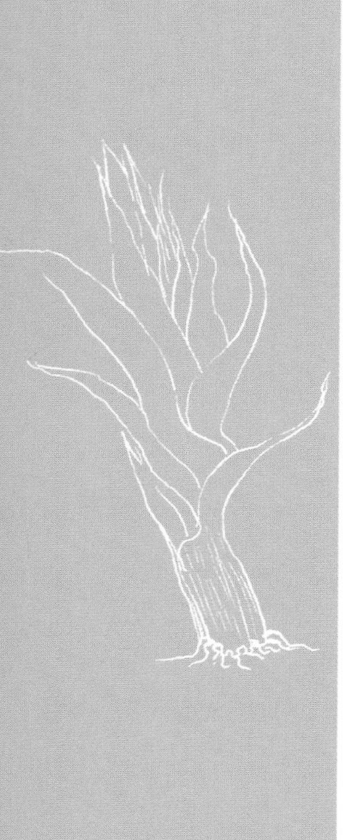

YIELD: 4 SERVINGS

NUTRITIONAL ANALYSIS PER SERVING:

Calories 263
Protein 33 gm.
Carbohydrates 13 gm.
Fat 8.5 gm.
Saturated fat 1.3 gm.
Cholesterol 71 mg.
Sodium 1,089 mg.

Salmon is rich in niacin and omega-3 fatty acids, which reduce the risk of heart disease.

Grilled Salmon Fillets

Salmon is available throughout the country now and can usually be found fresh. Grilling is one of the best ways to cook salmon, although if this is not an option for you, you can cook it in a skillet. (See Skillet-Cooked Salmon.)

The success of this dish depends on the use of unskinned salmon fillets. Ask your fish market to scale the skin when you buy the salmon, or do it yourself. I cook the fillets skin side down, which makes the skin appealingly crisp and protects the flesh, keeping it moist. You'll notice that I cook the salmon for only a few minutes; my family prefers it slightly rare.

4 pieces (6 to 7 ounces each, about 1 inch thick) boneless salmon fillets with the skin on, scaled
¼ teaspoon salt
1 teaspoon corn or canola oil
1 piece (4 to 6 inches) Japanese daikon radish
4 teaspoons virgin olive oil (optional) for sprinkling on salmon before serving

1. Preheat the oven to 180 degrees.
2. Heat a grill (preferably one with a lid) until it is very hot.
3. Sprinkle the fleshy inside of the salmon fillets with the salt, and pat the skin side with the oil.
4. Place the salmon, skin side down, on a clean rack on the very hot grill, and cover with the lid. Cook over high heat for about 2 minutes for 1-inch-thick steaks that are light pink and slightly underdone inside. (Decrease or increase the cooking time based on the thickness of your fillets and your taste preferences.)
5. When the salmon is cooked to your liking, place it, skin side up, in a nonstick ovenproof skillet, and place the skillet in a 180-degree oven for a few minutes while you finish the dish. The salmon will continue to cook in its own residual heat.
6. With a vegetable peeler, peel the outer skin of the daikon radish. Then cut the radish into strips, stack the strips, and cut them into a fine julienne.
7. To serve, arrange the salmon, skin side up, on individual plates, and sprinkle the julienne of radish on top. If desired, serve with Ragout of Asparagus (page 298) and Grilled Portobello Mushrooms (page 315). If the salmon is eaten on its own, sprinkle each fillet with 1 teaspoon of oil, if desired, just before serving.

SKILLET-COOKED SALMON

IF YOU DO NOT HAVE A GRILL, HEAT A STURDY CAST-IRON OR HEAVY ALUMINUM SKILLET FOR 2 TO 3 MINUTES OVER HIGH HEAT. ADD THE SALMON FILLETS, SKIN SIDE DOWN, AND COOK THEM, COVERED, FOR 2 MINUTES (SLIGHTLY LONGER OR LESS, AS YOU PREFER, FOR THE THICKNESS OF YOUR FILLETS). SET ASIDE, COVERED, FOR 2 OR 3 MINUTES, AND SERVE WHILE THE SALMON IS STILL SLIGHTLY PINK INSIDE.

YIELD: 4 SERVINGS

NUTRITIONAL ANALYSIS PER SERVING:

Calories 276
Protein 37 gm.
Carbohydrates 1 gm.
Fat 12.8 gm.
Saturated fat 1.9 gm.
Cholesterol 101 mg.
Sodium 221 mg.

SALMON POJARSKI

Pojarski is traditionally made with a puree of salmon, egg yolks, bread, and cream. In my healthier updated recipe, the salmon is coarsely chopped, yielding a better texture, and is held together with a small amount of bread crumbs and an egg white. Instead of moistening the crumbs with cream (making a panade*), I use chicken stock and other seasonings and add raw mushrooms, which give moisture and taste to the patties. Don't add the mushrooms more than a few hours ahead, however, as they tend to bleed and discolor the mixture. The salmon is served with a refreshing* crudité *sauce that is also good with grilled poultry or meat. To cook a complete steamed dinner with the salmon,* *see page 16.*

ABOUT SALMON

SALMON IS ONE OF THE FATTIER FISH RECOMMENDED BY DOCTORS; IT TENDS TO DECREASE CHOLESTEROL IN THE BLOOD AND REDUCE TRIGLYCERIDES. BE SURE TO CHECK THE SALMON FOR BONES. WHILE SOME FISHMONGERS REMOVE THE PIN BONES THAT RUN THE LENGTH OF THE BODY, OTHERS DO NOT. FEEL FOR THEM, AND REMOVE ANY YOU FIND BEFORE CHOPPING THE SALMON FOR PATTIES.

CRUDITÉ SAUCE

- ½ cucumber
- ⅓ red bell pepper
- 2 scallions
- 1 clove garlic
- 2 tablespoons vinegar
- ⅓ cup water
- 1 teaspoon sugar
- ½ teaspoon salt
- ⅛ teaspoon freshly ground black pepper
- ⅛ teaspoon Tabasco hot pepper sauce

SALMON PATTIES

- 1 medium onion (4 ounces)
- 2 ounces mushrooms
- 1 tablespoon canola oil
- 3 tablespoons water
- 2 slices white bread (2 ounces)
- ⅓ cup homemade unsalted and defatted chicken stock (see page 466), or lower-salt canned chicken broth
- 1 pound salmon, cleaned of skin, sinew, and bones (14 ounces trimmed)
- 1 egg white
- 2 tablespoons coarsely chopped fresh parsley
- 2 tablespoons chopped fresh chives
- ½ teaspoon salt (less if using canned broth)
- ¼ teaspoon freshly ground black pepper

For the *Crudité* Sauce

1. Peel the cucumber, remove the seeds, and chop finely to make about ½ cup. Place in a large bowl.
2. Using a vegetable peeler, remove the skin from the bell pepper, and finely chop the flesh to make ¼ cup. (See Peeling Peppers, page 312.) Add to the cucumbers.
3. Mince the scallions finely, and add to the bowl. Peel, crush, and finely chop the garlic, and add it to the bowl, along with the vinegar, water, sugar, salt, pepper, and Tabasco. Set aside until ready to serve.

For the Salmon Patties

4. Coarsely chop the onion and mushrooms. (You should have 1 cup of each.) Combine the onion, oil, and water in a skillet, and bring the mixture to a boil. Cook, covered, for 1 minute. Uncover, and add the mushrooms. Cook until most of the moisture has evaporated and the onion and mushrooms begin to fry. Cool.
5. Place the bread in a food processor, and process to make 1 cup of bread crumbs. Transfer to a bowl, and mix in the stock.
6. Coarsely chop the salmon, cutting it into ¼-inch pieces. Add the cooked onion and mushrooms, egg white, parsley, chives, salt, and pepper. Mix until well combined. Add the bread mixture, and mix just enough to incorporate. Divide the mixture into four equal parts, each about 6 ounces, and form into round or oval patties. (The mixture will be soft, so dampen your hands to help in the molding process.) Arrange the patties on an ovenproof plate that fits into a steamer (my steamer is bamboo).
7. Steam, covered, over boiling water for 6 to 7 minutes. The patties should still be moist in the center after steaming. Serve with the sauce.

Yield: 4 Servings

Nutritional Analysis per Serving:

Calories 244
Protein 23 gm.
Carbohydrates 14 gm.
Fat 10.5 gm.
Saturated fat 1.4 gm.
Cholesterol 55 mg.
Sodium 703 mg.

Salmon is an especially good source of omega-3 fatty acids.

SALMON IN SAVORY BROTH

In this recipe, salmon fillets are poached in a flavorful broth containing fennel, leek, carrot, mushrooms, wine, lemon juice, and lemon peel. The dish is flavored at the end with a little butter and oil, and garnished with a sprinkling of chives.

HOW TO JULIENNE LEMON PEEL

WHEN PEELING THE LEMON, USE A VEGETABLE PEELER, TAKING CARE TO REMOVE ONLY THE YELLOW OUTER SURFACE OF THE SKIN, WHICH CONTAINS THE ESSENTIAL OILS. THEN PILE THE STRIPS OF PEEL TOGETHER, AND CUT OR SHRED THEM FINELY INTO THIN STICKS TO CREATE A JULIENNE. FOLLOW THESE SAME STACKING AND CUTTING PROCEDURES WHEN PREPARING THE LEEK, CARROT, AND MUSHROOMS, ALL OF WHICH ARE JULIENNED.

- 1½ teaspoons julienned lemon peel
- 1½ tablespoons lemon juice
- About 3 ounces fennel, preferably from the center where it is most tender, washed and cut into ¼-inch pieces (¾ cup)
- About 2 ounces leek, both white and light green parts, washed and cut into julienne strips (1 cup loosely packed)
- 1 small carrot (2 ounces), peeled and cut into julienne strips (1 cup loosely packed)
- 2 large mushrooms (2 ounces), washed and cut into julienne strips (1 cup loosely packed)
- ½ cup dry white wine (such as sauvignon blanc or chardonnay)
- ½ cup water
- ¾ teaspoon salt
- ¼ teaspoon freshly ground black pepper
- 4 pieces salmon fillet (about 6 ounces each), cleaned of bones, skin, and sinew
- 1 tablespoon unsalted butter
- 2 tablespoons virgin olive oil
- 1 tablespoon minced fresh chives

1. Place the lemon peel, lemon juice, fennel, leek, carrot, mushrooms, wine, water, salt, and pepper in a large saucepan. Bring to a boil over medium to high heat, cover, and cook for 3 minutes.
2. Add the salmon fillets to the saucepan in one layer, and cook them, covered, over medium heat for 3 minutes, until the salmon is cooked but still slightly raw in the center.
3. To serve, lift the salmon pieces one at a time from the saucepan, and arrange a fillet on each of four plates. Using a slotted spoon, lift out the vegetables, and divide them among the plates, arranging them on top of and around the salmon. To the remaining juices in the saucepan add the butter and oil, and bring the mixture to a strong boil. Pour the sauce over the salmon pieces, and sprinkle the chives on top. Serve immediately.

YIELD: 4 SERVINGS

NUTRITIONAL ANALYSIS PER SERVING:

Calories 326
Protein 29 gm.
Carbohydrates 5 gm.
Fat 18.6 gm.
Saturated fat 4.1 gm.
Cholesterol 84 mg.
Sodium 502 mg.

Monkfish Roulade with Broccoli Rabe Stuffing

Monkfish, one of my favorites from the sea, was not really appreciated in the United States until recently. In this recipe, the textured, flavorful flesh of a large monkfish fillet is butterflied, wrapped around a broccoli rabe stuffing to form a roll or roulade, and then cooked on top of the stove. Broccoli rabe (also known as broccoli di rape*) is a mustard green that appears in Asian and Italian cooking and can be found in most Chinese markets. It is sautéed here with mushrooms and garlic to make a flavorful stuffing for the roulade, which is then served with a complementary tarragon and tomato sauce.* *(See photograph, page 184.)*

BROCCOLI RABE STUFFING

- 10 ounces broccoli rabe
- 1½ teaspoons virgin olive oil
- 2 cloves garlic, peeled, crushed, and finely chopped (1½ teaspoons)
- 4 ounces mushrooms, washed and chopped by hand or in a food processor (1½ cups)
- ¼ teaspoon salt
- ¼ teaspoon freshly ground black pepper

MONKFISH ROULADE

- 1 large fillet of monkfish (about 1½ pounds), black flesh and sinews removed (about 1 pound, 2 ounces trimmed)
- 1 tablespoon virgin olive oil
- 1 tablespoon unsalted butter
- ¼ teaspoon salt

TARRAGON-TOMATO SAUCE

- 3 tablespoons dry white wine
- Drippings from cooking the monkfish (above)
- 1 or 2 ripe tomatoes (7 ounces total), peeled, seeded, and cut into ½-inch pieces (1 cup)
- ¼ teaspoon salt
- ¼ teaspoon freshly ground black pepper
- 1 tablespoon chopped fresh tarragon

(continued)

ABOUT MONKFISH

MONKFISH—ALSO KNOWN AS GOOSEFISH, ANGELFISH, FROGFISH, SEA DEVIL, ANGLER, AND BELLYFISH—IS A FLAT, UGLY, SEA-BOTTOM DWELLER WITH A LARGE HEAD, HUGE TOOTH-FILLED MOUTH, AND WINGLIKE FINS. ONLY THE TAIL SECTION OF MONKFISH CONTAINS EDIBLE MEAT. WHITE, LOW IN FAT, AND FIRM-TEXTURED WITH FEW BONES, IT HAS A MILD, SWEET FLAVOR THAT HAS BEEN COMPARED TO LOBSTER. USUALLY SOLD IN FILLET FORM, MONKFISH FLESH IS SUITABLE FOR ALMOST ANY METHOD OF COOKING THAT PRODUCES A MEDIUM-TO-WELL-DONE RESULT, SINCE THE MEAT OF THIS FISH DOES NOT LEND ITSELF TO THE UNDERCOOKING ADVOCATED IN SOME MODERN RECIPES FOR FISH.

MONKFISH ROULADE WITH BROCCOLI RABE STUFFING (*continued*)

FOR THE BROCCOLI RABE STUFFING

1. Peel the fibrous outer layer of skin from the stems of the broccoli rabe, and cut off and discard the bottoms of the stems if they are tough. Wash the greens well, and cut them into ½-inch pieces.
2. Heat the 1½ teaspoons of oil in a large, heavy skillet. When it is hot, add the garlic, and sauté for 5 seconds, then add the broccoli, still wet from washing, along with the mushrooms and the ¼ teaspoon each of salt and pepper. Mix well, cover, and cook over medium heat for 5 minutes. The broccoli should be tender and the moisture gone from the pan. If any liquid remains, cook the mixture, uncovered, until the liquid has evaporated. Cool the stuffing to room temperature.

FOR THE MONKFISH ROULADE

3. Meanwhile, butterfly the monkfish to create a ½-inch-thick rectangle about 7 inches by 9 inches. (See Butterflying Chicken Breasts, page 212.) One side of the fillet will be whiter than the other; place the fillet white side down on a clean, flat work surface, and spread the cool stuffing mixture on top. Roll the monkfish to encase the filling, and tie it securely with kitchen string. The finished roll or roulade should be about 2½ inches in diameter. Cover and refrigerate the roulade until ready to cook. (It can be prepared up to 24 hours ahead.)
4. At cooking time, heat the tablespoon of oil and the butter in a deep skillet. Sprinkle the roulade with the ¼ teaspoon salt, and brown it on the smooth (unseamed) side over high heat for about 1 minute. Then turn the roulade over, cover the pan, reduce the heat to medium, and cook it for 12 to 15 minutes, or until the fish is tender when pierced with a fork. Transfer the roulade to a platter.

**YIELD:
4 SERVINGS**

NUTRITIONAL ANALYSIS PER SERVING:

***Calories 213
Protein 22 gm.
Carbohydrates 7 gm.
Fat 10.4 gm.
Saturated fat 2.5 gm.
Cholesterol 40 mg.
Sodium 469 mg.***

Broccoli rabe is high in vitamin A and folacin. Monkfish is an excellent source of protein, phosphorus, and selenium.

FOR THE TARRAGON-TOMATO SAUCE

5. Add the wine to the drippings in the skillet, and boil the mixture for 1 minute. Add the tomatoes and the ¼ teaspoon each of salt and pepper, and boil for another minute. Stir in the tarragon.
6. To serve the dish, remove the string from the monkfish, and cut the roulade into about eight slices, each ¾ inch thick. Divide the sauce among four hot plates, and arrange two slices of the roulade on top. Serve immediately.

TOP: STEAMED CAULIFLOWER WITH CHIVES (SEE PAGE 308).

BOTTOM: MONKFISH ROULADE WITH BROCCOLI RABE STUFFING (SEE PAGE 181).

FISH VARIATIONS

Any variety of thick fish fillet will work here. If you can't get a seawater fish like snapper, blackfish, or sea bass, use trout, perch, or catfish fillets instead, altering the cooking time to accommodate variations in thickness. The most important consideration when selecting the fish is freshness.

USING A MANDOLINE

I use a mandoline, a professional slicer made of stainless steel, to slice the potatoes for this recipe. Any slicer will work well, however, including the 1-millimeter blade of a food processor.

Red Snapper in Potato Jackets

Cooked between layers of sliced potato, these moist fish fillets make an impressive main course. The zucchini garnish makes a good first course, too. Serve the fish just as they emerge from the skillet, while the potatoes are still crisp.

- 2 large potatoes (about 1 pound)
- 4 1-inch-thick fish fillets (5 ounces each) from red snapper (or blackfish or sea bass)
- ¼ teaspoon salt
- ⅛ teaspoon freshly ground black pepper

ZUCCHINI GARNISH

- 1 medium zucchini (about 8 ounces)
- 1 tablespoon peanut oil
- 1 tablespoon soy sauce

- 2 tablespoons virgin olive oil
- 2 tablespoons peanut oil
- 2 tablespoons chopped fresh parsley

1. Preheat the oven to 400 degrees.
2. Peel the potatoes, and thinly slice them lengthwise. (See Using a Mandoline.) (You should have about fifty slices.) Wash the potatoes, drain off the water, and pat the slices dry with paper towels.
3. Place four pieces of plastic wrap (each 6 inches square) on the table. Arrange six overlapping slices of potato in the center of each square, and place a piece of fish on top. Sprinkle with the salt and pepper. Arrange another six slices of potato, also overlapping, on top of the fish, and fold the plastic around them so they are completely wrapped. Refrigerate until ready to cook (not too far ahead, or the potatoes will discolor), or cook immediately.

FOR THE GARNISH

4. Cut the zucchini into 2-inch chunks, then into ⅛-inch slices, and, finally, into a julienne (yielding about 3 cups). Spread the zucchini out on a cookie sheet and place in a 400-degree oven for 5 to 6 minutes to soften. Transfer the zucchini to a bowl, and toss with the 1 tablespoon of peanut oil and with the soy sauce.
5. At cooking time, divide the 2 tablespoons each of olive oil and peanut oil between two nonstick skillets, and place over medium heat. Carefully unwrap the potato-

(continued)

TOP: PEAS *À LA FRANÇAISE* (SEE PAGE 318).
BOTTOM: RED SNAPPER IN POTATO JACKETS (ABOVE).

fish packages, and, with a large spatula, transfer them to the skillets, placing two in each skillet. Sauté for 5 minutes. Carefully turn (so the arrangement is not disturbed), and sauté for 5 minutes or until the potatoes are nicely browned.

6. To serve, arrange the zucchini in a circle to border the plate, and place the fish in potato jackets in the center. Sprinkle with the parsley, and serve.

YIELD:
4 SERVINGS

NUTRITIONAL ANALYSIS PER SERVING:

Calories 369
Protein 32 gm.
Carbohydrates 17 gm.
Fat 18.9 gm.
Saturated fat 3.1 gm.
Cholesterol 52 mg.
Sodium 491 mg.

RED SNAPPER IN *BRUNOISE* SAUCE

I use red snapper fillets here, but the recipe can be prepared with fillets from any fresh, firm-fleshed fish. This is an easy, quick recipe. First, all the ingredients but the snapper are cooked together for a few minutes in a skillet. At serving time, the fish is added, cooked for a couple of minutes, and then served with a sauce created from the mixture in the pan. (See photograph, page 153.)

YIELD:
4 SERVINGS

NUTRITIONAL ANALYSIS PER SERVING:

Calories 306
Protein 31 gm.
Carbohydrates 9 gm.
Fat 11.7 gm.
Saturated fat 3.1 gm.
Cholesterol 60 mg.
Sodium 378 mg.

Snapper is an excellent source of protein and is low in fat.

1 small leek, washed and finely sliced (1½ cups)
3 ounces mushrooms, washed and cut into julienne strips (1½ cups)
¼ cup chopped shallots
⅓ cup peeled, diced (¼-inch dice) red bell pepper (See Peeling Peppers, page 312)
1 cup dry white wine
2 tablespoons virgin olive oil
½ teaspoon salt
¼ teaspoon freshly ground black pepper
4 red snapper fillets, about 5 ounces each, boneless but with skin on
1 tablespoon unsalted butter

1. Place all the ingredients except the fish and butter in a stainless steel saucepan. Cover, bring to a boil, reduce the heat to low, and boil gently for 3 minutes.
2. Add the fish, cover, and cook for 2½ to 3 minutes for fillets that are about ¾ inch thick. (Increase or decrease the cooking time proportionately for fillets of different thicknesses.)
3. Arrange a fillet on each of four plates. Add the butter to the drippings in the saucepan, and bring the mixture to a strong boil. Divide the mixture among the plates, spooning both sauce and vegetables on top of the fish. Serve immediately.

Tuna Steaks with Peppercorns

Tuna is an ideal replacement here for beef, the classic choice in pepper steak recipes. Thick tuna steaks are wonderfully moist and flavorful prepared this way and served rare. The total amount of pepper used can be adjusted to accommodate your taste preferences, although cracked pepper used in this way is much milder than you might imagine.

- **1 teaspoon Szechuan peppercorns**
- **½ teaspoon white peppercorns**
- **½ teaspoon black peppercorns**
- **1 teaspoon allspice berries (Jamaican peppercorns)**
- **4 tuna steaks, each 1 inch thick (about 6 ounces each)**
- **1 tablespoon corn oil**
- **½ teaspoon salt**

1. Crush the peppercorns with a meat pounder or the bottom of a saucepan (see Making a *Mignonnette,* page 352). Brush both sides of the steaks with the oil, and then sprinkle both sides with the salt and crushed pepper.
2. Heat a cast-iron pan for 2 to 3 minutes, until very hot. Place the steaks in the pan, and cook them over very high heat for about 1½ minutes on each side. Cover the pan, remove from the heat, and let stand for 3 to 5 minutes before serving. The steaks will continue to cook in their own residual heat but should remain pink inside.

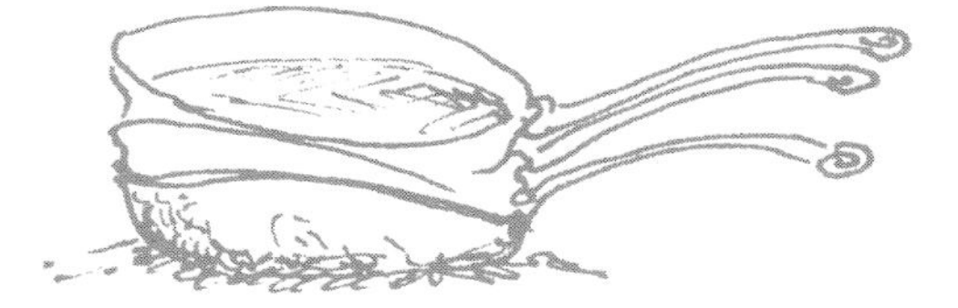

PEPPERCORN VARIETIES

I USE A MIXTURE OF FOUR DIFFERENT PEPPERCORNS IN THIS DISH: MILD, BROWN-SPECKLED SZECHUAN PEPPERCORNS; BLACK PEPPERCORNS; WHITE PEPPERCORNS, WHICH ARE THE SAME BERRY AS THE BLACK BUT WITH THE SKIN REMOVED; AND JAMAICAN PEPPERCORNS, BETTER KNOWN AS ALLSPICE. ONE OR ANOTHER OF THESE VARIETIES CAN BE OMITTED IF NOT AVAILABLE.

YIELD: 4 SERVINGS

NUTRITIONAL ANALYSIS PER SERVING:

Calories 278
Protein 40 gm.
Carbohydrates 1 gm.
Fat 11.8 gm.
Saturated fat 2.6 gm.
Cholesterol 65 mg.
Sodium 340 mg.

1993
Malolactic

Moules Maison (Mussels Home-Style)

This is the simplest way to cook mussels: all the ingredients are combined in a saucepan, and the mixture is cooked for a few minutes. The mussels, mushrooms, and tomatoes contain enough juice to create a nice sauce. Serve this dish for casual dining or as a first course.

- **4 pounds mussels, cleaned**
- **6 plum tomatoes (1 pound), seeded and cut into 1½-inch cubes (about 2½ cups)**
- **6 scallions, trimmed and cut into ¼-inch pieces**
- **½ pound mushrooms, cut into ½-inch dice (about 2½ cups)**
- **2 onions (8 ounces), peeled and coarsely chopped (2 cups)**
- **8 cloves garlic, peeled and sliced (2 tablespoons)**
- **1 cup dry white wine**
- **4 tablespoons virgin olive oil**
- **1½ teaspoons Tabasco hot pepper sauce**
- **½ teaspoon salt or to taste**
- **¼ cup coarsely chopped fresh flat-leaf parsley**

1. Place the mussels, tomatoes, scallions, mushrooms, onions, garlic, wine, oil, Tabasco, and salt in a large saucepan, and bring to a boil. Cook 6 to 7 minutes, covered, stirring occasionally, until all the mussels have opened. (Remove and discard any that fail to open.)
2. Divide the mussels among four dishes. Serve as is, or remove and discard the shell halves without meat, and serve the mussels in the half shell. Spoon sauce over the mussels, sprinkle with the parsley, and serve with French fries, if desired. (See page 327.)

YIELD: 4 SERVINGS

NUTRITIONAL ANALYSIS PER SERVING:

Calories 344
Protein 19 gm.
Carbohydrates 21 gm.
Fat 17.2 gm.
Saturated fat 2.5 gm.
Cholesterol 37 mg.
Sodium 721 mg.

Mussels are low in cholesterol and relatively low in fat.

ABOUT DRIED LIMA BEANS

I USE LARGE DRIED LIMA BEANS, WHICH COOK FASTER THAN MOST OTHER DRIED BEANS, FOR THIS RECIPE. AS THEY COOK, THE SKINS WILL SEPARATE FROM SOME OF THE BEANS AND RISE TO THE SURFACE; REMOVE AND DISCARD THE FLOATING SKINS, BUT DON'T ATTEMPT TO REMOVE THE SKINS FROM BEANS THAT DON'T SHED THEM ON THEIR OWN.

Stew of Lima Beans and Mussels with Spinach

For this recipe, mussels are cooked in a little wine and then removed from their shells. Some of the mussel-cooking liquid is added to the stew along with the drained beans and mussels, and this mixture is then served with sautéed spinach.

As a bonus recipe, the remainder of the juice from cooking the mussels—which years ago would have been transformed into a billi-bi with the addition of heavy cream, tarragon, and chives—is thickened lightly here with the reserved liquid from cooking the beans, a little sour cream, and chives. The result is a flavorful and less caloric soup (see Cold Mussel and Bean Soup on page 58).

- **8 ounces dried lima beans**
- **4 cups cold water**
- **1½ teaspoons salt**
- **3 pounds mussels**
- **1 cup dry, fruity white wine (such as chardonnay)**
- **4½ tablespoons virgin olive oil**
- **12 scallions, trimmed, washed, and coarsely chopped (1¼ cups)**
- **5 to 6 cloves garlic, peeled, crushed, and chopped (1 tablespoon)**
- **1 pound spinach, tough stems removed and the remainder washed (about 12 ounces, cleaned)**
- **½ teaspoon freshly ground black pepper**

1. Wash the lima beans, and discard any damaged beans or pebbles. Place the beans in a saucepan with the cold water. Add 1 teaspoon of the salt, and bring to a boil. Cover, reduce the heat, and boil gently for 30 to 40 minutes, until the beans are tender. (Remove and discard any skins that float to the surface.)
2. Drain the beans, reserving the cooking liquid for use in Cold Mussel and Bean Soup (see page 58). You should have about 2 cups of liquid; if you have less, add water.

(continued)

FOR THE ARTICHOKE BOTTOMS

3. Preheat the oven to 350 degrees.
4. Place the artichoke bottoms in a saucepan with the 1 cup of water, the oil, the lemon juice, and the salt. Bring to a boil, cover, reduce the heat, and boil the artichokes gently for about 20 minutes, until they are tender and most of the cooking liquid has evaporated. Let cool. When the artichokes are cool enough to handle, remove and discard the chokes.
5. Just before serving time, reheat the artichoke bottoms for about 1 minute in a microwave oven or for 10 to 15 minutes in a conventional oven set at 350 degrees. Place the roe in an ovenproof dish, and heat it for 5 minutes in a 350-degree oven to dry it. Chop the roe coarsely with a knife.
6. Reheat the lobster meat for 20 to 30 seconds in a microwave oven or for 8 to 10 minutes in a conventional oven set at 350 degrees. Bring the cup of reserved stock to a boil, and boil it until it is reduced to ½ cup. Add the butter, chives, and salt and pepper, and bring to a strong boil.
7. Arrange an artichoke bottom on each of four plates, and place the meat of half a lobster tail in the cavity of each with a piece of claw meat alongside. Spoon some sauce on top, and sprinkle with some of the roe. Serve, if desired, with Broccoli with Butter, page 304, arranging the broccoli around the artichoke bottoms.

**YIELD:
4 SERVINGS**

NUTRITIONAL ANALYSIS PER SERVING:

Calories 208
Protein 21 gm.
Carbohydrates 11 gm.
Fat 9.7 gm.
Saturated fat 4.1 gm.
Cholesterol 77 mg.
Sodium 577 mg.

Lobster is rich in selenium, a trace mineral associated with lower risk of cancer and heart disease.

LOBSTER IN ARTICHOKE BOTTOMS (SEE PAGE 197) AND BROCCOLI WITH BUTTER (SEE PAGE 304).

Couscous of Lobster

This impressive dish combines lobster meat with flavorful couscous and is served with a fresh chive sauce. For a decorative presentation, the shells from the bodies of the lobsters can be used as receptacles.

3 quarts water
2 lobsters (2 pounds each), preferably female

Couscous

1½ cups water
2 tablespoons virgin olive oil
1 medium onion, peeled and chopped (1 cup)
1½ cups couscous (about 10 ounces)
½ teaspoon salt
¼ teaspoon freshly ground black pepper

Chive Sauce

¼ cup virgin olive oil
4 tablespoons finely minced fresh chives
⅛ teaspoon salt
⅛ teaspoon freshly ground black pepper

1. Bring the 3 quarts of water to a boil in a large stockpot. Add the lobsters, cover, and bring the water back to a boil. Reduce the heat to low, and boil gently for 8 minutes. Remove the lobsters from the water, and set aside. When cool enough to handle, remove the meat from the shells (reserving the shells), and set aside the tomalley (liver) and coral (eggs), if any (about ½ cup combined).
2. To concentrate the taste of the stock, reduce it to 4 cups. You will need 1 cup to reheat the lobster meat and ½ cup for the sauce. Freeze the remainder.
3. Bring the 1½ cups water to a boil in a small saucepan.
4. Meanwhile, in a medium saucepan, heat the 2 tablespoons of oil, and sauté the onion over medium heat for about 2 minutes. Add the light green tomalley and dark green eggs, and mix well, crushing the eggs with a fork. Stir in the couscous, and then add the boiling water, ½ teaspoon salt, and ¼ teaspoon pepper. Mix well. Remove from the heat, cover, and set aside for 10 minutes.
5. Combine the lobster meat with the 1 cup of reduced stock in a saucepan. Slowly bring the stock almost to a boil, and keep it at this temperature for 3 to 4 minutes.
6. Combine the ½ cup of reserved reduced stock with the chive sauce ingredients in a saucepan, and bring to a strong boil.
7. Cut the reserved shells in half and fluff the couscous. Place some couscous on each of four plates and a shell receptacle on top. Fill the shell with couscous, arrange the warm lobster on top, and spoon on the sauce. Serve.

COOKING THE LOBSTER

Initially, cook the lobster for only 8 minutes—just enough so that it can be removed from the shell. Just before serving, reheat the lobster meat almost to a boil in the stock, and then set it aside for a few minutes to finish cooking in the residual heat remaining in the hot poaching liquid. Avoid boiling the stock; doing so will toughen the lobster meat.

Yield: 4 Servings

NUTRITIONAL ANALYSIS PER SERVING (WITHOUT TOMALLEY AND CORAL):

Calories 560
Protein 30 gm.
Carbohydrates 60 gm.
Fat 21.4 gm.
Saturated fat 2.9 gm.
Cholesterol 72 mg.
Sodium 731 mg.

ABOUT PAELLA

PAELLA COMES FROM THE SPANISH WORD FOR THE PAN (USUALLY A BIG IRON OR STEEL SKILLET OR SAUCEPAN) IN WHICH THIS CLASSIC CONCOCTION IS COOKED. IN KEEPING WITH TRADITION, PEOPLE IN SPAIN STILL OFTEN PREPARE THIS DISH OUTDOORS OVER A WOOD FIRE. THEY BRING THEIR CHICKEN FROM THE MARKET, AND PLUCK IT AND COOK IT WITH SAUSAGES AND RICE. ESSENTIALLY, PAELLA IS A BIG STEW OF RICE FLAVORED WITH POULTRY, MEAT, SEAFOOD—WHATEVER ONE CAN AFFORD—WITH SOME VEGETABLES ADDED NEAR THE END OF THE COOKING TIME.

Chicken and Seafood Paella

Paella contains a lot of rice; chorizo, the famed Spanish hot sausage; chicken legs; a seafood assortment of mussels, squid, and shrimp; and, finally, fresh vegetables. All of this is flavored with saffron, the best quality of which comes from Spain. This one-pot meal requires great attention to timing. First, the pork and sausage are browned, and then, in their drippings, the chicken is browned. The rice is added next and cooked with the seasonings, and then the seafood is added. Finally, the asparagus and peas are placed in the pot. Staggered in this way, everything is finished cooking at the same time.

3 ounces pancetta (best choice) or salt pork, cut into ¼-inch lardoons (½ cup)
8 ounces chorizo, cut into 1-inch pieces
3 tablespoons virgin olive oil
2 chicken legs (about 1 pound), skinned, carcass bone removed, and cut in half to separate thighs and drumsticks
1 medium onion (6 ounces), peeled and cut into ½-inch pieces (1¼ cups)
5 to 6 cloves garlic, peeled, crushed, and finely chopped (1 tablespoon)
2 cups long-grain Carolina rice
½ cup (about ½ ounces) dry mushroom pieces
1 teaspoon (loose) saffron pistils, crushed between thumb and fingers (see About Saffron, page 345)
1 teaspoon *herbes de Provence* (see page 467)
4 cups water
1 tomato (8 ounces), cut into ½-inch pieces (1⅓ cups)
1 red bell pepper (6 ounces), cut into ½-inch pieces
1 tablespoon chopped jalapeño pepper
1 teaspoon salt
½ teaspoon freshly ground black pepper
1 pound (about 12) mussels
¾ pound squid, cleaned and cut into 1½-inch pieces
12 shrimp (about 8 ounces), shelled
½ cup fresh shelled or frozen baby peas
6 stalks asparagus, peeled and cut into 1-inch pieces (1 cup)
1 tablespoon chopped fresh chives
½ teaspoon Tabasco hot pepper sauce

(continued)

CHICKEN CHASSEUR

In the original versions of this dish, unskinned chicken pieces were browned in a great amount of butter. Although the skin was crisp initially from the browning, it would soften and become gummy by the time the other ingredients were added and the dish cooked as a stew. I use skinless chicken thighs in my flavorful update of this dish. After sautéing the thighs in a little olive oil, I finish them in a chasseur *sauce containing onions and leeks, and flavored in the traditional manner with white wine, tomatoes, and mushrooms.*

COOKING IN ADVANCE

THIS DISH CAN BE PREPARED UP TO A DAY AHEAD; IF YOU DO SO, HOWEVER, COOK IT INITIALLY FOR 15 MINUTES INSTEAD OF 25. THE CHICKEN WILL CONTINUE TO COOK A LITTLE IN THE HOT SAUCE AS IT COOLS AND AGAIN AS THE DISH IS REHEATED LATER, SO IT WILL BE COOKED PROPERLY BY SERVING TIME.

- **1 tablespoon virgin olive oil**
- **8 skinless chicken thighs, with all surrounding fat removed (about 2 pounds)**
- **1 small leek (5 ounces), trimmed, cleaned, and coarsely chopped (1¾ cups)**
- **1 medium onion (4 ounces), peeled and chopped (1 cup)**
- **1½ tablespoons all-purpose flour**
- **1 cup dry white wine**
- **1 can (15 ounces) whole peeled tomatoes in juice**
- **5 to 6 cloves garlic, peeled, crushed, and finely chopped (1 tablespoon)**
- **20 medium mushrooms (about 12 ounces)**
- **1 teaspoon chopped fresh thyme**
- **1 teaspoon chopped fresh rosemary**
- **1 teaspoon salt**
- **½ teaspoon freshly ground black pepper**
- **1 tablespoon soy sauce**
- **1 tablespoon chopped fresh tarragon**

YIELD: 4 SERVINGS

NUTRITIONAL ANALYSIS PER SERVING:

Calories 330
Protein 37 gm.
Carbohydrates 22 gm.
Fat 10.7 gm.
Saturated fat 2.2 gm.
Cholesterol 138 mg.
Sodium 1,140 mg.

A tablespoon of soy sauce has half the sodium of a teaspoon of salt.

1. Heat the olive oil until it is hot in a large nonstick skillet. Add the chicken thighs in one layer, and cook them for 5 minutes on each side over medium to high heat. Transfer the thighs to a large, sturdy saucepan, arranging them side by side in a single layer in the pan.
2. To the drippings in the skillet add the leek and onion, and sauté for 30 seconds. Add the flour, mix it in well, and cook for about 30 seconds. Then mix in the wine and tomatoes. Bring the mixture to a boil over medium heat, and pour it into the

(continued)

TOP: POTATO AND SPINACH *GALETTE* (SEE PAGE 163).
BOTTOM: CHICKEN *CHASSEUR* (ABOVE).

saucepan containing the chicken. Stir in the garlic, mushrooms, thyme, rosemary, salt, pepper, and soy sauce.

3. Bring the mixture to a boil over high heat, stirring occasionally to prevent the chicken from scorching, then cover the pan, reduce the heat to low, and cook for 25 minutes. Sprinkle on the tarragon, and mix it in.
4. Serve two thighs per person with some of the vegetables and surrounding liquid.

GRILLED CHICKEN WITH CABBAGE *ANCHOYADE*

In this recipe, the chicken breasts are marinated for several hours in a finely chopped mixture of oregano, lemon peel, black pepper, and olive oil. A mini-chop, smaller and faster than a food processor, is ideal for chopping the herbs. Cooked on a hot grill, the breasts brown quickly and remain moist in the center.

- 8 strips lemon peel, removed with a vegetable peeler
- 2 teaspoons black peppercorns
- 4 tablespoons (loose) fresh oregano
- 4 boneless skinless chicken breasts (about 6 ounces each), from roasting chickens
- 3 tablespoons virgin olive oil
- 1 teaspoon salt

CABBAGE *ANCHOYADE*

- ½ red bell pepper, peeled and cut into ¼-inch dice (½ cup)
- 4 cloves garlic, peeled, crushed, and finely chopped (about 2 teaspoons)
- 6 anchovy fillets, finely chopped (4 teaspoons)
- ½ teaspoon salt
- ½ teaspoon freshly ground black pepper
- 4 teaspoons red wine vinegar
- 4 tablespoons virgin olive oil
- 18 ounces savoy cabbage, shredded (8 cups)

1. Place the lemon peel strips, peppercorns, and oregano in the bowl of a mini-chop, and process to a powder. (You should have about 4 tablespoons.) Sprinkle the mixture over the chicken, and arrange it in a dish. Sprinkle with the oil. Cover, and set aside in the refrigerator to macerate for at least ½ hour, or as long as overnight.
2. Preheat the oven to 180 degrees (warm).
3. At cooking time, sprinkle the chicken with the salt, and arrange it on a hot grill. Cook about 4 minutes on each side, and transfer to a 180-degree oven until serving time (up to 1 hour ahead).

For the Cabbage *Anchoyade*

4. Reserve 1 tablespoon of the red bell pepper for garnish.
5. In a bowl, combine the rest of the red pepper with the garlic, anchovies, salt, black pepper, vinegar, and oil. Add the cabbage, and mix well. (This can be made up to 3 to 4 hours ahead of time and refrigerated until serving time.)
6. At serving time, arrange the cabbage mixture in a mound in the center of each of four serving plates. Slice the chicken breasts lengthwise, and arrange the meat all around and on top of the cabbage. Sprinkle with the reserved red pepper, and serve immediately.

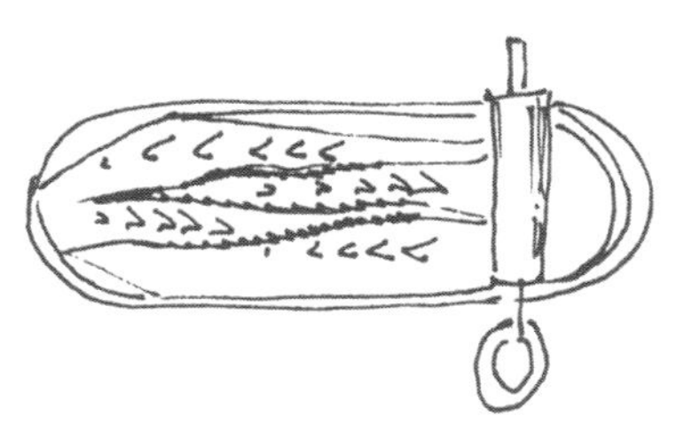

Yield:
4 Servings

NUTRITIONAL ANALYSIS PER SERVING:

Calories 458
Protein 44 gm.
Carbohydrates 11 gm.
Fat 26.6 gm.
Saturated fat 3.9 gm.
Cholesterol 102 mg.
Sodium 1,191 mg.

Anchovies are rich in omega-3 fatty acids.

Chicken Legs with Wine and Yams

This is one of those complete casserole dishes that make a whole meal by themselves. I use chicken legs for this dish because they stew better than chicken breasts, which tend to get stringy. Notice, however, that I remove the skin from the legs, which eliminates most of the fat. One chicken leg per person is sufficient when the legs are divided into thighs and drumsticks, especially since the dish is served with several vegetable garnishes.

4 chicken legs (about 2 pounds total)
2 tablespoons virgin olive oil
¼ cup chopped onion
4 large shallots (about 6 ounces), peeled
8 medium mushrooms (about 5 ounces)
4 yams (about 1 pound), peeled and halved lengthwise
1 cup dry white wine
8 large garlic cloves, peeled
½ teaspoon salt
½ teaspoon freshly ground black pepper
2 tablespoons chopped fresh parsley, for garnish

1. Remove the skin from the chicken legs, using a kitchen towel to help pull it off. In some markets, chicken legs are packaged with a piece of back carcass attached to the joint of the pelvis. In this case, remove any attached carcass bones from the chicken legs. Then separate the legs into thighs and drumsticks.
2. Heat the oil in one large or two smaller skillets, and brown the chicken pieces, partially covered to prevent splattering, on all sides for about 10 minutes.
3. Add the onion, and cook for 1 minute. Then add the shallots, mushrooms, yams, wine, garlic, salt, and pepper.
4. Bring to a boil, cover, and boil very gently for 20 minutes. Garnish with parsley, and serve.

YIELD: 4 SERVINGS

NUTRITIONAL ANALYSIS PER SERVING:

Calories 423
Protein 30 gm.
Carbohydrates 39 gm.
Fat 12.1 gm.
Saturated fat 2.2 gm.
Cholesterol 104 mg.
Sodium 405 mg.

Yams are a good source of fiber.

TOP: *CAROTTES À LA CIBOULETTE* (CARROTS WITH CHIVES) (SEE PAGE 306).
BOTTOM: CHICKEN LEGS WITH WINE AND YAMS (ABOVE).

BUTTERFLYING CHICKEN BREASTS

HOLDING YOUR KNIFE SO THE BLADE IS PARALLEL TO THE CUTTING SURFACE, SLICE ALMOST ALL THE WAY THROUGH THE THICKNESS OF EACH BREAST, STOPPING WHEN YOU CAN OPEN THE BREAST AS YOU WOULD A BOOK AND LAY THE ATTACHED HALVES FLAT.

Chicken Supreme Kiev-Style

I call this Kiev-style chicken to differentiate it from the famous Chicken Kiev that inspired it. In the original recipe, the chicken is usually left unskinned, stuffed with butter, dipped in eggs and bread crumbs, and then deep-fried—setting it a world apart from my rendition. I use skinless chicken, stuff it with a mushroom puree, and roll it in fresh bread crumbs that are seasoned with fresh herbs and only moistened with oil. Much lower in calories, my version is intensely flavored, moist, and delicious. (See photograph, page 246.)

- 4 boneless chicken breasts (about 7 ounces each), with skin and any visible fat removed
- 2 tablespoons coarsely chopped fresh cilantro (coriander or Chinese parsley)

Mushroom Filling

- 1½ tablespoons virgin olive oil
- 1½ cups chopped onions
- 8 ounces mushrooms, cleaned and chopped (3 cups)
- 4 to 5 cloves garlic, peeled, crushed, and chopped (1 tablespoon)
- ½ teaspoon salt
- ¼ teaspoon freshly ground black pepper

Coating

- 4 slices firm white bread, processed in a food processor to make crumbs (2 cups)
- 2 tablespoons virgin olive oil
- 2 tablespoons chopped fresh cilantro
- ½ teaspoon salt
- ½ teaspoon freshly ground black pepper
- ¼ cup nonfat milk

1. Preheat the oven to 400 degrees.
2. Butterfly the chicken breasts, and open the halves like a book. Pound the breasts lightly, and set them aside while you make the filling.

For the Filling

3. Heat the oil in a large skillet. When it is hot, add the onions, and sauté over medium to high heat for about 2 minutes. Stir in the mushrooms, garlic, salt, and pepper, and cook, covered, for about 3 minutes. Remove the lid, and continue cooking until there is no visible liquid remaining in the skillet. Add the cilantro, and transfer the mixture to a plate to cool.
4. When the filling is cool, divide it into four equal portions, and mound one portion in the center of each butterflied chicken breast. Fold all edges of the breast meat over the filling to enclose it completely.

For the Coating

5. Combine the bread crumbs, oil, cilantro, salt, and pepper in a bowl. Dip the stuffed chicken breasts in the milk, and then roll them in the seasoned bread crumbs.
6. Arrange the coated chicken breasts in a roasting pan, and bake them at 400 degrees for 20 to 25 minutes, until cooked through but still moist. Serve immediately with Bulgur Wheat Pilaf, page 342, if desired.

**Yield:
4 Servings**

NUTRITIONAL ANALYSIS PER SERVING:

Calories 391
Protein 42 gm.
Carbohydrates 21 gm.
Fat 15.0 gm.
Saturated fat 2.4 gm.
Cholesterol 95 mg.
Sodium 776 mg.

Olive oil and nonfat milk keep this dish low in fat.

Grilled Chicken with Tarragon Butter

I created this dish on my stovetop gas grill, but it could also be grilled outdoors on a freestanding gas or charcoal grill. The chicken is grilled long enough so that a great deal of the fat in the skin drains away, and the chicken takes on the characteristics of grilled meat; then it is transferred to a warm oven, where it finishes cooking in its own juices. The dish is less caloric if you remove and discard the chicken skin, but don't do this until just before serving, since the skin keeps the meat moist as it cooks.

A delicious tarragon butter, dotted on the chicken at serving time, replicates the flavor but not the calories of a béarnaise sauce.

LOWER-CHOLESTEROL ALTERNATIVE

IF YOU'RE AVOIDING BUTTER, SUBSTITUTE TARRAGON OIL (SEE PAGE 471) FOR THE TARRAGON BUTTER MIXTURE USED HERE. SIMPLY PAINT A THIN COATING OF IT ON THE CHICKEN PIECES WITH A PASTRY BRUSH JUST BEFORE SERVING.

- **1 chicken (about 3 pounds), quartered, with the carcass bones removed (and reserved for stock, if desired)**
- **½ teaspoon salt**

TARRAGON BUTTER

- **1½ tablespoons unsalted butter**
- **1½ tablespoons virgin olive oil**
- **2 tablespoons chopped fresh tarragon**
- **¼ teaspoon salt**

1. Preheat a grill.
2. Sprinkle the chicken pieces with the salt, and place them on the rack when the grill is medium to hot. Grill for about 20 minutes, turning the pieces occasionally, until they are nicely browned on all sides. While they are cooking, preheat the oven to 225 degrees.

FOR THE TARRAGON BUTTER

3. Meanwhile, place all the tarragon butter ingredients in the bowl of a blender or food processor, and process until smooth. Set aside.
4. When the chicken pieces are browned, transfer them to a tray, and bake them at 225 degrees, uncovered, for at least 20 minutes to finish cooking and "relax."
5. Remove the skin, if desired, and serve one quarter per person, each dotted with about 1 tablespoon of the tarragon butter.

GRILLED CHICKEN WITH TARRAGON BUTTER (ABOVE) AND SAUTÉED *HARICOTS VERTS* AND SHALLOTS (SEE PAGE 299).

YIELD: 4 SERVINGS

NUTRITIONAL ANALYSIS PER SERVING WITH SKIN:

Calories 443
Protein 41 gm.
Carbohydrates 0.3 gm.
Fat 29.8 gm.
Saturated fat 9.0 gm.
Cholesterol 144 mg.
Sodium 532 mg.

NUTRITIONAL ANALYSIS PER SERVING WITHOUT SKIN:

Calories 316
Protein 35 gm.
Carbohydrates 0.3 gm.
Fat 18.4 gm.
Saturated fat 5.8 gm.
Cholesterol 120 mg.
Sodium 514 mg.

TIMING CHICKEN

Notice that the dark meat is cooked for about 20 minutes and the breast meat for only 10 minutes. Delaying the addition of the white meat prevents it from becoming overcooked, which makes it stringy.

Yield: 4 Servings

Nutritional analysis per serving:

Calories 212
Protein 28 gm.
Carbohydrates 4 gm.
Fat 9.0 gm.
Saturated fat 4.3 gm.
Cholesterol 107 mg.
Sodium 402 mg.

Chicken is rich in protein and a good source of niacin, a B-complex vitamin.

Chicken in Tarragon Sauce

You can make this elegant dish easily and quickly. Buy boneless, skinless chicken breasts along with packaged thighs and drumsticks from the supermarket, and remove all skin from the chicken leg pieces. I add some cream at the end and garnish the dish with fresh tarragon, which goes particularly well with the chicken and cream.

6 pieces skinless chicken (2 drumsticks and 2 thighs with bones left in and 2 boneless breasts)
½ cup dry, fruity white wine
1 small onion (about 3 ounces), chopped (¾ cup)
½ cup homemade unsalted and defatted chicken stock (see page 466), or lower-salt canned chicken broth
2 bay leaves
1 sprig fresh thyme
½ teaspoon salt (less if using canned broth)
¼ teaspoon freshly ground black pepper
1 teaspoon potato starch dissolved in 1 tablespoon water (see About Potato Starch, page 394)
¼ cup heavy cream
1 teaspoon chopped fresh tarragon, for garnish

1. Place the chicken drumsticks and thighs, wine, onion, stock, bay leaves, thyme, salt, and pepper in a saucepan, and bring to a boil. Reduce the heat, cover, and boil gently for about 10 minutes.
2. Add the chicken breasts, cover, and boil gently for another 10 minutes.
3. Transfer the meat to a dish, and keep warm. Measure the cooking liquid. (There should be about 1 cup; if there is more, reduce it to 1 cup.)
4. Stir in the dissolved potato starch, and bring to a boil. Then add the cream, and return to a boil. Return the chicken pieces to the pan, and heat them through. Remove from the heat, sprinkle with the tarragon, and serve.

Brown Rice Chicken Fricassee

For this fricassee, I use short-grain brown rice, which takes about 1 hour to cook. To reduce the cooking time by 15 minutes, substitute medium-grain white rice. Only the chicken wing pieces have skin on them, but these render enough fat to brown the rest of the bones. Use a sturdy skillet, and cook the bones until they are nicely browned.

- About 1¾ pounds chicken bones, including neck, gizzard, and wing sections
- 1 medium onion (6 ounces), peeled and coarsely chopped (1¼ cups)
- 1½ cups short-grain brown rice
- 1 ripe tomato, chopped, or 1 cup drained canned tomato, crushed
- 2 to 3 cloves garlic, peeled, crushed, and finely chopped (about 2 teaspoons)
- 1 small jalapeño pepper, seeded and chopped (2 teaspoons)
- ¼ cup coarsely chopped cilantro (coriander or Chinese parsley), with stems
- 1 teaspoon salt
- ¼ teaspoon freshly ground black pepper
- ¾ cup Spanish salad olives, cut into ½-inch pieces
- ⅓ cup dark raisins
- 3 cups water

1. In a large saucepan, sauté the chicken bones over medium to high heat for 15 minutes, until nicely browned.
2. Add the onion, and sauté 1 minute. Then stir in the rice.
3. Add the tomato, garlic, jalapeño, cilantro, salt, pepper, olives, raisins, and water, and bring the mixture to a boil. Reduce the heat, cover, and boil gently for 50 minutes.
4. Remove the bones. When cold enough to handle, pick the meat from them, and return it to the dish. Serve.

CLAUDINE'S FRICASSEE

My daughter, Claudine, has a favorite chicken fricassee dish, too. In her version, cooked chicken gizzards are combined with the same rice, garlic, and onion that I use, and she flavors her fricassee with cilantro, but she extends it with zucchini and eggplant.

YIELD: 6 SERVINGS

NUTRITIONAL ANALYSIS PER SERVING:

Calories 285
Protein 13 gm.
Carbohydrates 46 gm.
Fat 6.3 gm.
Saturated fat 1.3 gm.
Cholesterol 21 mg.
Sodium 841 mg.

Brown rice includes the outer layer of fiber-rich bran.

A MODERN COQ AU VIN

POULET AU VIN ROUGE IS A CLASSIC COQ AU VIN, ALTHOUGH HISTORICALLY THE "COCK"—AN OLDER CHICKEN—WAS SO TOUGH THAT IT HAD TO BE COOKED A LONG TIME; THEN THE JUICES WERE THICKENED WITH THE BLOOD OF THE CHICKEN. NOW, WITH THE TENDER CHICKENS WE HAVE AVAILABLE, THIS DISH CAN BE MADE QUICKLY. THE SKIN OF THE CHICKEN IS REMOVED AND THE MEAT COOKED IN RED WINE. HAPPILY, MOST OF THE WINE'S CALORIES DISAPPEAR THROUGH THE COOKING PROCESS.

Poulet au Vin Rouge (Chicken with Red Wine)

This is a modern version of the classic coq au vin—rich in flavor but lower in calories than the original, and much faster to make. I divide the chicken into pieces, remove the skin, brown it, and cook it in red wine, adding the breast pieces at the end so they don't overcook. The onions are glazed separately in a little olive oil and sugar, with the mushrooms added near the end of the cooking time. Finally, everything is combined and served with croutons.

- 1 chicken (3½ to 4 pounds)
- 12 small pearl onions (6 ounces), peeled
- 2 tablespoons virgin olive oil
- ½ teaspoon sugar
- ½ cup water
- 4 large mushrooms (4 ounces), quartered
- ⅓ cup finely chopped onion
- 3 cloves garlic, peeled, crushed, and finely chopped (2 teaspoons)
- 1¼ cups dry, fruity red wine
- ½ teaspoon dried thyme leaves or 1 sprig fresh thyme
- 2 bay leaves
- ¾ teaspoon salt
- ¾ teaspoon freshly ground black pepper
- 1 teaspoon potato starch dissolved in 2 tablespoons red wine (see About Potato Starch, page 394)

CROUTONS

- 4 slices white bread (4 ounces)
- 1 teaspoon canola oil
- 2 tablespoons finely chopped fresh parsley

1. Cut the chicken into four pieces (two breasts with wings and two legs). Cut off the wings, and divide them at the joints into three pieces each. Skin and bone the breasts. Set the breasts aside with the two meatier wing pieces. (Freeze the bones and wing tips for future use.) Skin the legs, and separate the thighs from the drumsticks by cutting through them at the joint. Cut the ends off the drumsticks. Leave in the thigh and drum bones. Set the legs aside with the breasts and reserved wing pieces.
2. Place the pearl onions with 1 tablespoon of the oil, the sugar, and the water in a

(continued)

TOP: TURNIPS AND MASHED POTATOES (SEE PAGE 323).
BOTTOM: *POULET AU VIN ROUGE* (CHICKEN WITH RED WINE) (ABOVE).

POULET AU VIN ROUGE (CHICKEN WITH RED WINE) (*continued*)

large saucepan, and bring to a boil over high heat. Boil for a few minutes, or until the water has evaporated and the onions start frying. Cook until the onions are browned on all sides. Add the mushrooms, and sauté for 1 minute. Set aside, covered.

3. In a large skillet, heat the remaining 1 tablespoon of oil. When hot, sauté the chicken wing pieces for 2 to 3 minutes, until lightly browned on all sides. Add the leg pieces, and brown them for 2 to 3 minutes on each side. Repeat with the breasts. Set all the chicken pieces aside.
4. To the drippings in the skillet, add the chopped onion, and sauté for 1 minute. Then add the garlic, and cook for about 10 seconds. Add the wine, thyme, bay leaves, salt, and pepper, and bring to a boil. Return the dark meat and the wings to the pan, cover, and boil very gently for 8 minutes.
5. Add the chicken breasts, and boil gently for another 7 minutes. This brings the total cooking time to 15 minutes for the dark meat and only 7 minutes for the breast meat.
6. Add the dissolved potato starch to the pan, and stir until the pan juices are thickened. Then add the pearl onions and mushrooms with their juices to the red wine sauce.

FOR THE CROUTONS

7. Preheat the oven to 400 degrees.
8. Trim the crusts from the bread, and cut the slices diagonally to form two triangles. Trim each triangle to form a heart-shaped crouton.
9. Spread the oil on a cookie sheet, and press the croutons into the oil so they are moistened on both sides. Bake at 400 degrees for 8 to 10 minutes, until nicely browned.
10. At serving time, dip the tip of each crouton in the sauce to moisten it and then into the chopped parsley. Cut the chicken breast pieces in half, and serve one piece of breast, one piece of drum or thigh meat, and one piece of wing per person with two croutons. Sprinkle the remaining chopped parsley over the chicken and garnishes.

YIELD: 4 SERVINGS

NUTRITIONAL ANALYSIS PER SERVING:

Calories 476
Protein 47 gm.
Carbohydrates 22 gm.
Fat 15.3 gm.
Saturated fat 2.8 gm.
Cholesterol 143 mg.
Sodium 717 mg.

Chicken is a relatively low-fat source of protein and a good source of niacin.

Poule au Pot (Chicken Stew)

Poule *is actually the French name for "hen," and this famous "chicken in a pot" dish originated in the sixteenth century under the rule of Henry IV. Conventionally, it is not as refined as I make it here by removing the meat from the bones and making the stock fat-free. Notice that in addition to using all the chicken meat, I use the stock in which the chicken is cooked, so no nutrients or vitamins are lost.*

- 1 chicken (about 3½ pounds)
- 4 quarts water
- 1 teaspoon dried thyme leaves
- 1 teaspoon dried rosemary
- 3 bay leaves
- 12 cloves
- 2 teaspoons salt
- 1 teaspoon black peppercorns

VEGETABLES

- 2 large leeks (about 12 ounces total), cleaned
- 4 medium onions (10 ounces total), peeled
- 4 carrots (about 1 pound), peeled
- 1 small butternut squash (1 pound), peeled, seeded, and quartered
- 1 small Savoy cabbage (about 1 pound), quartered
- 4 large mushrooms (about 4 ounces)

- 16 slices from a baguette (2 ounces total), toasted in the oven
- ½ cup grated Gruyère cheese
- *Cornichons*
- Hot mustard

1. Place the chicken, breast side down, with the neck and heart in a narrow stainless steel stockpot. (Reserve the liver to sauté or freeze for future use.) Add the water, and bring it to a boil over high heat. Reduce the heat, and boil gently for 10 minutes. Skim the cooking liquid to remove the fat and impurities that come to the surface.
2. Add the thyme, rosemary, bay leaves, cloves, salt, and peppercorns to the stock. Cover, and continue boiling gently for another 25 minutes. Remove the chicken from the pot; save the stock. When the chicken is cool enough to handle, pull off and discard the skin. Pull the meat from the bones, keeping it in the largest possible pieces. Set the meat aside, covered, in about ½ cup of the stock. Place the bones back in the remaining stock, and boil gently for another hour.

(continued)

REMOVING FAT FROM STOCK

CONVENTIONALLY, STOCK IS STRAINED THROUGH PAPER TOWELS TO ELIMINATE MOST OF THE FAT. IF TIME PERMITS, IT IS A GOOD IDEA TO CHILL THE STOCK UNTIL ANY REMAINING FAT SOLIDIFIES ON TOP. AFTER IT HARDENS, YOU CAN REMOVE AND DISCARD IT WITH EASE.

YIELD: 4 TO 6 SERVINGS

NUTRITIONAL ANALYSIS PER SERVING:

Calories 402
Protein 42 gm.
Carbohydrates 40 gm.
Fat 9.4 gm.
Saturated fat 3.5 gm.
Cholesterol 119 mg.
Sodium 1,172 mg.

Gruyère is a rich source of calcium.

POULE AU POT (CHICKEN STEW) (*continued*)

3. Strain the stock twice through a strainer lined with paper towels. Rinse out the pot, and return the stock to the pot. (You should have 8 to 9 cups. If necessary, adjust with water.)

FOR THE VEGETABLES

4. Add the leeks, onions, carrots, squash, and cabbage to the stock, and bring to a boil. Boil, covered, for 15 minutes. Add the mushrooms, and cook for another 5 minutes.
5. Reheat the meat and the surrounding liquid, and arrange the meat in the center of a large platter. Remove the vegetables with a slotted spoon, and arrange them around the chicken. Ladle some of the stock into four to six small bowls, and serve it with the baguette slices and cheese. Pass around the *cornichons* and hot mustard at the table.

POULET RÔTI (ROASTED CHICKEN)

This classic way to cook chicken is still the simplest and best method. Roasting the bird at a high temperature crystallizes the skin, so it becomes delectably crisp while it protects the flesh, keeping it moist. For best results, do not cover the chicken while it is roasting; if covered with a piece of aluminum foil, for example, it will start steaming and taste reheated when served. For maximum flavor, the chicken should be served no more than 45 minutes after roasting.

YIELD: 4 SERVINGS

NUTRITIONAL ANALYSIS PER SERVING:

Calories 428
Protein 48 gm.
Carbohydrates 0.1 gm.
Fat 24.9 gm.
Saturated fat 6.8 gm.
Cholesterol 154 mg.
Sodium 279 mg.

Discarding the chicken skin can cut the fat content in half.

- 1 chicken (about 3½ pounds)
- ¼ teaspoon salt
- ¼ teaspoon freshly ground black pepper
- 1 teaspoon virgin olive oil
- 2 to 3 tablespoons water (optional)
- 1 recipe *Coquillettes au Gruyère* (page 338), with variations indicated in steps 7 and 8 below (optional)
- 1 bunch watercress, for garnish

1. Preheat the oven to 425 degrees.
2. Sprinkle the chicken inside and out with the salt and pepper. Truss the chicken if you like, although this is not required.
3. Heat the oil in a large ovenproof nonstick skillet until it is hot but not smoking. Place the chicken on its side in the skillet, and brown it over medium to high heat for about 2½ minutes. Then turn the chicken over, and brown it on the other side for 2½ minutes.
4. Place the skillet, with the chicken still on its side, in the 425-degree oven. Roast it, uncovered, for 20 minutes. Then turn the chicken onto its other side, and roast it for another 20 minutes. Finally, turn the chicken onto its back, baste it with the fat that has emerged during the cooking, and roast it, breast side up, for 10 minutes.
5. Remove the chicken from the oven, and place it, breast side down, on a platter. Pour the drippings from the skillet into a bowl, and set them aside for a few minutes to allow the fat to rise to the top.
6. To serve, carve the chicken, separating the legs from the thighs and cutting each breast in half. Arrange a piece of dark meat and a piece of white meat on each of four plates.
7. If you *are* serving *Coquillettes au Gruyère* (Pasta Shells with Swiss Cheese), cook the pasta as directed in step 1 of the recipe on page 338, except place the ½ cup of reserved pasta-cooking liquid in the unwashed skillet used to cook the chicken. Bring to a boil, stirring to release and dissolve any solidified juices in the skillet, and place this deglazing liquid in a bowl large enough to hold the pasta.
8. Skim off about 3 tablespoons of clear fat that has risen to the top of the bowl of reserved chicken drippings, and add those tablespoons to the deglazing liquid in the large bowl instead of the olive oil in step 2. Remove and discard any remaining surface fat from the drippings, and add the defatted drippings to the large bowl. Add the drained pasta, and complete the recipe as indicated on page 338. Serve immediately with the chicken.
9. If you *are not* serving the *Coquillettes au Gruyère* with the chicken, deglaze the skillet by adding the 2 to 3 tablespoons of water and stirring to loosen and melt any solidified juices. Add to the drippings in the bowl. Skim off and discard most of the fat from the reserved drippings, and serve the defatted drippings with the chicken, garnishing each serving with a few sprigs of watercress.

REDUCING THE FAT

THE SKIN OF THE ROASTED CHICKEN CAN BE REMOVED AND DISCARDED AT THE END OF THE COOKING PERIOD, IF YOU WANT THE DISH TO BE LESS CALORIC. FROM A HEALTH STANDPOINT, IT IS ESSENTIAL THAT YOU DISCARD ALMOST ALL THE FAT THAT HAS ACCUMULATED AROUND THE CHICKEN DURING THE COOKING PROCESS, RETAINING ONLY ENOUGH TO SEASON THE *COQUILLETTES AU GRUYÈRE*, SHOULD YOU ELECT TO SERVE THEM WITH THE CHICKEN. THE SOLIDIFIED DRIPPINGS AND JUICE THAT REMAIN AFTER THE FAT IS SKIMMED OFF BECOME A FLAVORFUL SAUCE FOR THE CHICKEN.

CUTTING THE CALORIES

By removing the chicken skin from the *ballottine* slices before they are served, you can eliminate about half the calories in the dish. Don't attempt to remove the skin from the whole *ballottine* before it is sliced, since it is essentially holding the chicken together. Rather, remove and discard the skin from each slice as it is cut.

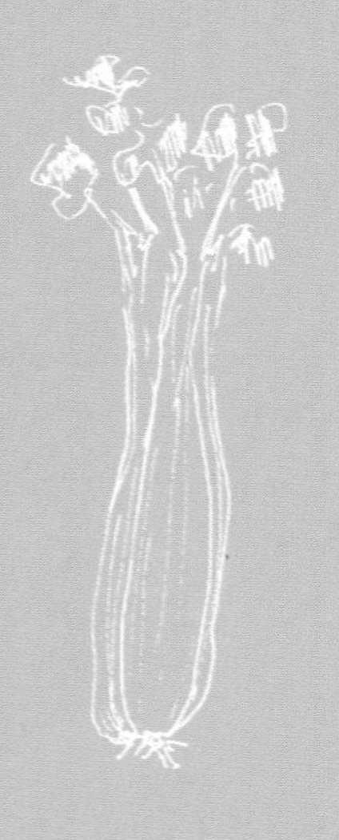

Chicken *Ballottine* Stuffed with Red Rice

A ballottine *is a whole chicken that has been boned and stuffed. This version is good family fare and also showy enough to serve company. It can be prepared up to 1 day ahead. Freeze the bones and gizzard for later use in soup or stock. When chicken is roasted at a high temperature, as here, the fat drips to the bottom of the pan and can be discarded. This dish is best cooked in a sturdy aluminum roasting pan, which assures a good crystallization of the cooking juices, used to create a sauce.*

The long-grain wehani rice used in the stuffing has a chewy texture that I love. I cook it here with mushrooms in stock and eventually flavor it with leeks and onions. The ballottine *is served with a rich wine sauce containing the defatted chicken drippings and finely diced vegetables (a* brunoise*).*

Red Rice Stuffing

- ½ cup long-grain red wehani rice
- 1¼ cups homemade unsalted and defatted chicken stock (see page 466), or lower-salt canned chicken broth
- ¼ teaspoon salt (less if using canned broth)
- ½ ounce dried mushrooms, broken into pieces
- About ½ leek (3 ounces), trimmed, washed, and sliced (1 cup)
- 1 onion (4 ounces), peeled and chopped (¾ cup)
- 1½ teaspoons virgin olive oil
- ¼ cup water

Chicken *Ballottine*

- 1 chicken (about 3¾ pounds), defatted and boned, with bones and giblets reserved for other uses (2¼ pounds boned)
- ¼ teaspoon salt
- ¼ teaspoon freshly ground black pepper

Red Wine Sauce

- Drippings from cooking the chicken
- ½ cup water
- ½ cup red wine (such as cabernet sauvignon)
- 1 stalk celery (2 ounces), peeled and cut into ¼-inch dice (½ cup)

- 1 small onion (3 ounces), peeled and chopped (½ cup)
- 1 carrot (2 ounces), peeled and cut into ¼-inch dice (⅓ cup)
- ½ teaspoon potato starch dissolved in 1 tablespoon water (see About Potato Starch, page 394)
- 1 tablespoon soy sauce
- 1 tablespoon chopped fresh parsley

For the Red Rice Stuffing

1. Place the rice, stock, salt, and mushrooms in a large saucepan. Bring the mixture to a boil, cover, reduce the heat to low, and cook for 1 hour. Set the rice aside in the pan, uncovered, to cool.
2. Meanwhile, place the leek, onion, oil, and water in a saucepan. Bring the mixture to a boil, cover, reduce the heat to low, and cook at a gentle boil for 5 minutes. Remove the lid, and continue to cook until all the moisture is gone. Add the mixture to the pan containing the rice, mix well, and cool to room temperature.

For the Chicken *Ballottine*

3. Preheat the oven to 400 degrees.
4. Sprinkle the boned chicken with the salt and pepper, and stuff it with the cool rice mixture. Then roll the chicken up, tie it securely with string, and place it in a roasting pan. Roast the *ballottine* at 400 degrees for 1 hour, then lift it from the pan, and place it on a platter.

For the Red Wine Sauce

5. Remove and discard all fat from the drippings in the pan, and add the water and wine to the drippings. Heat the mixture, stirring to loosen and melt the solidified juices in the pan, and cook for 30 seconds. Strain into a saucepan, and add the celery, onion, and carrot. Bring the mixture to a boil over high heat. Cover, reduce the heat to low, and boil gently for 5 mintues. Stir in the dissolved potato starch and soy sauce, and bring the mixture back to a boil to thicken it.
6. Transfer the *ballottine* to a cutting board, cut half of it into four or five slices, each about 1 inch thick, and remove and discard the skin from each slice. Place the uncut half of the *ballottine* on the serving platter, and arrange the cut slices in front of it. Pour the wine sauce over and around the *ballottine,* and garnish with the parsley. Cut and skin additional slices of *ballottine* as needed at the table.

Yield: 4 Servings

NUTRITIONAL ANALYSIS PER SERVING:

Calories 215
Protein 24 gm.
Carbohydrates 16 gm.
Fat 4.4 gm.
Saturated fat 0.1 gm.
Cholesterol 72 mg.
Sodium 377 mg.

Red wehani rice has four times the fiber of white rice and more potassium and phosphorus.

Stuffed and Roasted Cornish Hens

For an even leaner presentation, you can remove the skin from the hens before serving them. However, this isn't essential, since the hens are cooked at such a high temperature that most of the fat in the skin emerges and collects in the bottom of the roasting pan. Discard this liquid fat at the end of the cooking period and combine the remaining drippings with a little water to form a natural juice that is delicious with the hens.

1½ cups water
⅓ cup bulgur wheat
2 Cornish hens, about 1¼ pounds each
4 teaspoons canola oil
1 leek (4 ounces), roots and damaged or wilted leaves removed, remainder chopped (1¼ cups)
1 onion (3 ounces), chopped (about ¾ cup)
2 cloves garlic, peeled, crushed, and chopped (about 1½ teaspoons)
1 teaspoon chopped jalapeño pepper (more or less, depending on your tolerance for hotness)
1 Granny Smith apple (7 ounces), cored and cut (unpeeled) into ⅜-inch pieces (about 1¼ cups)
¼ teaspoon freshly ground black pepper
½ teaspoon salt

1. Bring 1 cup of the water to a boil in a saucepan, stir in the bulgur wheat, and set the pan aside off the heat for 1 hour. Drain. (You should have 1 cup.)
2. Preheat the oven to 425 degrees.
3. Bone the Cornish hens from the neck opening without tearing the skin. Reserve the bones to make stock or soup at another time.
4. Heat 3 teaspoons of the oil in a large skillet. When it is hot, add the leek and onion, and sauté for 2 to 3 minutes, until the vegetables are wilted and translucent. Add the garlic and jalapeño, and mix well. Stir in the apple, the black pepper, three-fourths of the salt, and the bulgur. Mix well, and cook, uncovered, over medium heat for 2 to 3 minutes, until any additional moisture in the wheat is absorbed and it is fluffy. Cool.
5. Stuff the boned hens with the cooled apple and wheat mixture, and tie the hens with twine to enclose the stuffing.

(continued)

BUYING BULGUR WHEAT

TRY TO BUY YOUR BULGUR WHEAT IN A HEALTH FOOD STORE, WHERE IT IS USUALLY MUCH LESS EXPENSIVE AND BETTER IN QUALITY THAN THAT SOLD ELSEWHERE. BE SURE TO BUY TRUE BULGUR, NOT JUST CRACKED WHEAT. THE LATTER IS UNCOOKED; THE FORMER IS CRACKED WHEAT THAT HAS BEEN STEAMED AND DRIED; IT NEEDS ONLY TO BE RECONSTITUTED IN WATER.

YIELD: 4 SERVINGS

NUTRITIONAL ANALYSIS PER SERVING:

Calories 435
Protein 36 gm.
Carbohydrates 23 gm.
Fat 21.9 gm.
Saturated fat 5.1 gm.
Cholesterol 110 mg.
Sodium 385 mg.

Bulgur is high in fiber.

utes. Drain, press (reserving the soaking liquid in the bowl), and coarsely chop the mushrooms. Set the mushrooms aside separately from the soaking liquid.

8. Heat the oils in a large skillet or saucepan. When hot, sauté the onion and celery for 3 minutes. Add the *herbes de Provence,* garlic, and mushrooms, mix well, and remove from the heat.
9. Toast the bread slices well, and cut them into ⅜-inch croutons. (You should have 3 cups.) Stir the croutons and raisins into the mixture in the skillet.
10. Pour the reserved mushroom-soaking liquid into a measuring cup, leaving behind and discarding the sandy residue in the bottom of the bowl. (You should have about ¾ cup.)
11. Add to the mixture in the skillet the salt and pepper, and toss gently to combine. Pack lightly into a loaf pan, and cover with aluminum foil. Bake at 400 degrees for 30 minutes.

FOR THE GRAVY

12. If you want to include the pureed vegetables in your gravy, push the vegetables and cooking juices from the roasting pan through a sieve or a food mill into a saucepan.
13. Let rest for 4 to 5 minutes, until most of the fat has risen to the top, and skim off as much of it as possible. (You should have approximately 2 cups of cooking juices.)
14. Add the reserved diced neck, gizzard, and heart meat, and simmer the mixture for 10 minutes to reduce it slightly. Stir in the dissolved potato starch and soy sauce until smooth.
15. Carve the turkey, and serve it with the gravy and mushroom stuffing.

YIELD: 8 TO 10 SERVINGS

NUTRITIONAL ANALYSIS PER SERVING (6 OUNCES OF TURKEY):

Calories 466
Protein 59 gm.
Carbohydrates 23 gm.
Fat 14.8 gm.
Saturated fat 3.3 gm.
Cholesterol 187 mg.
Sodium 677 mg.

ROASTED TURKEY WITH MUSHROOM STUFFING (SEE PAGE 228);
PUREE OF CARROT WITH GINGER (SEE PAGE 307).

Poached Turkey in Vegetable Consommé

Skinless, boneless turkey breasts are available now in most supermarkets around the country. Here, I cook a breast briefly in a flavorful vegetable stock composed of mushrooms, leek, carrots, turnip, celery, and water, then set the breast aside, covered, to finish cooking in the residual heat of the surrounding broth. This technique produces a very moist breast, which is a plus, since turkey breast meat is so lean that it tends to be dry if not properly cooked.

½ cup dried mushrooms (about ⅓ ounce)
7 cups (1¾ quarts) water
1 leek (6 ounces), trimmed (leaving most of the green parts), washed, and cut into ¼-inch dice (1¾ cups)
3 carrots (6 ounces), peeled and cut into ¼-inch dice (1 cup)
1 white turnip, peeled and cut into ¼-inch dice (1 cup)
2 ribs celery, cleaned and cut into ¼-inch dice (⅔ cup)
1 teaspoon salt
1 boneless turkey breast (2 pounds), skin removed
Crusty bread
Horseradish and hot mustard (optional)

1. Place the mushrooms in a large pot with the water. Bring to a boil, and immediately remove the mushrooms, retaining the liquid in the pot. Chop the mushrooms coarsely, and return them to the pot.
2. Add all the remaining vegetables and the salt to the pot, bring the mixture to a boil, and boil gently for 5 minutes. Add the breast of turkey, and bring the mixture back to a boil. Reduce the heat, cover, and boil gently for 10 minutes. Remove the pot from the heat, and let the meat and vegetables stand in the hot broth, covered, for 30 minutes. Remove the turkey to a cutting board, and slice it.
3. Place one or two slices of the turkey breast in each of four soup bowls, ladle the hot broth with vegetables on top, and serve with crusty bread. Offer horseradish and hot mustard on the side, if desired. Or the turkey slices can be transferred to side plates to be eaten with the bread, mustard, and horseradish, while the broth and vegetables are consumed separately.

Yield: 4 Servings

NUTRITIONAL ANALYSIS PER SERVING:

Calories 262
Protein 46 gm.
Carbohydrates 15 gm.
Fat 1.5 gm.
Saturated fat 0.4 gm.
Cholesterol 111 mg.
Sodium 701 mg.

Turkey breast is rich in niacin, an essential water-soluble vitamin.

Turkey Fricadelles with Vegetable Sauce

This is my variation of a dish that my wife prepares occasionally. I make a mousse with very lean ground turkey meat, an egg, and ice cubes (which make the meat sufficiently spongy and juicy). Then I quickly mix in some blanched vegetables for color and texture, and form the mixture into patties. Served with a mushroom and tomato sauce, the fricadelles *are tasty, attractive, and very low in calories.*

- ½ cup water
- 1 cup shredded or finely sliced carrot (2 ounces)
- 3 cups (lightly packed) spinach leaves, cleaned (3 ounces)
- 1 pound ground raw turkey meat
- ⅓ cup small ice cubes
- 1 egg
- ¾ teaspoon salt
- ½ teaspoon freshly ground black pepper

Vegetable Sauce

- 1 tablespoon virgin olive oil
- ¼ cup chopped onion
- 4 ounces mushrooms, cut into ¼-inch pieces (1½ cups)
- 12 ounces tomatoes, cut into ½-inch pieces (2½ cups)
- 3 cloves garlic, peeled, crushed, and chopped (2 teaspoons)
- ½ teaspoon salt

- 1 tablespoon canola oil

1. Bring the water to a boil in a saucepan. Add the carrot, and cook for 1 minute. Then add the spinach, and cook for 1 minute. Drain, reserving the cooking liquid (you should have ½ cup) for use in the sauce, and cool the vegetables.
2. Place the turkey meat, ice, and egg in the bowl of a food processor, and process for 20 seconds, scraping down the sides of the bowl after 10 seconds. Add the salt, pepper, carrots, and spinach, and process for about 5 seconds. Transfer the mixture to a bowl, and form it into four patties. Wrap the patties in plastic wrap, and refrigerate them while you make the sauce.

For the Vegetable Sauce

3. Heat the olive oil in a skillet. When it is hot but not smoking, sauté the onion over medium to high heat for 1 minute. Add the mushrooms, cook for 2 minutes, and

then add the tomatoes, garlic, and salt along with the reserved ½ cup vegetable-cooking liquid. Bring the mixture to a boil, cover, reduce the heat to low, and cook for 5 minutes.

4. About 15 minutes before serving time, heat the canola oil over medium heat in a nonstick skillet large enough to hold the turkey patties in one layer.
5. When the oil is hot, add the patties, and cook them, uncovered, for 3 minutes on one side. Turn them over, and cook them, covered, for 3 minutes on the other side. Discard the fat, and set the patties aside to rest, covered, in the skillet for 5 minutes before serving.
6. Serve one patty per person, with some sauce.

**YIELD:
4 SERVINGS**

**NUTRITIONAL
ANALYSIS
PER SERVING:**

Calories 311
Protein 24 gm.
Carbohydrates 9 gm.
Fat 19.9 gm.
Saturated fat 4.2 gm.
Cholesterol 110 mg.
Sodium 801 mg.

Turkey is a good source of tryptophan, an amino acid associated with improved sleep patterns.

750 ml

Grilled Quail on Quinoa with Sunflower Seeds

Quinoa, a grain that dates back to the Incas, is hailed as the "super grain of the future." Containing more protein than any other grain, it is a rich source of vital nutrients. Quinoa becomes almost transparent as it cooks, and has a delicate, nutty flavor. I add sautéed sunflower seeds and dried currants to the quinoa in this recipe, which also features grilled boneless quail.

Quail

- 1 medium-size shallot, peeled
- 1 large clove garlic, peeled
- 1 tablespoon *nuoc nam* (see About Southeast Asian Ingredients, page 52)
- ½ teaspoon sugar
- ¼ small jalapeño pepper
- 1 tablespoon water
- 4 boneless quail (about 4 ounces each)

Quinoa

- 2 tablespoons peanut oil
- 1 small onion (about 2 ounces), chopped (½ cup)
- 2 tablespoons sunflower (or pumpkin) seeds, hulled
- 2 tablespoons dried currants
- 1 cup (6 ounces) quinoa
- 1¾ cups homemade unsalted and defatted chicken stock (see page 466), or lower-salt canned chicken broth
- ¾ teaspoon salt (less if using canned broth)
- ¼ teaspoon freshly ground black pepper

For the Quail

1. Preheat the oven to 180 degrees (warm).
2. Place the shallot, garlic, *nuoc nam,* sugar, jalapeño, and water in a small mini-chop, and process until liquefied. Place the quail in a flat dish, and pour the marinade over the quail, turning until they are coated. Cover, and refrigerate for at least 1 hour.
3. At cooking time, place the quail on a very hot grill, and cook 2½ to 3 minutes on each side.
4. Transfer to a dish, and keep warm in a 180-degree oven until serving time (up to 45 minutes).

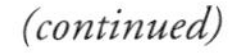

(continued)

Garbure Soup Farmer-Style

I love garbure *prepared in the classical style, but I also enjoy this lighter version containing pork shoulder as the only meat. I trim the shoulder first, removing the "skin" and surrounding fat, then cook it with a selection of vegetables based on those in the original version. Served in the traditional manner with a layer of bread and crusty cheese on top, it makes a great main course.*

About *Garbure*

Garbure is a soup from the southwest of France. Traditionally very rich, it often encompasses goose or duck confit (pieces of duck or goose poached in their own fat), a variety of sausages, pork shoulder, and other types of meat, including pig's feet.

- 1 boneless fully cooked smoked pork shoulder (about 2 pounds), trimmed of "skin" and surrounding fat (1½ pounds trimmed)
- 8 ounces dried white kidney beans
- 12 cups water
- 2 potatoes (12 ounces), peeled and cut into 1-inch pieces (1¾ cups)
- 1 leek (6 ounces), trimmed, washed, and cut into 1-inch pieces (2 cups), including most green portions
- 1 stalk celery (2 ounces), washed and cut into ½-inch pieces (1 cup)
- 3 carrots (6 ounces), peeled and cut into ½-inch pieces (1 cup)
- 3 parsnips (6 ounces), peeled and cut into ½-inch pieces (1 cup)
- 1 8-ounce piece savoy cabbage, cut into 2-inch pieces (4 cups)
- About ½ teaspoon salt (depending on the saltiness of the pork)
- 4 thin (¼-inch) slices country bread (4 ounces)
- 1½ cups (lightly packed) grated swiss cheese (5 ounces), preferably Gruyère

1. Place the pork in a large kettle, and add the beans and water. Bring the mixture to a boil over high heat, cover, reduce the heat to low, and boil gently for 1 hour.
2. Add the potatoes, leek, celery, carrots, parsnips, cabbage, and salt, and bring the mixture back to a boil. Cover, reduce the heat to low, and boil gently for 1 hour longer. By this time the meat will have separated into pieces. (You will have 4 quarts of soup. If you have less, add water to make 4 quarts.) To have 4 to 6 servings now, reserve 2 quarts (8 cups) of the soup to use within the next 2 or 3 days, or freeze it for future use.
3. At serving time, preheat a broiler. Bring 2 quarts of the soup to a boil on top of the stove, and pour it into a 2½-quart casserole dish or enameled cast-iron pot. (The

(continued)

Yield: 4 Servings

Nutritional analysis per serving:

Calories 294
Protein 23 gm.
Carbohydrates 33 gm.
Fat 8.2 gm.
Saturated fat 3.8 gm.
Cholesterol 36 mg.
Sodium 769 mg.

Pork is high in thiamine, iron, and vitamin B_{12}. Carrots are high in beta-carotene. White kidney beans and parsnips are high in folacin.

Garbure Soup Farmer-Style (above) with assorted breads (see pages 477–81).

pot should be nearly full.) Arrange the bread slices on top to cover the soup in one layer, and push them gently into the liquid until they are moist.

4. Sprinkle the cheese on top, and place the dish under the hot broiler, about 4 inches from the heat. Broil for about 10 minutes, until the cheese on top is bubbly and brown. Carry the dish to the table, and serve in 4 to 6 bowls or soup plates.

SLOW-COOKED PORK ROAST

Often people don't realize that some cuts of pork—such as the loin and fillet I use here—are lean and very low in cholesterol and fat. This boneless sirloin roast from the end of the loin where it attaches to the fillet (or tenderloin) is so lean, in fact, that it would be dry if cooked in a conventional manner.

YIELD: 6 SERVINGS

NUTRITIONAL ANALYSIS PER SERVING:

Calories 208
Protein 24 gm.
Carbohydrates 4 gm.
Fat 10.1 gm.
Saturated fat 2.8 gm.
Cholesterol 72 mg.
Sodium 400 mg.

Pork provides excellent protein, and this sirloin roast has relatively few calories.

SPICY SOY MARINADE

- **2 tablespoons soy sauce**
- **1 tablespoon honey**
- **½ teaspoon dry mustard**
- **½ teaspoon ground ginger**
- **1 teaspoon cumin powder**
- **¼ teaspoon cayenne pepper**
- **1 tablespoon canola oil**

PORK ROAST

- **1 boneless pork sirloin roast, about 1½ pounds, trimmed of all surface fat**
- **About 1 cup water**

1. Preheat the oven to 275 degrees.
2. Mix all the marinade ingredients together in a small bowl.
3. Place the roast in a roasting pan, and rub it on all sides with the marinade. Roast it at 275 degrees for 2 hours, turning the meat in the juices every 45 minutes and adding a few tablespoons of water to the pan if a little additional moisture is needed.
4. When the roast reaches an internal temperature of 155 degrees, remove it, and add enough water to the pan to create about ½ cup of juice.
5. Cut the roast into ¼-inch slices, and serve three slices per person with a generous spoonful of the juice.

√

Puerto Rican Pork and Beans

My wife, Gloria, is of Puerto Rican ancestry, and she often prepares this type of dish when we have guests, especially family visiting from Europe. A satisfying, one-dish meal, it can be cooked ahead and frozen, and it is even better reheated.

Buy the meatiest, leanest country-style spareribs you can find. Note that the cilantro stems are cooked with the beans to give them an unusual and definitive flavor, and then the leaves are added at the end. We particularly like the flavor of cilantro, but if you object to its taste, omit it from the recipe.

- 1 tablespoon canola oil
- 4 country-style pork loin spareribs (about 1½ pounds)
- 4 cups cold water
- 1 medium carrot, peeled and cut into ½-inch cubes (about ½ cup)
- 2 medium onions (about 10 ounces total), peeled and cut into ½-inch cubes (2 cups)
- 6 cloves garlic, peeled, crushed, and chopped (about 1 tablespoon)
- 3 bay leaves
- 1 teaspoon dried oregano
- 1 can (1 pound) whole tomatoes
- 1 small jalapeño pepper, chopped (about 2 teaspoons)
- 2 teaspoons salt
- 1 pound dried red kidney beans, sorted to remove any stones and washed
- 1 bunch cilantro (coriander or Chinese parsley), stems and leaves chopped separately (¼ cup chopped stems, 2 teaspoons chopped leaves)

1. Heat the oil in a sturdy saucepan. When it is hot, add the pork in one layer, and cook it over medium heat for about 30 minutes, turning it until it is brown on all sides.
2. Add all the remaining ingredients except the chopped cilantro leaves. Bring to a boil, reduce the heat to low, cover, and simmer gently for 1¾ to 2 hours, until the meat is tender.
3. Divide among four individual plates, sprinkle with the chopped cilantro leaves, and serve with Yellow Rice with Orange Rind (see page 344).

Yield: 4 Servings

NUTRITIONAL ANALYSIS PER SERVING:

Calories 767
Protein 46 gm.
Carbohydrates 82 gm.
Fat 29.7 gm.
Saturated fat 9.6 gm.
Cholesterol 85 mg.
Sodium 1,400 mg.

Kidney beans are an excellent source of iron and soluble fiber. Pork is a good source of thiamine, a B-complex vitamin needed for a healthy nervous system.

ALTERNATIVE TO GRILLING

IF YOU DON'T HAVE ACCESS TO A GRILL, SAUTÉ SIX PATTIES AT A TIME IN A NONSTICK PAN, COOKING THEM IN 2 TEASPOONS OF SAFFLOWER OIL FOR ABOUT 5 MINUTES ON EACH SIDE.

Saucisses au Chou (Sausages with Savoy Cabbage) on Lentils

It is best to buy a lean piece of pork and grind it yourself for the sausage patties in this recipe. Be sure to mix the sausage ingredients at least 2 hours and up to 1 day ahead so the seasonings can flavor the meat well. Highly seasoned with coriander, cumin, and hot pepper, the patties are wrapped in blanched savoy cabbage leaves, so the meat stays juicy as it cooks. Lentils, very high in soluble fibers, are cooked with seasonings here and then combined with a little olive oil, garlic, pepper, Tabasco, and mustard. They could also be served on their own as a first course or as a meat accompaniment.

Sausage Patties

- 1¼ pounds lean ground pork
- 1½ teaspoons salt
- ¼ teaspoon freshly ground black pepper
- ¾ teaspoon fennel seeds
- ½ teaspoon ground coriander seeds
- ½ teaspoon ground cumin
- ⅛ teaspoon cayenne pepper
- ⅛ teaspoon ground allspice
- ½ cup coarsely chopped mushrooms (about 2 ounces)

Cabbage

- 6 cups water
- 6 large outer leaves from a savoy cabbage (about 10 ounces)

Lentils

- ½ pound (1 cup) lentils
- 3 cups water
- 2 small onions (3 ounces), peeled and chopped (¾ cup)
- 4 large cloves garlic, peeled, crushed, and finely chopped (3 teaspoons)
- 2 bay leaves
- ¾ teaspoon salt
- ¼ cup virgin olive oil
- ¼ teaspoon freshly ground black pepper
- ¼ teaspoon Tabasco hot pepper sauce
- 1½ tablespoons Dijon-style mustard

- 1 tablespoon chopped fresh parsley or cilantro (coriander or Chinese parsley)

For the Sausage Patties

1. Thoroughly mix the sausage ingredients in a bowl, and refrigerate, covered. (If you prepare the meat 1 day ahead, reserve the mushrooms, which might darken and discolor the mixture, and mix them in just before forming the mixture into patties.)

For the Cabbage

2. In a large saucepan, bring the 6 cups of water to a boil, add the cabbage leaves, and bring the water back to a boil.
3. Cook the cabbage for 5 minutes, until soft but still firm. Drain, and refresh under cool water.
4. Cut each leaf on either side of the center stem. Discard the stems (or add them to soup). Form the sausage mixture into twelve patties about 1½ to 2 ounces each, and wrap each patty in a piece of cooked cabbage leaf.

For the Lentils

5. Wash the lentils under cool, running water, and place them in a pot with the 3 cups of water, the onions, 2 teaspoons of the chopped garlic, the bay leaves, and the salt.
6. Bring to a boil, cover, and boil gently for 20 to 25 minutes. The lentils should be tender and a little wet; if an excess of liquid remains, drain it off. (One cup of raw lentils will yield 3 cups of cooked lentils.)
7. Add the oil, the remaining teaspoon of garlic, the black pepper, the Tabasco, and the mustard, and mix well. Set aside.

To Cook the Patties

8. Place the patties on a hot, well-cleaned grill, and cook for about 5 minutes on each side.
9. To serve, divide the lentils among six plates, and arrange two sausage patties on each plate. Sprinkle with the chopped parsley, and serve immediately.

Yield: 6 Servings

NUTRITIONAL ANALYSIS PER SERVING:

Calories 381
Protein 30 gm.
Carbohydrates 27 gm.
Fat 17 gm.
Saturated fat 3.8 gm.
Cholesterol 63 mg.
Sodium 1,004 mg.

Pork is remarkably rich in thiamine, a B-complex vitamin essential for nerve functioning. Lentils provide soluble fiber and iron.

√ Fillet of Pork *Charcutière*

For this classic pork recipe, pork fillets are trimmed of all fat, so they have no more cholesterol than chicken breasts and are also relatively low in calories. The acidic sauce served with the pork is particularly complementary. It consists of dried tomatoes and the liquid used to reconstitute them, onions, garlic, scallions, white wine, and cornichons *(see About* Cornichons*).*

1 cup water
1 ounce dried tomatoes
1 tablespoon unsalted butter
1 tablespoon virgin olive oil
2 pork fillets (about 10 ounces each), totally trimmed of fat and sinew and cut into 4 equal pieces (about 16 ounces total, trimmed)
½ cup red onion, cut into ¼-inch dice
1 teaspoon chopped garlic
⅓ cup minced scallions
¼ cup dry white wine
1 teaspoon Dijon-style mustard
¼ cup sliced *cornichons* (French-style gherkins)
¼ teaspoon salt
¼ teaspoon Tabasco hot pepper sauce

1. Bring the water to a boil in a saucepan, add the dried tomatoes, and set aside for 30 to 45 minutes. Drain, reserving the soaking liquid (about ½ cup), and cut the tomatoes into ½-inch pieces. (You should have about 1 cup.)
2. Heat the butter and oil in a heavy skillet. When they are hot, add the meat, and sauté it on one side for 4 to 5 minutes. Then turn it over, cover the pan, reduce the heat, and cook the pork another 5 minutes.
3. Remove the meat to a plate, cover it, and set it aside to continue cooking in its own residual heat.
4. Add the onion, garlic, and scallions to the skillet, and sauté over medium to high heat for 1 minute. Stir in the wine, and cook for 30 seconds. Add the reconstituted tomato pieces and their reserved soaking liquid. Bring to a boil, and boil for 2 minutes to reduce the liquid. Then stir in the mustard, *cornichons,* salt, and Tabasco.
5. Arrange some of the sauce on top of and around each piece of meat, and serve with Gnocchi *Maison* (see page 340), if desired.

TOP: CHICKEN SUPREME KIEV-STYLE (SEE PAGE 212).
BOTTOM: FILLET OF PORK *CHARCUTIÈRE* (ABOVE) ACCOMPANIED BY GNOCCHI *MAISON* (SEE PAGE 340).

ABOUT *CORNICHONS*

CORNICHONS ARE TINY FRENCH-STYLE GHERKINS PRESERVED IN VINEGAR. IF THESE ARE NOT AVAILABLE AT A SPECIALTY FOOD STORE IN YOUR AREA, SUBSTITUTE STANDARD COMMERCIAL OR HOMEMADE DILL PICKLES TO LEND CRUNCH AND FLAVOR TO THE DISH.

YIELD: 4 SERVINGS

NUTRITIONAL ANALYSIS PER SERVING:

Calories 232
Protein 26 gm.
Carbohydrates 9 gm.
Fat 9.5 gm.
Saturated fat 3.2 gm.
Cholesterol 81 mg.
Sodium 448 mg.

Pork fillets are high in iron and vitamin B_{12}.

SMOKED PORK ROAST WITH MUSTARD-HONEY GLAZE

Guests will love to help themselves to this flavorful glazed pork roast. Served with Braised Sour Cabbage (see page 305) and a simple salad, it makes a wonderful party menu.

1 smoked picnic pork shoulder, bone in (about 6¼ pounds)

GLAZE

2 tablespoons honey
2 teaspoons dry mustard
½ teaspoon paprika
⅛ teaspoon cayenne pepper

½ cup water
1 tablespoon cider vinegar

1. Place the pork shoulder in a stockpot, and cover it with enough cold water to extend ½ inch above the meat. Bring the water to 180 degrees (this will take about 15 to 20 minutes), and cook at 180 to 190 degrees for 1¼ hours. (Watch the temperature closely; the liquid should not boil.)
2. Meanwhile, in a small bowl, mix together the honey, mustard, paprika, and cayenne. Set aside.
3. Preheat the oven to 375 degrees.
4. Let the pork cool in the cooking liquid, and then trim it, removing most of the exterior fat and rind from around the bones. Trim, also, the surface of the meat that is dark and leathery. Score the top of the ham every ¾ inch, and spread the glaze over the surface.
5. Place the pork in a roasting pan or saucepan, and roast at 375 degrees for 1 hour. The surface should be nicely browned.
6. Transfer the meat to a serving platter, and add the water and vinegar to the drippings in the pan. Using a wooden spatula, scrape the bottom of the pan to dissolve any solidified cooking juices, and mix them with the water and vinegar. Strain the juices over the pork shoulder, and serve, slicing it at the table.

RIGHT: SMOKED PORK ROAST WITH HONEY-MUSTARD GLAZE (ABOVE).
LEFT: BRAISED SOUR CABBAGE (SEE PAGE 305).

ABOUT SMOKED PORK SHOULDER

SMOKED PORK SHOULDERS, OFTEN CALLED PICNIC HAMS, ARE AVAILABLE AT MOST SUPERMARKETS. TO ENHANCE THE TASTE OF THIS "FULLY COOKED" CUT, RECOOK IT IN WATER KEPT AT 180 TO 190 DEGREES; THE WATER WILL DRAW SALT FROM THE MEAT AND MAKE IT SUBSTANTIALLY MORE MOIST AND FLAVORFUL. TAKE CARE THAT THE WATER DOESN'T EXCEED THIS 180- TO 190-DEGREE RANGE, HOWEVER, OR THE HAM MAY SPLIT OPEN AND ACTUALLY LOSE MOISTURE.

YIELD: 10 SERVINGS

NUTRITIONAL ANALYSIS PER SERVING:

Calories 238
Protein 33 gm.
Carbohydrates 4 gm.
Fat 9.3 gm.
Saturated fat 3.1 gm.
Cholesterol 63 mg.
Sodium est. 1,000 mg.

Couscous of Lamb

Couscous is usually served with meat, but it is sometimes combined with fish and vegetables, vegetables alone, or even fruit and sugar for a dessert not unlike rice pudding. When prepared as it is customarily with lamb or chicken, couscous is almost always served with a hot sauce, called harissa *or* arissa, *which is a puree of hot peppers. I make my own* harissa *here, but it can be purchased in cans at some supermarkets and most specialty food stores. Some of this puree is mixed with the broth created by the stew, and the remainder is served with the dish itself.*

About Couscous

Couscous is a national dish of the Maghreb, the fertile strip of land in North Africa comprising Morocco, Algeria, and Tunisia. There are variations among the couscous made in Algeria (which has tomato), Tunisia (which tends to be the hottest), and Morocco (which uses saffron). The dish is named for the wheat semolina that is one of its ingredients. The grain is classically prepared in a *couscoussier* through a long, complicated steaming process. To simplify matters, I customarily use the instant couscous found in supermarkets, which is quite good.

Harissa

- 2 ounces dried red chili pods (anchos) (6 to 8 peppers)
- 5 cups cold water
- 8 cloves garlic, peeled
- 2 tablespoons virgin olive oil
- 1 tablespoon tomato paste
- ¼ teaspoon cayenne pepper
- ½ teaspoon salt

Stew

- 1½ pounds very lean lamb (preferably from the shank or shoulder), cut into 1½-inch chunks
- 3 cups water
- 5 cloves garlic, peeled
- 1 piece fresh ginger about the same size as the combined garlic cloves, peeled
- 2 teaspoons cumin powder
- 2 teaspoons salt
- 2 tablespoons tomato paste
- 2 tablespoons homemade (or canned) *harissa*
- 1 large onion (8 ounces), peeled and sliced
- ½ pound kohlrabies or white turnips (about 2), peeled and cut into 1½-inch chunks
- 1 small butternut squash (about 12 ounces), peeled, seeded, and cut into 1½-inch chunks
- 1 small eggplant (about 8 ounces), trimmed and cut into 1½-inch chunks
- 2 carrots (about 3 ounces), peeled and cut into 1½-inch chunks
- 1 ripe tomato (about 8 ounces), cut in half, seeded, and cut into 1-inch dice
- 1 medium zucchini (about 6 ounces), cut into 1½-inch chunks
- 1 can (16 ounces) chickpeas (garbanzo beans)

COUSCOUS

- 1¾ cups water
- ¼ teaspoon freshly ground black pepper
- ¼ teaspoon salt
- ⅓ stick unsalted butter
- 2 cups instant couscous
- 4 ounces (about ¾ cup) dried figs, cut into ½-inch pieces

FOR THE *HARISSA*

1. Place the peppers in a bowl with the water. Set a plate on top to hold the peppers underwater, and let them soak overnight.
2. Remove the peppers from the water, and reserve ½ cup of the soaking water. Pull out and discard the pepper stems, and cut the peppers into 1-inch pieces. Place some of the pepper pieces in a mini-chop with some of the garlic, some of the oil, and a little of the pepper-soaking water, and process until pureed. Remove to a bowl. Process (in batches, if necessary) the remainder of the peppers with the remainder of the garlic, oil, and soaking liquid, and combine with the puree in the bowl. Add the tomato paste, cayenne, and salt to the puree, mix well, and place in a jar. (See Using *Harissa.*)

FOR THE STEW

3. If you like mild-flavored lamb, cover the lamb chunks with cold water, bring to a boil, drain in a colander, and rinse under cold water. Eliminate this step if you like stronger-flavored lamb.
4. Place the lamb in a large dutch oven or pot, and add the 3 cups of water. Puree the garlic cloves and ginger together in a mini-chop or food processor (you will have about ¼ cup), and add the puree to the dutch oven with the cumin powder, salt, tomato paste, and *harissa.*
5. Bring the mixture to a boil, and boil gently, covered, for 45 minutes. Add the onion, kohlrabies, butternut squash, eggplant, and carrots. Return to a boil, and boil gently for 15 minutes. Then add the tomato, zucchini, and chickpeas with their liquid. Return to a boil, and boil gently for 15 minutes longer. Set aside until serving time.

FOR THE COUSCOUS

6. Bring the water to a boil in a small saucepan, and add the pepper and salt. Meanwhile, melt the butter in a larger saucepan, add the couscous, and stir until the grains are coated with butter. Stir in the figs, and then mix in the seasoned boiling water. Stir well, cover, and set aside for about 10 minutes.

(continued)

USING *HARISSA*

MY RECIPE MAKES ABOUT 1 CUP OF FIERY *HARISSA* SAUCE, MORE THAN YOU WILL NEED FOR SERVING WITH THE COUSCOUS OF LAMB. REFRIGERATE THE REMAINDER (IT WILL KEEP FOR WEEKS), AND SERVE IT AS A SEASONING FOR STEWS, SOUPS, OR VEGETABLE DISHES.

YIELD: 4 SERVINGS

NUTRITIONAL ANALYSIS PER SERVING:

Calories 924
Protein 57 gm.
Carbohydrates 134 gm.
Fat 18.4 gm.
Saturated fat 7.6 gm.
Cholesterol 129 mg.
Sodium 1,817 mg.

Couscous, the grain, is a complex carbohydrate, the cornerstone of healthful eating.

Couscous of Lamb (*continued*)

For the *Harissa* Sauce

7. At serving time, place 1 cup of broth from the hot lamb stew into a serving bowl, and add about 2 tablespoons (depending on the hotness you desire) of the remaining homemade *harissa.* Stir well, and place the sauce on the table so guests can, at their discretion, add this to the stew.
8. To serve, fluff the couscous, and mound it on individual plates. Make a well in the center of each mound, and fill with a few pieces of meat, vegetables, and juice. Serve immediately.

Irish Lamb Stew

In this recipe, I cook the vegetable garnishes separately in water. That water, which contains all the vegetables' nutrients, is then used to cook the lamb. The trimmings from these vegetables are added to the stew and become the thickening agent for a gravy made from the natural cooking juices. This makes for a flavorful and hearty dish that is also low in calories and fat.

1½ pounds potatoes
3 carrots (about 10 ounces)
3 to 4 ribs celery (about 5 ounces)
3 cups water
1½ pounds lamb from the leg or shoulder, well trimmed and cut into 1-inch cubes
2 medium onions (about 8 ounces), peeled and quartered
3 large cloves garlic, peeled
3 sprigs fresh thyme or 1 teaspoon dried thyme
2 bay leaves
1 teaspoon salt
½ teaspoon freshly ground black pepper
2 teaspoons Worcestershire sauce
1 tablespoon chopped fresh parsley

1. Peel the potatoes, and cut them into eighteen pieces of about equal size. Round off the cut corners of each potato piece, and reserve the trimmings. (You should have about 2 cups of trimmings and eighteen small, "roundish" potatoes, all approximately the same size.) Peel the carrots, and cut them into sticks 1¾ inches long by ½ inch thick. Trim the celery ribs (reserving the trimmings), and cut them into sticks 2 inches long by ½ inch wide.
2. Place the potatoes in a saucepan, and add the water. Bring to a boil, reduce the heat, and boil gently, covered, for 12 minutes. Drain, reserving the cooking liquid, and set the potatoes aside. Return the reserved cooking liquid to the saucepan, add the carrots and celery, and bring back to a boil. Boil gently for 5 minutes. Drain, reserving the cooking liquid. (You should have about 2 cups of liquid; adjust with water as needed.)
3. Place the lamb in a dutch oven or cooking pot with a tight lid, and add the reserved cooking liquid and the potato and celery trimmings. Then stir in the onions, garlic, thyme, bay leaves, salt, pepper, and Worcestershire sauce, and bring to a boil. Reduce the heat, cover, and boil gently for 45 minutes.
4. Remove the meat. Push the cooking juices and vegetable pieces through a food mill (or process momentarily in a food processor), and place them back in the pot with the meat. Add the reserved small potatoes, the celery, and the carrot sticks to the pot, and bring to a boil. Simmer 5 minutes.
5. Sprinkle with parsley, and serve immediately.

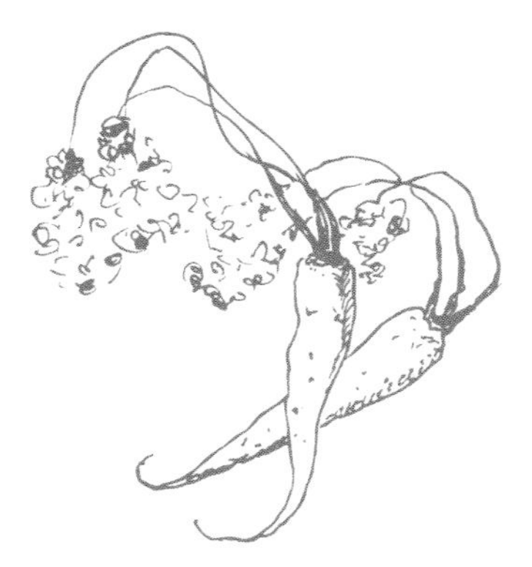

YIELD:
6 SERVINGS

NUTRITIONAL ANALYSIS PER SERVING:

Calories 255
Protein 26 gm.
Carbohydrates 25 gm.
Fat 5.4 gm.
Saturated fat 1.9 gm.
Cholesterol 73 mg.
Sodium 498 mg.

This dish is high in complex carbohydrates and fiber.

Grilled Lamb Chops Riviera

This dish is named Riviera because it is prepared in the style of the French Riviera, where tomatoes, eggplant, and olives are common ingredients, along with spinach, which serves here as a base for the lamb chops. I prepare only one chop per person, selecting chops 1¾ inches thick with a trimmed weight of 6 ounces, which provides about 3 to 4 ounces of meat per serving.

I like the taste of grilled meat, so I cook these outside on a hot grill in summer. To broil the chops instead, place them about 3 inches from the heat, and cook them for about 4 minutes on each side. Let them rest in a warm oven before serving, as instructed in the recipe.

- **2 tablespoons virgin olive oil**
- **1 small onion (about 3 ounces), peeled and chopped (½ cup)**
- **3 cloves garlic, peeled, crushed, and chopped (2 teaspoons)**
- **1 pound spinach, trimmed of tough stems and washed (12 ounces trimmed)**
- **1¼ teaspoons salt**
- **½ teaspoon freshly ground black pepper**
- **6 plum tomatoes (about 12 ounces), peeled, seeded, and cut into ½-inch pieces (1½ cups)**
- **1 eggplant (about 1 pound), ends trimmed and remainder cut into 4 slices, each 1 inch thick**
- **4 loin lamb chops (about 2 pounds), each about 1¾ inches thick, trimmed of all surrounding fat (about 1 pound, 8 ounces, trimmed)**
- **16 oil-cured black olives**

1. Preheat a grill. Preheat the oven to 350 degrees. Preheat a second oven to 160 degrees.
2. Heat 1 tablespoon of the olive oil in a large skillet. When the oil is hot, add the onion, and sauté it for 1 minute. Stir in the garlic, then add the spinach, ½ tea-

(continued)

Top: Potato *Gaufrettes* (see page 328).
Bottom: Grilled Lamb Chops Riviera (above).

spoon of the salt, and ¼ teaspoon of the pepper. Cover and cook for 1 minute over high heat, just until the spinach wilts. Mix well, bringing the garlic and onions to the top so they don't burn, cover, and continue cooking over medium heat for another 4 minutes. Transfer the spinach mixture to a bowl, and keep it warm until serving time.

3. Add the tomatoes to the unwashed skillet along with ¼ teaspoon of the salt. Cover, and cook for about 1 minute over medium heat, just long enough to heat through. Set aside, covered, until serving time.
4. Sprinkle the eggplant slices with ¼ teaspoon of the salt, and brush them lightly on both sides with about 2½ teaspoons of the oil. Place the slices on the rack of the grill, and cook them for a total of 4 minutes, turning them once midway through, so they are nicely marked by the grill on both sides. Transfer the slices to a tray, and place them in the 350-degree oven for at least 10 minutes to finish cooking.
5. Meanwhile, sprinkle the lamb chops with the remaining ¼ teaspoon salt and ¼ teaspoon pepper. Brush them on both sides with the remaining ½ teaspoon oil, and place them on the rack of the grill. Cook them for a total of 7 to 8 minutes, turning them occasionally, until they are nicely browned on both sides. Arrange the chops on a tray, and place them in the 160-degree oven for at least 15 minutes and as long as 30 minutes, to finish cooking. (If your chops are thinner, cook them for proportionately less time.)
6. At serving time, spread the spinach on four warmed plates, and divide the tomatoes among the plates, sprinkling them on top of the spinach. Arrange a slice of eggplant in the center of each plate, and place a lamb chop on top of each slice. Place 4 olives on each plate. Spoon any natural juices from the lamb over the chops, and serve immediately.

YIELD: 4 SERVINGS

NUTRITIONAL ANALYSIS PER SERVING:

Calories 352
Protein 30 gm.
Carbohydrates 17 gm.
Fat 19.3 gm.
Saturated fat 4.1 gm.
Cholesterol 81 mg.
Sodium 1,161 mg.

Plum tomatoes provide vitamins A and C. Eggplant is a good source of plant fiber. Lamb chops are rich in iron and zinc.

Grilled Leg of Lamb

In this recipe, a mini-chop comes in handy to reduce the marinade ingredients to a puree. Marinate the lamb for at least a few hours and up to a day before grilling it. If you don't have a grill, you can cook the meat under your oven broiler. After grilling, transfer the lamb to a warm oven, where it finishes cooking in its own residual heat.

Marinade

- **24 mint leaves (about ⅓ cup, lightly packed)**
- **½ small jalapeño pepper**
- **1 piece ginger about the size of a large olive, peeled**
- **2 cloves garlic, peeled**
- **2 tablespoons apricot jam**
- **1 tablespoon soy sauce**
- **3 tablespoons water**

- **1 1½-pound-piece boneless lamb from the back leg, trimmed of most of the fat**

1. Place the mint leaves, jalapeño, ginger, garlic, jam, soy sauce, and water in the bowl of a mini-chop, and process until liquefied.
2. Transfer to a plastic bag. Place the lamb in the bag with the seasonings, and seal the bag. Refrigerate for at least 2 hours or overnight to allow the meat to macerate in the seasonings.
3. To cook, remove the lamb from the bag, and dry it off with paper towels.
4. Preheat the oven to 200 degrees.
5. Place the lamb on a grill over very high heat for about 7 minutes on each side. Transfer the meat to a roasting pan, pour the reserved marinade around it, and place it in the 200-degree oven for at least 15 minutes.
6. Slice, and serve with some of the juices.

Yield: 4 Servings

NUTRITIONAL ANALYSIS PER SERVING:

Calories 276
Protein 37 gm.
Carbohydrates 8 gm.
Fat 10.0 gm.
Saturated fat 3.5 gm.
Cholesterol 114 mg.
Sodium 349 mg.

This recipe uses a flavorful marinade containing no fat.

Roasted Leg of Lamb

This classic French bourgeois dish is great for entertaining, since even a small leg of lamb like this will easily serve eight people. Garlic slivers are customarily inserted into the flesh of the leg before it is cooked. In addition, I add a garnish of flavored bread crumbs, patting them onto the leg to form a beautiful coating. Leftovers can be served cold the following day with a salad.

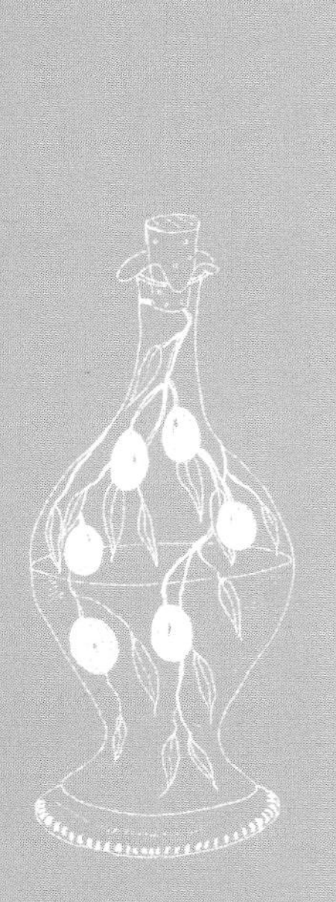

Yield: 8 Servings

Nutritional analysis per serving:

Calories 298
Protein 39 gm.
Carbohydrates 8 gm.
Fat 11.2 gm.
Saturated fat 3.4 gm.
Cholesterol 117 mg.
Sodium 241 mg.

The heme iron found in lamb and other animal sources is absorbed better than the nonheme iron found in vegetables.

- **1 small leg of spring lamb (5 pounds with shank and pelvis bone), trimmed of most visible fat, with pelvis bone removed (about 4 pounds, trimmed)**
- **12 small slivers of garlic from one very large or 2 medium-size cloves of garlic**
- **1½ tablespoons virgin olive oil**
- **¼ teaspoon salt**
- **¼ teaspoon freshly ground black pepper**
- **2 cloves garlic, peeled**
- **3 shallots, peeled**
- **1½ cups (loose) fresh flat-leaf parsley leaves**
- **4 to 5 slices firm-textured white bread, processed in a food processor to make crumbs (2 cups)**

1. Preheat the oven to 425 degrees.
2. Make twelve small, randomly placed incisions about ½ inch deep on both sides of the leg of lamb, and insert a garlic sliver in each incision. Rub the leg with ½ tablespoon of the oil. Combine the salt and pepper, and sprinkle on the lamb. Place the leg top side down in a roasting pan, and roast it at 425 degrees for 15 minutes.
3. Meanwhile, place the peeled garlic, shallots, and parsley in the bowl of a food processor, and process until finely chopped. Place the bread crumbs in a bowl, and gently stir in the processed mixture and the remaining tablespoon of oil, mixing just long enough to moisten the crumbs. (Don't overmix; the mixture should be loose, not gooey or lumpy.)
4. After 15 minutes, turn over the leg of lamb, and pat the bread mixture on top. Reduce the oven temperature to 400 degrees, and cook the lamb for another 30 minutes, until it reaches an internal temperature of about 130 degrees. Let it rest in a lukewarm place (on top of the stove or in a 180-degree oven) for 20 minutes before carving.

TOP: ROASTED LEG OF LAMB (ABOVE).
BOTTOM: LAMB SHANKS AND BEANS MULLIGAN (SEE PAGE 257).

Long-Roasted Lamb

Although I usually serve leg of lamb rare, I occasionally enjoy it long-roasted until well done. Flavored with an anchovy-garlic mixture, the lamb is browned and then cooked slowly until tender on top of the stove in a dutch oven or pot with a tight lid. This represents a different and delicious way of preparing leg of lamb.

1 3½-pound boneless leg of lamb roast, as lean as possible
5 to 6 cloves garlic, peeled, crushed, and chopped (1 tablespoon)
4 anchovy fillets, coarsely chopped
1 teaspoon *herbes de Provence* (see page 467)
½ teaspoon salt
1 tablespoon virgin olive oil
2 onions (12 ounces), peeled and cut into 1-inch pieces (2 cups)
½ cup water
1 tablespoon chopped fresh chives

1. If the lamb roast is rolled and tied, cut the string and unroll it; if it is not rolled, lay it as flat as possible. Trim off most of the fat and sinews. (The trimmed weight should be about 2¼ pounds.) Combine the garlic, anchovies, and *herbes de Provence* in a small bowl, and spread the mixture on what will be the interior of the roast after you roll it. Roll the roast up, and tie it securely with kitchen twine. Sprinkle the exterior of the roast with the salt.
2. Heat the oil in a cast-iron dutch oven or similar pot with a tight lid. When the oil is hot, add the roast, and brown it over medium heat, partially covered (to prevent spattering), for 30 minutes, turning the meat occasionally with tongs so it browns evenly on all sides.
3. Add the onions and water, bring to a boil, cover the pan completely with the lid, and reduce the heat to very low. Continue to cook the roast for 2½ hours.
4. Pour the cooking liquid into a measuring cup. (You will have about 2 cups.) Let it rest for a few minutes, then scoop as much fat as possible from the top (about ⅓ cup). Return the remaining liquid to the pan containing the roast to serve as a natural sauce with the meat.
5. Cut the meat into slices, and arrange on a platter. Pour the sauce around and on top of the meat, and sprinkle with the chives. Serve.

YIELD: 8 SERVINGS

NUTRITIONAL ANALYSIS PER SERVING:

Calories 290
Protein 42 gm.
Carbohydrates 4 gm.
Fat 10.9 gm.
Saturated fat 3.5 gm.
Cholesterol 128 mg.
Sodium 335 mg.

Anchovies are a good source of omega-3 fatty acids, which decrease blood cholesterol.

Fricassee of Veal

This recipe could serve as many as eight or as few as four, depending on the size of your guests' appetites and how extensive the menu is. For this type of dish, it is best to make a large quantity; you can divide it afterward and freeze a portion for later.

I finish this classic dish with cream, but that can be omitted, and the dish can be served simply with the garnishes of onions and mushrooms.

VEAL FOR A FRICASSEE

BE SURE TO USE LEAN MEAT FROM THE SHOULDER, CHUCK, OR SHANK HERE. MEAT FROM THESE PARTS OF THE ANIMAL WILL RETAIN ITS MOISTNESS WHEN STEWED AND WILL BE MUCH LESS EXPENSIVE THAN MEAT FROM THE BACK LEG (TOP OR BOTTOM ROUND), WHICH IS GOOD FOR SCALLOPINI BUT DRY PREPARED IN THIS MANNER.

- **1 tablespoon canola oil**
- **1 tablespoon unsalted butter**
- **2 pounds very lean veal from the shoulder, chuck, or shank, cut into 12 large cubes (2 inches each)**
- **4 medium onions (12 ounces total), peeled and chopped (2½ cups)**
- **2 tablespoons all-purpose flour**
- **1½ cups water**
- **1 bouquet garni (see Bouquet Garni, page 468)**
- **¾ teaspoon salt**
- **5 cloves garlic, peeled, crushed, and coarsely chopped (1½ tablespoons)**

GARNISHES

- **½ pound (12 to 15) pearl onions, peeled**
- **½ cup water**
- **½ pound mushrooms (domestic and/or wild), washed**
- **⅓ cup heavy cream**

1. Heat the oil and butter in a sturdy saucepan or dutch oven. When they are hot, add the meat, and cook it over medium to low heat for 20 minutes, turning it often, until browned on all sides.
2. Add the chopped onions, and cook for 5 minutes. Then add the flour, and cook for 1 minute longer. Stir in the water, bouquet garni, salt, and garlic. Bring to a boil, cover, and boil gently for 1 hour. (The recipe can be prepared to this point up to one day ahead, cooled, and refrigerated.)

FOR THE GARNISHES

3. Place the pearl onions and water in a saucepan. Bring to a boil, and boil for 5 minutes. (Most of the water should have evaporated.) Add the onions with the mushrooms to the fricassee, and boil gently 5 minutes.
4. Stir in the cream. Serve the fricassee with Wehani Brown Rice, page 346.

YIELD: 6 SERVINGS

NUTRITIONAL ANALYSIS PER SERVING:

Calories 306
Protein 32 gm.
Carbohydrates 12 gm.
Fat 13.8 gm.
Saturated fat 5.8 gm.
Cholesterol 153 mg.
Sodium 426 mg.

Veal Bitochki

This lean recipe for bitochki*—the Russian name for ground meat patties—features ground veal, but ground turkey, chicken, or even beef could be used instead. To keep it moist and juicy, the meat is mixed with bread crumbs and milk before it is flavored with onion, garlic, parsley, salt, and pepper.*

The combination of horseradish and yogurt in the sauce gives it a distinctively Russian flavor that complements the veal nicely. To prevent the sauce from curdling, add the yogurt at the last minute, and then don't heat the mixture above 160 degrees.

- 3 slices bread (about 2½ ounces)
- ½ cup milk
- ⅓ cup chopped onion
- ½ teaspoon chopped garlic
- 3 tablespoons chopped fresh parsley
- ¼ teaspoon freshly ground black pepper
- ½ teaspoon salt
- 1 pound lean ground veal

Horseradish-Yogurt Sauce

- 1 tablespoon virgin olive oil
- 2 tablespoons chopped onion
- 4 ounces mushrooms, washed and cut into julienne strips (1¾ cups)
- ¼ cup homemade unsalted and defatted chicken stock (see page 466), or lower-salt canned chicken broth
- 1 tablespoon grated horseradish, either fresh or bottled
- 1 cup plain yogurt
- ¼ teaspoon salt (less if using canned broth)
- ¼ teaspoon freshly ground black pepper
- 2 tablespoons coarsely chopped fresh cilantro (coriander or Chinese parsley)

Yield: 4 Servings

Nutritional Analysis per Serving:

Calories 317
Protein 29 gm.
Carbohydrates 19 gm.
Fat 13.7 gm.
Saturated fat 5.0 gm.
Cholesterol 101 mg.
Sodium 664 mg.

Calcium-rich yogurt is an easy-to-digest dairy product.

1. Process the bread into crumbs. (You should have 1½ cups.) Combine the crumbs and milk thoroughly in a bowl. Add the onion, garlic, parsley, pepper, and salt, and mix well. Mix in the ground veal.
2. Divide the mixture into four patties, each about ¾ to 1 inch thick. Arrange the patties on a plate, and place them in a steamer set over boiling water. Cook for 10 minutes. Remove them from the steamer, and let them "rest" at room temperature while you prepare the sauce.

For the Sauce

3. Heat the oil until it is hot but not smoking in a saucepan or skillet. Add the onion, and sauté for 1 minute. Stir in the mushroom strips, and cook for another 20 seconds. Add the stock, bring to a boil, and boil for about 2 minutes. Stir in the remainder of the ingredients, and heat until warm, not boiling. (The sauce will break down if the mixture is brought to a boil.)
4. Serve the patties, one per person, coated with some of the sauce.

Veal Chops with Mushrooms

I use relatively small veal chops here, each weighing about ½ pound with the bone. Veal is low in calories, and most markets offer a good-quality, milk-fed variety. If you can, buy your veal, as I do, from farms that feed their cows organic foods. The quality is dramatically better. In this dish, I sauté the mushrooms in the veal drippings, creating a delicious sauce for serving on the chops.

- **2 teaspoons virgin olive oil**
- **2 teaspoons unsalted butter**
- **4 veal loin chops, about ¾ inch thick (8 ounces each), preferably white milk-fed veal (called *plume de veau* or Provimi)**
- **½ teaspoon salt**
- **½ teaspoon freshly ground black pepper**
- **2 shallots, peeled and chopped (¼ cup)**
- **12 ounces mushrooms, sliced (about 5 cups)**
- **¼ cup dry white wine**
- **2 cloves garlic, peeled, crushed, and finely chopped (1 teaspoon)**
- **¼ cup chopped fresh parsley**

1. Heat the oil and butter in a large skillet. Sprinkle the veal chops with half the salt and pepper, and sauté in the hot oil and butter for 4 minutes on each side. Remove to a platter.
2. In the pan drippings, sauté the shallots for 10 seconds over medium heat. Add the mushrooms and wine, and cook, covered, for 1 minute.
3. Uncover, and cook for another minute. Add the garlic and the remaining salt and pepper. Toss, and cook for 10 seconds; then stir in the parsley.
4. Pour the mushroom sauce over the veal chops. Serve immediately.

Yield: 4 Servings

Nutritional Analysis per Serving:

Calories 293
Protein 27 gm.
Carbohydrates 6 gm.
Fat 16.6 gm.
Saturated fat 6.6 gm.
Cholesterol 109 mg.
Sodium 393 mg.

Veal is a good source of iron, vitamin B_{12}, and niacin.

COOKING

VEAL CHOPS

Be sure you don't overcook the chops. Although veal is not served rare as beef is, it should be slightly pink inside and juicy throughout.

Grilled Veal Chops with Caper Sauce

This is a good summer recipe. I use veal chops here, but a breast of poultry or even a piece of fish would go well with the caper sauce. Cook the chops briefly on a very hot grill, to give them the distinctive taste and color of grilled meat, and then transfer them to a warm oven, where they continue to cook slowly in their own residual heat. The sauce is made separately and the chops coated with it before they are served. (See photograph, page 333.)

- 4 veal rib chops, each about 1 inch thick (about 10 ounces each, with bones)
- 1 teaspoon canola oil
- ¼ teaspoon salt
- ¼ teaspoon freshly ground black pepper

Caper and Sage Sauce

- ½ cup diced (¼-inch dice) red onion
- 2 tablespoons capers, drained
- 1 tablespoon minced fresh sage
- 2 teaspoons julienned lemon peel
- 1 tablespoon lemon juice
- 2 tablespoons virgin olive oil
- 2 tablespoons chopped fresh flat-leaf parsley
- ¼ teaspoon freshly ground black pepper
- ¼ teaspoon salt (less if using canned chicken broth)
- 2 tablespoons homemade unsalted and defatted chicken stock (see page 466), or lower-salt canned chicken broth

1. Heat a grill until it is very hot. Preheat the oven to 180 degrees.
2. Rub the chops with the oil, and sprinkle them with the ¼ teaspoon each of salt and pepper. Cook the chops on the clean rack of the hot grill for about 2½ minutes on each side. Transfer them to the 180-degree oven, and let them rest for at least 10 minutes and no longer than 30 minutes before serving.
3. Meanwhile, mix all the sauce ingredients in a bowl.
4. At serving time, place a chop on each of four plates, and coat with the sauce.

Yield: 4 Servings

Nutritional analysis per serving:

Calories 320
Protein 35 gm.
Carbohydrates 3 gm.
Fat 18.0 gm.
Saturated fat 3.8 gm.
Cholesterol 155 mg.
Sodium 519 mg.

Veal is a good source of vitamin B_{12}, a water-soluble vitamin critical for growth, healthy nerve tissue, and blood production.

VEAL CHOPS WITH OLIVE SHAVINGS

If you take into account that the bone in each of these well-trimmed chops weighs an ounce or so, you end up with 5 to 6 ounces of meat per person in this dish, an adequate—but not excessive—amount. The chops are sautéed briefly, then finished in the oven. A sauce is created from the pan drippings, with the addition of a little onion, wine, water, butter, ketchup, and, finally, olive shavings.

- **1 tablespoon canola oil**
- **4 veal chops (about 8 ounces each, ¾ inch thick), trimmed of as much surrounding fat as possible (about 7 ounces each trimmed)**
- **¼ teaspoon salt**
- **¼ teaspoon freshly ground black pepper**
- **1 small onion (2 to 3 ounces), peeled and chopped (½ cup)**
- **¼ cup dry white wine**
- **⅓ cup water**
- **1 tablespoon unsalted butter**
- **1 tablespoon ketchup**
- **8 ounces olives (a mixture of green, purple, and black varieties), pitted and cut into shavings (about 6 ounces)**
- **1 tablespoon chopped fresh parsley or chives**

1. Prewarm the oven to 180 degrees.
2. Heat the oil in a very large, sturdy skillet. Sprinkle the chops with the salt and pepper, and cook them in the hot oil over high heat for 3 minutes. Turn them over, and cook them on the other side for 3 minutes.
3. Remove the chops from the skillet (reserving the drippings), and place them on an ovenproof platter. Place the platter in the warm oven to allow the chops to "rest" while you make the sauce.
4. Add the onion to the drippings in the skillet, and sauté for 1½ minutes, stirring continuously. Add the wine, mix it in well, bring the mixture to a boil, and boil it for about 30 seconds. Add the water, butter, ketchup, and olive shavings, and boil for 1½ to 2 minutes.
5. Arrange the chops on individual plates, and spoon the sauce on top. Sprinkle with the parsley, and serve immediately.

**YIELD:
4 SERVINGS**

NUTRITIONAL ANALYSIS PER SERVING:

Calories 307
Protein 32 gm.
Carbohydrates 4 gm.
Fat 16.5 gm.
Saturated fat 4.2 gm.
Cholesterol 133 mg.
Sodium 1,020 mg.

Veal chops provide lean protein and vitamin B_{12}.

Veal Roast with Artichokes

Shoulder is the best choice of veal to use for this recipe. If you buy the large muscle of the shoulder, you may not have to tie the meat; if, however, the piece is separating or is longer and flatter, roll it and tie it with twine. If you are in a part of the United States where you can obtain baby artichokes, use them instead of the large ones, cutting them into halves rather than quarters. If you don't find the larger pearl onions I used here, substitute more of the smaller ones. This roast is good served cold with a green salad, tomato salad, or pasta salad.

- **1 2½-pound boneless veal shoulder roast, trimmed of most surface fat**
- **½ teaspoon salt**
- **½ teaspoon freshly ground black pepper**
- **1 teaspoon dried thyme leaves**
- **1 tablespoon unsalted butter**
- **1 tablespoon virgin olive oil**
- **5 medium artichokes, with stems (about 1 pound, 12 ounces total)**
- **12 onions (14 ounces), each about the size of a table tennis ball, peeled**
- **18 large cloves garlic, peeled**
- **1 tomato (6 ounces), cut in half, seeded, and cut into ½-inch pieces (1 cup)**
- **1 tablespoon soy sauce**
- **2 tablespoons water**

1. Preheat the oven to 400 degrees.
2. Tie the trimmed roast with twine if necessary, and sprinkle it with ¼ teaspoon each of the salt and pepper and with the thyme. In an ovenproof skillet, heat the butter and oil. When hot, add the meat, and brown it on all sides for a total of 8 to 10 minutes. Remove the roast to a platter, and reserve the drippings in the skillet.
3. With a sharp knife, remove the top third of the artichokes. Then, with scissors, trim off the upper half of the remaining leaves to remove the thorny projections. Cut the artichokes into fourths, and remove and discard the chokes.
4. Add the artichokes, onions, garlic, and remaining salt and pepper to the drippings in the skillet, and toss the vegetables to coat them with the drippings. Arrange the roast on top of the vegetables, and place the pan in the 400-degree oven for 20 min-

(continued)

Yield: 4 Servings

Nutritional Analysis per Serving:

Calories 483
Protein 62 gm.
Carbohydrates 25 gm.
Fat 15.2 gm.
Saturated fat 4.9 gm.
Cholesterol 252 mg.
Sodium 876 mg.

Veal provides iron, niacin, and vitamin B_{12}.

LEFT: VEAL ROAST WITH ARTICHOKES (ABOVE).
RIGHT: CORN AND PEPPER SAUTÉ (SEE PAGE 312).

1992
VINTNER'S RESERVE
KENDALL-JACKSON

utes. Turn the roast over, stirring the vegetables as you do so, and return the pan to the oven for another 20 minutes.

5. Stir in the tomato, soy sauce, and water, and cook for 10 additional minutes, for a total cooking time of 1 hour, not including the browning. (*Note:* I use a roast about 8½ inches long by 2½ inches in diameter. If your roast is shorter and thicker than mine, cook it a little longer.)
6. Remove the roast from the oven, and allow it to rest for 10 minutes. Carve, and serve.

Osso Buco

Osso buco literally means "bone with a hole" (or "with a mouth") in Italian. It is a reference to the large bones that are about half the content of the slices of veal shank traditionally used as the main ingredient in this classic dish. I brown the meat in the standard way in a large, sturdy pot, then add wine, water, and a multitude of garnishes, and cook the dish slowly until the veal is very tender. At the end, the osso buco is flavored with grated orange and lemon rind, and shredded basil leaves are sprinkled on top. Quite delicious, it goes particularly well with Brown Saffron Rice (see page 345).

4 10-ounce slices of veal shank with bones, each about 1½ inches thick (2½ pounds total, about half bones and half meat)
1 tablespoon unsalted butter
1 tablespoon virgin olive oil
1 medium onion (5 to 6 ounces), peeled and finely chopped (1¼ cups)
1 small leek (about 4 ounces), trimmed (with most green parts left on), coarsely chopped, and washed in a sieve (¾ cup)
1 medium carrot (3 ounces), trimmed, peeled, and coarsely chopped (½ cup)
6 cloves garlic, peeled, crushed, and finely chopped (4 teaspoons)

- 2 stalks celery (4 ounces), washed and coarsely chopped (⅔ cup)
- 1 teaspoon *herbes de Provence* (see page 467)
- ⅔ cup fruity white wine
- ⅔ cup water
- 1 teaspoon salt
- ½ teaspoon freshly ground black pepper
- 2 ripe medium tomatoes (10 to 11 ounces), halved, seeded, and cut into ½-inch pieces (1¼ cups)
- 1 tablespoon grated orange rind
- 1 tablespoon grated lemon rind
- 1 teaspoon potato starch (see About Potato Starch, page 394) or cornstarch dissolved in 1 tablespoon white wine
- ½ cup shredded fresh basil leaves

1. Pat the veal dry with paper towels. Heat the butter and oil in a large, sturdy saucepan or dutch oven. When they are hot, add the meat in one layer, and brown it over medium to high heat on all sides for about 12 minutes. Add the onion, leek, and carrot, mix well, and cook for 2 minutes. Then add the garlic, celery, *herbes de Provence,* wine, water, salt, and pepper, mix well, and bring the mixture to a strong boil. Reduce the heat to low, cover, and cook gently for 1½ hours, until the meat is tender when pierced with the point of a sharp knife.
2. Add the tomato, orange rind, and lemon rind, mix well, and bring back to a boil. Boil, uncovered, for 2 to 3 minutes. Add the dissolved starch mixture, and bring to a boil again. Remove the pan from the heat, add the basil, mix gently, cover, and set aside until ready to serve. (The dish is more flavorful if allowed to sit for at least 30 minutes before serving. It can be made up to 8 hours ahead and reheated, with the basil added at the time of reheating.)
3. Serve a slice of shank with bone to each person. Pour sauce over and around the shanks, and serve them with Brown Saffron Rice (see page 345).

YIELD: 4 SERVINGS

NUTRITIONAL ANALYSIS PER SERVING:

Calories 280
Protein 33 gm.
Carbohydrates 16 gm.
Fat 9.2 gm.
Saturated fat 3.0 gm.
Cholesterol 118 mg.
Sodium 687 mg.

Veal shanks provide iron-rich protein.

Breast of Veal Cocotte

Of all meat juices, those rendered by veal have the most concentrated taste, especially when the veal is cooked slowly, as it is here, in a type of dutch oven or cocotte. *I use veal breast, which is usually quite lean and relatively inexpensive. The amount of meat is small; at least two-thirds of the weight of a veal breast is bones and cartilage, both of which add flavor to the sauce. Carrots, onions, and garlic extend and enhance the dish.*

Yield: 6 Servings

Nutritional analysis per serving:

Calories 225
Protein 18 gm.
Carbohydrates 15 gm.
Fat 10.5 gm.
Saturated fat 3.7 gm.
Cholesterol 69 mg.
Sodium 290 mg.

Flavorful* herbes de Provence *keep the sodium content of this dish relatively low.

- 1 veal breast, about 3½ pounds (4 to 5 meaty ribs)
- 1 tablespoon *herbes de Provence* (see page 467)
- ½ teaspoon salt
- 1 tablespoon virgin olive oil
- 1 cup water
- 1 cup dry white wine
- 1 pound baby carrots (about 30), peeled
- 1 pound pearl onions (about 30), peeled
- 1 head garlic (15 to 20 cloves), peeled

1. Place the veal breast, *herbes de Provence,* salt, oil, and ½ cup of the water in a large *cocotte* (a high-sided cooking pot or casserole with a lid). Bring to a boil over high heat, reduce the heat to medium, and boil, covered, for 15 minutes. At this point most of the liquid will have evaporated. Continue to cook, uncovered, over medium heat for about 25 minutes, turning the meat often to brown it well on all sides.
2. Add the wine, cover, reduce the heat to low, and simmer slowly for about 1¼ hours, until the meat is tender when pierced with a fork.
3. Mix in the carrots, onions, garlic, and remaining ½ cup of water. Cover, and cook over low heat for 30 minutes longer.
4. Divide the meat, carrots, onions, and garlic among six individual plates, and serve immediately.

Seared Calves' Liver with Tarragon-Lemon Sauce

I like my calves' liver pink inside—medium rare—and this is reflected in the recipe, but you can adjust the cooking time to your taste. After the steaks are cooked briefly in a skillet on top of the stove, they are transferred to a plate and set aside, covered, to finish cooking in their own residual heat, while a tarragon-and-lemon-flavored sauce is created from the liver drippings in the skillet.

- 2 tablespoons unsalted butter
- 1 tablespoon virgin olive oil
- ½ teaspoon salt
- ½ teaspoon freshly ground black pepper
- 4 calves' liver steaks, each about ⅜ inch thick and 5 ounces (about 1¼ pounds total), cleaned of skin and as many sinews as possible

Tarragon-Lemon Sauce

- ½ cup coarsely chopped red onion
- 2 scallions, trimmed and finely minced (¼ cup)
- 2 tablespoons lemon juice
- ¼ cup water
- 1 tablespoon drained capers
- 2 teaspoons chopped fresh tarragon

1. Heat the butter and oil until hot in one very large (12-inch) or two smaller (8-inch) skillets. Sprinkle the salt and pepper on both sides of the liver steaks, and place them in the skillet(s) in one layer with no overlap. Sauté the steaks over high heat for about 1½ minutes on each side for medium rare (adjust the cooking time if your liver is thicker or thinner, or if you like it cooked more or less). Transfer the steaks to a plate, and cover them with an overturned plate. (They can wait like this for 10 to 15 minutes, while you prepare the sauce.)

For the Tarragon-Lemon Sauce

2. Add the onion and scallions to the drippings in the skillet(s). Sauté for about 20 seconds, then add the lemon juice, and stir until all the solidified juices have melted. If you are using two skillets, at this point combine their contents in one, and boil the mixture for another 20 seconds, until most of the liquid has evaporated. Add the water, the capers, and the tarragon, mix well, and bring to a boil.
3. Arrange the liver steaks on individual plates, top with the tarragon-lemon sauce, and serve immediately.

About Calves' Liver

Be sure to select calves' liver, not beef liver, for this dish. Much paler in color, it has a more pleasant odor, has a milder flavor, and is more tender than liver from a mature animal. Store fresh liver slices loosely wrapped in the refrigerator, and use within a day of purchase.

Yield: 4 Servings

Nutritional Analysis per Serving:

Calories 384
Protein 26 gm.
Carbohydrates 10 gm.
Fat 15.4 gm.
Saturated fat 6.3 gm.
Cholesterol 454 mg.
Sodium 422 mg.

Calves' liver is rich in vitamin B_{12}, copper, folacin, and chromium.

Barley-Stuffed Cabbage Rolls

Cooked barley lends body and texture to the stuffing for these savoy cabbage rolls, which are made with very lean ground beef. The rolls can be cooked ahead in the sweet-and-sour sauce and then reheated at serving time in a conventional or microwave oven.

- ½ cup pearl barley
- 9½ cups water
- 1 head savoy cabbage (about 1½ pounds)
- 1½ tablespoons canola oil
- 1 medium onion (about 7 ounces), peeled and chopped (1½ cups)
- 5 to 6 cloves garlic, peeled, crushed, and finely chopped (1 tablespoon)
- 4 tablespoons cider vinegar
- 1 pound lean ground beef (10 percent fat or less)
- ½ teaspoon freshly ground black pepper
- ½ teaspoon dried dill weed
- ½ teaspoon caraway seeds
- ½ teaspoon dried thyme leaves

Cider-Tomato Sauce

- 1 cup tomato sauce
- 1½ cups homemade unsalted and defatted chicken stock (see page 466), or lower-salt canned chicken broth
- ¼ teaspoon salt (less if using canned broth)
- 1 tablespoon brown sugar
- 2 tablespoons cider vinegar

1. Preheat the oven to 400 degrees.
2. Place the barley and 1½ cups of the water in a large saucepan. Bring the water to a boil, reduce the heat, cover, and boil the barley gently for 30 minutes, until it is tender. Set aside. Most of the water will be absorbed at this point.
3. Remove and reserve the core of the cabbage, and gently pull off nine or ten of the large outer leaves one at a time without tearing them. Bring the remaining 8 cups of water to a boil in a large pot. Drop the leaves into the water, and bring it back to a boil, gently pushing the leaves down under the water. Boil the leaves, covered, for 6 to 8 minutes, then drain them, and cool them under cold water. Remove the leaves from the water, shaking them gently to remove as much of the water clinging to them as possible, and set them aside.
4. Heat the oil in a large skillet. When it is hot, add the onion, and cook over medium to high heat, stirring occasionally, for 2 minutes. Trim the cabbage core, and cut it and the remaining cabbage leaves into ½-inch pieces. (You should have about 4 cups.) Add the garlic to the onion, stir well, and immediately add the cabbage heart

pieces and vinegar. Cover, and cook over medium heat for 8 to 10 minutes, until the cabbage is wilted and tender and most of the moisture is gone from the pan. Cool.

5. When the cabbage mixture is cold, combine it in a bowl with the barley, ground beef, pepper, dill, caraway, and thyme.
6. Spread the reserved cabbage leaves on a flat work surface, and cut out and discard the thick part of the central rib in each. You will need eight of the leaves for stuffing; the remaining one or two leaves are for any patching that is necessary.
7. Divide the stuffing mixture among the eight leaves, and fold in the sides and ends of the leaves to enclose the stuffing. Place the stuffed leaves seam side down in a large gratin dish in one layer.
8. Combine the sauce ingredients in a saucepan, and bring the mixture to a boil. Pour the sauce over the cabbage rolls, cover the dish with aluminum foil, and bake at 400 degrees for 1 hour. Remove the foil, baste the rolls with the surrounding sauce, and continue baking them, uncovered, for 20 minutes, basting them once or twice more to create a nice glaze on top.
9. Run the dish under a hot broiler for a few minutes if you want the rolls browner on top, and serve them immediately, two rolls per person.

**YIELD:
4 SERVINGS**

NUTRITIONAL ANALYSIS PER SERVING:

Calories 444
Protein 31 gm.
Carbohydrates 45 gm.
Fat 17.7 gm.
Saturated fat 5.1 gm.
Cholesterol 70 mg.
Sodium 691 mg.

Barley is a good source of thiamine, niacin, and potassium. Cabbage contains fiber, which helps reduce the risk of cancer.

BREAKING WITH TRADITION

REAL CHILI AFICIONADOS DON'T USE BEANS, OF COURSE, IN THEIR RENDITIONS OF THIS CLASSIC DISH; IN TEXAS, FOR EXAMPLE, MEAT—USUALLY FATTY BEEF, OFTEN FROM THE SHOULDER—IS THE MAIN INGREDIENT. BEANS ARE A PROMINENT PART OF MY CHILI, WITH MEAT USED MORE AS A SEASONING. I SELECT LEAN (10 PERCENT FAT) GROUND BEEF, AVAILABLE NOW IN SUPERMARKETS, AND EXTEND THE CHILI WITH RED KIDNEY BEANS.

YIELD: 4 TO 6 SERVINGS

NUTRITIONAL ANALYSIS PER SERVING (FOR 6):

Calories 344
Protein 20 gm.
Carbohydrates 56 gm.
Fat 4.8 gm.
Saturated fat 1.6 gm.
Cholesterol 23 mg.
Sodium 618 mg.

CHILI CON CARNE WITH RED BEANS

Notice that the beans and beef are cooked together first for an hour before the onions, scallions, garlic, jalapeño, and an assortment of herbs and spices are added; then the mixture is cooked for another hour. This gives the dish a fresher flavor, I think, than adding all the seasoning ingredients at the beginning. Spooned over Boiled Rice (see page 343), this soupy chili makes a satisfying one-dish meal for four or six people. I serve it with Romaine with Creamy Yogurt Dressing (see page 295) for a refreshing complementary taste.

8 ounces dried red kidney beans
8 ounces very lean ground beef (10-percent fat or less)
1½ teaspoons salt
4 cups cold water
2 small or 1 medium onion (4 ounces), peeled and cut into 1-inch pieces (1½ cups)
6 scallions, trimmed, keeping most of the green, and cut into ½-inch pieces (1 cup)
5 to 6 cloves garlic, peeled, crushed, and chopped (1 tablespoon)
1 jalapeño pepper, seeded and chopped (2 teaspoons)
1 can (14 ounces) tomatoes in sauce
½ teaspoon dried thyme leaves
1 teaspoon ground cumin
1½ tablespoons chili powder
2 bay leaves
⅓ cup finely chopped cilantro stems
1 recipe Boiled Rice (see page 343)
⅓ cup (loose) coarsely chopped cilantro leaves

1. Sort through the beans, removing and discarding any damaged ones, and rinse in a sieve under cold water. Place the beans, beef, salt, and water in a stockpot, and bring the mixture to a boil over high heat. (This will take about 10 minutes.) Reduce the heat to low, cover, and boil gently for 1 hour.
2. Add the onions, scallions, garlic, jalapeño, tomatoes (with sauce), thyme, cumin, chili powder, bay leaves, and cilantro stems. Bring the mixture to a boil over high heat, reduce the heat to low, cover, and boil gently for 1 hour. (The mixture will still be somewhat soupy.)
3. To serve, spoon the chili over the rice, and sprinkle the cilantro leaves on top.

Spicy Beef Shell Roast

If you allow only a small portion of meat per serving and trim the meat completely, beef is a perfectly acceptable component of a well-balanced diet. It is, in fact, a good source of iron. Moreover, you can cut back on the amount of salt by using dry herbs to flavor the meat, as I do here. Notice that the beef is cooked initially on top of the stove and finished in the oven; this produces an exterior crust that intensifies the taste of the meat.

- **1 beef shell roast (also called New York strip), about 1½ pounds untrimmed**
- **1 teaspoon dried thyme**
- **1 teaspoon dried oregano**
- **1 teaspoon dried rosemary**
- **¼ teaspoon freshly ground black pepper**
- **¼ teaspoon cayenne pepper**
- **¼ teaspoon salt**
- **1 tablespoon virgin olive oil**
- **¼ cup homemade unsalted and defatted chicken stock (see page 466), or lower-salt canned chicken broth**

1. Preheat the oven to 450 degrees.
2. Remove all surface fat from the roast. The trimmed roast should weigh 1¼ pounds and be 1¾ inches thick.
3. Crush the dried herbs between your thumb and finger, and mix them with the black and cayenne peppers. Pat the mixture on both sides of the meat.
4. When ready to cook, sprinkle the roast with the salt. Heat the oil in a heavy ovenproof skillet or saucepan. When hot, add the meat, and cook over medium to high heat for 3 minutes on each side.
5. Transfer the roast to the 450-degree oven, and cook for 8 to 10 minutes for medium rare. Add the chicken stock, and let rest 10 minutes before carving. Serve with the natural meat-cooking juices.

Yield: 4 Servings

NUTRITIONAL ANALYSIS PER SERVING:

Calories 220
Protein 30 gm.
Carbohydrates 1 gm.
Fat 9.9 gm.
Saturated fat 2.7 gm.
Cholesterol 87 mg.
Sodium 230 mg.

Beef is rich in iron.

PROVENÇAL TOUCHES

A mixture of hazelnuts, toasted bread, garlic, and parsley is transformed into a powder and added to this dish just before it is served. Other last-minute additions are capers, olives, and tomatoes, ingredients that are special to the Provence region of France.

Daube of Beef Arlésienne

This dish comes from Arles, the small town in Provence made famous by Vincent van Gogh. A beef stew, the daube is flavored with small potatoes, pearl onions, baby carrots, white wine, and herbes de Provence. *I like to use shoulder blade steaks (sometimes called chicken steaks) in this dish, because they are very lean, except for a strip of nerve tissue in the center that becomes gelatinous as the meat cooks and keeps it moist and flavorful.*

- 8 small red potatoes (about 8 ounces), peeled
- 1½ cups water
- 8 small pearl onions (about 5 ounces), peeled
- About 12 to 16 baby carrots (4 ounces), peeled
- 1½ teaspoons virgin olive oil
- 4 boned shoulder blade beef steaks or chicken steaks, trimmed of all surrounding fat and cut in half (20 to 24 ounces total trimmed weight)
- 1 medium onion (about 5 ounces), peeled and chopped (1 cup)
- 1 cup dry white wine
- 1¼ teaspoons salt
- 1 teaspoon *herbes de Provence* (see page 467)

Arlésienne Mixture

- 12 to 15 shelled hazelnuts (about 2 tablespoons)
- 1 slice toasted country bread (about 1 ounce)
- 2 cloves garlic, peeled
- ½ cup (loose) fresh parsley leaves
- 2 tablespoons drained capers
- ¼ cup *Niçoise* olives
- 1 medium tomato (6 ounces), seeded and cut into 1-inch dice (¾ cup)

1. Place the potatoes and water in a saucepan, and bring to a boil over high heat. Cover the pan, reduce the heat to low, and boil the potatoes gently for 8 minutes.
2. Add the pearl onions and carrots, bring the mixture back to a boil over high heat, cover, reduce the heat to low, and boil gently for another 8 minutes, or until all the vegetables are tender but still firm when pierced with the point of a sharp knife. Drain off and reserve the vegetable cooking liquid (you should have about 1½ cups), and set the vegetables aside in the pan.
3. Heat the oil in a large, sturdy pot. When it is hot, add the steaks and cook them over medium to high heat for 8 to 10 minutes, turning them once midway through, so they are browned on both sides. Add the chopped onion, and cook it with the steaks for 2 minutes, stirring occasionally. Then mix in the reserved

vegetable-cooking liquid, white wine, salt, and *herbes de Provence.* Bring the mixture to a boil, cover, reduce the heat to very low, and boil very gently for 1 hour. (The recipe can be prepared to this point a day ahead.)

For the *Arlésienne* Mixture

4. Preheat the oven to 400 degrees.
5. Spread the hazelnuts on a tray, and toast them at 400 degrees for 10 minutes. Place the bread, hazelnuts, garlic, and parsley in the bowl of a food processor, and process the mixture until it is finely chopped.
6. At serving time, add the bread and hazelnut mixture along with the reserved vegetables to the beef mixture in the pot. Mix well, bring the daube to a boil, and cook it gently for 5 minutes to heat it through completely. Add the capers, olives, and tomato, cook 1 additional minute, and serve immediately.

**Yield:
4 Servings**

NUTRITIONAL ANALYSIS PER SERVING:

Calories 389
Protein 34 gm.
Carbohydrates 25 gm.
Fat 16.9 gm.
Saturated fat 4.9 gm.
Cholesterol 101 mg.
Sodium 1,058 mg.

The largest amounts of vitamins and minerals in red potatoes are found just beneath the skin.

Wine Merchant Steak

Although the steaks in this dish can be grilled and served plain, I extend the dish with a sauce made of shallots, mushrooms, garlic, and a good, earthy wine, thickened with Dijon-style mustard and garnished with chopped chives.

- 4 New York strip, shell, or sirloin tip steaks (9 ounces each), about ¾ inch thick
- ¾ teaspoon salt
- ½ teaspoon freshly ground black pepper
- 2 tablespoons virgin olive oil
- 2 shallots, peeled and finely chopped (4 tablespoons)
- 4 large mushrooms (about 4 ounces), cut into julienne strips
- 2 large cloves garlic, peeled, crushed, and finely chopped (1½ teaspoons)
- 1 cup red wine (Beaujolais type)
- 1 cup homemade unsalted and defatted chicken stock (see page 466), or lower-salt canned chicken broth
- 1 tablespoon Worcestershire sauce
- 1 tablespoon Dijon-style mustard
- ½ teaspoon potato starch dissolved in 2 teaspoons water (see About Potato Starch, page 394)
- 1 tablespoon finely chopped fresh chives

1. Trim the steaks, removing all visible surface fat and sinews. The trimmed steaks should weigh about 7 ounces each.
2. Sprinkle the steaks with ½ teaspoon of the salt and with the pepper.
3. Heat the oil in a large skillet. When hot, add the steaks, and sauté for 2½ minutes on each side for medium rare.
4. Remove the steaks to a platter, and set aside in a warm place. To the drippings in the skillet, add the shallots, and sauté for about 10 seconds. Add the mushrooms and garlic, and sauté for 1 minute. Stir in the wine, and boil down until only about 2 tablespoons remain. Add the stock, and reduce the mixture to about ¾ cup.
5. Add the Worcestershire sauce, mustard, and remaining salt, and mix well. Stir in the dissolved potato starch, and bring the mixture to a boil.
6. Arrange the steaks on individual plates, and spoon some sauce on top and around each steak. Garnish with the chives, and serve.

WINE MERCHANT STEAK (ABOVE)
AND *POMMES PERSILLADE* (POTATOES WITH PARSLEY AND GARLIC) (SEE PAGE 322).

LESS IS MORE . . . HEALTHY

THE STEAKS IN THIS CLASSIC BISTRO DISH ARE RELATIVELY SMALL COMPARED TO THOSE SERVED IN RESTAURANTS A FEW YEARS AGO. IN ADDITION, THE MEAT IS TRIMMED OF ALL FAT, LEAVING EACH PORTION WITH A WEIGHT OF ABOUT 7 OUNCES, AN AMPLE SERVING.

YIELD: 4 SERVINGS

NUTRITIONAL ANALYSIS PER SERVING:

Calories 355
Protein 44 gm.
Carbohydrates 6 gm.
Fat 16.2 gm.
Saturated fat 4.2 gm.
Cholesterol 121 mg.
Sodium 714 mg.

MOIST CUTS OF BEEF

IT IS IMPORTANT IN THIS RECIPE TO USE BEEF SHOULDER BLADE OR SHANK. THESE ARE LEAN YET GELATINOUS CUTS THAT WILL RETAIN THEIR MOISTNESS AFTER COOKING—A QUALITY ESSENTIAL TO THE SUCCESS OF THIS DISH.

Braised Beef in Red Wine

An intensely flavored red wine sauce is the hallmark of this dish, and my recipe contains nearly a whole bottle of red wine, along with a little soy sauce, vinegar, garlic, onions, and carrots for flavor. Even though the dish is a bit complicated, it makes an outstanding winter main dish that is well worth the effort.

- 2 onions (about 8 ounces), peeled and quartered
- 2 carrots (about 6 ounces), peeled and cut into 1-inch pieces
- 1 whole head garlic, separated into cloves (12 to 15), unpeeled
- 4 bay leaves
- 1 teaspoon dried thyme
- 1 teaspoon dried oregano
- 3 tablespoons red wine vinegar
- 4 tablespoons balsamic vinegar
- 2 tablespoons dark soy sauce
- 1 tablespoon black peppercorns, coarsely crushed
- 3 cups dry red wine (preferably a cabernet sauvignon variety or a deep, fruity red from the Rhône Valley)
- 1 piece of beef, about 3 pounds, from the shoulder blade (top blade) or a whole boned shank
- 1 tablespoon virgin olive oil
- ½ teaspoon salt
- 1 tablespoon potato starch dissolved in 2 tablespoons water (see About Potato Starch, page 394)

GARNISHES

- About 18 small baby carrots (8 to 10 ounces total), peeled
- About 18 small pearl onions (about 8 ounces total), peeled
- ½ cup water
- About 18 small potatoes (about 1 pound total), peeled
- About 18 medium mushrooms (about 12 ounces total)
- 1 tablespoon chopped fresh parsley

1. Place the onions, carrots, garlic, bay leaves, thyme, oregano, vinegars, soy sauce, peppercorns, and red wine in a saucepan, and bring the mixture to a boil over high heat.
2. Meanwhile, place the meat in a heat-proof container. When the mixture in the saucepan comes to a boil, pour it over the meat, and set it aside to cool. When it is cool, cover the container with plastic wrap, and refrigerate it for at least 6 hours and as long as 3 days.

(continued)

DUTCH OVEN ALTERNATIVE

I COOK THE BEEF IN A PRESSURE COOKER TO SAVE TIME, BUT YOU CAN COOK IT INSTEAD IN A DUTCH OVEN. BROWN THE MEAT AS DIRECTED IN THE RECIPE, THEN COOK IT, TIGHTLY COVERED, OVER LOW HEAT FOR 3 HOURS IN A DUTCH OVEN, AND FINISH WITH THE GARNISHES. ENCLOSING THE MEAT AS IT COOKS—IN EITHER A PRESSURE COOKER OR A DUTCH OVEN—CONTRIBUTES TO ITS MOISTURE RETENTION.

3. When you are ready to cook, remove the beef, reserving the marinade, and pat the beef dry with paper towels. Heat the oil in a pressure cooker over medium to high heat until hot; then add the beef, and sprinkle it with the salt. Cook, uncovered, over medium heat for about 15 minutes, turning occasionally, until the meat has browned on all sides. Add the marinade mixture, and bring to a boil. Cover, and bring the cooker to the appropriate pressure, following the manufacturer's guidelines. Then reduce the heat to very low, and cook for 1½ hours.
4. Depressurize the cooker according to the manufacturer's instructions, and remove the meat. Transfer the cooking juices to a smaller saucepan, and let them rest for 10 minutes to allow the fat to rise to the top. Place the meat back in the cooker.
5. Skim all visible fat from the surface of the juices, and bring the remaining liquid to a boil. Boil gently for 5 minutes, and then stir in the dissolved potato starch to thicken the juices. Using a strainer with a fine mesh, strain the resulting sauce, and pour all but 1 cup of it over the meat.

FOR THE GARNISHES

6. Place the carrots, onions, and water in a saucepan. Bring to a boil, cover, and boil over medium heat for 5 minutes. (Most of the liquid should be gone.) Set aside.
7. Place the potatoes in another saucepan, and cover them with cold water. Bring to a boil, and boil gently for 10 to 12 minutes, uncovered, until they are almost cooked but still firm. Drain. Combine with the carrots and onions. Set aside until serving time.
8. Place the reserved cup of wine sauce in a large saucepan. Wash the mushrooms, and add them to the sauce. Cover, bring to a boil, and boil gently for 5 minutes. Set aside until serving time.
9. At serving time, reheat the meat in the sauce over low heat until it is heated through. Add the carrots, onions, and potatoes to the mushrooms, and heat until hot.
10. Arrange the meat on a large platter, and cut it into 1-inch slices. Surround the meat with the vegetables, and pour the sauce over and around them. Sprinkle with the parsley. Serve.

YIELD: 6 SERVINGS

NUTRITIONAL ANALYSIS PER SERVING:

Calories 524
Protein 49 gm.
Carbohydrates 37 gm.
Fat 19.7 gm.
Saturated fat 6.7 gm.
Cholesterol 148 mg.
Sodium 838 mg.

This recipe is a good source of protein, iron, vitamin B_{12}, and thiamin.

Venison Steaks in Sweet-Sour Sauce

Be sure to obtain your venison from a reputable source, so you know that the meat has been aged and is tender. Thoroughly trimmed of fat, the steaks are very lean, quite flavorful, and rich, so 4 to 5 ounces of meat per person are adequate. Venison is traditionally served with a sweet-sour sauce. The sauce I have created here contains currant jelly for sweetness, and vinegar—cooked with shallots and added to the sauce at the end—for a contrasting sour taste. I particularly enjoy this main course served with Skillet Sweet Potatoes (recipe on page 329). (See photograph, page 290.)

- **1 loin of venison (about 1½ pounds), completely trimmed of fat (about 1 pound trimmed)**
- **1 teaspoon canola oil**
- **1 teaspoon chopped fresh thyme leaves**
- **1 tablespoon ketchup**
- **1 tablespoon currant jelly or seedless raspberry jam**
- **2 teaspoons soy sauce**
- **¼ cup cold water**
- **1 tablespoon peanut oil**
- **1 tablespoon unsalted butter**
- **¼ teaspoon salt**
- **¼ teaspoon freshly ground black pepper**
- **1 tablespoon chopped shallots**
- **2 tablespoons red wine vinegar**

1. Cut the trimmed loin into four steaks, each about 4 ounces. Pound the steaks gently until each is about ¾ inch thick. Rub the steaks with the canola oil, and sprinkle them with the thyme. Arrange the steaks in a single layer on a plate, cover with plastic wrap, and refrigerate for at least 1 hour and as long as 8 hours before cooking.
2. Mix the ketchup, jelly, soy sauce, and water together in a small bowl, and set aside.
3. When you are ready to cook the steaks, prewarm the oven to 180 degrees.
4. Heat the peanut oil and butter until hot in a large, sturdy saucepan. Sprinkle the steaks with the salt and pepper, place them in the saucepan, and sauté over medium to high heat for 2 to 2½ minutes on each side for medium-rare meat. Transfer the steaks to an ovenproof plate (retaining the drippings in the pan), cover with aluminum foil, and keep warm in the oven while you make the sauce.
5. Add the shallots to the drippings in the pan, and sauté them for about 20 seconds. Add the vinegar, and cook until most of the moisture has evaporated (about

(continued)

VENISON STEAKS IN SWEET-SOUR SAUCE (*continued*)

1½ minutes). Add the jelly mixture, and mix well. Boil for 10 seconds, and strain through a fine mesh strainer.

6. Place each steak on a plate, coat with some of the sauce, and serve immediately with Skillet Sweet Potatoes (see page 329).

YIELD:
4 SERVINGS

NUTRITIONAL ANALYSIS PER SERVING:

Calories 224
Protein 26 gm.
Carbohydrates 5 gm.
Fat 10.1 gm.
Saturated fat 3.5 gm.
Cholesterol 104 mg.
Sodium 412 mg.

Venison has only one-third the saturated fat of lean beef, and it is rich in iron.

TOP: RAW RELISH OF GRAPEFRUIT AND PEACH (SEE PAGE 347).
BOTTOM: VENISON STEAKS IN SWEET-SOUR SAUCE (SEE PAGE 289) WITH SKILLET SWEET POTATOES (SEE PAGE 329).

Side Dishes

Arugula and Olive Salad

Arugula, called roquette *in France and sometimes rocket in this country, is a pungent, garlicky salad green that goes particularly well with the lemon dressing in this recipe. You can, however, substitute other greens if arugula is not available, combining them with the dressing in the same manner and serving the salad garnished with olives and croutons.* *(See photograph, page 94.)*

About 14 ounces arugula
20 oil-cured black olives
2 slices firm-textured white bread (2 ounces)
1½ teaspoons virgin olive oil

LEMON DRESSING

1½ tablespoons lemon juice
2 tablespoons virgin olive oil
¼ teaspoon salt
⅛ teaspoon freshly ground black pepper

1. Preheat the oven to 400 degrees.
2. Wash the arugula, removing and discarding the tough outer leaves and stems. Dry it thoroughly, taking care not to bruise the leaves. (You should have 8 lightly packed cups.)
3. Pit the olives and cut them into ½-inch pieces. (You should have ½ cup.)
4. Trim the crusts from the bread slices, and cut the bread into ½-inch cubes. (You should have 1¼ cups.) Place the bread cubes in a bowl, add the 1½ teaspoons of olive oil, and rub the oil gently into the cubes to coat them well. Arrange the cubes on a baking tray, and bake them at 400 degrees for 8 minutes, until they are well browned. Set aside.
5. In a bowl large enough to hold the arugula greens, mix all the dressing ingredients.
6. At serving time, add the arugula to the bowl containing the dressing, and toss well to combine. Divide the arugula among four plates, and sprinkle the olives and croutons on top and around the greens. Serve immediately.

YIELD:
4 SERVINGS

NUTRITIONAL ANALYSIS PER SERVING:

Calories 161
Protein 3 gm.
Carbohydrates 9 gm.
Fat 13.3 gm.
Saturated fat 1.7 gm.
Cholesterol 0 mg.
Sodium 637 mg.

Arugula has twice as much vitamin A as butter lettuce.

Romaine with Creamy Yogurt Dressing

Romaine lettuce holds up particularly well to a light dressing that substitutes plain, nonfat yogurt for most of the oil. Cool and tangy, the yogurt gives the dressing a creamy consistency and a refreshingly sour taste that makes it a good accompaniment for Chili con Carne with Red Beans *(see page 278).*

1 tablespoon white wine vinegar
¼ teaspoon salt
¼ teaspoon freshly ground black pepper
3 tablespoons nonfat plain yogurt
1 tablespoon virgin olive oil
8 to 10 ounces romaine lettuce, ribs cut in half and leaves torn into 1½- to 2-inch pieces (6 cups)
1 tablespoon chopped fresh herb mixture (tarragon, chives, basil, and chervil)

1. In a bowl large enough to hold the lettuce, whisk together the vinegar, salt, pepper, and yogurt. Whisk in the oil.
2. Wash the lettuce pieces well in cold water and spin them dry in a salad spinner.
3. Add the lettuce to the dressing in the bowl, and toss it until coated with the dressing. Sprinkle on the fresh herbs, and serve immediately.

Yield: 4 Servings

NUTRITIONAL ANALYSIS PER SERVING:

Calories 47
Protein 2 gm.
Carbohydrates 3 gm.
Fat 3.5 gm.
Saturated fat 0.5 gm.
Cholesterol 3 mg.
Sodium 148 mg.

The darker green the leaves of lettuces, the more vitamin A they contain.

JULIENNED CARROTS

TO MAKE THE JULIENNED CARROT STRIPS, CUT A PEELED AND TRIMMED CARROT INTO VERY THIN, LENGTHWISE SLICES (USING A VEGETABLE PEELER, IF DESIRED). STACK THE SLICES AND CUT THEM, FIRST LENGTHWISE, THEN CROSSWISE, TO CREATE MATCHLIKE STICKS ABOUT 2 INCHES LONG.

Asian Savoy Salad

Savoy cabbage is quite attractive, with its pale and darker green colors, and its wrinkled leaves tend to hold a dressing well. I macerate the leaves here in an interesting mixture containing oyster sauce and garlic that goes particularly well with the cabbage. This salad is great as a garnish for roasted or grilled poultry, meat, or fish, and it also makes a good first course.

Asian Dressing

- 2 tablespoons rice wine vinegar
- 1½ tablespoons soy sauce
- 1 tablespoon oyster sauce
- ¼ teaspoon Tabasco hot pepper sauce
- 1 teaspoon sugar
- 2 cloves garlic, peeled, crushed, and finely chopped (2 teaspoons)

Savoy Salad

- ½ pound tender savoy cabbage leaves, with tough lower part of central ribs removed and discarded, leaves finely shredded (about 6 cups, lightly packed)
- ½ cup julienned carrot strips (see Julienned Carrots)

1. Combine the dressing ingredients in a plastic bag large enough to hold the cabbage. Add the cabbage, toss it with the dressing, and allow the mixture to macerate for at least 2 hours.
2. Transfer the salad and dressing to a serving bowl, sprinkle with the carrot, and serve.

YIELD: 4 SERVINGS

NUTRITIONAL ANALYSIS PER SERVING:

Calories 34
Protein 2 gm.
Carbohydrates 7 gm.
Fat 0.1 gm.
Saturated fat 0 gm.
Cholesterol 0 mg.
Sodium 585 mg.

Carrots, a rich source of beta-carotene, help reduce the risk of cancer.

Tomatoes and Onion with Parsley Vinaigrette

This sauce is especially good when tomatoes—preferably organically grown—are at their peak. The seasonings are simple: vinegar, oil, salt, and pepper. If you don't have a red onion, you can use a mild Texas or Vidalia onion instead, and you can replace the parsley with basil, tarragon, or another herb to your liking.

2 large ripe tomatoes (about 1 pound)
1 medium red onion (about 3 ounces)
¼ teaspoon salt
¼ teaspoon freshly ground black pepper
1 tablespoon red wine vinegar
3 tablespoons virgin olive oil
2 tablespoons chopped fresh flat-leaf parsley

1. Cut the tomatoes into ¼-inch slices, and arrange the slices on a platter.
2. Peel the onion, cut it into very thin slices, and arrange the slices on top of the tomato.
3. Sprinkle with the salt, pepper, vinegar, and oil.
4. Sprinkle with the parsley, and serve.

Yield: 4 Servings

Nutritional Analysis per Serving:

Calories 123
Protein 1 gm.
Carbohydrates 7 gm.
Fat 10.5 gm.
Saturated fat 1.4 gm.
Cholesterol 0 mg.
Sodium 148 mg.

Tomatoes are rich in vitamin C.

PEELING ASPARAGUS

I FIND IT WORTHWHILE TO PEEL THE LOWER PART OF ASPARAGUS STALKS. REMOVING THE FIBROUS OUTER LAYER FROM THE BASE OF THE TIP TO THE CUT END MAKES THE ENTIRE SPEAR EDIBLE; OTHERWISE, ONLY THE TIPS ARE PALATABLE.

Ragout of Asparagus

This stew of asparagus can be ready in about 5 minutes and so should be prepared at the last moment. The spears can be peeled and cut in advance and refrigerated until cooking time. Most of the small amount of water used to cook the asparagus will evaporate, and the little bit remaining will mix and emulsify with the butter that is added at the end, creating a smooth, creamy, flavorful sauce. This dish makes an ideal first course.

½ cup water
16 asparagus spears (about 1 pound), peeled and cut into 1½-inch pieces (about 3 cups)
2 tablespoons unsalted butter
¼ teaspoon salt

1. Bring the water to a boil in a saucepan. Add the asparagus, and bring the water back to a boil. Cover. Boil for 2½ minutes over high heat.
2. Add the butter and salt, bring back to a strong boil, and boil for about 1 minute longer. The cooking liquid will bind with the butter, creating a light, delicate sauce.
3. Serve immediately.

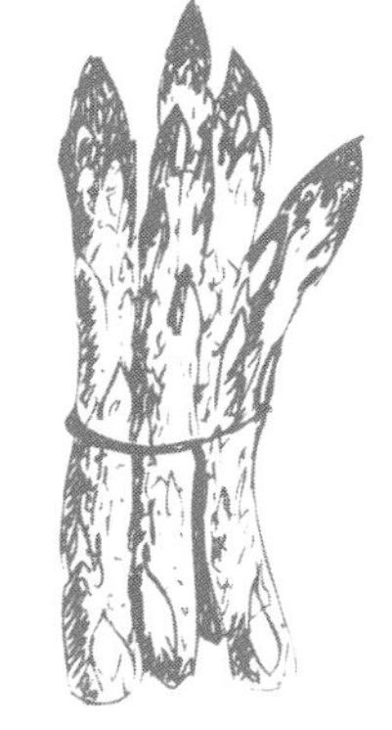

YIELD: 4 SERVINGS

NUTRITIONAL ANALYSIS PER SERVING:

Calories 73
Protein 3 gm.
Carbohydrates 4 gm.
Fat 6.0 gm.
Saturated fat 3.6 gm.
Cholesterol 16 mg.
Sodium 138 mg.

This dish is a delicious way to meet a healthy fiber goal.

√ Sauteéd Haricots Verts and Shallots

Try to find authentic haricots verts, *thin French green beans—sometimes available in specialty food stores or at farmers' markets—for this classic dish. If these are impossible to locate, however, cook the smallest, firmest regular string beans you can find until they are tender but still firm, and finish them with sautéed shallots and seasonings.* *(See photograph, page 214.)*

- **1½ cups water**
- **1 pound *haricots verts* (very thin French green beans), or very small regular string beans, tips removed**
- **1 tablespoon unsalted butter**
- **1 tablespoon peanut oil**
- **2 shallots, peeled and finely chopped (2 tablespoons)**
- **¼ teaspoon salt**
- **¼ teaspoon freshly ground black pepper**

1. Bring the water to a boil in a large saucepan. Rinse the beans, and add them to the boiling water. Cook, covered, over high heat for 7 or 8 minutes, until the beans are tender but still firm to the bite. Drain the beans (most of the water will have evaporated), and spread them on a large platter to cool.
2. At serving time, heat the butter and oil in a skillet. When they are hot, add the shallots, and sauté for about 10 seconds. Add the beans, salt, and pepper, and continue to sauté for about 2 minutes, until the beans are heated through. Serve with Grilled Chicken with Tarragon Butter (see page 215), if desired.

Yield: 4 Servings

NUTRITIONAL ANALYSIS PER SERVING:

Calories 90
Protein 2 gm.
Carbohydrates 8 gm.
Fat 6.4 gm.
Saturated fat 2.4 gm.
Cholesterol 8 mg.
Sodium 142 mg.

Haricots verts *are a good source of soluble fiber.*

Flageolets in *Mirepoix*

*Flageolets are a French bean variety. Although you can occasionally find them fresh here, they are more likely to be available dried and can usually be found in specialty food stores. Long and narrow, they are light green in color because they are picked when only half ripe. They look somewhat like small dried lima beans and take about the same length of time to cook. I cook them here with finely diced vegetables (*mirepoix*) that add flavor. A traditional lamb accompaniment, flageolets go very well with Long-Roasted Lamb (see page 264).*

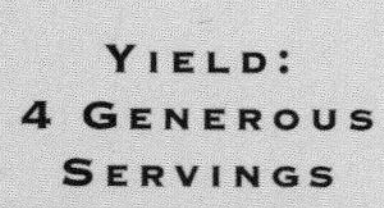

Yield: 4 Generous Servings

NUTRITIONAL ANALYSIS PER SERVING:

Calories 268
Protein 13 gm.
Carbohydrates 44 gm.
Fat 5.3 gm.
Saturated fat 0.7 gm.
Cholesterol 0 mg.
Sodium 632 mg.

Dried flageolets are an excellent source of fiber, iron, potassium, and magnesium.

- ½ **pound dried flageolets**
- 1 **small onion (3 ounces), peeled and chopped (½ cup)**
- 1 **carrot (2 ounces), peeled and cut into ¼-inch dice (⅓ cup)**
- 1 **small rib celery (1½ ounces), peeled and cut into ¼-inch dice (⅓ cup)**
- 1 **piece leek (2 ounces), white and green parts thinly sliced (½ cup) and washed under cold water in a sieve**
- ½ **teaspoon *herbes de Provence* (see page 467)**
- 1½ **cups homemade unsalted and defatted chicken stock (see page 466), or lower-salt canned chicken broth**
- 1½ **cups water**
- 1 **teaspoon salt (less if using canned broth)**
- 1 **tomato, seeded and cut into ½-inch dice (¾ cup)**
- 1 **tablespoon virgin olive oil**

1. Wash the flageolets, removing and discarding any stones or foreign matter, and place them in a pot with all the rest of the ingredients except the tomato and the oil. Bring the mixture to a boil, cover, reduce the heat to low, and boil gently for about 1½ hours, until the beans are tender and most of the liquid has evaporated.
2. Using a hand blender in the pot, puree a small amount of the mixture (or remove a cup of the beans, puree them in a food processor or mini-chop, and add the puree to the pot). Stir the puree into the pot to thicken the whole mixture slightly.
3. Stir in the tomato and oil, and serve immediately, or cool, cover, refrigerate, and reheat for later serving.

Dried Lima Bean Puree

Dried lima beans cook quickly and are very good pureed. I cook them here in chicken stock flavored with a little salt and herbes de Provence, *although you can substitute water for the stock if you want a vegetarian dish. When tender, the beans are transformed into a smooth, delicate puree in a food processor.*

4 ounces large dried lima beans
1½ cups homemade unsalted and defatted chicken stock (see page 466), lower-salt canned chicken broth, or water
⅓ teaspoon salt (less if using canned chicken broth)
⅛ teaspoon *herbes de Provence* (see page 467)
1 tablespoon virgin olive oil

1. Wash the lima beans, and sort through them, removing and discarding any pebbles or damaged beans. Place the beans, stock, salt, and *herbes de Provence* in a saucepan, and bring the mixture to a boil over high heat. Then cover the pan, reduce the heat to low, and cook the beans gently for about 35 minutes, until they are soft and tender. There should be only a little liquid remaining in the pan.
2. Transfer the beans and liquid to the bowl of a food processor, and process the mixture for 15 to 20 seconds. Add the oil, and process for a few seconds, until it is incorporated.
3. Serve immediately, or set aside and reheat at serving time in a double boiler or microwave oven.

ADVANCE PREPARATION

THE PUREE CAN BE PREPARED AHEAD. REHEAT IT IN A DOUBLE BOILER OR MICROWAVE OVEN, HOWEVER, SINCE IT TENDS TO BURN IF WARMED CONVENTIONALLY ON TOP OF THE STOVE IN A SAUCEPAN.

YIELD: 4 SERVINGS

NUTRITIONAL ANALYSIS PER SERVING:

Calories 139
Protein 7 gm.
Carbohydrates 19 gm.
Fat 4.1 gm.
Saturated fat 0.6 gm.
Cholesterol 0 mg.
Sodium 239 mg.

Dried lima beans provide fiber, magnesium, iron, and vitamin E.

A LOW-CALORIE DINNER

For a complete low-calorie steamed dinner, serve the Broccoli Piquant with Salmon Pojarski (see page 178) and *Pommes à l'Anglaise* (see page 321). For cooking instructions, see page 16.

Broccoli Piquant

In this recipe, the broccoli is steamed briefly so that it keeps all of its nutrients and its deep green color. Flavored with a simple sauce made of lemon juice, olive oil, and Tabasco, this vegetable dish could be served as a first course.

Lemon Sauce

1½ tablespoons lemon juice
2 tablespoons virgin olive oil
¼ teaspoon Tabasco hot pepper sauce
¼ teaspoon salt

1½ pounds broccoli, cleaned

1. Combine the lemon juice, olive oil, Tabasco, and salt in a bowl. Mix well, and set aside.
2. Separate the broccoli florets from the stems. Peel the stems, if the exterior is tough or fibrous, and cut them into slices about ½ inch thick by 2 inches long.
3. Arrange the broccoli florets and stems on an ovenproof plate, and place it in a steamer (mine is bamboo). Steam, covered, over boiling water for 11 to 12 minutes.
4. Toss gently with the sauce, and serve.

Yield: 4 Servings

Nutritional analysis per serving:

Calories 90
Protein 3 gm.
Carbohydrates 6 gm.
Fat 7.1 gm.
Saturated fat 1.0 gm.
Cholesterol 0 mg.
Sodium 173 mg.

Broccoli is high in soluble fiber, vitamin C, and calcium.

Clockwise from left: Broccoli Piquant (above); Salmon Pojarski (see page 178); *Pommes à l'Anglaise* (Steamed Potatoes) (see page 321); all served together as a steamed dinner.

Broccoli with Butter

I love broccoli in everything from salads to soups, but this simple preparation is one of my favorites. Choose bunches with heads that are very tight and deep green; then peel the tough outer layer of the stems. This enables people to eat the entire stalk, which I think is the best part of the broccoli.

I cook the broccoli here in a minimum of water—most of it evaporates during the cooking time, leaving all the nutrients behind in the vegetable. I add a little butter for flavor at the last moment. (See photograph, page 198.)

1 pound broccoli, separated into florets about 2 inches wide at the flower, with stems peeled (14 ounces peeled)
1 cup water
1½ tablespoons unsalted butter
¼ teaspoon salt

1. Place the broccoli in a large saucepan with the water. Bring to a boil, and cook, covered, over medium heat for 5 minutes. (Most of the liquid will have evaporated.)
2. Add the butter and salt, mix gently, and serve immediately.

Yield: 4 Servings

Nutritional Analysis per Serving:

Calories 66
Protein 3 gm.
Carbohydrates 5 gm.
Fat 4.7 gm.
Saturated fat 2.7 gm.
Cholesterol 12 mg.
Sodium 162 mg.

Broccoli is high in beta-carotene, vitamin C, and fiber; it helps to reduce cancer risk.

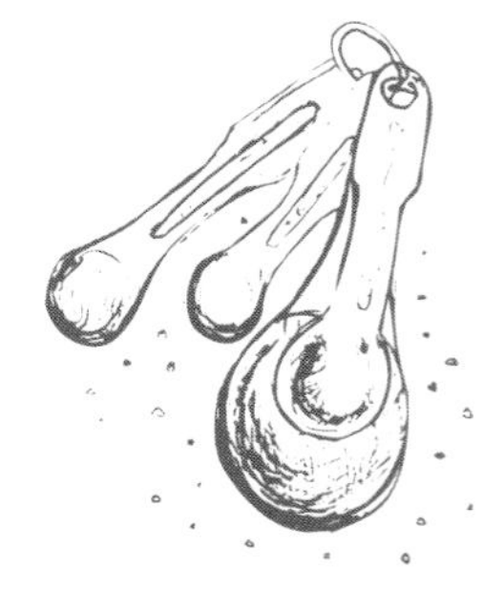

Braised Sour Cabbage

A combination of sweet apple cider and cider vinegar gives this dish a sweet-and-sour taste that complements pork especially well but that also goes well with goose or duck. You can substitute red cabbage for the savoy cabbage and add some sliced apple, if you like. (See photograph, page 251.)

1 pound savoy cabbage, cored and cut into 1-inch slices
1 medium onion (about 6 ounces), peeled and thinly sliced
¾ cup dark raisins
1 cup sweet apple cider
3 tablespoons cider vinegar
¾ teaspoon salt
¼ teaspoon freshly ground black pepper
½ tablespoon canola oil

1. Combine all the ingredients in a stainless steel saucepan.
2. Bring to a boil, cover, reduce the heat to medium, and boil for 45 minutes. Most of the liquid should have evaporated by then, but the cabbage should be moist; cook longer if excess moisture remains in the bottom of the pan. The small amount of liquid still in the pan should be caramelized and brown, and the cabbage a little crunchy. Serve.

Yield: 4 Servings

Nutritional Analysis per Serving:

Calories 167
Protein 3 gm.
Carbohydrates 38 gm.
Fat 2.0 gm.
Saturated fat 0.2 gm.
Cholesterol 0 mg.
Sodium 444 mg.

Raisins are a good source of iron, potassium, and soluble fiber.

Carottes à la Ciboulette (Carrots with Chives)

These carrots are cooked in a little water, butter, and seasonings. By the time the carrots are cooked and tender, the water has evaporated, leaving all the nutrients and the concentrated taste of the seasoned carrots. *(See photograph, page 211.)*

1 pound carrots, peeled and thinly sliced (about 3½ cups)
1 tablespoon unsalted butter
¾ cup water
1 teaspoon sugar
¾ teaspoon salt
¼ teaspoon freshly ground black pepper
2 tablespoons chopped fresh chives, for garnish

1. Combine the carrots, butter, water, sugar, salt, and pepper in a saucepan.
2. Bring to a boil, cover, and cook for 5 minutes, until most of the moisture has evaporated and the carrots are just tender. (If an excess amount of liquid remains in the pan, cook, uncovered, for a few minutes, or until most of the liquid has evaporated and the carrots start sizzling.)
3. Sprinkle with the chives, and serve as soon as possible.

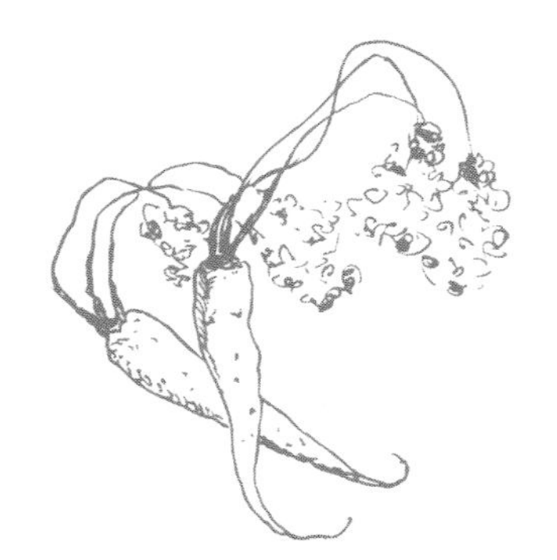

Yield: 4 Servings

NUTRITIONAL ANALYSIS PER SERVING:

Calories 74
Protein 1 gm.
Carbohydrates 11 gm.
Fat 3.1 gm.
Saturated fat 1.8 gm.
Cholesterol 8 mg.
Sodium 448 mg.

Carrots are a wonderful source of beta-carotene, the precursor to vitamin A.

Puree of Carrot with Ginger

In this dish, the nutrient-rich water remaining in the saucepan after the carrots and ginger are cooked is added to the food processor. It lends low-calorie moisture and flavor to the puree. *(See photograph, page 230.)*

1½ pounds carrots, peeled
1 tablespoon peeled diced ginger
3 cups water
2 tablespoons virgin olive oil
¾ teaspoon salt
¼ teaspoon freshly ground black pepper
¼ cup milk

1. Cut the peeled carrots into 1½-inch chunks, and place them in a saucepan. Add the ginger and water, and bring to a boil.
2. Cover the pan, reduce the heat, and boil gently for 15 minutes, until tender. (Only about ½ cup of water should remain in the pan.)
3. Transfer the carrots and ginger with the cooking juices to the bowl of a food processor, and process for a few seconds. Then add the remaining ingredients. Process until very smooth. Serve.

Yield: 4 Servings (2½ Cups)

Nutritional Analysis per Serving:

Calories 136
Protein 2 gm.
Carbohydrates 16 gm.
Fat 7.5 gm.
Saturated fat 1.3 gm.
Cholesterol 2 mg.
Sodium 473 mg.

STEAMED CAULIFLOWER WITH CHIVES

Especially flavorful if prepared at the last moment, this dish features florets of cauliflower that are steamed and then tossed with a little butter, peanut oil, chives, salt, and pepper. Be sure to use firm, white cauliflower for this dish. Older specimens with dark spots on top have a much stronger flavor. (See photograph, page 182.)

- **1 firm, white cauliflower, trimmed of all green leaves (1½ pounds)**
- **3 cups water**
- **¼ teaspoon salt**
- **¼ teaspoon freshly ground black pepper**
- **1 tablespoon unsalted butter**
- **1 tablespoon peanut oil**
- **¼ cup minced fresh chives**

1. Wash the cauliflower, and divide it into 12 to 16 florets of approximately equal size.
2. Bring the water to a boil in the base of a steamer or pot, preferably stainless steel. Place a steamer basket in the pot, add the cauliflower florets, cover, and cook over medium to high heat for about 10 minutes, until the florets are tender but still firm.
3. Transfer the cauliflower to a serving bowl, add the salt, pepper, butter, peanut oil, and chives, and toss briefly to mix. Serve immediately.

**YIELD:
4 SERVINGS**

NUTRITIONAL ANALYSIS PER SERVING:

Calories 72
Protein 1 gm.
Carbohydrates 3 gm.
Fat 6.4 gm.
Saturated fat 2.4 gm.
Cholesterol 8 mg.
Sodium 146 mg.

Cauliflower, a member of the cancer-protective cabbage family, provides excellent plant fiber.

Cauliflower in Scallion Sauce

Crisp, tender cauliflower florets are served with a flavorful sauce of sautéed scallions. Lightly browned bread crumbs are sprinkled over the hot cauliflower at the last moment.

- **1 head cauliflower with greens removed (about 1¼ pounds)**
- **1 cup water**
- **1 slice bread (1 ounce)**
- **3 tablespoons safflower oil**
- **4 scallions, finely minced (½ cup)**
- **¼ teaspoon salt**
- **¼ teaspoon freshly ground black pepper**

1. Separate the cauliflower into florets (making fourteen to sixteen pieces). Bring the water to a boil in a large saucepan. Add the florets in one layer, cover, and boil over high heat for about 8 to 10 minutes or until tender. (Most of the water should have evaporated.)
2. Meanwhile, toast the bread, and break it into the bowl of a food processor; process it until crumbed. (You should have about 3 tablespoons.)
3. Heat the oil in a skillet. When hot, add the scallions and bread crumbs, and sauté over medium heat for about 1½ minutes. Stir in the salt and pepper, and sprinkle the mixture over the hot cauliflower. Serve immediately.

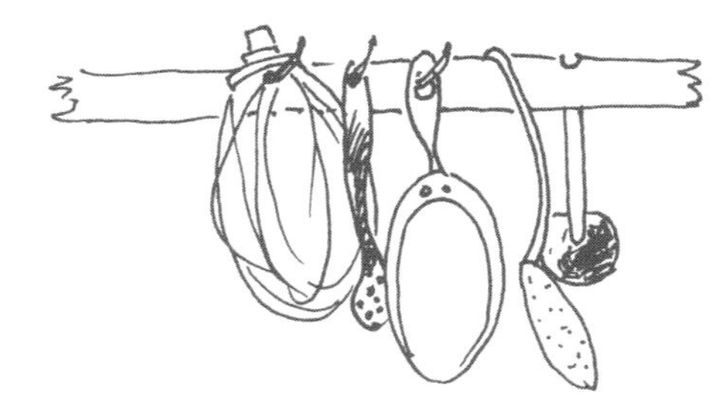

PRESERVING NUTRIENTS

In this recipe, cauliflower florets are cooked in just enough water so that most of the liquid has evaporated by the time the florets are tender, and the nutrients and vitamins are preserved in the vegetable. If the dish is done ahead, reheat the cauliflower in a little water on top of the stove or in the oven.

Yield: 4 Servings

NUTRITIONAL ANALYSIS PER SERVING:

Calories 141
Protein 3 gm.
Carbohydrates 10 gm.
Fat 10.7 gm.
Saturated fat 1.0 gm.
Cholesterol 0 mg.
Sodium 192 mg.

Cauliflower has twice as much soluble fiber as zucchini.

CELERIAC AND POTATO PUREE

Although of the same family as celery stalks, celeriac is a different vegetable entirely, with a flavor almost too intense to enjoy on its own. I cook it here with potatoes and then puree the vegetables together. The result is delightful.

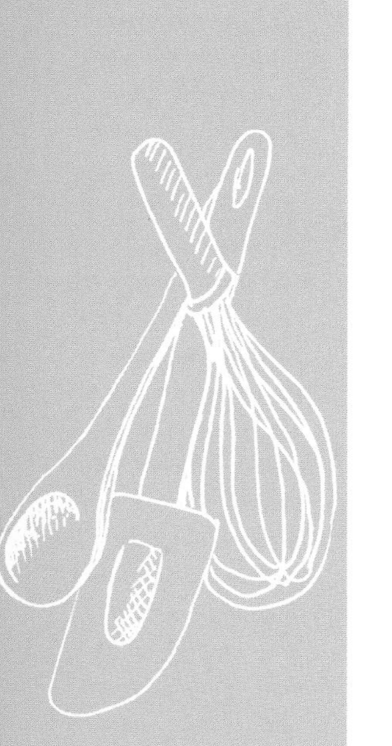

1 celeriac (about 1 pound, 6 ounces)
1¼ pounds potatoes
1¼ cups water
¾ teaspoon salt
1 tablespoon unsalted butter
¾ cup milk

1. Peel the celeriac and cut it into 2-inch chunks. Peel the potatoes, wash them, and cut them into 2-inch chunks.
2. Place the celeriac and potatoes in a saucepan with the water and ¼ teaspoon of the salt. Bring to a boil, reduce the heat, cover, and boil the vegetables gently until tender, about 30 minutes.
3. Push the vegetables and their cooking liquid through a food mill set over a saucepan. Whisk in the butter, then add the remaining salt and the milk, and whisk them into the puree. Serve hot.

YIELD: 4 SERVINGS (4 TO 5 CUPS)

NUTRITIONAL ANALYSIS PER SERVING:

Calories 190
Protein 6 gm.
Carbohydrates 34 gm.
Fat 4.9 gm.
Saturated fat 2.8 gm.
Cholesterol 14 mg.
Sodium 576 mg.

Celeriac, resembling the turnip, is a versatile low-calorie vegetable.

Red Swiss Chard with Ginger

I can usually find small red Swiss chard at my market in the spring. The ribs are quite tender in these early specimens and can be cooked successfully with the leaves. A beautiful red color, the chard is seasoned here with ginger and jalapeño pepper, with the quantity of the latter adjusted to individual tastes. If you cannot find red Swiss chard, substitute regular chard or another green, such as Romaine lettuce or watercress.

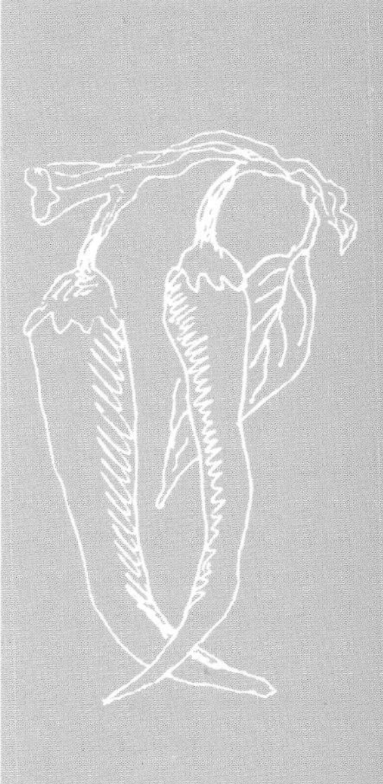

1¼ pounds small red Swiss chard
3 tablespoons virgin olive oil
4 large shallots (about 4 ounces), peeled and finely chopped (½ cup)
1 1½-ounce piece of ginger, peeled and finely chopped (2 tablespoons)
1 small jalapeño pepper, seeded and finely chopped (2 teaspoons)
¾ teaspoon salt

1. Trim about 2 inches from the tops of the chard leaves, and discard the trimmings. Cut the remaining chard ribs and leaves into 2-inch pieces. Wash and drain the chard. (You should have about 12 cups, lightly packed.)
2. Heat the oil in a large saucepan. When it is hot, add the shallots, and sauté them for 30 seconds over high heat. Add the ginger and jalapeño, mix well, and cook for 10 seconds.
3. Add about a third of the chard, still wet from the washing, turning it over in the pan several times to incorporate the shallots and garlic and prevent them from burning in the bottom of the pan. Then add the rest of the chard and the salt. Cover, reduce the heat to medium, and cook the mixture for 6 to 8 minutes, stirring occasionally, until the chard leaves are wilted and tender but the ribs are still slightly firm.
4. Transfer the mixture to a serving dish, and serve immediately.

Yield: 4 Servings

NUTRITIONAL ANALYSIS PER SERVING:

Calories 137
Protein 3 gm.
Carbohydrates 10 gm.
Fat 10.4 gm.
Saturated fat 1.4 gm.
Cholesterol 0 mg.
Sodium 717 mg.

Red Swiss chard is rich in vitamin A and also provides potassium, folacin, and fiber.

Corn and Pepper Sauté

This is one of my favorite ways to prepare corn and red bell pepper. Fresh corn kernels are sautéed briefly in a skillet, and since the starch in them doesn't cook long enough to set, the corn remains crunchy and sweet. Red pepper remains quite firm and thick-walled when peeled and is easily digested. This is an easy dish to make and is especially good if the corn is fresh from the garden. (See photograph, page 271.)

PEELING PEPPERS

For this recipe, I peel the red pepper with a vegetable peeler, instead of placing it under the broiler and peeling off the blistered skin, as is done conventionally. Use a good vegetable peeler, and peel off as much of the skin from the whole vegetable as possible before cutting it into segments and removing additional skin from the recessed areas.

Yield: 4 Servings

Nutritional analysis per serving:

Calories 130
Protein 3 gm.
Carbohydrates 18 gm.
Fat 6.7 gm.
Saturated fat 3.7 gm.
Cholesterol 16 mg.
Sodium 149 mg.

Corn is high in vitamins A and B; red bell pepper is a good source of vitamins A, B, C, and E.

- **2 ears fresh corn**
- **1 large red bell pepper (8 ounces)**
- **2 tablespoons unsalted butter**
- **¼ teaspoon salt**
- **¼ teaspoon freshly ground black pepper**

1. Husk the ears of corn, and cut off the kernels. (You should have about 2 cups.) Set aside.
2. Using a vegetable peeler, remove as much of the skin as you can from the red pepper. (The firmer the pepper, the easier it is to peel.) Cut the pepper into sections, remove the seeds from each section, and peel off any remaining skin. Cut the pepper into ¼-inch pieces. (You should have about 1 cup.)
3. Heat the butter in a skillet. Add the corn, and sauté in hot butter over high heat for about 2 minutes. Then add the red pepper, and sauté the mixture for 1½ minutes longer. Stir in the salt and black pepper, and serve immediately.

Cucumber with Tarragon

Even though cucumbers are usually eaten raw, cooked cucumbers make an absolutely delightful, light, and delicate garnish, particularly for fish. I use a "seedless" cucumber here and then cut it in such a way that most of the few seeds are trimmed away. The chopped tarragon is a welcome addition and gives the dish a special accent. *(See photograph, page 153.)*

1 English-style "seedless" cucumber (about 1 pound)
3 cups water
1 tablespoon unsalted butter
¼ teaspoon salt
¼ teaspoon freshly ground black pepper
1 tablespoon chopped fresh tarragon

1. Trim off and discard both ends of the cucumber, and cut it crosswise into 1½-inch chunks. (You should have about seven chunks.) Cut each chunk lengthwise into six wedges, and, using a small paring knife, round the sharp edges and shape the wedges into ovals, eliminating most of the seeds as you do so.
2. Bring the water to a boil in a saucepan. Add the cucumber ovals, and bring the water back to a strong boil. Immediately drain the ovals in a sieve or colander, and set aside.
3. At serving time, melt the butter in a large skillet. Add the cucumber ovals, salt, and pepper, and toss to mix. Cook 2 to 3 minutes, just until the ovals are hot throughout. Add the tarragon, and toss it with the cucumber.
4. Serve about ten cucumber ovals per person.

Yield: 4 Servings

NUTRITIONAL ANALYSIS PER SERVING:

Calories 41
Protein 1 gm.
Carbohydrates 4 gm.
Fat 3.0 gm.
Saturated fat 1.8 gm.
Cholesterol 8 mg.
Sodium 138 mg.

Fresh herbs are best for taste; otherwise use dried herbs at one-third the amount.

Gratin of Eggplant and Tomato

To begin this dish, lightly oiled slices of eggplant are spread on a tray and baked. Far easier than cooking them the conventional way (in batches in a skillet), this approach is healthier, too, since much less oil is required. The slices are then layered with tomatoes in a gratin dish, topped with flavored bread crumbs, and finished in the oven. *(See photograph, page 172.)*

- **2 long, narrow, firm eggplants (1 pound total)**
- **2 tablespoons corn oil**
- **½ teaspoon salt**
- **1 slice fine-textured white bread, processed into crumbs in a food processor (⅔ cup)**
- **⅓ cup grated parmesan cheese**
- **1 teaspoon chopped fresh thyme leaves**
- **1 tablespoon virgin olive oil**
- **4 ripe medium tomatoes (about 1 pound), cut into ⅜-inch slices**

1. Preheat the oven to 400 degrees.
2. Trim (but do not peel) the eggplants, and cut them lengthwise into ½-inch slices. (You will have about eight slices.)
3. Coat the bottom of a jelly roll pan or roasting pan with the corn oil. Lay the eggplant slices in a single layer in the oiled pan, and then immediately turn them over in the pan so they are lightly oiled on both sides.
4. Sprinkle the slices with the salt, and bake them for 15 minutes. Then turn the slices carefully with a large metal spatula (they will be soft), and bake them for another 10 minutes. Set the eggplant aside in the pan, and let it cool to lukewarm.
5. Meanwhile, in a small bowl, mix the bread crumbs, parmesan cheese, thyme, and olive oil.
6. Arrange alternating slices of eggplant and tomato in a 4- to 6-cup gratin dish, overlapping the slices as required to fit them all into the dish. Sprinkle the bread crumb mixture evenly on top. (At this point, the dish can be covered and refrigerated for up to 8 hours.)
7. When ready to cook the gratin, preheat the oven to 400 degrees. Bake the gratin for 20 to 25 minutes, until the vegetables are soft and heated through, and the crumb topping is nicely browned. Serve immediately.

Yield: 4 Servings

NUTRITIONAL ANALYSIS PER SERVING:

Calories 194
Protein 6 gm.
Carbohydrates 16 gm.
Fat 12.9 gm.
Saturated fat 2.7 gm.
Cholesterol 6 mg.
Sodium 448 mg.

Grilled Portobello Mushrooms

These large, meaty, big-capped mushrooms are available now in most supermarkets around the country and are ideal for grilling. They make an attractive, flavorful, and unusual garnish for fish, poultry, or meat. I grill only the caps here, but the stems can be cooked alongside the caps on the grill or reserved and frozen for later use—preferably chopped, since they are tougher than the caps—in soups or stuffings.

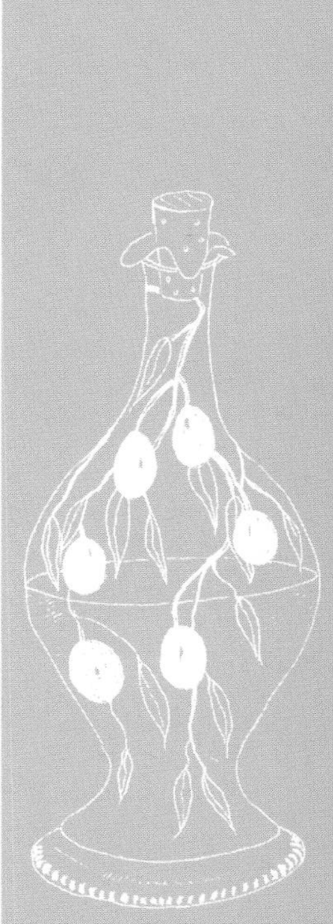

- 4 **large Portobello mushrooms (about 1 pound total), stems removed and reserved for soup or stuffing (12 ounces of caps)**
- 1½ **tablespoons virgin olive oil**
- ¼ **teaspoon salt**

1. Preheat the oven to 180 degrees.
2. Rub the top surface of the mushroom caps with the oil, which will be absorbed quickly, and sprinkle them with the salt.
3. Place the caps on a very hot grill, and cook them, top side down, for 3 minutes. Turn them over, and cook them for 3 minutes on the other side.
4. If serving the mushrooms within 30 minutes, place them in a pan in a 180-degree oven until serving time.
5. Otherwise, allow the mushrooms to cool, and reheat them in a 400-degree oven or in a skillet on top of the stove just before serving.

Yield: 4 Servings

NUTRITIONAL ANALYSIS PER SERVING:

Calories 66
Protein 2 gm.
Carbohydrates 4 gm.
Fat 5.4 gm.
Saturated fat 0.7 gm.
Cholesterol 0 mg.
Sodium 138 mg.

Mushrooms are naturally rich in chromium, an essential trace mineral.

Caramelized Mushrooms with Shallots

I like to use medium to large mushrooms in this recipe, preferring the older, somewhat darker specimens with visible gills because they are more flavorful. To achieve the concentrated taste I want here, I cook the mushrooms for a long time—it takes a while for the moisture to emerge from them and evaporate, and then for them to brown. When done, the mushrooms are almost meatlike in texture and have an intense flavor that is further enhanced by the addition of shallots and parsley.

1½ tablespoons virgin olive oil
1 pound mushrooms, preferably older specimens, with slightly opened and darkened gills, washed
3 to 4 shallots (3 ounces), peeled and thinly sliced (1 cup)
1 tablespoon unsalted butter
⅓ cup chopped fresh flat-leaf parsley
½ teaspoon salt
½ teaspoon freshly ground black pepper

1. Heat the oil in a skillet with a lid. When it is hot, add the mushrooms, and cook them, covered, over medium heat for 20 to 25 minutes, until all the liquid that emerges from them has disappeared and the mushrooms are nicely browned.
2. Add the shallots to the skillet, and sauté them, uncovered, for 2 to 3 minutes, until they are soft and brown.
3. Add the butter, parsley, salt, and pepper, and sauté for 10 seconds longer. Serve immediately.

Yield: 4 Servings

NUTRITIONAL ANALYSIS PER SERVING:

Calories 114
Protein 3 gm.
Carbohydrates 9 gm.
Fat 8.4 gm.
Saturated fat 2.5 gm.
Cholesterol 8 mg.
Sodium 283 mg.

PAN-SEARED OR GRILLED MARINATED FLANK STEAK (SEE PAGE 285),
CARAMELIZED MUSHROOMS WITH SHALLOTS (ABOVE),
AND SAUTÉED LETTUCE PACKAGES (SEE PAGE 330).

Buttered Potatoes with Parsley

A time-honored combination, potatoes with parsley are always welcome. Trim the potato pieces to form ovals of nearly equal size, then boil them in water until tender. After the water is discarded, return the potatoes to the stove briefly to eliminate any remaining moisture—a simple step that produces potatoes with a creamy, smooth interior. Finish the dish with butter, salt, and parsley.

1½ pounds potatoes, peeled and cut into 2-inch pieces (about 20 pieces)
1½ tablespoons unsalted butter
¼ teaspoon salt
3 tablespoons chopped fresh parsley

1. Trim the potato pieces (reserving the trimmings for soup, if desired), rounding them off to make ovals of about the same size and shape. Rinse the potato pieces well, place them in a saucepan, and add enough cold tap water to cover. Bring to a boil, reduce the heat to low, and boil gently for 15 to 20 minutes.
2. Drain the water, and place the saucepan containing the potatoes back on the stove over high heat for about 30 seconds to evaporate any remaining moisture from the potatoes. (This step is important, as it will give you a very moist and smooth-textured potato.)
3. Add the butter, salt, and parsley, toss gently (to avoid breaking the potatoes), and serve immediately.

YIELD: 4 SERVINGS

NUTRITIONAL ANALYSIS PER SERVING:

Calories 140
Protein 3 gm.
Carbohydrates 23 gm.
Fat 4.4 gm.
Saturated fat 2.7 gm.
Cholesterol 12 mg.
Sodium 144 mg.

Parsley is rich in vitamins A and C, potassium, and iron.

Pommes à l'Anglaise (Steamed Potatoes)

It is important that you use potatoes of approximately the same size for this dish. If you can't find small, round, red-skinned potatoes, cut larger potatoes into equal-size chunks, and round off the corners to make them more uniformly shaped. Prepared at the last moment and eaten freshly steamed, these are moist and delicate, much more so than potatoes cooked and left standing in water. For a complete steamed dinner, serve Pommes à l'Anglaise *with Salmon Pojarski (page 178) and Broccoli Piquant (page 302). Preparation instructions are given on page 16. (See photograph, page 303.)*

12 **small new potatoes (1½ pounds), peeled**

1. Peel the potatoes, and place them in a bowl of cold water until cooking time.
2. When ready to cook and serve, arrange them on an ovenproof plate, and place in a steamer (mine is bamboo). Steam, covered, over boiling water for about 25 minutes or until tender.

Yield: 4 Servings

NUTRITIONAL ANALYSIS PER SERVING:

Calories 124
Protein 3 gm.
Carbohydrates 28 gm.
Fat 0.3 gm.
Saturated fat 0 gm.
Cholesterol 0 mg.
Sodium 12 mg.

Potatoes provide nutritiously satisfying complex carbohydrates and are naturally low in sodium.

POTATOES IN ADVANCE

FOR THIS RECIPE, THE POTATOES CAN BE PEELED AND CUT INTO CUBES AHEAD, PROVIDED THEY ARE KEPT IN WATER TO COVER SO THEY DON'T DISCOLOR. JUST BEFORE SERVING, DRAIN, DRY WITH PAPER TOWELS, AND SAUTÉ QUICKLY IN A LITTLE CANOLA OIL, WHICH CAN WITHSTAND HIGH TEMPERATURES.

Pommes Persillade (Potatoes with Parsley and Garlic)

These potatoes are a standard item on most bistro menus. Cut into little cubes, they can be sautéed in just a few minutes. They are best served immediately after cooking; if cooked ahead, they soften and lose the exterior crispness that contrasts so well with their soft interior. *(See photograph, page 282.)*

- **2 large potatoes (18 ounces), peeled**
- **2 tablespoons canola oil**
- **3 cloves garlic, peeled**
- **¼ cup (loose) fresh parsley leaves**
- **1 teaspoon salt**
- **1 teaspoon freshly ground black pepper**

1. Cut the potatoes into ⅜-inch cubes. Place in a sieve, and rinse well under cool tap water. Place in a bowl with water to cover until ready to cook.
2. In a large nonstick skillet, heat the oil. Drain the potatoes, pat dry with paper towels, and add to the hot oil. Sauté over high heat for 12 to 14 minutes, stirring occasionally, until the potatoes are browned on all sides.
3. Meanwhile, chop the garlic and parsley together until finely minced, and set the mixture aside. (This is a *persillade.*) Add the salt, pepper, and *persillade* to the potatoes in the skillet, tossing to combine. Serve immediately.

YIELD: 4 SERVINGS

NUTRITIONAL ANALYSIS PER SERVING:

Calories 102
Protein 2 gm.
Carbohydrates 19 gm.
Fat 2.4 gm.
Saturated fat 0.2 gm.
Cholesterol 0 mg.
Sodium 558 mg.

Potatoes are high in soluble fiber and potassium.

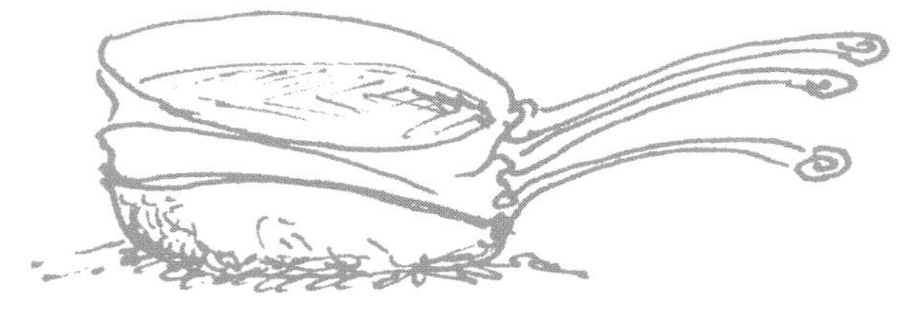

Turnips and Mashed Potatoes

In this recipe, potatoes and turnips are cooked in just enough water so that there is about ½ cup of liquid remaining in the pan when the vegetables are tender—enough to incorporate with them to create a nice puree. If a little more liquid is required, add a dash of water or stock; if too much liquid remains in the pan after the vegetables are cooked, remove the lid, and quickly boil to reduce the liquid to ½ cup. *(See photograph, page 219.)*

3 large potatoes (18 ounces total)
2 turnips (6 ounces total)
1 large clove garlic, peeled
½ teaspoon salt
1 cup water
2 tablespoons unsalted butter

1. Peel the potatoes and turnips, and cut them into 2-inch pieces.
2. Place in a saucepan with the garlic, salt, and water. Bring to a boil, cover, reduce the heat, and boil gently for 20 minutes, until the vegetables are tender. (About ½ cup of liquid should remain. Adjust to this level, if necessary.)
3. Transfer the mixture to the bowl of a food processor, add the butter, and process until smooth and creamy. Serve.

ABOUT BUTTER FLAVOR

Although I don't use milk or cream in this recipe, I do use a little butter. Select a good-quality butter, and add it at the last moment for maximum taste enhancement.

Yield: 4 Servings (2½ Cups)

NUTRITIONAL ANALYSIS PER SERVING:

Calories 137
Protein 2 gm.
Carbohydrates 20 gm.
Fat 5.9 gm.
Saturated fat 3.6 gm.
Cholesterol 16 mg.
Sodium 303 mg.

This combination of root vegetables is a good source of potassium.

Potato Sauté à Cru

SLICE AND SOAK

FOR THIS DISH, THE POTATOES CAN BE PEELED AND EVEN SLICED AHEAD, AS LONG AS THEY ARE KEPT IN WATER TO COVER AND THEN ARE CAREFULLY DRAINED AND PATTED DRY JUST BEFORE SAUTÉING.

Potatoes that are sautéed raw have a totally different taste from hash browns, which are made from cooked potatoes.

These potatoes are best served immediately after cooking—20 minutes is the maximum waiting time. If the dish is prepared ahead and reheated, the taste will be disappointingly different.

I cook the potatoes for this dish in canola oil because it can withstand higher temperatures than butter without burning; for these potatoes to brown properly, they must be cooked at a fairly high temperature. If you want the flavor of butter, add a little at the end of the cooking period for maximum taste enhancement.

4 **baking potatoes (1¾ to 2 pounds)**
3 **tablespoons canola oil**
¼ **teaspoon salt**

1. Peel the potatoes, and cut them crosswise into ¼-inch slices. Rinse them, and set them aside in a bowl of cool water to cover. (This can be done a couple of hours ahead.)
2. About 20 minutes before serving, drain the potato slices, and pat them dry with paper towels.
3. Heat the oil in one very large or two smaller skillets (preferably nonstick). When it is hot, add the potatoes, and cook them over medium to high heat, half covered (to prevent splattering), for about 15 minutes, tossing them every 2 minutes or so to prevent them from burning and to enable them to brown on all sides. (Some of the slices will be browner than others, but this gives contrast of texture, color, and taste to the dish.) When the potatoes are tender, toss them with the salt. Serve immediately.

YIELD: 4 SERVINGS

NUTRITIONAL ANALYSIS PER SERVING:

Calories 217
Protein 3 gm.
Carbohydrates 29 gm.
Fat 10.4 gm.
Saturated fat 0.8 gm.
Cholesterol 0 mg.
Sodium 145 mg.

French Fries

These French fries are cooked as fries are in professional kitchens. First blanch them in oil that is not too hot, so they will cook without taking on any color. This can be done hours ahead. Just before serving, brown the fries quickly in very hot oil until crisp on the outside and soft and moist inside.

ABOUT FRENCH FRIES

NOTICE THAT I START THIS RECIPE WITH 1½ CUPS OF OIL. AFTER THE SECOND COOKING, ABOUT 1¼ CUPS OF OIL SHOULD REMAIN; THE POTATOES ABSORB ONLY ABOUT ¼ CUP OF OIL, OR 1 TABLESPOON PER PORTION. THIS IS LESS OIL THAN WOULD HAVE BEEN USED IN THE DRESSING IF THE POTATOES HAD BEEN MADE INTO A SALAD INSTEAD.

- **3 large Idaho (russet) potatoes (2 pounds)**
- **1½ cups vegetable oil**
- **Salt to taste**

1. Peel the potatoes, and cut them lengthwise into sticks ½ inch thick. Wash the sticks in cold water, drain them, and pat them dry.
2. In a 12-inch nonstick skillet, heat the oil to 350 degrees. Add the potatoes, and cook for 5 minutes, until they are tender but still whitish. Remove, and set aside until serving time. (You can prepare the recipe up to this point hours ahead.)
3. At serving time, reheat the oil to 400 degrees, and finish frying the potatoes, half at a time, for 4 to 5 minutes (shaking the pan occasionally to prevent them from sticking) until nicely browned and crisp.
4. Remove the potatoes from the oil, set them aside on absorbent paper, and repeat with the second batch. Sprinkle with salt, and serve immediately.

YIELD: 4 SERVINGS

NUTRITIONAL ANALYSIS PER SERVING:

Calories 286
Protein 4 gm.
Carbohydrates 37 gm.
Fat 14.0 gm.
Saturated fat 1.7 gm.
Cholesterol 0 mg.
Sodium 16 mg.

Potato Gaufrettes or Chips

There are two possible recipes here: Large potatoes can be cut either into waferlike slices on a mandoline to make gaufrettes, *or—using the slicing disk on a food processor—into paper-thin slices for chips. Instead of frying the potatoes in a deep fryer, where they would absorb a great deal of oil, I arrange the slices on an oiled tray and bake them in the oven. Much lower in calories than conventional* gaufrettes *or chips, they make a great meat accompaniment or a good snack on their own.* *(See photograph, page 259.)*

3 tablespoons canola oil
1 large white or sweet potato (about 12 ounces), peeled and cut into about 20 waferlike slices on a mandoline, or into paper-thin slices in a food processor fitted with the slicing disk
⅛ teaspoon salt

1. Preheat the oven to 400 degrees.
2. Coat the bottom of a jelly roll pan with 2 tablespoons of the oil. Arrange a single layer of the sliced potatoes in the pan so they fit snugly against one another. Then turn the slices over once in the oil (so they are lightly oiled on both sides).
3. Place the pan in the hot oven for 16 to 18 mintues, until the potato slices are dry and nicely browned. (Some of the slices will brown faster than others; as they brown, carefully remove them with a spatula.) Place the slices on a rack to cool.
4. Repeat with the rest of the potato slices, replenishing the tray with the remaining tablespoon of oil as needed.
5. Lightly salt the *gaufrettes* or chips, and serve.

Yield: 4 Servings

NUTRITIONAL ANALYSIS PER SERVING:

Calories 141
Protein 1 gm.
Carbohydrates 11 gm.
Fat 10.3 gm.
Saturated fat 0.8 gm.
Cholesterol 0 mg.
Sodium 73 mg.

Potatoes are a source of satisfying and nutritious complex carbohydrates.

Skillet Sweet Potatoes

For this recipe, I like to use bright orange yam slices, beginning them in a mixture of butter, oil, and water, then continuing to cook them until nicely browned after the water has evaporated. An easy dish, it is good with almost any meat or fish main course. *(See photograph, page 290.)*

1 large sweet potato (about 1 pound), peeled and cut crosswise into 12 slices, each about ¼ inch thick
1 tablespoon unsalted butter
1 tablespoon corn oil
½ cup water
¼ teaspoon salt

1. Arrange the potato slices in a single layer in one very large or two slightly smaller nonstick skillets. Add the butter, oil, water, and salt. Bring the mixture to a boil, cover, and boil gently over high heat for about 5 minutes. Most of the water will have evaporated, and the potatoes will be soft.
2. Continue to cook, uncovered, over medium heat, turning until the slices are nicely browned on both sides, about 1 additional minute per side. Serve immediately.

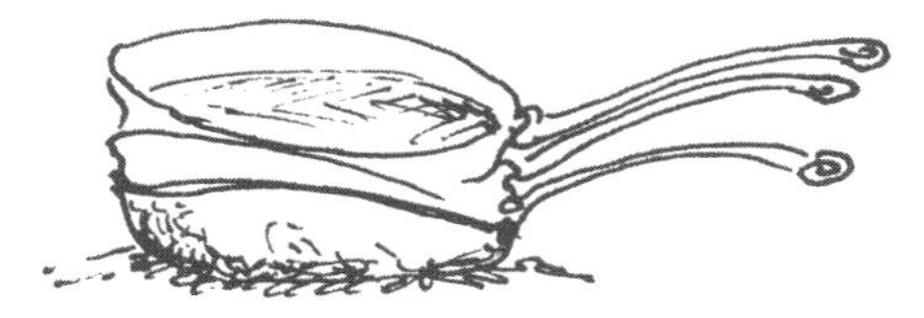

YIELD: 4 SERVINGS

NUTRITIONAL ANALYSIS PER SERVING:

Calories 141
Protein 1 gm.
Carbohydrates 20 gm.
Fat 6.5 gm.
Saturated fat 2.3 gm.
Cholesterol 8 mg.
Sodium 146 mg.

One sweet potato provides five times the recommended daily allowance of vitamin A.

Sautéed Lettuce Packages

Unfortunately, people don't often cook lettuce. I am very fond of it sautéed with garlic, mixed into soufflés, or combined with peas or carrots in a stew. Here, I poach whole heads of Boston lettuce, then halve them, fold them into triangle-shaped packages, and sauté them in a little butter and oil. These make a great accompaniment for Veal Chops with Olive Shavings (see page 269) or almost any roast meat. (See photograph, page 317.)

Yield: 4 Servings

NUTRITIONAL ANALYSIS PER SERVING:

Calories 96
Protein 3 gm.
Carbohydrates 8 gm.
Fat 6.9 gm.
Saturated fat 2.4 gm.
Cholesterol 8 mg.
Sodium 156 mg.

- 3 **quarts water**
- 4 **firm heads Boston lettuce (2 pounds total)**
- 1 **tablespoon unsalted butter**
- 1 **tablespoon peanut oil**
- ¼ **teaspoon salt**
- ⅛ **teaspoon freshly ground black pepper**

1. Bring the water to a boil in a large pot. Meanwhile, wash the lettuce thoroughly, gently opening the leaves to let water flow over and around them, but taking care not to separate the leaves from the cores.
2. Add the lettuce heads to the boiling water, and cover them with an inverted plate to keep them submerged. Bring the water back to a boil, reduce the heat to medium, and boil the lettuce gently for 20 minutes. Remove the plate, drain the water, and add enough ice to the pot to cover the lettuce and cool it quickly.
3. When the lettuce heads are cold, remove them from the pot, and, holding them gently to preserve their original shape, press each head between your palms to remove as much liquid as possible. Cut the heads in half lengthwise (top to core), then fold each half head into a triangle-shaped package. Set aside until cooking time. (The lettuce can be prepared to this point up to a day ahead, covered, and refrigerated.)
4. When you are ready to proceed, heat the butter and oil until hot in a large skillet. Add the lettuce packages, folded side up, and sprinkle them with half the salt and pepper. Cook over medium to high heat for 3 to 4 minutes. Turn the packages over, sprinkle them with the remaining salt and pepper, and sauté 3 to 4 minutes longer, until lightly browned.
5. Arrange the lettuce packages on a serving platter, and serve immediately, two packages per person, or place them in a gratin dish, and warm them in a 180-degree oven for up to 30 minutes before serving.

Skillet Spinach with Nutmeg

The combination of nutmeg and spinach is classic in French cooking. Here, I cook freshly cleaned spinach, still wet from washing, in a little butter and oil for a minute, then season it with salt, pepper, and nutmeg, and cook it a few minutes longer to boil away excess liquid. Fast and easy, this dish is very flavorful.

1 pound spinach, trimmed of large stems and damaged leaves (about 13 ounces trimmed)
1 tablespoon unsalted butter
1 tablespoon virgin olive oil
¼ teaspoon salt
¼ teaspoon freshly ground black pepper
¼ teaspoon freshly grated nutmeg

1. Wash and drain the spinach. At serving time, heat the butter and oil until very hot in a large skillet. Add half the spinach (still wet from washing), and stir well. When it begins to wilt, add the remainder of the spinach to the skillet, and cover with a lid.
2. Cook the spinach for 1 minute over high heat, and then remove the lid. The spinach will be wilted, and liquid will have emerged from it. Add the salt, pepper, and nutmeg, and mix well. Continue cooking, uncovered, over high heat for 3 to 4 minutes, stirring occasionally, until most of the liquid has boiled away. Serve.

Yield: 4 Servings

NUTRITIONAL ANALYSIS PER SERVING:

Calories 77
Protein 3 gm.
Carbohydrates 3 gm.
Fat 6.6 gm.
Saturated fat 2.3 gm.
Cholesterol 8 mg.
Sodium 208 mg.

Spinach is rich in vitamin A and folacin as well as iron and potassium.

Gratin of Tomato and Bread

This is a terrific summer dish; cherry tomatoes are inexpensive then and at their peak. For variety, I sometimes substitute yellow cherry tomatoes for the red or use small pear-shaped tomatoes. The combination of flavors—tomatoes, bread, garlic, olive oil, parsley, and parmesan cheese—makes this everybody's favorite.

- **1¼ pounds cherry tomatoes (about 3½ cups)**
- **3 ounces day-old bread (preferably from a French baguette), cut into 1-inch cubes (about 3½ cups)**
- **6 cloves garlic, peeled and sliced (2 tablespoons)**
- **½ cup coarsely chopped fresh parsley**
- **½ teaspoon freshly ground black pepper**
- **2 tablespoons virgin olive oil**
- **½ teaspoon salt**
- **¼ cup grated parmesan cheese**

1. Preheat the oven to 375 degrees.
2. Wash the tomatoes, and remove and discard any stems. Place the tomatoes in a bowl, and mix in the remainder of the ingredients. Transfer the mixture to a 6-cup gratin dish.
3. Bake at 375 degrees for 40 minutes. Serve immediately.

Yield: 4 Servings

NUTRITIONAL ANALYSIS PER SERVING:

Calories 185
Protein 6 gm.
Carbohydrates 21 gm.
Fat 9.4 gm.
Saturated fat 2.1 gm.
Cholesterol 5 mg.
Sodium 506 mg.

Tomatoes are a good source of cancer-protective beta-carotene.

TOP: GRILLED VEAL CHOPS WITH CAPER SAUCE (SEE PAGE 268).
BELOW: GRATIN OF TOMATO AND BREAD (ABOVE).

Vegetable Burgers

For this interesting recipe, several vegetables are first cooked together. (I use spinach, corn, peas, and red pepper, but other vegetables could be substituted.) Then the vegetable-cooking juices—in combination with some chicken stock—are used as a base for cooking the grits. While I use white grits here, semolina or farina could also be used to create the thick mass needed to hold the vegetables together.

- 1 cup water
- 3 cups (loosely packed) trimmed and washed spinach
- 1 ear sweet corn, husked, with kernels removed (½ cup)
- ½ cup fresh peas or frozen baby peas
- ⅓ cup peeled, diced (¼-inch dice) red bell pepper (see Peeling Peppers, page 312)
- 1¼ cups homemade unsalted and defatted chicken stock (see page 466), or lower-salt canned chicken broth
- ½ teaspoon salt (less if using canned broth)
- ¼ teaspoon freshly ground black pepper
- ½ cup white grits
- 1½ tablespoons canola oil
- ½ teaspoon unsalted butter

1. Bring the water to a boil in a saucepan. Add the spinach, corn kernels, peas, and red pepper, and bring the water back to a boil. Immediately drain the vegetables in a colander set over a pan, pressing lightly on the vegetables to extrude most of the water. (You should have about 1 cup of cooking liquid.)
2. Place the cooking liquid in a saucepan with the chicken stock, salt, and black pepper, and bring to a boil. Add the grits, and mix well.
3. Cook, covered, over low heat, stirring occasionally so the grits don't stick to the bottom of the pan, for 20 to 25 minutes. The mixture will be quite thick.
4. Transfer the grits to a dish, spreading them out so they cool more quickly. When they are lukewarm, add the vegetables, and mix well. Cool completely, and then form the mixture into four patties.

PREPARATION TIPS

The burgers can be assembled in advance but should not be sautéed until the last moment. Be sure to sauté them in a nonstick pan and turn them carefully with a large hamburger spatula. Although they are moist and delicious, they are delicate and have a tendency to break apart.

Yield: 4 Servings

NUTRITIONAL ANALYSIS PER SERVING:

Calories 177
Protein 6 gm.
Carbohydrates 25 gm.
Fat 6.7 gm.
Saturated fat 0.9 gm.
Cholesterol 1 mg.
Sodium 333 mg.

5. At serving time, heat the oil and butter in a nonstick pan. When they are hot, add the patties, and cook, covered (to prevent splattering), for about 8 minutes on the first side.
6. Turn carefully (the patties tend to break apart), and cook for another 8 minutes on the second side. Serve.

Julienne of Zucchini

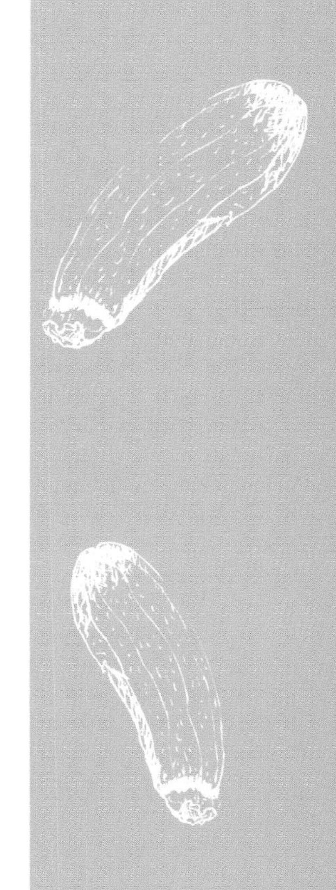

The zucchini are cut in an interesting way here: long, thin strips are sliced from the firm, fleshy sides of the vegetable, and the cottony, seedy centers are discarded. When sliced this way, into what we call julienne strips, zucchini has a special "bite" and crunchiness, and it makes an attractive presentation. You can also make a "nest" of these strips and serve them topped with a grilled lamb chop, scallops, shrimp, or fish.

4 or 5 small, firm zucchini (about 1½ pounds total)
1 tablespoon unsalted butter
2 tablespoons virgin olive oil
4 tablespoons chopped shallots
¼ teaspoon salt
¼ teaspoon freshly ground black pepper

1. Wash the zucchini, and trim off and discard both ends. Using a mandoline or a sharp knife, cut each zucchini lengthwise into long julienne strips ⅛ inch thick, stopping when you reach the cottony center of the zucchini. Rotate the zucchini, and continue cutting until all the firm flesh has been removed. Discard the centers, and set aside the julienne strips. (You should have about 6 cups.)
2. Heat the butter and oil in a large skillet. When they are hot, add the shallots, and sauté for 15 seconds over medium to high heat. Add the zucchini, salt, and pepper, and sauté over high heat for 4 minutes.
3. Serve immediately.

YIELD: 4 SERVINGS

NUTRITIONAL ANALYSIS PER SERVING:

Calories 116
Protein 2 gm.
Carbohydrates 7 gm.
Fat 9.9 gm.
Saturated fat 2.7 gm.
Cholesterol 8 mg.
Sodium 142 mg.

Zucchini are a good source of soluble fiber.

Pasta and Zucchini

I make this extra-simple pasta sauce with zucchini, garlic, salt, pepper, and olive oil. The combination of vegetables and cooking liquid creates a rich, satisfying, colorful pasta sauce that is not too high in calories.

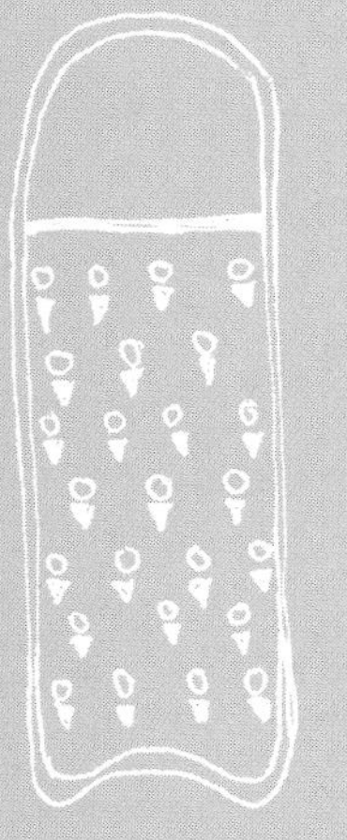

10 cups water
6 ounces (2 rounded cups) farfalle (bow-tie pasta)
2 small zucchini (9 ounces)
3 tablespoons virgin olive oil
8 cloves garlic, peeled and thinly sliced (about 2 tablespoons)
½ teaspoon salt
¼ teaspoon freshly ground black pepper
2 tablespoons grated parmesan cheese

1. Bring the water to a boil in a large saucepan. Add the farfalle, bring back to a boil, and boil for 13 to 15 minutes, until done as desired.
2. Meanwhile, wash and trim the zucchini, cut them in half crosswise, and then cut them lengthwise into ¼-inch slices. Stack the slices, and cut them lengthwise into ¼-inch sticks that are 2½ to 3 inches long. (You should have 2 cups.)
3. Heat the oil in a skillet. When hot, sauté the zucchini sticks over high heat for 4 minutes, until lightly browned and cooked through. Add the garlic, and sauté for 30 seconds longer.
4. When the pasta is cooked, remove ⅓ cup of the cooking liquid, and place it in a bowl large enough to hold the pasta. Drain the pasta through a colander, and add it to the bowl. Add the zucchini, salt, and pepper, and toss to combine.
5. Serve with the grated cheese.

Yield: 4 Servings

NUTRITIONAL ANALYSIS PER SERVING:

Calories 277
Protein 8 gm.
Carbohydrates 36 gm.
Fat 11.7 gm.
Saturated fat 1.9 gm.
Cholesterol 2 mg.
Sodium 326 mg.

Pasta and other complex carbohydrates are a vital part of a healthful diet.

TOP: PASTA AND ZUCCHINI (ABOVE).
BOTTOM: BRAISED STUFFED ARTICHOKES (SEE PAGE 75).

Coquillettes au Gruyère (Pasta Shells with Swiss Cheese)

If you are serving this dish with Poulet Rôti *(see page 222), replace the olive oil with a little of the fat that emerges from the chicken and the deglazed drippings from the skillet in which the chicken was roasted. This unites the pasta with the taste of the chicken, making them wonderfully compatible.*

- **8 cups water**
- **10 ounces medium-size pasta shells, preferably imported**
- **3 tablespoons virgin olive oil**
- **½ teaspoon salt**
- **¼ teaspoon freshly ground black pepper**
- **1 tablespoon chopped fresh chives**
- **1 cup (loosely packed) freshly grated swiss cheese (3 ounces), preferably Gruyère**

1. Bring the water to a boil in a saucepan. Add the pasta, and cook until tender (about 15 minutes). Remove ½ cup of the pasta-cooking liquid, and put it in a stainless steel bowl large enough to hold the shells. Then drain the pasta in a colander.
2. To the cooking liquid in the bowl add the oil, salt, and pepper. Mix well. Add the pasta and chives, toss to mix, and stir in the cheese.
3. Spoon the pasta onto four plates, and serve immediately.

YIELD: 4 SERVINGS

NUTRITIONAL ANALYSIS PER SERVING:

Calories 441
Protein 15 gm.
Carbohydrates 53 gm.
Fat 18.1 gm.
Saturated fat 5.5 gm.
Cholesterol 23 mg.
Sodium 350 mg.

Gruyère is rich in calcium.

Curried Bulgur with Currants

You can make a salad with bulgur by simply reconstituting it in water and tossing it with vinegar, lemon juice, and seasonings—anything from scallions to garlic. Here, I cook the bulgur with onions, flavor it with curry, and mix in some currants. A filling, high-carbohydrate dish that is quick, easy, and inexpensive to make, it goes particularly well with Grilled Savory Lamb Chops (page 256).

- **1 tablespoon virgin olive oil**
- **1 small onion (2 ounces), chopped**
- **2 scallions, coarsely chopped (about ¼ cup)**
- **2 tablespoons dried currants**
- **1 teaspoon curry powder**
- **1 cup bulgur wheat**
- **2 cups homemade unsalted and defatted chicken stock (see page 466), or lower-salt canned chicken broth**
- **½ teaspoon salt (less if using canned broth)**

1. In a skillet, heat the oil. When hot, add the onion and scallions, and sauté for 1 minute.
2. Stir in the currants and curry powder, and then add the bulgur wheat, chicken stock, and salt. Mix well. Bring to a boil, cover, reduce the heat, and cook gently for 20 minutes. Fluff with a fork, and serve immediately.

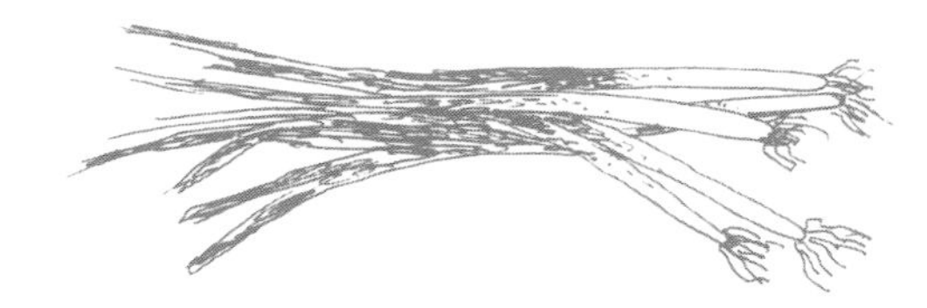

About Bulgur

Bulgur wheat—steamed, sun-dried, and crushed wheat berries—is indigenous to Middle Eastern cooking, like its uncooked relative, cracked wheat. Although bulgur is available now boxed in supermarkets, I prefer the coarser grinds I find loose in health food stores.

Yield: 4 Servings

Nutritional analysis per serving:

Calories 186
Protein 7 gm.
Carbohydrates 33 gm.
Fat 5.2 gm.
Saturated fat 0.9 gm.
Cholesterol 0 mg.
Sodium 382 mg.

Bulgur is high in fiber; currants provide iron and potassium.

Gnocchi Maison

For this recipe, I use elements of both potato and Parisian gnocchi (see About Gnocchi). The mixture can be prepared and even poached ahead, either by dropping spoonfuls of it into boiling water or piping it, as I do here, from a pastry bag held directly over the pot. As the mixture emerges from the bag, I cut it at the tip into 1½-inch lengths and let them drop into the pot. This technique is faster and produces gnocchi of a more uniform size and shape than the spoon method.

Gnocchi make an excellent garnish for poultry, fish, or meat. (See photograph, page 246.)

ABOUT GNOCCHI

THERE ARE DIFFERENT TYPES OF GNOCCHI: ROMAN-STYLE GNOCCHI ARE MADE WITH SEMOLINA THAT IS FIRST COOKED INTO A MUSH AND THEN COOLED, MOLDED, AND CUT INTO SHAPES; POTATO GNOCCHI, ANOTHER TYPE, USE POTATOES AS THE MAIN INGREDIENT; PARISIAN GNOCCHI ARE MADE WITH A PÂTE À CHOUX (CREAM PUFF DOUGH) MIXTURE.

1 medium potato (about 5 ounces)
5½ cups water
2 tablespoons virgin olive oil
¼ teaspoon salt
⅛ teaspoon freshly ground black pepper
½ cup all-purpose flour
2 tablespoons parmesan cheese
2 eggs
2 tablespoons chopped fresh parsley

1. Place the potato in a small saucepan, and cover it with water. Bring to a boil, cover, reduce the heat to low, and boil gently for about 40 minutes, until tender. Drain, and let cool. When the potato is cool enough to handle, peel it. Set aside.
2. Place ½ cup of the water, 1 tablespoon of the oil, the salt, and the pepper in a saucepan, and bring to a boil. Remove from the heat, and add the flour all at once. Mix well with a wooden spoon until the mixture forms a ball, and then place the pan back over the heat for 15 or 20 seconds to dry out the dough a little.
3. Preheat the oven to 400 degrees.
4. Bring the remaining 5 cups of water to a boil in a saucepan.
5. Meanwhile, transfer the ball of dough to the bowl of a food processor, and add the potato in pieces. Process for about 10 seconds. Add 1 tablespoon of the cheese and one of the eggs, and process for 5 seconds. Add the other egg, and process until smooth. Place the mixture in a pastry bag fitted with a ¾-inch plain round tip.
6. Pipe the mixture from the pastry bag into the boiling water, cutting it with a knife into 1½-inch pieces as it emerges from the tip and letting the pieces drop into the

YIELD: 4 SERVINGS

NUTRITIONAL ANALYSIS PER SERVING:

Calories 187
Protein 6 gm.
Carbohydrates 17 gm.
Fat 10.2 gm.
Saturated fat 2.2 gm.
Cholesterol 108 mg.
Sodium 216 mg.

water. (You should have thirty-five to forty pieces.) Bring the water back to a light boil, reduce the heat, and boil very gently, uncovered, for 5 minutes.

7. With a slotted spoon, transfer the gnocchi to a bowl of ice water. When they are cold, drain them and place them in a 3- to 4-cup gratin dish. Add the remaining tablespoon each of oil and cheese along with the parsley, and mix well.
8. At serving time, heat the gnocchi in the oven at 400 degrees for 12 to 15 minutes. Serve immediately.

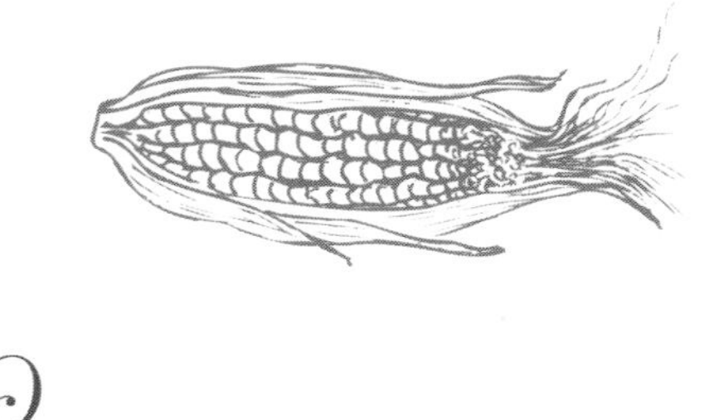

Cornmeal au Gruyère

Ready to eat in a few minutes, this fast polenta consists primarily of cornmeal and leeks, cooked together in a good chicken stock. The Gruyère cheese adds texture and taste that go quite well with stews and roasted meat. If you want to decrease the calories, however, serve the dish without the cheese.

YIELD: 4 SERVINGS

NUTRITIONAL ANALYSIS PER SERVING:

Calories 147
Protein 8 gm.
Carbohydrates 17 gm.
Fat 6.3 gm.
Saturated fat 3.2 gm.
Cholesterol 16 mg.
Sodium 437 mg.

Gruyère is rich in calcium.

- **2¼ cups homemade unsalted and defatted chicken stock (see page 466), or lower-salt canned chicken broth**
- **1 piece leek, trimmed and finely chopped (½ cup)**
- **½ teaspoon salt (less if using canned chicken broth)**
- **¼ teaspoon freshly ground black pepper**
- **½ cup stone-ground yellow cornmeal**
- **2 ounces Gruyère cheese, cut into ¼-inch dice (½ cup)**

1. In a saucepan, combine the stock, leek, salt, and pepper. Bring the mixture to a boil. Whisk in the cornmeal, and return to a boil.
2. Lower the heat, cover, and cook gently for 4 to 5 minutes, stirring occasionally.
3. Add the cheese, and mix until it has melted into the mixture. Serve immediately.

THE BEST BULGUR

THE QUALITY OF BULGUR VARIES; I PREFER TO BUY MINE IN HEALTH FOOD STORES, BECAUSE I FIND THEIR VERSION IS GENERALLY COMPOSED OF BIGGER PIECES RATHER THAN JUST FLAKES AND IS MUCH LESS EXPENSIVE THAN THE PACKAGED BULGUR AVAILABLE IN SUPERMARKETS.

Bulgur Wheat Pilaf

Bulgur is a steamed and dried cracked wheat that is reconstituted for use by soaking it in hot water for about 1 hour or cold water for at least 2 hours, or by boiling it in water for about 30 minutes. This grain has a chewy, nutty texture that makes it particularly good with stews or roasted meats or poultry. I especially like it with Chicken Supreme Kiev-Style (see page 212).

- ½ cup cracked bulgur wheat
- 1½ cups boiling water
- 1 tablespoon peanut oil
- 1 red onion (5 ounces), peeled and chopped (1¼ cups)
- 2 cloves garlic, peeled, crushed, and chopped (1 teaspoon)
- ¼ teaspoon salt
- ⅛ teaspoon freshly ground black pepper
- ½ cup frozen petite peas
- 1½ teaspoons unsalted butter

1. Place the bulgur in a heat-proof bowl, and pour the boiling water over it. Let stand for 45 minutes to 1 hour, until most of the water is absorbed by the wheat. Drain in a sieve.
2. Heat the oil in a saucepan. When the oil is hot, sauté the onion in it for about 3 minutes. Add the garlic, salt, and pepper, and sauté for 10 seconds.
3. Stir the drained bulgur into the mixture in the saucepan. Cook for 4 to 5 minutes. Excess moisture will cook away initially, and then the wheat will begin to brown and become fluffy. Add the frozen peas, mix well, and cook for about 1 minute longer. Stir in the butter.
4. Serve immediately with Chicken Supreme Kiev-Style (see page 212).

YIELD: 4 SERVINGS

NUTRITIONAL ANALYSIS PER SERVING:

Calories 132
Protein 4 gm.
Carbohydrates 19 gm.
Fat 5.2 gm.
Saturated fat 1.5 gm.
Cholesterol 4 mg.
Sodium 174 mg.

Bulgur supplies fiber, B vitamins, and important trace minerals.

Boiled Rice

Simply boiled in salted water, long-grain white rice is useful as a garnish for any type of stew, some soups, and Chili con Carne with Red Beans (see page 278). Some varieties of rice are stickier than others. If you prefer a sticky rice—and many people do—whether for serving as a side dish or as the base for a rice pudding, use a rice that is not converted.

2 **cups water**
¼ **teaspoon salt**
1 **cup long-grain white rice**

1. Bring the water and salt to a boil in a large saucepan. Add the rice, mix well, and bring back to a boil. Then reduce the heat to low, cover, and boil gently for 20 minutes.
2. Fluff the rice with a fork, and serve immediately.

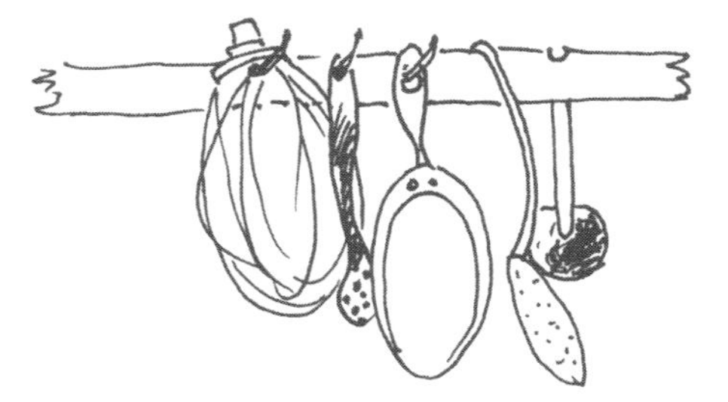

Yield: 4 Servings

NUTRITIONAL ANALYSIS PER SERVING:

Calories 167
Protein 3 gm.
Carbohydrates 37 gm.
Fat 0.3 gm.
Saturated fat 0.1 gm.
Cholesterol 0 mg.
Sodium 137 mg.

Yellow Rice with Orange Rind

American Indians painted their faces with the dye from achiote seeds. Virtually tasteless, they lend bright color to the rice. They soften somewhat after cooking and are edible, but you can sauté them in the oil and butter until they have released their color and then remove and discard them before adding the onions and pepper flakes to the pan. For a more conventional white rice, omit the achiote seeds and orange rind.

1 tablespoon canola oil
1½ teaspoons unsalted butter
1 medium onion (about 6 ounces), peeled and chopped (1 cup)
1 teaspoon achiote (annatto) seeds
¼ teaspoon crushed red pepper flakes
1 cup long-grain white rice
2 cups water
½ teaspoon salt
1½ teaspoons grated orange rind

1. Heat the oil and butter in a saucepan. When they are hot, add the onion, achiote seeds, and red pepper flakes. Cook over medium heat for 3 to 4 minutes.
2. Mix in the rice. Add the water, salt, and orange rind. Bring to a boil, cover, reduce the heat to low, and cook gently for 20 minutes. Serve with Puerto Rican Pork and Beans (see page 243).

Yield: 4 Servings

NUTRITIONAL ANALYSIS PER SERVING:

Calories 228
Protein 4 gm.
Carbohydrates 41 gm.
Fat 5.2 gm.
Saturated fat 1.2 gm.
Cholesterol 4 mg.
Sodium 277 mg.

Rice, a versatile complex carbohydrate, is at the base of the food guide pyramid.

Brown Saffron Rice

Although you conventionally need about twice as much liquid as rice by volume, the ratios vary more widely with brown rice varieties, which also take longer to cook than white rice. The cup of short-grain brown rice I use for this recipe requires 2¼ cups of liquid and takes 45 minutes to cook, but you should make adjustments when preparing this dish to accommodate the peculiarities of the brown rice you are using.

- 2 **teaspoons unsalted butter**
- 2 **teaspoons peanut oil**
- 1 **small onion or piece of large onion (about 2 ounces), peeled and finely chopped (⅓ cup)**
- 6 **to 7 ounces short-grain brown rice (1 cup)**
- ½ **teaspoon dried thyme**
- 2¼ **cups homemade unsalted and defatted chicken stock (see page 466), or lower-salt canned chicken broth**
- ¼ **teaspoon salt (less if using canned broth)**
- 1½ **teaspoons dried saffron**
- ¼ **cup grated parmesan cheese**

1. Heat the butter and oil in a sturdy saucepan. When they are hot, add the onion, and sauté for 1 minute over medium heat. Add the rice, thyme, stock, salt, and saffron, and mix well.
2. Bring the mixture to a full boil, stirring occasionally, over high heat. Then reduce the heat to very low, cover, and cook at a very gentle boil for about 45 minutes (some varieties may cook faster than others), until the rice is tender, slightly sticky, and still somewhat chewy. Add the grated cheese, and mix it gently into the rice with the tines of a fork.
3. Serve the rice with Osso Buco (see page 272).

ABOUT SAFFRON

THIS ANCIENT YELLOW-ORANGE SPICE—ACTUALLY THE STIGMAS OF A SMALL PURPLE CROCUS (*CROCUS SATIVUS*)—IS SO COSTLY BECAUSE THE STIGMAS MUST BE REMOVED FROM MORE THAN 80,000 BLOSSOMS AND THEN DRIED TO PRODUCE A POUND OF SAFFRON. FORTUNATELY, IT DOESN'T TAKE MANY OF THE THREADLIKE STRANDS TO LEND VIVID COLOR AND DELICATE, BITTERSWEET FLAVOR TO A DISH. STORE SAFFRON IN A COOL, DARK PLACE, AND FOR BEST RESULTS USE WITHIN SIX MONTHS.

YIELD: 4 SERVINGS

NUTRITIONAL ANALYSIS PER SERVING:

Calories 257
Protein 7 gm.
Carbohydrates 39 gm.
Fat 7.9 gm.
Saturated fat 3.0 gm.
Cholesterol 9 mg.
Sodium 311 mg.

Wehani Brown Rice

I was first introduced to wehani rice a few years ago, and it has since become one of my favorites. The extra-long, reddish brown kernels require a long time to cook, but they then have a nutty, chewy texture that I love. Even though wehani rice is not available everywhere in the country, it is carried or can be ordered by many health food stores. It is well worth the search!

2 tablespoons virgin olive oil
1 medium onion (about 6 ounces), peeled and chopped (1 cup)
⅓ cup pumpkin seeds
1 cup (6 ounces) wehani brown rice
¾ teaspoon salt
2½ cups warm water

1. Heat the oil in a saucepan until it is hot but not smoking. Add the onion, and sauté for 2 minutes. Add the pumpkin seeds, and cook for 1 minute. Mix in the rice thoroughly, and add the salt and water. Bring to a boil, stirring occasionally.
2. Cover, reduce the heat to low, and boil gently for 1 hour, or until the water has been absorbed by the rice and it is tender. Serve immediately.

YIELD: 4 SERVINGS

NUTRITIONAL ANALYSIS PER SERVING:

Calories 253
Protein 5 gm.
Carbohydrates 38 gm.
Fat 9.1 gm.
Saturated fat 1.3 gm.
Cholesterol 0 mg.
Sodium 417 mg.

Wehani rice provides fiber, and pumpkin seeds are rich in zinc.

Raw Relish of Grapefruit and Peach

I enjoy relishes and try always to have some on hand. Whereas combinations that are cooked a long time will often keep for several weeks in the refrigerator, this relish—primarily a raw fruit mixture—will not last more than about a week. A fresh-tasting blend of peach and grapefruit, with a little mint and jalapeño pepper added for extra flavor, it is an ideal accompaniment for everything from game to pâtés to cold cuts to roasts, and it goes well with Venison Steaks in Sweet-Sour Sauce (recipe on page 289). (See photograph, page 290.)

- About ¼ red bell pepper, peeled and coarsely chopped (about 2 ounces)
- 1 ripe yellow peach (about 4 ounces), peeled, pitted, and coarsely chopped
- 1 small grapefruit (about 10 ounces), peeled, flesh segments separated from surrounding membrane, and flesh coarsely chopped (about ½ cup)
- ¼ cup (loose) fresh mint leaves, minced
- 1 small jalapeño pepper, seeded and finely chopped (about 1½ teaspoons)
- 2 teaspoons cider vinegar
- ¼ teaspoon cumin powder
- ⅛ teaspoon salt
- 1 teaspoon sugar

1. Mix all the ingredients in a bowl. (You will have about 1½ cups.) Cover, and refrigerate for up to 1 week.
2. Serve as needed to garnish game or other meats or cold cuts.

Yield: 4 Servings

NUTRITIONAL ANALYSIS PER SERVING:

Calories 30
Protein 1 gm.
Carbohydrates 7 gm.
Fat 0.1 gm.
Saturated fat 0 gm.
Cholesterol 0 mg.
Sodium 70 mg.

Grapefruit is rich in potassium and vitamin C.

DESSERTS

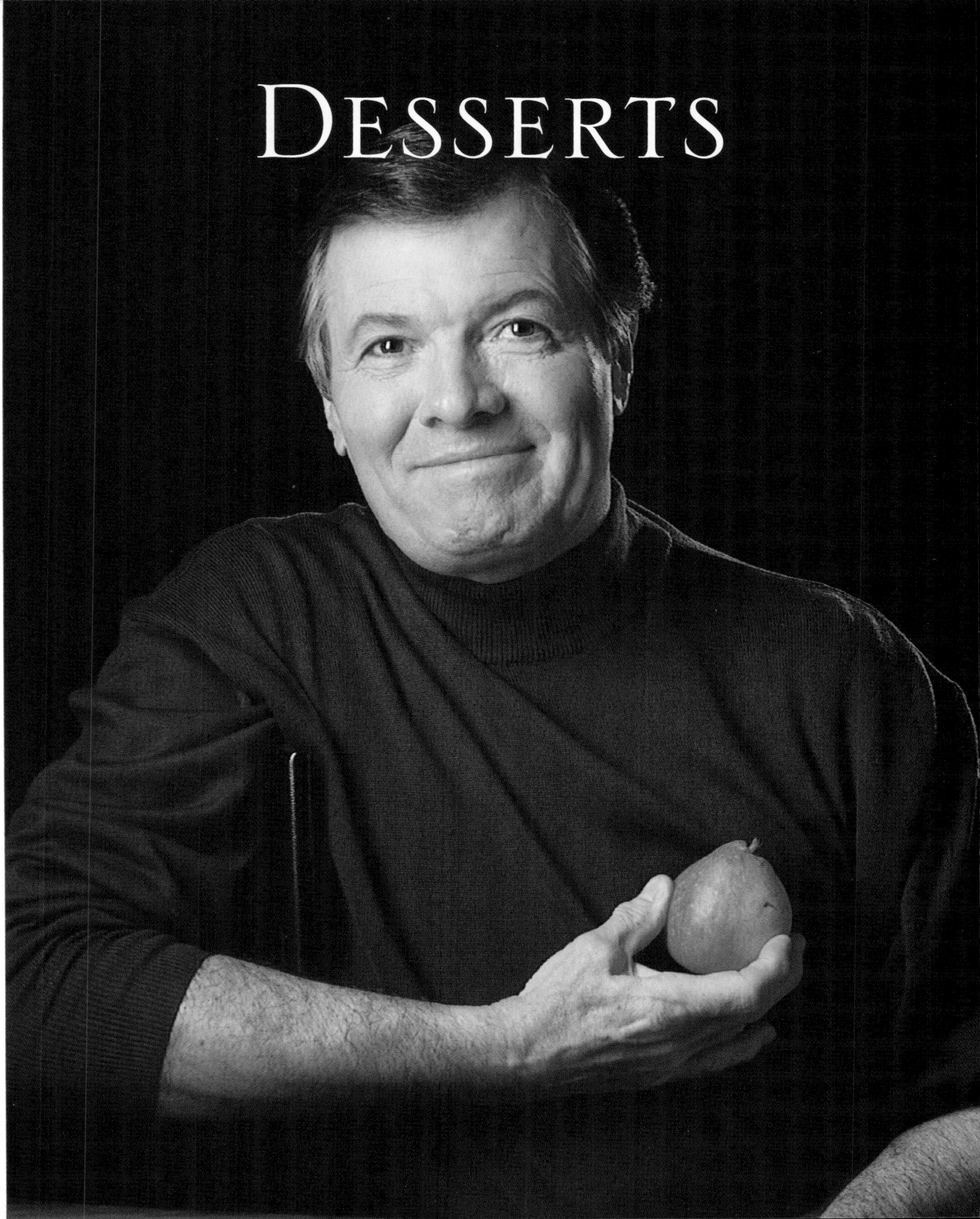

Sweet Apple Flake Confections

When dried in a convection oven, thin, unpeeled apple slices are transformed into crisp flakes with a flavor I find almost addictive. Pressed into scoops of frozen yogurt, as they are in this recipe, the flakes are a delicious substitute for cookies. They also make a great, healthful snack on their own and can be served as a garnish for custard or ice cream.

1 firm apple (8 ounces), preferably Golden Delicious, russet, or Rome Beauty

1 pint frozen low-fat vanilla or coffee yogurt

1. Preheat a convection oven to 250 degrees.
2. Using a sharp, thin-bladed or serrated knife, cut the unpeeled apple crosswise into slices ⅛ inch thick. You should have about sixteen slices. If desired, remove the pits from the center slices. Arrange the slices in one layer, side by side, on an aluminum cookie sheet.
3. Place the cookie sheet in the oven, and cook the apple slices for about 1 hour, until they are fairly dry and very lightly browned. Remove the slices from the sheet while they are still warm and flexible, and arrange them on a platter. Cool them to room temperature. The flakes should then be dry and crunchy. Place them in a metal or plastic storage container with a tight lid, and store at room temperature until ready to use.
4. About 1½ to 2 hours before serving time, transfer the frozen yogurt from the freezer to the refrigerator to soften.
5. At serving time, place a large scoop of frozen yogurt in the center of each of four dessert plates. Press four of the apple flakes around the sides and across the top of each scoop, encasing the scoop with the apples. (Or, arrange the apple flakes on or around the yogurt scoops in another design to your liking.) Serve immediately.

YIELD: 4 SERVINGS

NUTRITIONAL ANALYSIS PER SERVING:

Calories 131
Protein 4 gm.
Carbohydrates 26 gm.
Fat 1.2 gm.
Saturated fat 0 gm.
Cholesterol 5 mg.
Sodium 55 mg.

Apples contain fiber that is particularly helpful in lowering cholesterol.

Caramelized Apple Timbales

This dessert can be made ahead. Arrange the cooked, caramelized apples in tiny, plastic-lined soufflé molds so they are easy to unmold. Notice that the apples are not peeled; the skin gives some chewiness and texture to the dish. The concentrated taste is particularly pleasing when the timbales are served with a little sour cream or plain yogurt. (See photograph, page 356.)

- **4 large Golden Delicious apples (about 1½ pounds)**
- **2 tablespoons lemon juice**
- **4 tablespoons granulated sugar**
- **3 tablespoons water**
- **2 teaspoons julienned lemon rind**
- **⅓ cup water**
- **1 tablespoon unsalted butter**
- **4 tablespoons sour cream or yogurt**

1. Remove the apple stems with a little adjoining skin and flesh, and place them in a bowl with the lemon juice. Set aside for use as a decoration.
2. Cut the apples in half lengthwise, and core them. Then cut each half crosswise into ¼-inch-thick slices to make about 6 loosely packed cups.
3. In a skillet, combine the sugar and the 3 tablespoons of water, and cook over medium-high heat until the mixture turns into a dark brown caramel (about 3 to 4 minutes). Add the apple slices, the lemon rind, the ⅓ cup of water, and the butter. Mix well, reduce the heat, and cook at a gentle boil, covered, for about 7 minutes. (The apples should be tender and most of the moisture gone.) Remove the lid, and cook, rolling the apples in the caramel, for about 5 minutes over high heat until the juice has turned again into caramel and the apple pieces are browned. Let cool to lukewarm.
4. Meanwhile, line four small soufflé molds or ramekins (about ½- to ¾-cup capacity) with plastic wrap. Pack the lukewarm apple mixture into the molds, cover with plastic wrap, and refrigerate until cold.
5. At serving time, unmold the timbales, and decorate them with the reserved apple stems. Serve each with a tablespoon of sour cream or yogurt.

Yield: 4 Servings

NUTRITIONAL ANALYSIS PER SERVING:

Calories 199
Protein 1 gm.
Carbohydrates 38 gm.
Fat 6.5 gm.
Saturated fat 3.7 gm.
Cholesterol 14 mg.
Sodium 10 mg.

Apples are high in pectin.

MAKING A *MIGNONNETTE*

TO COARSELY CRUSH WHOLE PEPPERCORNS (CREATING WHAT THE FRENCH CALL A *MIGNONNETTE*), SPREAD THEM ON A CLEAN, FLAT WORK SURFACE, AND PRESS ON THEM WITH THE BASE OF A SAUCEPAN UNTIL THEY CRACK OPEN. PEPPER CRUSHED THIS WAY IS MUCH LESS HOT THAN PEPPER GROUND CONVENTIONALLY. IF YOU MUST USE A PEPPER MILL, HOWEVER, SET IT TO GRIND THE PEPPER AS COARSELY AS POSSIBLE.

Cheese, Apple, and Nut Mélange

The combination of flavors here—cheese, nuts, and apples that have been rolled in lemon juice and sprinkled with black pepper—is delicious.

Although I usually serve the mélange as a dessert, it also makes an ideal brunch or light lunch main dish.

2 large apples (russet, Golden Delicious, or Rome Beauty)
2 tablespoons lemon juice
½ teaspoon black peppercorns, coarsely crushed (see Making a *Mignonnette*)
⅔ cup pecans (about 25 halves)
5 ounces blue cheese (Gorgonzola, Stilton, or Roquefort), cut into 4 pieces
4 sprigs basil or arugula (about 5 ounces)
French bread

1. Preheat the oven to 375 degrees.
2. Cut the unpeeled apples into quarters, remove and discard the cores, and roll the quarters in the lemon juice. Sprinkle the apples with the pepper. Spread the pecans on a cookie sheet, and bake at 375 degrees for 8 minutes.
3. To serve, arrange two pieces of apple, one piece of cheese, and a few pecans on each of four plates. Arrange a few leaves from the basil or arugula sprigs around the apples. Serve with crusty French bread.

YIELD: 4 SERVINGS

NUTRITIONAL ANALYSIS PER SERVING:

Calories 303
Protein 10 gm.
Carbohydrates 18 gm.
Fat 22.8 gm.
Saturated fat 7.7 gm.
Cholesterol 27 mg.
Sodium 511 mg.

TOP: CHEESE, APPLE, AND NUT MÉLANGE (ABOVE).
BOTTOM: *PAIN AU CHOCOLAT ET NOISETTES* (BREAD WITH CHOCOLATE AND HAZELNUTS) (SEE PAGE 441).

Spicy Apple Charlotte

I use russet apples here, but another variety can be substituted. The apples are cooked on top of the stove initially in a flavorful mixture of sugar, honey, and spices. Then, when most of the moisture has evaporated and the apple slices are brown, they are baked between layers of bread in a cake pan. Coat the unmolded charlotte with peach jam, and serve it in slices, warm or at room temperature, with a spoonful of sour cream or plain yogurt, if desired.

1 tablespoon unsalted butter
1½ tablespoons corn oil or safflower oil
2 pounds russet apples (about 5), peeled, cored, and cut into ¼-inch slices
¼ cup sugar
¼ cup honey
1 teaspoon ground cinnamon
¼ teaspoon ground allspice
⅛ teaspoon ground cloves
11 slices very thin, fine-textured white bread (6½ ounces)
3 tablespoons strained peach jam
1½ teaspoons Calvados (apple brandy) (optional)
Sour cream or plain yogurt (optional)

1. Preheat the oven to 375 degrees.
2. Heat the butter and 1 tablespoon of the oil in a large saucepan. When they are hot, add the apples, and sauté for 1 minute. Then add the sugar, honey, cinnamon, allspice, and cloves, mix gently, cover, and cook over medium heat for 10 minutes. Most of the moisture from the apples should be gone at this point; remove the lid, and cook the apples, uncovered, for 5 to 6 minutes, until they are nicely browned.
3. Using the remaining ½ tablespoon of oil, oil a round cake pan 8 inches in diameter and 1½ inches deep.
4. Cut 7 slices of the bread into triangles by first cutting the slices in half diagonally, then trimming the crusts from each to create smaller triangles. Lay the triangles side by side to cover the bottom of the prepared pan. Trim the remaining 4 slices of bread, cut each of them in half to make rectangles, and arrange them around the sides of the pan.
5. Spoon the apple mixture on top of the bread, and spread it evenly into the corners of the pan. Smooth the surface, and arrange the bread trimmings on top of the apples so most of them are covered.
6. Bake the charlotte at 375 degrees for 20 to 25 minutes. Meanwhile, combine the strained peach jam with the Calvados, if desired, in a small bowl.

Yield: 6 to 8 Servings

NUTRITIONAL ANALYSIS PER SERVING:

Calories 260
Protein 2 gm.
Carbohydrates 52 gm.
Fat 5.8 gm.
Saturated fat 1.6 gm.
Cholesterol 5 mg.
Sodium 146 mg.

Apples are a source of pectin, a soluble fiber that slows sugar absorption and helps to lower blood cholesterol.

7. Let the charlotte cool on a rack for 10 minutes, then invert it onto a plate. No more than 20 to 30 minutes before serving, coat the surface with the peach mixture (if applied earlier, the coating will be absorbed by the dessert).
8. Cut the charlotte into slices, and serve with a dollop of sour cream or yogurt, if desired.

Gratin of Apples, Walnuts, and Granola

This recipe couldn't be easier. No need to peel the apples; just cut them into chunks, combine them with the granola, walnuts, and orange juice, press the mixture into a gratin dish, and bake. The dessert is delicious served with a little sour cream, whipped cream, or even nonfat plain yogurt.

Yield: 4 Servings

- **2 apples (preferably russet or Opalescent)**
- **1 cup low-fat granola mixture**
- **¼ cup walnut pieces**
- **2 tablespoons sugar**
- **¼ cup orange juice**
- **4 tablespoons sour cream or whipped cream for garnish (optional)**

1. Preheat the oven to 400 degrees.
2. Cut the apples in half, core them, and cut them into 1-inch pieces. (You should have about 4 cups.)
3. Thoroughly mix the apple cubes with the granola, walnuts, sugar, and orange juice in a bowl, and press the mixture lightly into a 6-cup gratin dish. Bake for 1 hour, until the apples are soft and the dessert is nicely browned on top.
4. Serve lukewarm or at room temperature, topping each serving with 1 tablespoon of sour cream or whipped cream, if desired.

NUTRITIONAL ANALYSIS PER SERVING:

Calories 202
Protein 3 gm.
Carbohydrates 38 gm.
Fat 6.0 gm.
Saturated fat 0.5 gm.
Cholesterol 0 mg.
Sodium 32 mg.

Granola is a good source of fiber, potassium, zinc, and magnesium.

Baked Apple Tart

In this dish cored, halved apples filled with apricot jam are wrapped in a round of pastry dough and dusted with a sprinkling of sugar before baking. The classic dough for this dessert is suitable for most baking needs and is easily made in a food processor.

Dough

- 3 tablespoons unsalted butter, cold
- ¾ cup all-purpose flour (3 ounces)
- ½ teaspoon granulated sugar
- 2 tablespoons ice-cold water

Filling

- 2 large Golden Delicious apples (1 pound)
- 2 tablespoons apricot jam
- 1 tablespoon granulated sugar
- ½ tablespoon unsalted butter

1. Preheat the oven to 400 degrees.
2. Cut the butter into ½-inch pieces. Place the flour, butter, and sugar in the bowl of a food processor. Process for 5 seconds, add the water, and process for another 5 seconds. Remove the dough, even if not compactly mixed, then press it and roll it out between two layers of plastic wrap to form a circle about 10 inches in diameter. Remove the top layer of wrap, and invert the dough onto a cookie sheet. Peel off the remaining wrap, and refrigerate the dough.
3. Meanwhile, peel the apples, cut them in half, and remove the cores. Hollow the apples out a little with a measuring spoon, and chop the trimmings. (You should have about ¾ cup.) Place ½ tablespoon of the jam in the hollow of each apple half, and arrange the halves, cut side down, in the center of the circle of dough. Sprinkle the chopped apple around the halves.
4. Bring the edge of the dough up over the apples to create a border, 1 to 2 inches high, around the edge. (This will hold the cooking juices inside.)
5. Sprinkle the top of the tart with sugar, and dot with butter. Bake at 400 degrees for 45 minutes to 1 hour, until well browned. Serve warm or at room temperature.

Top: Caramelized Apple Timbales (see page 351).
Bottom: Baked Apple Tart (above).

About Classic Pastry Dough

It is important that you not overmix the dough ingredients. The butter should not be totally incorporated into the flour; visible pieces will melt as the dough cooks, and it will develop some of the flakiness of puff pastry. Notice that there is no waste; the dough is rolled free-form on a cookie sheet and the edges folded over the apples, so trimming is not required.

Yield: 4 Servings

Nutritional Analysis per Serving:

Calories 260
Protein 3 gm.
Carbohydrates 41 gm.
Fat 10.6 gm.
Saturated fat 6.3 gm.
Cholesterol 27 mg.
Sodium 6 mg.

Tartelettes aux Fruits Panachés

A minimum of flour and butter is used in the dough for these small, flavorful fruits panachés, *or mixed fruit, tarts. Thin dough disks are baked with a topping of lightly sugared apricot and plum wedges until the pastry is crisp and the fruit soft.*

- **⅔ cup all-purpose flour, plus a little flour for use in rolling out the dough**
- **3 tablespoons cold unsalted butter, cut into 3 equal pieces**
- **1 tablespoon canola oil**
- **½ teaspoon sugar**
- **⅛ teaspoon salt**
- **1 tablespoon ice water, if needed**
- **4 small ripe apricots (8 to 10 ounces)**
- **4 small ripe dark plums (8 to 10 ounces)**
- **2 tablespoons sugar**

1. Preheat the oven to 400 degrees.
2. Place the flour, butter, oil, ½ teaspoon sugar, and salt in the bowl of a food processor, and process for about 10 seconds. Feel the dough; if it is soft enough to gather together into a ball, remove it from the bowl, and form a ball. If it is still dry to the touch, add the ice water, and process for another 5 or 6 seconds before removing the dough from the bowl and forming a ball. Refrigerate the dough or roll it out immediately.
3. Lightly flour a flat work surface, and roll the ball of dough into a very thin layer (no more than ⅛ inch thick). Using a round cutter with a 5-inch diameter, cut four disks, gathering up and rerolling the trimmings as required. Carefully transfer the disks to a large cookie sheet or jelly roll pan, leaving a few inches of space between them.
4. Cut the apricots and plums into thin wedges, and arrange them alternating in a wedge spiral on top of each dough disk. Sprinkle the fruit with the 2 tablespoons of sugar, and bake the *tartelettes* at 400 degrees for 30 to 35 minutes, until the fruit is soft and the dough cooked through and nicely browned. Some of the juice from the fruit will have leaked out onto the cookie sheet. Before it hardens and makes the disks stick to the sheet, lift the tarts with a broad spatula, and transfer them to a cooling rack or platter.
5. At serving time, place a *tartelette* on each of four dessert plates, and serve lukewarm or at room temperature.

YIELD: 4 SERVINGS

NUTRITIONAL ANALYSIS PER SERVING:

Calories 277
Protein 4 gm.
Carbohydrates 39 gm.
Fat 12.8 gm.
Saturated fat 5.7 gm.
Cholesterol 23 mg.
Sodium 71 mg.

This high-fiber dessert includes apricots, which are rich in potassium and vitamin A.

White Peach and Walnut Tart

White peaches, one of my favorite fruits, are baked here in a tart shell created from a dough containing a minimum of flour and butter. To absorb some of the peach juices and lend added flavor to the tart, the shell and the peaches are sprinkled before baking with a mixture of walnuts, flour, and sugar, ground together with the dough trimmings into a powder. The baked dessert is glazed, while still warm, with a coating of jam and served at room temperature.

Tart Dough

- **⅔ cup all-purpose flour**
- **2 tablespoons unsalted butter**
- **1 tablespoon corn oil**
- **⅛ teaspoon salt**
- **½ teaspoon sugar**
- **1 tablespoon cold water**

Walnut Mixture

- **¼ cup walnut pieces**
- **1 tablespoon all-purpose flour**
- **1 tablespoon sugar**
- **Dough trimmings**

- **3 ripe white peaches (about 1 pound), cut into quarters**
- **¼ cup apricot preserves**

1. Preheat the oven to 400 degrees.
2. Place all the dough ingredients except the water in the bowl of a food processor. Process for about 15 seconds, just until the mixture looks sandy. Add the water, and process for another 5 seconds, just until the mixture begins to gather together. Transfer the dough to a piece of plastic wrap and, using the wrap, gather the dough into a ball. Roll the dough between two sheets of plastic wrap until it is about 10 inches in diameter (it will be very thin). Place an 8-inch metal flan ring or removable-bottom quiche or tart pan on a cookie sheet, and fit the dough inside the ring, pressing it into place. Trim the top edge to remove any excess dough, and reserve the trimmings.
3. Place all the walnut mixture ingredients, including the dough trimmings, in the bowl of a food processor. Process until well combined, and set aside.
4. Spread half of the walnut mixture on the bottom of the tart shell. Arrange the peach quarters in one layer, skin side down, around the circumference of the shell. (You should have two peach quarters remaining.) Cut each of the remaining peach quarters in half and arrange them skin side down, in the middle of the tart shell. Sprinkle the rest of the walnut mixture evenly on top.

Yield: 6 Servings

Nutritional Analysis per Serving:

Calories 208
Protein 2.7 gm.
Carbohydrates 30 gm.
Fat 9.4 gm.
Saturated fat 2.9 gm.
Cholesterol 11 mg.
Sodium 53 mg.

5. Bake the tart at 400 degrees for 1 hour. Cool to lukewarm on a cooling rack, and then, using a spoon, spread the apricot preserves carefully over the top. Remove the ring from around the tart (the dough will shrink enough in cooking to allow easy removal).
6. Using two large hamburger spatulas, transfer the tart to a serving platter. Cut it into six wedges, and serve at room temperature. Refrigerate any leftovers, and enjoy them the next day.

Baked Apricots with Almonds

The success of this dish depends on the quality of the apricots you use. If you have very ripe, full-flavored fruit, preferably from an organic farm, you will have terrific results. I used to make this dessert with a lot of heavy cream; now I use just a little half-and-half. If you want to go one step further, eliminate the half-and-half and add a few tablespoons of water to lend a little moisture to the fruit.

- **1 pound ripe apricots (about 6 or 7)**
- **3 tablespoons apricot jam**
- **¼ cup half-and-half**
- **2 tablespoons sliced almonds**
- **1 tablespoon granulated sugar**

1. Preheat the oven to 350 degrees.
2. Cut the apricots in half, and remove their pits.
3. Arrange the apricot halves, cut side down, in a gratin dish. Spoon the jam over the fruit, and pour the half-and-half around the fruit. Sprinkle the almonds and sugar on top.
4. Bake at 350 degrees for 30 to 35 minutes. Serve lukewarm or at room temperature.

Yield: 6 Servings

NUTRITIONAL ANALYSIS PER SERVING:

Calories 91
Protein 2 gm.
Carbohydrates 17 gm.
Fat 2.5 gm.
Saturated fat 0.8 gm.
Cholesterol 4 mg.
Sodium 9 mg.

Apricots are high in potassium and vitamin A.

Apricot *Délice*

Délice *is the French word for "delight," which accurately describes this fruit dessert. Fresh apricots are cooked in a sweet wine that is flavored with basil, and then cooled. With the addition of diced kiwi, the cooking liquid is transformed into a sauce and spooned over the apricots at serving time.* *(See photograph, page 407.)*

½ cup apricot or peach preserves
1 cup Sauternes (sweet wine)
1 stalk fresh basil
2 tablespoons water
8 ripe apricots (1¼ pounds), washed
1 kiwi (about 3 ounces)
8 fresh basil leaves, for decoration

1. Place the apricot preserves, Sauternes, basil stalk, and water in a saucepan measuring about 7 inches across (just large enough to hold the apricots snugly in one layer). Bring the mixture to a boil, and add the apricots. (They should be barely covered with the liquid.) Bring back to a boil, cover, and boil the apricots gently for 5 minutes, or until they are just tender. Let cool, covered, in the liquid.
2. Meanwhile, peel the kiwi, and cut the flesh into ¼-inch dice.
3. At serving time, arrange two apricots on each plate. Discard the basil stalk, and toss the kiwi pieces in the cooking juice. Coat the apricots with the juice, and divide the remaining juice and kiwi pieces among the four plates. Decorate each apricot with a basil leaf, and serve.

**YIELD:
4 SERVINGS**

NUTRITIONAL ANALYSIS PER SERVING:

Calories 211
Protein 2 gm.
Carbohydrates 44 gm.
Fat 0.7 gm.
Saturated fat 0 gm.
Cholesterol 0 mg.
Sodium 21 mg.

Apricots are rich in potassium, and kiwis are an excellent source of vitamin C.

Lemon Bananas in Crisp Shells

Instead of using rich cookie dough or puff pastry for the dessert shells here, I make them from packaged square wonton wrappers, which are fat-free. (See About Wonton Wrappers or Skins, page 190.) The wrappers are first blanched in boiling water, then lightly oiled, and baked until brown and crisp. When cool, the wrappers are filled, sandwich-style, with banana slices flavored with lemon juice and rind, dark rum, and peach preserves.

2 quarts water
8 wonton wrappers, each about 3 inches square (2 ounces)
2 teaspoons canola oil
1½ tablespoons confectioners' sugar, plus 1 teaspoon for decoration
2 teaspoons grated lemon rind
2 tablespoons lemon juice
¼ cup peach preserves
2 tablespoons dark rum
2 ripe bananas (about 1 pound)

1. Preheat the oven to 375 degrees.
2. Bring the water to a boil in a pot. Drop in the wonton wrappers one at a time, and bring the water back to a boil. Boil the wrappers 1½ minutes, then drain them carefully into a colander, and return them to the pot. Fill the pot with cold water to stop the wrappers from cooking further and cool them.
3. Brush a large cookie sheet with the oil. Using both hands, carefully lift the wrappers from the cold water, shaking off as much of the water clinging to them as you can, and arrange them side by side on the oiled sheet. Place the 1½ tablespoons of confectioners' sugar in a sieve, and sprinkle it on top of the wet wonton wrappers.
4. Place the wrappers in the 375-degree oven for 16 to 18 minutes, until they are nicely browned, crisp, and glazed on the surface. Using a thin hamburger spatula, remove the hot wrappers from the cookie sheet, and place them on a rack to cool completely.
5. Mix the lemon rind, lemon juice, peach preserves, and rum in a bowl large enough to hold the bananas. Peel the bananas, and cut them in half crosswise, then into thin (⅓-inch) lengthwise slices. Add them to the bowl, and mix gently to coat the banana slices with the sauce.
6. At serving time, arrange a wonton crisp on each of four dessert plates. Divide the banana mixture among the plates, spooning it on top of the crisps. Place the remaining wonton crisps on top of the bananas, and sprinkle the remaining teaspoon of sugar on top. Serve immediately.

YIELD: 4 SERVINGS

NUTRITIONAL ANALYSIS PER SERVING:

Calories 209
Protein 2 gm.
Carbohydrates 42 gm.
Fat 2.9 gm.
Saturated fat 0.4 gm.
Cholesterol 1 mg.
Sodium 92 mg.

Bananas are an exceptionally good source of potassium.

Baked Bananas in Lemon-Rum Sauce

Available year-round, bananas are best when little black spots begin to form on the peels, indicating they are very ripe. For this recipe, bananas are baked in the peels, which blacken completely after 15 minutes of cooking. When they are cool enough to handle, the fruit is removed from the peels and served with the tart lemon-rum sauce, or simply with a little lemon juice.

4 very ripe bananas, with black-spotted skin (about 2 pounds)

Lemon-Rum Sauce

1 tablespoon grated lemon rind
2 tablespoons lemon juice
2 tablespoons granulated sugar
3 tablespoons orange marmalade
¼ cup water
2 tablespoons dark rum

Garnishes

Mint leaves
Strips of orange peel

1. Preheat the oven to 400 degrees.
2. Trim the ends of the bananas, removing about ½ inch from each end, and cut a slit through the peel extending the length of the fruit. Arrange the unpeeled bananas on a cookie sheet, and place in a 400-degree oven for 15 minutes. (The peel will turn black.)
3. Meanwhile, in a saucepan, mix together the lemon rind, lemon juice, sugar, marmalade, and water, and bring the mixture to a boil. Boil for 1 minute. Transfer to a serving dish.
4. As soon as the bananas are cool enough to handle, remove the peels, and place the bananas in the sauce. Using a spoon, coat the bananas on all sides with the sauce.
5. When cool, stir in the rum, and decorate the bananas with mint leaves and orange peel. Serve.

Yield: 4 Servings

Nutritional Analysis per Serving:

Calories 216
Protein 2 gm.
Carbohydrates 52 gm.
Fat 0.7 gm.
Saturated fat 0.3 gm.
Cholesterol 0 mg.
Sodium 10 mg.

Bananas are high in potassium.

Cherry Bread Pudding

This is a great dessert to make when Bing cherries are in full season. You can make the same recipe with berries or pieces of plum instead of cherries, and flavor them with the almond-sugar mixture, too. This dessert is best served lukewarm with a little sour cream or, if you prefer, yogurt.

1 pound ripe cherries (14 ounces pitted)
3 slices white bread (3 ounces), toasted
1 cup milk
½ cup sliced almonds, toasted
½ cup cherry preserves
4 teaspoons granulated sugar
1 teaspoon unsalted butter
½ teaspoon confectioners' sugar
1 cup sour cream or yogurt (optional)

1. Preheat the oven to 350 degrees.
2. Pit the cherries. Coarsely crumble the toasted bread (you should have 1 cup), and place it in a bowl with the milk. Mix well, and add the cherries, almonds (reserving 2 tablespoons), and cherry preserves.
3. In another bowl, mix the reserved almonds with 2 teaspoons of the sugar.
4. Grease a 6-cup gratin dish with the butter, and sprinkle it with the remaining 2 teaspoons of sugar. Pour the cherry mixture into the dish and top with the almond-sugar mixture.
5. Bake at 350 degrees for 35 to 40 minutes. Cool to lukewarm, sprinkle with confectioners' sugar, and serve with sour cream or yogurt, if desired.

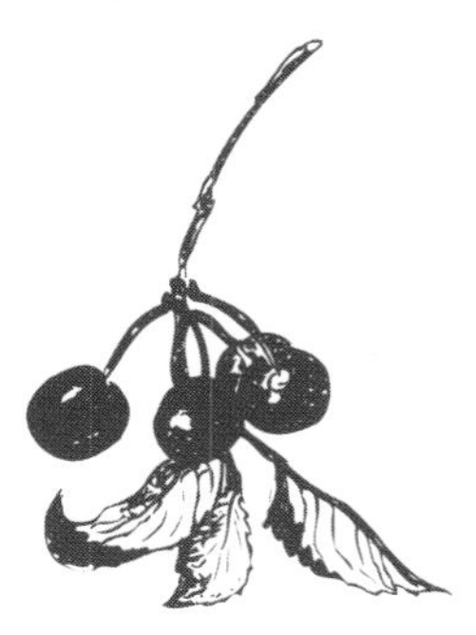

**YIELD:
6 SERVINGS**

NUTRITIONAL ANALYSIS PER SERVING:

Calories 322
Protein 6 gm.
Carbohydrates 44 gm.
Fat 15.3 gm.
Saturated fat 6.9 gm.
Cholesterol 24 mg.
Sodium 128 mg.

Cherries are a source of potassium. Yogurt is rich in calcium and riboflavin.

SUMMER CHERRY PUDDING WITH RUM SAUCE

This cherry pudding is a classic summer offering in England. Sour cherries are cooked briefly in wine and sugar, then layered with cake crumbs in a bowl lined with pound cake. After a few hours, the juices from the cherry mixture seep into the cake, and the dessert becomes a solid mass that takes on the shape of the bowl. Unmolded at serving time, it is presented with a sauce made from mango, honey, and rum.

1½ pounds sour cherries
½ cup dry, fruity red wine
¼ cup sugar
1 10¾-ounce pound cake

RUM SAUCE
1 ripe mango (about 1 pound)
2 tablespoons honey
1 tablespoon dark rum
⅓ cup water

½ cup champagne grapes, if available, or equivalent amount of Red Flame grapes cut into ¼-inch dice, for garnish

YIELD: 4 SERVINGS

NUTRITIONAL ANALYSIS PER SERVING:

Calories 432
Protein 5 gm.
Carbohydrates 74 gm.
Fat 12.7 gm.
Saturated fat 6.9 gm.
Cholesterol 135 mg.
Sodium 249 mg.

Cherries are a good source of vitamin A, and mangoes are rich in vitamin A, vitamin C, potassium, and fiber.

1. Pit the cherries, and place them in a stainless steel saucepan with the wine and sugar. Bring the mixture to a boil, uncovered, over medium heat, and cook for 5 minutes to reduce the juices. Cool. (You will have 2¼ cups.)
2. Trim off the brown sides of the pound cake, reserving the trimmings. Cut the trimmed cake lengthwise into five slices, each about ½ inch thick.
3. Place a strip of parchment paper in a 4- to 6-cup bowl so that the paper covers the bottom and comes up the sides of the bowl. (This will help in the unmolding later.) Arrange three slices of the cake on top of the parchment so the cake covers the bottom and sides of the bowl.
4. Place half the cherry mixture on top of the cake and crumble half the reserved cake trimmings over the cherries. Spoon the remaining cherry mixture on top and crumble the remaining cake trimmings over it. Finish with the remaining two slices of cake, arranging them so that all the cherries are covered.
5. Cover the bowl with plastic wrap touching the cake. Place a weight of about 1 pound on top of the dessert so it presses and compacts the layers of cake and cherries. Refrigerate. (The recipe can be prepared to this point up to 2 days ahead.)

(continued)

FOR THE RUM SAUCE

6. Peel the mango, and cut the flesh from the pit. Place the flesh in a food processor or blender with the honey, rum, and water, and process until smooth. (You will have 1¾ cups.)
7. When ready to serve, unmold the cake onto a serving plate, pour the mango sauce around it, and sprinkle with the grapes. Spoon onto dessert dishes at the table.

RUSSIAN CRANBERRY *KISSEL*

Kissel *is a classic Russian dessert that usually consists of a puree of acidic fruit. Any tart berries can be used, but cranberries are the classic choice. Sometimes the berries are merely combined with sugar and thickened with a little cornstarch. I add orange juice and rind to my version and serve the* kissel *with a little yogurt (or, if I want it richer, sour cream) and garnishes of pomegranate seeds and mint.* *(See photograph, page 396.)*

YIELD: 4 SERVINGS

NUTRITIONAL ANALYSIS PER SERVING:

Calories 128
Protein 1 gm.
Carbohydrates 31 gm.
Fat 0.4 gm.
Saturated fat 0.1 gm.
Cholesterol 1 mg.
Sodium 12 mg.

Cranberries are low in calories and high in fiber.

1 package (12 ounces) fresh cranberries
1½ teaspoons grated orange rind
¾ cup orange juice
¼ cup sugar
1 teaspoon cornstarch
¼ cup plain yogurt or sour cream
2 tablespoons pomegranate seeds
A few sprigs mint
4 cookies (optional)

1. Put the cranberries, orange rind and juice, sugar, and cornstarch in a stainless steel saucepan, and bring the mixture to a boil over high heat, stirring occasionally. Cover, reduce the heat, and cook gently for approximately 10 minutes. The mixture will be thick and bright red. Set it aside to cool. (You should have about 2 cups.)
2. When it is cool, divide it among four glass goblets. Garnish with yogurt (or sour cream), a sprinkling of pomegranate seeds, and mint, and serve with cookies, if desired.

Jam Omelet Soufflé

This is a simple soufflé, made with egg whites and a little egg yolk for color and flavor. Baked in an oval-shaped tray, it resembles a classic omelet.

The egg mixture used here is the base, too, for the classic French omelette norvégienne *or* omelette surprise—*what we in this country call Baked Alaska. The traditional ice-cream filling is replaced in my version with cake slices spread with fruit preserves and moistened with espresso coffee.*

1 teaspoon unsalted butter
4 ounces pound cake, sponge cake, or cookies
¼ cup black currant (or other fruit) preserves
2 egg yolks
2 teaspoons pure vanilla extract
6 egg whites
½ cup granulated sugar
¼ cup freshly brewed espresso coffee
1 teaspoon confectioners' sugar

1. Preheat the oven to 400 degrees.
2. Grease an oval, stainless steel tray (about 12 inches long by 7 inches wide) with the butter. Cut the cake into ½-inch slices (if using cookies, leave them whole), and spread them with the preserves.
3. Mix the egg yolks lightly with the vanilla, and set aside.
4. No more than an hour before cooking, beat the egg whites until firm. Add the granulated sugar in one stroke, and mix for an additional 10 seconds, just long enough to incorporate the sugar. Using a large spatula, fold the egg yolk mixture into the egg whites. Place about one-fourth of the mixture on the buttered tray, and spread it out so the entire length and most of the width of the tray is covered.
5. Arrange the cake slices in a single layer, preserves side down, on top of the egg mixture on the tray. Sprinkle the cake slices evenly with the espresso, and then cover them with one-fourth of the remaining egg mixture, spreading and smoothing it with a spatula.
6. Place the remaining egg mixture in a pastry bag fitted with a star tube, and use it to decorate the top and sides of the soufflé. Bake the tray at 400 degrees for about 15 minutes, until the surface of the soufflé is nicely browned and the mixture is just set inside.
7. Sprinkle with the confectioners' sugar, and serve immediately.

YIELD: 6 SERVINGS

NUTRITIONAL ANALYSIS PER SERVING:

Calories 239
Protein 6 gm.
Carbohydrates 36 gm.
Fat 7.9 gm.
Saturated fat 2.3 gm.
Cholesterol 100 mg.
Sodium 80 mg.

Apricot and Fig Soufflé

Flavored with a puree containing both dried apricots and apricot preserves, this soufflé has an intense taste that I like. Dried figs lend texture and provide interesting color contrast.

The soufflé will puff nicely and can be served hot in the mold. It can also be made ahead and served cold as a kind of apricot pudding. As it cools, it will deflate, falling to about the level of the uncooked mixture in the mold. It is good either way on its own, or it can be served with yogurt or sour cream.

6 ounces dried apricots
1 cup water
¼ cup apricot preserves
⅓ cup diced (¼-inch dice) dried figs
½ teaspoon unsalted butter
5 egg whites
1 tablespoon sugar
Confectioners' sugar (optional)
Yogurt or sour cream (optional)

1. Place the apricots and water in a saucepan. Bring to a boil, cover, reduce the heat, and boil gently for 15 minutes. (All but about ⅓ cup of the water should have evaporated. If there is more, reduce it to this amount by boiling; if there is less, add enough water to make this amount.) Transfer the contents of the saucepan to the bowl of a food processor, add the preserves, and process until smooth.
2. Place the processed mixture in a bowl, fold in the figs, and set aside. (The recipe can be prepared to this point a few hours ahead.)
3. Preheat the oven to 375 degrees.
4. Grease a 4-cup soufflé mold with the butter, and set it aside.
5. About ½ hour before serving, beat the egg whites until stiff, add the sugar, and beat for a few more seconds to incorporate it. Gently fold and mix the apricot mixture into the egg whites, and transfer the mixture to the buttered mold.
6. Bake the mold at 375 degrees for about 20 minutes, until the soufflé is puffy and barely set inside. Sprinkle with the confectioners' sugar, if desired, and serve immediately, as is or with a spoonful of yogurt or sour cream.

YIELD: 4 SERVINGS

NUTRITIONAL ANALYSIS PER SERVING:

Calories 234
Protein 7 gm.
Carbohydrates 54 gm.
Fat 0.9 gm.
Saturated fat 0.3 gm.
Cholesterol 1 mg.
Sodium 63 mg.

Dried apricots are high in potassium and vitamin A.

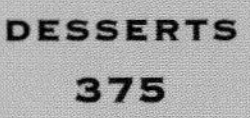

Cranberry Soufflés with Cranberry–Red Wine Sauce

Fresh cranberries, available much of the year now at most supermarkets, are used in this dessert. The berries are cooked first with a little sugar and jam, then some of the mixture is pureed and combined with wine to create a flavorful sauce, and the remainder is folded into egg whites for the soufflé. Small, disposable aluminum molds can be used here, or the soufflés can be baked in conventional glass, ceramic, or metal molds. (See photograph, page 376.)

FREEZE AND BAKE

THE ASSEMBLED SOUFFLÉS CAN BE COOKED IMMEDIATELY, OF COURSE, BUT THEY CAN ALSO BE REFRIGERATED FOR A FEW HOURS, OR EVEN FROZEN, BEFORE COOKING. IF YOU DECIDE TO MAKE THEM AHEAD AND FREEZE THEM, TRANSFER THE FROZEN MOLDS DIRECTLY FROM THE FREEZER TO THE HOT OVEN, AND COOK THE SOUFFLÉS AS INDICATED IN THE RECIPE.

- **1 tablespoon unsalted butter (to butter the molds)**
- **1 10-ounce package fresh cranberries**
- **⅓ cup sugar**
- **½ cup apricot or peach jam**
- **¼ cup water**
- **¾ cup fruity, dry red wine**
- **3 egg whites**
- **Confectioners' sugar, for sprinkling on the finished soufflés**

1. If you will bake the soufflés immediately after preparing them, preheat the oven to 375 degrees.
2. Butter four ¾-cup aluminum, ovenproof glass, or ceramic molds. Set them aside.
3. Combine the cranberries, sugar, jam, and water in a large stainless steel saucepan, and bring the mixture to a boil over medium to high heat. Cover the saucepan, reduce the heat to very low, and cook gently for 20 minutes. (You will have about 1¾ cups.)
4. Place ¾ cup of the cranberry mixture in the bowl of a food processor, and process it until smooth. Add the red wine, process briefly, and strain the mixture through a fine strainer set over a bowl. Set the sauce aside until serving time.
5. Beat the egg whites until they are firm. Working as quickly as you can, fold them into the remaining cup of cooked cranberries. Fill the prepared molds with the mixture, and either bake immediately, or refrigerate the molds for up to 2 hours before baking, or freeze them (uncovered until firm, then covered) for up to 2 weeks before baking.
6. If you are baking the soufflés immediately or after a brief refrigeration, arrange the filled molds on an aluminum tray, and place them in the 375-degree oven for 13 to

(continued)

CRANBERRY SOUFFLÉS WITH CRANBERRY–RED WINE SAUCE (*continued*)

15 minutes, until they are puffy on top and set in the center. If you are baking frozen soufflés, place them on a tray directly from the freezer, and bake in a preheated 375-degree oven for 15 to 18 minutes. (If the soufflés begin to darken on top after 10 to 12 minutes, place a sheet of aluminum foil loosely on top of them for the remainder of the cooking period.) When they are done, sprinkle the hot soufflés with the confectioners' sugar.

7. To serve the soufflés, divide the sauce among four plates. Using a large spoon, scoop the soufflés from the molds, and place one in the center of each plate. Serve immediately.

**YIELD:
4 SERVINGS**

NUTRITIONAL ANALYSIS PER SERVING:

Calories 265
Protein 3 gm.
Carbohydrates 52 gm.
Fat 3.1 gm.
Saturated fat 1.8 gm.
Cholesterol 8 mg.
Sodium 61 mg.

*Cranberries are a good source of fiber.
Egg whites provide high-quality, fat-free protein.*

CLOCKWISE FROM TOP: CARAMEL CUPS WITH COFFEE FROZEN YOGURT (SEE PAGE 446) AND CRYSTALLIZED ROSE PETALS (SEE PAGE 451); ICE-CREAM PHYLLO NAPOLEONS (SEE PAGE 449); CRANBERRY SOUFFLÉS WITH CRANBERRY–RED WINE SAUCE (SEE PAGE 375).

Soufflé of Mango with Mango Sauce

The flesh of two ripe mangoes is pureed here, with half the puree strained to make a sauce and the remainder combined with beaten egg whites for the soufflé. Because there are no egg yolks in the base of this soufflé—it consists solely of mango puree and a little sugar—the assembled dish will keep, refrigerated, for a few hours before baking, provided the egg whites are well beaten and stiff. In fact, the unbaked soufflé can even be frozen for up to 2 weeks. Place it in the freezer uncovered until firm (so the covering material won't stick to its exposed surface), then cover it for the remainder of its time in the freezer. When you are ready to cook the soufflé, let it defrost partially, uncovered, at room temperature for an hour or so before baking it.

1 teaspoon unsalted butter
4 tablespoons granulated sugar
2 very ripe mangoes (about 1 pound each)
2 tablespoons grenadine syrup
2 tablespoons Grand Marnier
2 tablespoons water
3 egg whites
1 teaspoon confectioners' sugar
2 kiwis (about 3 ounces each), peeled and cut into ½-inch dice (⅔ cup)

1. If you will bake the soufflé immediately after preparing it, preheat the oven to 375 degrees.
2. Using the butter and 1 tablespoon of the granulated sugar, butter and sugar a 3½-to-4-cup soufflé mold.
3. Peel and pit the mangoes, and puree the flesh in a food processor. (You should have 2 cups.) Set 1 cup of the puree aside in a bowl large enough to hold the soufflé mixture. Strain the remaining cup of puree through a fine strainer set over a small bowl. (You should have about ¾ cup strained.)
4. Add the grenadine, Grand Marnier, and water to the strained puree, cover, and refrigerate. (You should have about 1¼ cups of mango sauce.)
5. Beat the egg whites by hand or with a mixer until stiff, then add the remaining 3 tablespoons of granulated sugar, and beat a few more seconds. Add about half of the beaten whites to the reserved cup of mango puree, and mix with a whisk. Then,

working as quickly as you can, gently but thoroughly fold in the rest of the egg whites with a rubber spatula.

6. Fill the prepared mold with the soufflé mixture. Smooth the top, then decorate it with ridges or lines, if desired, using the blade of a knife or metal spatula.
7. If baking the soufflé immediately, place it in the 375-degree oven for about 25 minutes, until it is puffed and golden on top. Alternatively, refrigerate the soufflé, uncovered, for up to an hour, and then bake it; or freeze it, uncovered, for at least 12 hours until solid, then cover it with plastic wrap (which won't stick to the frozen soufflé), and freeze for up to 2 weeks. Remove the soufflé from the freezer 1 hour before baking, immediately peel off the plastic wrap, and let the soufflé sit at room temperature to partially defrost, while you preheat the oven to 350 degrees. Bake the soufflé for 35 to 40 minutes, until it is puffed, golden, and set.
8. Sprinkle the hot soufflé with the confectioners' sugar. Divide the sauce among four dessert plates, and sprinkle the diced kiwi on top. Bring the soufflé to the table, and serve large spoonfuls of it on top of the sauce.

YIELD: 4 SERVINGS

NUTRITIONAL ANALYSIS PER SERVING:

Calories 233
Protein 4 gm.
Carbohydrates 52 gm.
Fat 1.5 gm.
Saturated fat 0.7 gm.
Cholesterol 3 mg.
Sodium 46 mg.

Mangoes are high in potassium, fiber, and vitamin A.

ANGEL HAIR

"SPINNING" THESE GOLDEN THREADS OF SUGAR IS A SOMETIMES TRICKY, OFTEN MESSY PROPOSITION—BEST SUITED TO THE MORE ADVENTUROUS. IT HELPS TO ADD A LITTLE BEESWAX TO THE HOT CARAMEL (A TRICK I LEARNED FROM MY GOOD FRIEND AND FELLOW CHEF JEAN-CLAUDE SZURDAK). THE WAX COATS THE SUGAR THREADS, MAKING THEM LESS LIKELY TO STICK TOGETHER. DON'T TRY THIS IN HOT, HUMID WEATHER.

Oeufs à la Neige in Peach Sauce

A classic French dessert, oeufs à la neige, *or snow eggs, consists of egg-shaped portions of meringue dropped into hot water and cooked briefly on top of the stove. I serve the snow eggs with a sauce made of canned peaches pureed with yogurt, a little sugar, Cointreau, and vanilla. Although similar in color and consistency to crème anglaise, the rich custard sauce traditionally served with the "eggs," it is much less caloric.*

The snow eggs may be finished in the conventional manner, with a drizzle of caramel on top, or, for a more dramatic effect, with strands of caramel angel hair.

PEACH SAUCE

- ¾ cup nonfat plain yogurt
- ¾ cup sliced peaches in syrup
- 1½ tablespoons sugar
- 1½ tablespoons Cointreau or Grand Marnier
- ½ teaspoon vanilla extract

SNOW EGGS

- 6 cups water
- 3 large egg whites
- ¼ cup sugar

CARAMEL

- 3 tablespoons sugar
- 1 tablespoon water

ANGEL HAIR (ALTERNATIVE TOPPING)

- 1 cup sugar
- ¼ cup water
- 2 teaspoons grated edible wax, such as beeswax

FOR THE PEACH SAUCE

1. Place the yogurt, peaches (with syrup), 1½ tablespoons sugar, Cointreau, and vanilla in a blender or food processor, and process until smooth and foamy. If desired, strain the peach sauce through a fine-mesh strainer set over a bowl.

FOR THE SNOW EGGS

2. Bring the water to a boil in a large pot. Meanwhile, beat the egg whites in a mixer until they are firm (3 to 4 minutes). Add the ¼ cup sugar, and continue beating the

whites at medium to high speed for 30 seconds. At this point, reduce the heat of the water so that it is no more than 180 degrees (just under the simmer/boil).

3. Using a ladle or a large spoon, scoop out four mounds of meringue one at a time, and, using another spoon, slide them into the hot (not boiling) water. Poach the egg white mounds for about 2½ minutes, then use a skimmer to gently turn them over, and cook for another 2½ minutes. Lift them carefully from the water, and drain them on paper towels.

For the Caramel

4. Not more than 3 hours before serving the snow eggs, place the 3 tablespoons of sugar and 1 tablespoon of water in a small, unlined copper or stainless steel saucepan. Mix just enough to combine them, then bring to a boil over high heat. Reduce the heat to medium, and continue boiling the mixture for about 3 minutes, until it thickens into a syrup and turns a rich caramel color, taking care that it doesn't burn.
5. While the caramel is cooking, pour the peach sauce into a serving dish or shallow glass bowl, and arrange the snow eggs on top in one layer. Remove the caramel from the stove, and immediately pour it directly on top of the "eggs," dividing it equally among them. Serve, preferably within an hour.

For the Angel Hair (Alternative Topping)

6. Combine the sugar and water in a small saucepan, bring to a boil over medium heat, and cook until a light ivory in color (about 335 degrees). Remove from the heat, and stir in the wax.
7. Cover the floor surrounding your work table with newspapers, and secure a long-handled spatula or wooden spoon so that the entire handle extends beyond the edge of the table.
8. When the syrup has cooled for a few minutes, hold two forks side by side in one hand (or use a small whisk with the wires clipped off where they begin to curve), and dip the tines into the pan. Lift some syrup, and wave the forks high over the spatula so that the dripping threads solidify in the air before falling over the extended handle.
9. Slide the collected strands off the handle, and use immediately to garnish the "eggs" or store in an airtight container.

Yield: 4 Servings

Nutritional Analysis per Serving (with Caramel Topping):

Calories 192
Protein 5 gm.
Carbohydrates 41 gm.
Fat 0.1 gm.
Saturated fat 0.1 gm.
Cholesterol 1 mg.
Sodium 77 mg.

Nonfat yogurt is rich in calcium and riboflavin.

FONSECA'S
1970
NTAGE PORT

Pistachio Floating Island with Black Currant Sauce

This elegant dessert must be made ahead so it can chill and set before being unmolded. I make this recipe in a loaf pan, but it can be made in a round pan, too. Except for the small amount of butter used to grease the baking pan, the dessert contains no fat and only about 280 calories per serving. The colorful, easy-to-make sauce combines two distinct flavors—strawberries and black currants.

- **½ teaspoon unsalted butter**
- **5 large egg whites (¾ cup)**
- **½ cup granulated sugar**
- **⅓ cup coarsely chopped shelled pistachio nuts**
- **2 large strawberries, hulled and cut into ¼-inch dice (⅓ cup)**

Sauce

- **10 ounces strawberries, hulled**
- **½ jar natural black currant preserves (with berries; 10 ounces)**
- **2 tablespoons crème de cassis (black currant liqueur)**

- **2 tablespoons chopped pistachio nuts, for garnish**

1. Preheat the oven to 350 degrees.
2. Grease a 6-cup loaf pan with the butter. Beat the egg whites until stiff. Add the sugar all at once, and beat for a few seconds. Fold the pistachios and the diced berries into the beaten whites, and transfer the mixture to the loaf pan.
3. Place the pan in a larger vessel (a small roasting pan works well), and surround it with warm tap water. Bake at 350 degrees for 30 minutes, and then remove the pan from the water bath and allow it to cool on a rack. The dessert will deflate slightly. (The recipe can be prepared to this point up to 1 day ahead, covered with plastic wrap, and refrigerated.)

(continued)

Yield: 6 Servings

Nutritional Analysis per Serving:

Calories 281
Protein 6 gm.
Carbohydrates 55 gm.
Fat 5.3 gm.
Saturated fat 0.8 gm.
Cholesterol 1 mg.
Sodium 66 mg.

Egg whites provide high-quality protein with no fat.

Pistachio Floating Island with Black Currant Sauce (above).
Figs Vilamoura (see page 391).

Crêpes à la Confiture

As children, my brother and I would sit and watch my mother prepare crêpes and eat them as quickly as they came out of the pan—usually with homemade jam, but sometimes with just a sprinkling of sugar or a little grated chocolate. I duplicate this taste treat for my daughter for breakfast from time to time. It is easily done in a few minutes and is always a winner!

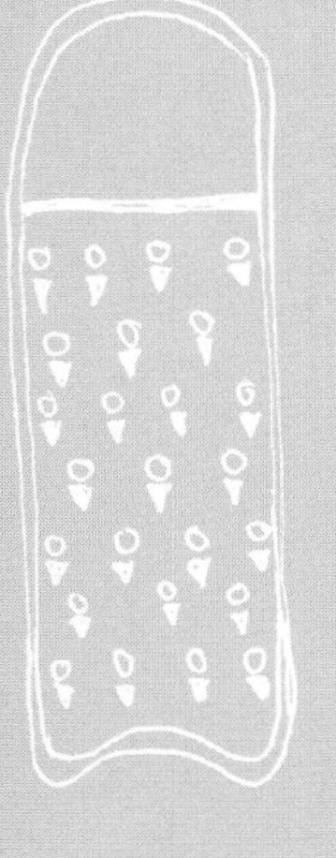

Crêpes

⅔ cup all-purpose flour
2 large eggs
½ teaspoon sugar
¾ cup nonfat milk
1 tablespoon corn or canola oil
A little additional oil for greasing the skillet

Fillings

The best-quality jam or preserves: strawberry, apricot, quince, blackberry, plum, or the like
Sugar
Grated chocolate

1. Combine the flour, eggs, sugar, and ¼ cup of the milk in a bowl, and mix with a whisk until smooth. (The mixture will be fairly thick.) Add the remaining milk and the tablespoon of oil, and mix until smooth.
2. Lightly grease the bottom of an 8- or 9-inch nonstick skillet with a little oil, and heat the pan over medium to high heat. When it is hot, add about 3 tablespoons of the crêpe batter, and quickly tilt and move the skillet so the batter coats the entire bottom of the pan. (Move quickly, or the batter will set before the bottom of the skillet is coated, and the crêpe will be thicker than desired.)
3. Cook for about 45 seconds on one side, and then turn and cook for about 20 seconds on the other side. As you make the crêpes, stack them on a plate, first-browned side down, so that when they are filled and folded this nicer side will be visible. The crêpes are best made and filled just before eating.
4. To fill, spread each crêpe with about 2 teaspoons of jam, 1 teaspoon of sugar, or 2 teaspoons of grated chocolate. Fold in half, enclosing the filling, and then in half again. Eat immediately.

Yield: 4 Servings (16 Crêpes)

Nutritional Analysis per Serving:

Calories 314
Protein 8 gm.
Carbohydrates 44 gm.
Fat 13.4 gm.
Saturated fat 4.3 gm.
Cholesterol 107 mg.
Sodium 59 mg.

CRÊPE TECHNIQUE

I USE A VERY LIGHT CRÊPE BATTER THAT CONTAINS ONLY ONE EGG AND COOK THE CRÊPES IN AN 8-INCH NONSTICK SKILLET. PERHAPS THE MOST IMPORTANT THING TO REMEMBER WHEN MAKING CRÊPES IS TO SPREAD THE BATTER VERY QUICKLY IN THE HOT SKILLET SO IT WILL NOT SOLIDIFY BEFORE IT COATS THE BOTTOM OF THE PAN; IF YOU MOVE TOO SLOWLY, YOU WILL NEED MORE BATTER, AND THE RESULTING CRÊPE WILL BE TOO THICK. USE A TWISTING, TILTING, AND SHAKING MOTION TO MOVE THE BATTER QUICKLY OVER THE SURFACE OF THE PAN, COATING IT LIGHTLY.

Crêpe Soufflés in Grapefruit Sauce

These crêpes can be made ahead and served unstuffed on their own, with the grapefruit sauce, or with jam. In this recipe, I fill them with a low-calorie soufflé mixture made from a combination of stiffened, slightly sweetened egg whites and grated lime rind. This same mixture could be baked without the crêpes in a large greased soufflé mold (1½- or 2-quart size) for approximately 30 minutes and then served with the grapefruit sauce alongside.

Grapefruit Sauce

1 Ruby Red grapefruit (1 pound)
¼ cup grenadine syrup
1 tablespoon lemon juice

Crêpes

½ cup flour
1 egg
¾ cup milk
2 tablespoons canola oil plus ¼ teaspoon for greasing skillet
⅛ teaspoon salt
¼ teaspoon granulated sugar

Soufflé Mixture

5 egg whites
¼ cup granulated sugar
1 tablespoon grapefruit rind, from grapefruit used in sauce
1 teaspoon unsalted butter

6 fresh mint leaves, coarsely chopped, for garnish (optional)

1. Grate the grapefruit (colored skin only) to obtain 1 tablespoon of rind. Reserve.

For the Grapefruit Sauce

2. Peel the remaining skin and underlying white pith from the grapefruit. With a sharp knife, remove the flesh segments from the surrounding membranes. Squeeze the membranes to obtain ½ cup of juice.
3. Cut the segments into ½-inch pieces (½ cup), and combine in a bowl with the grapefruit juice, grenadine, and lemon juice.

(continued)

Grapefruit and Kiwi Ambrosia

This refreshing, satisfying dessert is the ideal finish for an elegant menu. The grapefruit is cut into membrane-free wedges and mixed with pieces of kiwi and sweet white Sauternes-type wine. Intensely flavored Sauternes, the greatest dessert wine in the world, is made from grapes attacked by the fungus botrytis, *which shrivels them and concentrates their juice. This wine also can be served with the dessert.*

- 2 Ruby Red grapefruits (1 pound each)
- 3 kiwis
- ½ cup Sauternes-type sweet white wine
- 2 tablespoons Grand Marnier liqueur
- 8 Bing cherries

1. Peel the grapefruits with a sharp knife, removing all the skin and the underlying white pith so the flesh of the fruit is totally exposed. Cut between the membranes, and remove the flesh in wedgelike pieces. Place the grapefruit pieces in a bowl, and squeeze any remaining juice from the membranes over them before discarding the membranes.
2. Peel the kiwis, and cut them into ½-inch pieces. Add them to the grapefruit along with the wine and Grand Marnier. Mix, and allow to macerate for at least a few minutes and as long as a few hours before serving.
3. To serve, spoon the fruit into glass goblets or dessert dishes, and top each serving with a couple of cherries.

Yield: 4 Servings

Nutritional Analysis per Serving:

Calories 119
Protein 1 gm.
Carbohydrates 22 gm.
Fat 0.5 gm.
Saturated fat 0.03 gm.
Cholesterol 0 mg.
Sodium 4 mg.

Kiwis and grapefruit are rich in vitamin C and potassium.

Clockwise from top: Grapefruit and Kiwi Ambrosia (above);
Russian Cranberry *Kissel* (see page 372);
Frozen Black Velvet (see page 443).

Oranges in Grand Marnier

Make this refreshing dessert far enough ahead so that the oranges can cool completely in the cooking syrup. Julienned orange rind, blanched first to eliminate bitterness, lends texture to and intensifies the taste of the dessert. The oranges are poached just briefly and flavored with Grand Marnier.

4 seedless navel oranges (6 ounces each)
3 cups water
¼ cup granulated sugar
2 tablespoons Grand Marnier
Mint leaves, for garnish

1. With a vegetable peeler, cut two long strips of peel, each about 1 inch wide, from each orange. Stack the strips, and cut them lengthwise into a julienne (very thin strips). Place the julienne in a saucepan, and cover with 2 cups of the water. Bring to a boil, drain in a colander, rinse under cool water, and return the julienne to the rinsed saucepan with the remaining cup of water and the sugar. Cook for 3 to 4 minutes, until large bubbles form and the mixture becomes a syrup.
2. Meanwhile, cut some additional strips from the orange peels, julienne them, and reserve for garnish, if desired. Finish peeling the oranges, removing the white pith under the skin as well. Cut the oranges in half crosswise, and add to the syrup. Cover and cook over low heat for 3 to 4 minutes, checking occasionally and adding 1 or 2 tablespoons of water if no liquid is visible in the pan.
3. Let the oranges cool in the juice, and then add the Grand Marnier. Arrange two orange halves and some juice in each dessert dish. Garnish with the reserved orange julienne if desired, and with the mint leaves, and serve.

Yield: 4 Servings

NUTRITIONAL ANALYSIS PER SERVING:

Calories 124
Protein 1 gm.
Carbohydrates 29 gm.
Fat 0.1 gm.
Saturated fat 0 gm.
Cholesterol 0 mg.
Sodium 1 mg.

Oranges are a good source of soluble fiber, potassium, and vitamin C.

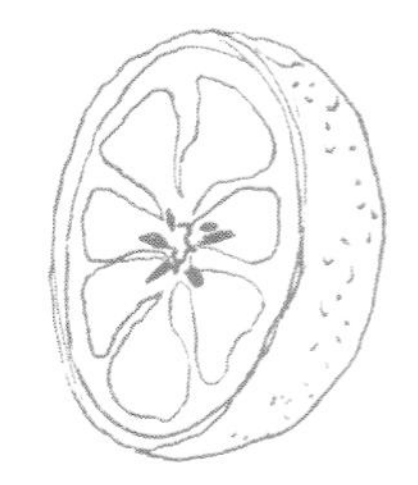

Guava Paste Toast with Mint

This dish holds happy taste memories of childhood for my wife. Her Puerto Rican mother served guava paste often, and I have learned to like it too, especially in combination with a little cream cheese and mint. You'll find it in the ethnic food sections of most supermarkets and in Latin American specialty food stores. This is good not only as a dessert but also as an afternoon snack or buffet dish.

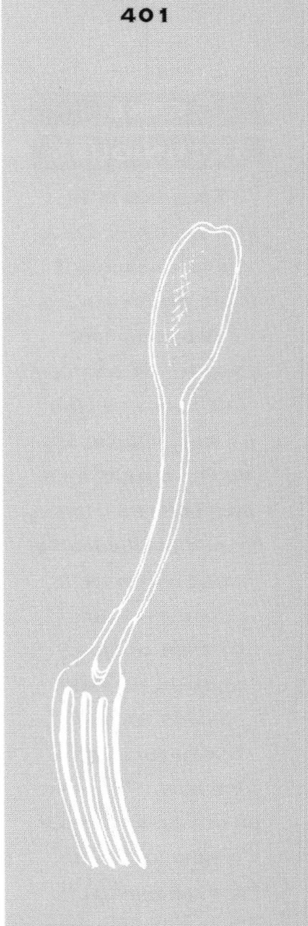

- 4 **thin slices white bread, crusts removed**
- 4 **ounces cream cheese**
- 1 **can (1½ pounds) guava paste**
- 24 **fresh mint leaves**

1. No more than 30 minutes before serving, toast the bread slices lightly, and cut each of them into six pieces.
2. On each piece, place a small slice of cream cheese, and top it with a small slice of guava paste. Garnish each toast with a mint leaf, and arrange them on a plate. Serve as a dessert or snack.

Note: Leftover guava paste, well wrapped, will keep for several weeks in the refrigerator.

Yield: 4 Servings

NUTRITIONAL ANALYSIS PER SERVING:

Calories 308
Protein 4 gm.
Carbohydrates 48 gm.
Fat 11.3 gm.
Saturated fat 6.4 gm.
Cholesterol 32 mg.
Sodium 222 mg.

Guava is a rich source of potassium.

Pears in Espresso

I like to use espresso in this recipe, but any leftover brewed coffee will do. I think that Bosc pears, which take longer to cook than most, lend themselves especially well to this preparation, although you can use another variety instead. If you can obtain tiny Seckel pears in your area, they are also good in this dessert.

- **4 Bosc pears (about 1½ pounds total), peeled and cored from the base with a small round scoop or a sharp-edged metal measuring teaspoon**
- **2 cups espresso coffee**
- **About 2 cups water**
- **⅓ cup light brown sugar**
- **1 teaspoon grated lemon rind**
- **2 tablespoons Kahlua or another coffee-flavored liqueur**
- **4 cookies (optional)**

1. Stand the peeled and cored pears upright in a saucepan that will hold them snugly. Add the coffee and enough of the water to cover the pears completely; then add the sugar. Bring the coffee mixture to a boil, cover, reduce the heat to low, and boil gently until the pears are tender, 30 to 35 minutes.
2. Remove the pears from the liquid, and arrange them in a serving bowl. Boil the liquid until it is reduced to 1 cup, stir in the lemon rind, and pour the mixture over the pears. Cool.
3. Add the Kahlua to the cooled dish, and serve the pears cold, with cookies, if desired.

Yield: 4 Servings

Nutritional Analysis per Serving:

Calories 183
Protein 1 gm.
Carbohydrates 44 gm.
Fat 0.6 gm.
Saturated fat 0.03 gm.
Cholesterol 0 mg.
Sodium 8 mg.

Pears are a good source of fiber.

Baked Pears with Figs

Replace the figs with raisins, if you prefer, or bake the pears alone with the citrus juices, butter, and apricot preserves. This dessert should be made with fully ripened pears. Serve at room temperature.

2 ripe Anjou pears (about 1 pound total)
16 dried Black Mission figs (8 ounces total)
1 tablespoon orange juice
1 tablespoon lemon juice
¾ cup water
1 tablespoon unsalted butter
1 tablespoon apricot preserves
½ cup sour cream (optional)

1. Preheat the oven to 400 degrees.
2. Peel, halve, and core the pears. Cut the figs crosswise into slices, and arrange them in a gratin dish. Place the pears, flat side down, on top of the figs, and sprinkle them with the orange and lemon juices. Then pour in the water. Dot with butter, and spoon the preserves on top of the pears.
3. Bake the pears at 400 degrees for 45 minutes, checking occasionally to ensure that the mixture stays wet so it doesn't burn; if it gets too dry, add a couple of tablespoons of water.
4. Let cool, and serve at room temperature with some sour cream, if desired.

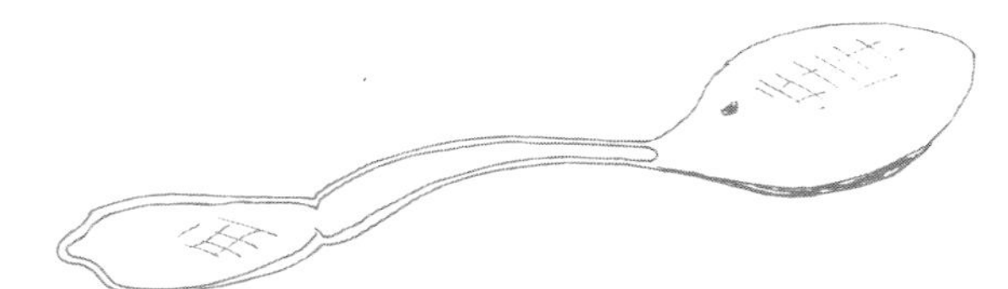

**YIELD:
4 SERVINGS**

NUTRITIONAL ANALYSIS PER SERVING:

Calories 246
Protein 2 gm.
Carbohydrates 57 gm.
Fat 4.0 gm.
Saturated fat 1.9 gm.
Cholesterol 8 mg.
Sodium 9 mg.

Figs are high in fiber and potassium.

PREVENTING DISCOLORATION IN PEARS

FOLDED PAPER TOWELS ARE PLACED ON TOP OF THE PEARS IN THE PAN TO ABSORB SOME OF THE SURROUNDING LIQUID AND KEEP THE PEAR TOPS MOIST, THUS PREVENTING THEM FROM DISCOLORING AS THEY COOK.

Pears in Grenadine

The time required to cook pears varies dramatically, and this must be taken into account when preparing this and other recipes. I use firm Bosc pears here, peeling and coring them before cooking, and even though the cooking liquids boil up inside the pears in this preparation, it takes them 30 minutes to get tender. Well-ripened Anjou or Bartlett pears, on the other hand, cook in as little as 2 or 3 minutes, while Seckels can take as long as 1 hour. When cooked, the pears—saturated with the cooking juices—sink into the liquid.

6 medium Bosc pears (2 pounds)
⅓ cup lime juice
⅓ cup sugar
⅓ cup grenadine
1 cup dry white wine
1 cup water

1. Peel and core the pears, leaving the stems attached and a little of the skin in place around the stems for decoration. Stand the pears upright in a saucepan that will hold them snugly in one layer, and add the lime juice, sugar, grenadine, white wine, and water. (The liquid should barely cover the pears.) Fold a length of paper towel in half and then in half again, and place it over the pears to cover their tops completely.
2. Bring the liquid to a boil over medium to high heat, then reduce the heat to low, cover, and boil the pears gently for about 30 minutes, or until they are very tender when pierced with the point of a sharp knife.
3. Set the pears off the heat, and let them cool in the pan for about 15 minutes, then lift them from the pan, and stand them upright in a serving dish. There should be about 2½ cups of cooking liquid remaining. Return the pan to the stove, and boil the liquid over high heat until it is reduced to a syrup. (You will have 1 cup.)
4. Pour the syrup over the pears, cover, and refrigerate until cold. Serve one pear per person with some of the surrounding syrup.

YIELD: 6 SERVINGS

NUTRITIONAL ANALYSIS PER SERVING:

Calories 147
Protein 1 gm.
Carbohydrates 33 gm.
Fat 0.5 gm.
Saturated fat 0 gm.
Cholesterol 0 mg.
Sodium 3 mg.

Pears are higher in soluble fiber than apples, oranges, or bananas.

CLOCKWISE FROM TOP: PEARS IN GRENADINE (ABOVE);
APRICOT *DÉLICE* (SEE PAGE 366);
BROILED FIGS IN PEACH SAUCE (SEE PAGE 393).

Pears au Gratin

This is a nice way to use leftover French bread. Leftover cookies or cake can be substituted, in which case eliminate the butter and sugar.

It is important that the pears be well ripened for this dish, even if this means buying fruit that is slightly damaged or has darkened skin; the skin will be removed and any remaining spots on the flesh of the sliced pears will be concealed under the crumbs of the topping.

Sour cream or whipped heavy cream makes a nice addition, but the dish is very good without either garnish.

4 very ripe pears (about 1½ pounds), peeled, halved lengthwise, and cored
3 ounces day-old French-style bread
2 tablespoons unsalted butter
¼ cup sugar
½ cup pecan halves
Sour cream or whipped heavy cream (optional)

1. Preheat the oven to 375 degrees.
2. Cut the pears lengthwise into ¼-inch slices, and arrange them in one slightly overlapping layer in the bottom of a 6-cup gratin dish.
3. Break the bread into the bowl of a food processor, and process it until coarsely chopped. (You should have about 1¾ cups of coarse crumbs.) Add the butter, sugar, and pecans. Process until the mixture is mealy, and then sprinkle it evenly over the pears.
4. Bake at 375 degrees for 30 minutes, until the topping is nicely browned. Allow to cool slightly.
5. Serve the pears lukewarm, with a little sour cream or whipped heavy cream, if desired.

Yield: 4 Servings

NUTRITIONAL ANALYSIS PER SERVING:

Calories 343
Protein 4 gm.
Carbohydrates 50 gm.
Fat 16.1 gm.
Saturated fat 4.5 gm.
Cholesterol 16 mg.
Sodium 124 mg.

A pear has three times the fiber of a fresh peach.

Pineapple Délice

The quality of this dessert depends entirely on the quality of the pineapple. If your pineapple is ripe and flavorful, this quick and easy preparation will be delicious; if it's not, the dessert is not worth making.

- **½ teaspoon grated lime peel**
- **1½ tablespoons lime juice**
- **2 tablespoons honey**
- **2 tablespoons kirsch (cherry brandy)**
- **1 small ripe pineapple (about 2¼ pounds), leaves removed**
- **4 slices pound cake or cookies (optional)**

1. Mix the grated lime peel, lime juice, honey, and kirsch together in a large bowl.
2. Peel the pineapple, removing the skin and most of the black holes on the surface of the flesh. Stand the pineapple upright, and begin cutting it vertically into ¼-inch slices, stopping when you get to the core, turning it 90 degrees, and cutting again, until the pineapple has been rotated 360 degrees on its base and all the flesh has been removed. Stack up the slices, and cut them into 1½-inch-wide strips.
3. Add the pineapple strips to the bowl containing the other ingredients, and mix well. Allow the pineapple to macerate in the lime juice mixture for at least 1 hour.
4. Serve as is or with slices of pound cake or cookies.

PINEAPPLE RIPENESS

SOME PEOPLE INSIST THAT IF YOU CAN PULL OUT A LEAF FROM THE CROWN OF A PINEAPPLE, THE FRUIT IS RIPE. I THINK YOU SHOULD RELY ON YOUR NOSE. A RIPE PINEAPPLE WILL HAVE A PLEASANT, FRUITY SMELL.

YIELD: 4 SERVINGS

NUTRITIONAL ANALYSIS PER SERVING:

Calories 115
Protein 1 gm.
Carbohydrates 27 gm.
Fat 0.5 gm.
Saturated fat 0.03 gm.
Cholesterol 0 mg.
Sodium 2 mg.

Pineapple is a good source of fiber.

Pineapple in Cantaloupe Sauce

Three fruits are represented here: pineapple and plum slices are served in a beautiful sauce created by processing the flesh of cantaloupe. This dish is best if made with only ripe, full-flavored fruit. *(See Pineapple Ripeness on page 409.)* *The cantaloupe sauce can be used as a marinade for other fruit if ripe pineapple and plums are not available. Good substitutes would be watermelon, honeydew melon, or apples.*

About ½ of a ripe cantaloupe (1 pound)
3 tablespoons honey
2 tablespoons Grand Marnier
About ⅓ of a ripe pineapple (1 pound)
2 red Santa Rosa plums (about 6 ounces total)

1. Remove the rind and seeds from the cantaloupe, and cut the flesh into 1-inch pieces. You should have about 2 cups. Place the pieces in the bowl of a food processor with the honey, and process until smooth. Pour the puree into a bowl, and stir in the Grand Marnier. Cover, and refrigerate until ready to serve. (You should have about 1½ cups.)
2. Remove the rind and core from the pineapple, and cut the flesh crosswise into ⅛-inch-thick slices. You should have about twenty slices.
3. Cut the plums in half crosswise, remove the pits, and cut the flesh into slices ⅛ inch thick. You should have about twenty slices.
4. At serving time, divide the cantaloupe sauce among four dessert plates. Arrange four or five slices of pineapple on top of the sauce on each plate, and place a plum slice on top of the pineapple. Arrange the remaining plum slices around the periphery of each plate to create a decorative border. Serve.

Yield: 4 Servings

Nutritional Analysis per Serving:

Calories 470
Protein 6 gm.
Carbohydrates 111 gm.
Fat 4.4 gm.
Saturated fat 0.3 gm.
Cholesterol 0 mg.
Sodium 6 mg.

This dessert is rich in potassium, vitamin C, and fiber.

Salpicon of Pineapple (Diced Pineapple)

Salpicon *means "a mixture cut into dice," and this dessert consists of diced ripe pineapple seasoned with crème de cassis, cognac, and brown sugar. Ripeness is important here.* *(See Pineapple Ripeness on page 409.)* *If you are fortunate enough to find a particularly sweet pineapple, cut down on the sugar. The dark raisins add color and a chewy texture that is appealing with the crisp pineapple.*

1 ripe pineapple (3 pounds)
¼ cup crème de cassis
2 tablespoons cognac
3 tablespoons light brown sugar
1 tablespoon dark raisins, for garnish

1. Trim the pineapple at both ends, and cut it lengthwise into quarters. Cut out the core. Cut each quarter in half, and remove the wedges of fruit from the skin. Cut each wedge into eight pieces.
2. In a bowl, combine the pineapple pieces with the crème de cassis, cognac, and brown sugar. Refrigerate until serving time.
3. Spoon into six dessert bowls. Serve very cold, garnished with the raisins.

Yield: 6 Servings

Nutritional Analysis per Serving:

Calories 198
Protein 1 gm.
Carbohydrates 25 gm.
Fat 0.5 gm.
Saturated fat 0 gm.
Cholesterol 0 mg.
Sodium 4 mg.

Pineapple is high in vitamin C and iron.

Blackberries in Creamy Honey Sauce

For this dessert, ripe blackberries are tossed in a little sugar and mounded on plates coated with a sauce composed of honey, orange juice, yogurt, and mint. Quick and easy, the dish is as attractive as it is flavorful. Any other berries—strawberries, raspberries, boysenberries—can be substituted here. Be sure to choose very ripe berries for maximum sweetness.

2 cups (1 pint) blackberries
1 tablespoon sugar
3 tablespoons honey
¼ cup orange juice
1 cup nonfat plain yogurt
1 tablespoon shredded fresh peppermint leaves

1. Gently toss the blackberries and sugar in a small bowl. Cover, and refrigerate until serving time.
2. Meanwhile, mix the honey and orange juice in another small bowl. When the mixture is smooth, add the yogurt and mint, and mix just until smooth. Cover, and refrigerate until serving time.
3. To serve, divide the yogurt sauce among four dessert plates. Mound some berries in the center, dividing them equally among the plates. Serve immediately.

Yield: 4 Servings

NUTRITIONAL ANALYSIS PER SERVING:

Calories 137
Protein 4 gm.
Carbohydrates 31 gm.
Fat 0.4 gm.
Saturated fat 0.1 gm.
Cholesterol 1 mg.
Sodium 44 mg.

Blackberries are high in fiber and a good source of vitamin C.

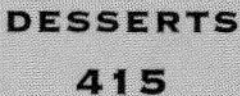

BLUEBERRIES WITH BROWN SUGAR

This is a simple, delicious summer recipe. Look over the blueberries carefully, and remove and discard any damaged ones. If you wash them, dry them off with paper towels so the water doesn't dilute the yogurt. The best way to serve the berries is to arrange them on individual plates, create a well in the center of each plate, spoon the yogurt into the wells, and sprinkle with brown sugar. If you desire a richer dessert, substitute sour cream or whipped cream for the yogurt, and sprinkle it with brown sugar.

1 pint blueberries
8 tablespoons plain yogurt
4 tablespoons dark brown sugar
Mint leaves, for garnish

1. Divide the blueberries among four plates. Make a well in the center of the berries, and spoon in some yogurt.
2. Sprinkle the berries and yogurt with the brown sugar, decorate with a few mint leaves, and serve. The sugar will melt and spread somewhat on the yogurt, giving the dessert an interesting look.

YIELD: 4 SERVINGS

NUTRITIONAL ANALYSIS PER SERVING:

Calories 110
Protein 1 gm.
Carbohydrates 25 gm.
Fat 1.2 gm.
Saturated fat 0.6 gm.
Cholesterol 4 mg.
Sodium 23 mg.

Blueberries provide fiber, and yogurt provides calcium.

Custard with Blueberry Sauce

This custard is quite lean; I use nonfat milk and a minimum of sugar. On its own, it might not be as rich-tasting as you would like, but in combination with a sauce of fresh blueberries, good-quality apricot preserves, and cognac, it makes a beautiful dessert.

Remove the molds from the oven as soon as the custard is lightly set yet still somewhat jellylike if shaken. It will continue to firm as it cools.

Custard

- 2 large eggs
- ¼ cup sugar
- 1 teaspoon pure vanilla extract
- 1¾ cups nonfat milk

Blueberry Sauce

- ¼ cup apricot preserves, best possible quality
- 2 tablespoons cognac
- 1 tablespoon water
- 1 cup fresh blueberries

For the Custard

1. Preheat the oven to 350 degrees.
2. Break the eggs into a mixing bowl, and beat them with a fork until they are well combined and there is no visible sign of egg white. Add the sugar, vanilla, and milk, and mix well to dissolve the sugar.
3. Arrange four small (¾-cup) soufflé molds in a roasting pan, and strain the custard mixture into the molds. Surround the molds with enough lukewarm tap water to extend about three-quarters of the way up the sides of the molds.
4. Place the pan in the 350-degree oven, and bake the molds for about 35 minutes, until the custard is barely set. Remove the molds from the water bath, and cool them for at least 3 hours.

For the Blueberry Sauce

5. Mix the preserves and cognac together in a small bowl, adding the water, if needed, to thin to the consistency of a sauce. Stir in the blueberries, and set aside.
6. At serving time, unmold the custards on individual plates, spoon some blueberry sauce over and around them, and serve immediately.

Top: Potted Plums with Phyllo Dough (see page 412).
Bottom: Custard with Blueberry Sauce (above).

Regulating the Water Bath

The water bath surrounding the custard molds as they bake should not be allowed to boil, or the custard will overcook. If the water begins to boil, add a few ice cubes (removing enough water to compensate for the ice as it melts) to quickly lower the water temperature.

Yield: 4 Servings

Nutritional analysis per serving:

Calories 220
Protein 7 gm.
Carbohydrates 37 gm.
Fat 2.8 gm.
Saturated fat 0.9 gm.
Cholesterol 108 mg.
Sodium 92 mg.

Blueberries contribute to vitamin C intake.

Blueberry Crumble

This is an easy recipe that I prepare often in the summer, when berries are plentiful. I especially like it made with blueberries, but blackberries, boysenberries, and raspberries are good like this, flavored with a fruit preserve or jam, moistened with a little orange juice, and topped before baking with leftover cake or cookie crumbs. The crumble can be served on its own, with yogurt, or—if you want to splurge—with sour cream or whipped cream.

2 cups fresh or frozen blueberries (about 10 ounces)
¼ cup apricot preserves
2 tablespoons orange juice
3 ounces pound cake, sponge cake, or cookies, crumbled
1 cup yogurt

1. Preheat the oven to 375 degrees.
2. Mix the blueberries, preserves, and orange juice together in a bowl, and then transfer the mixture to a 3-cup gratin dish.
3. Crumble the cake or cookies on top, covering the blueberries entirely.
4. Bake at 375 degrees for 30 minutes.
5. Serve lukewarm, topped with 2 generous tablespoons of yogurt per person.

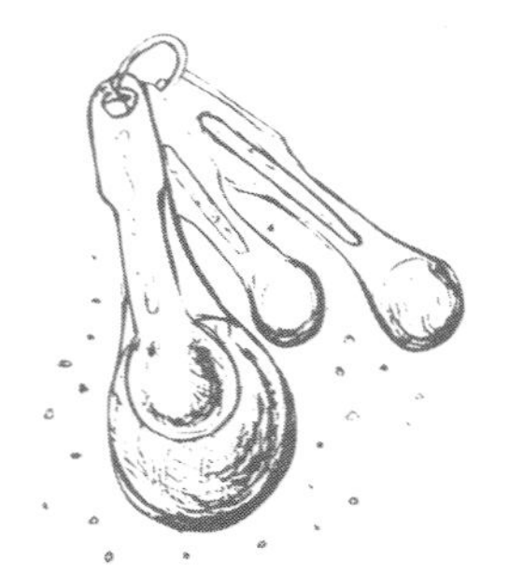

Yield: 4 Servings

NUTRITIONAL ANALYSIS PER SERVING:

Calories 234
Protein 5 gm.
Carbohydrates 39 gm.
Fat 7.4 gm.
Saturated fat 2.2 gm.
Cholesterol 35 mg.
Sodium 70 mg.

Raspberry Granité

Especially attractive when served in champagne glasses, this refreshing sherbet is flavored with raspberry brandy and garnished with mint sprigs. It makes a perfect finish to an elegant meal.

- **¾ pound fresh raspberries or 1 package (12 ounces) frozen unsweetened raspberries**
- **1 cup raspberry preserves**
- **1 tablespoon fresh lemon juice**
- **4 teaspoons raspberry brandy**
- **4 sprigs fresh mint, for garnish**
- **Additional fresh raspberries, for garnish**

1. Place the berries and preserves in the bowl of a food processor, and process until pureed. Strain through a fine strainer into a bowl. (You should have 2 cups.)
2. Add the lemon juice, and mix. Place the bowl in the freezer for about 2½ hours. The mixture should be hard-set but still soft enough in the center so it can be mixed.
3. Transfer the puree to the bowl of a food processor, and process for about 20 seconds. (It will "whiten" slightly.) Return the puree to a bowl, and place it back in the freezer for another 2½ to 3 hours.
4. To serve, scoop into glass dishes, and spoon 1 teaspoon of the raspberry brandy over each serving. Decorate with a sprig of fresh mint and a few berries, if desired.

EASY-TO-MAKE GRANITÉ

THIS GRANITÉ CAN BE MADE WITH FRESH RASPBERRIES OR WITH UNSWEETENED FROZEN RASPBERRIES. RASPBERRY PRESERVES INTENSIFY THE TASTE OF THE BERRIES AND SWEETEN THE MIXTURE. THE RESULTING PUREE IS FROZEN, THEN LIGHTLY EMULSIFIED IN A FOOD PROCESSOR AND FROZEN AGAIN. THIS DESSERT IS BEST SERVED WHEN JUST HARD ENOUGH SO THAT YOU CAN SCOOP IT OUT TO FORM A LARGE "CURL."

YIELD: 4 SERVINGS

NUTRITIONAL ANALYSIS PER SERVING:

Calories 250
Protein 1 gm.
Carbohydrates 63 gm.
Fat 0.6 gm.
Saturated fat 0 gm.
Cholesterol 0 mg.
Sodium 32 mg.

Raspberry Velvet

I often use individually quick frozen (IQF) berries. Available year round at most supermarkets, they are generally berries of high quality that have been picked and frozen (without sugar) at the peak of ripeness. Of course, if you have access to fresh raspberries, by all means use them.

The berries are liquefied and strained here first, then the mixture is partially frozen and, finally, the slush is served in sugar-rimmed glasses. If you prepare the dessert ahead and freeze the mixture until hard, be sure to defrost it under refrigeration for an hour or so before serving, to achieve the desired slushy consistency.

- 1 **package (12 ounces) IQF (individually quick frozen) unsweetened raspberries, defrosted, or an equivalent amount of fresh raspberries (about 12 ounces)**
- ⅓ **cup seedless black raspberry preserves**
- ¼ **cup water**
- 2 **teaspoons lime juice**
- 1 **tablespoon sugar**
- 4 **sprigs fresh mint**

1. Push the raspberries through a food mill with the black raspberry preserves, then strain the mixture through a fine-mesh strainer set over a bowl to eliminate any remaining seeds. Add the water, and mix well. (You will have about 2 cups.)
2. Place the bowl containing the berry mixture in the freezer, and stir it occasionally until it is half frozen and slushy in consistency.
3. Meanwhile, place the lime juice in one small saucer and the sugar in another. Dip the rims of four stemmed glasses (preferably tulip champagne glasses) first into the lime juice and then into the sugar, to create a border. Place the glasses in the freezer or refrigerator until serving time.
4. At serving time, divide the raspberry velvet among the prepared glasses, and decorate each with a sprig of mint. Serve immediately.

Yield: 4 Servings

NUTRITIONAL ANALYSIS PER SERVING:

Calories 124
Protein 1 gm.
Carbohydrates 32 gm.
Fat 0.9 gm.
Saturated fat 0 gm.
Cholesterol 0 mg.
Sodium 11 mg.

Red Wine and Cassis Strawberries

In wine-growing regions, berries—particularly strawberries—are typically combined with the wine from that area, and sometimes a liqueur, and served as a dessert. Here, I mix strawberries with a fruity red wine and black currant or blackberry liqueur and serve them in the classic way, spooned into wine goblets. If desired, top the desserts with a little sour cream, and serve them with cookies.

- **3 cups ripe strawberries, washed and hulled**
- **3 tablespoons sugar**
- **3 tablespoons cassis (black currant–flavored liqueur) or *crème de mûres* (blackberry-flavored liqueur)**
- **¾ cup dry, fruity red wine**
- **1 tablespoon shredded peppermint leaves**
- **4 tablespoons sour cream (optional)**
- **Cookies (optional)**

1. Quarter the berries, and place them in a bowl with the sugar, liqueur, wine, and mint. Mix well, and serve immediately, or refrigerate (for up to 8 hours) until serving time.
2. Spoon the berries and marinade into wine goblets for serving. If desired, top each dessert with a dollop of sour cream, and serve it with a cookie.

Yield: 4 Servings

Nutritional Analysis per Serving:

Calories 133
Protein 0.1 gm.
Carbohydrates 22 gm.
Fat 0.4 gm.
Saturated fat 0 gm.
Cholesterol 0 mg.
Sodium 3 mg.

Strawberries contain more vitamin C than oranges.

Strawberry Buttermilk Shortcakes

Homemade strawberry shortcake is a hit with just about everyone, and this very easy version is no exception. The shortcakes are served with a garnish of sour cream, although yogurt would make a good, lower-calorie substitute.

1 pint strawberries
½ cup strawberry jam

SHORTCAKES
½ cup all-purpose flour
½ cup cake flour
1 teaspoon baking powder
½ teaspoon baking soda
1½ tablespoons sugar
½ teaspoon salt
3 tablespoons unsalted butter, softened
⅓ cup buttermilk

½ cup sour cream
4 sprigs mint, for garnish

1. Rinse and hull the berries. Cut off about ¼ inch from the stem end of each berry. (This part of the berry tends to be less sweet, especially if the berries are not completely ripe.) Reserve these trimmings for the sauce. (You should have about 1½ cups of trimmings.)
2. Cut the trimmed berries into wedges, and place them in a bowl. Transfer the trimmings to the bowl of a food processor. Add the jam to the berry trimmings, and process until smooth. Pour the sauce over the berries, toss well, and set aside in the refrigerator for at least 1 hour, or as long as 6 hours.

FOR THE SHORTCAKES

3. Preheat the oven to 450 degrees.
4. In a bowl, combine the flours, baking powder, soda, sugar, and salt with the butter, mixing gently with a spoon for 30 seconds at most. (The mixture should not be completely smooth.) Add the buttermilk, and mix with a spoon just enough to combine the ingredients into a soft dough.
5. Invert the dough onto a nonstick cookie sheet, and cover it with a piece of plastic wrap. Press on the dough until you have extended it to a thickness of about ⅜ inch, and then cut it into 2½-inch squares. Bake at 450 degrees for 10 to 12 minutes. Remove to a rack; cool.
6. At serving time, cut the shortcakes in half horizontally. Arrange the bottoms on four dessert dishes, and spoon the berry mixture on top. Cover with the shortcake tops, and garnish each with sour cream and a sprig of mint. Serve.

ABOUT SHORTCAKE

IN THIS RECIPE, I USE BOTH BAKING POWDER AND BAKING SODA. BAKING POWDER IS MADE FROM A MIXTURE OF BAKING SODA AND CREAM OF TARTAR (TARTARIC ACID); I USE BAKING SODA IN ADDITION BECAUSE OF THE SOURNESS AND ACIDITY OF THE BUTTERMILK. IT IS IMPORTANT THAT YOU MIX THE INGREDIENTS FOR THE SHORTCAKES LIGHTLY AND QUICKLY, COMBINING THEM JUST ENOUGH SO THEY HOLD TOGETHER.

YIELD: 4 SERVINGS

NUTRITIONAL ANALYSIS PER SERVING:

Calories 392
Protein 5 gm.
Carbohydrates 61 gm.
Fat 15.4 gm.
Saturated fat 9.3 gm.
Cholesterol 37 mg.
Sodium 607 mg.

Jam Sandwiches

Jam "sandwiches" are fun to make for a party. Consisting of thin slices of firm-textured pound cake spread with different-flavored jams, these can be served stacked up together, in traditional sandwich fashion, or open-faced, with a colorful jam spread on the surface of each cake slice. To add diversity to your dessert tray, select other jam flavors you like, and cut the sandwiches into unusual shapes. I begin with a piece of pound cake 6 inches long by 5 inches wide.

6 ounces fine-textured pound cake
1½ tablespoons raspberry jam
1½ tablespoons apricot jam
1½ tablespoons strawberry jam

1. Trim the outside of the pound cake, and cut it into six slices, each ¼ inch thick. Spread the raspberry jam on the top surface of one slice, the apricot jam on the top surface of another slice, and the strawberry jam on the top surface of a third slice.
2. Top with the remaining pound cake slices to create three sandwiches. Cut each into different shapes: one into squares, one into triangles, and one into rectangles.
3. Arrange on a plate, and serve.

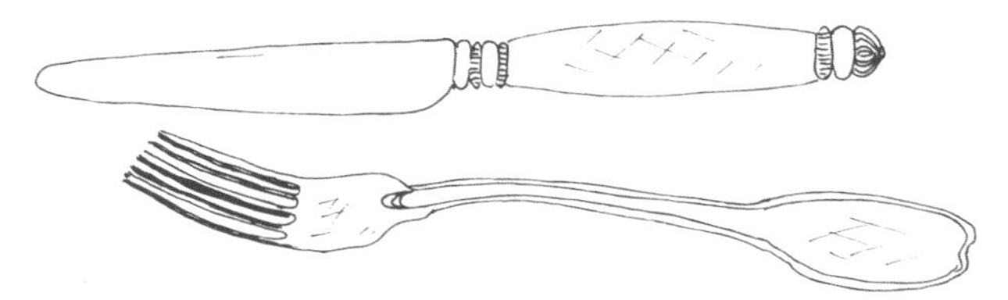

**Yield:
4 Servings**

NUTRITIONAL ANALYSIS PER SERVING:

Calories 206
Protein 2 gm.
Carbohydrates 34 gm.
Fat 7.8 gm.
Saturated fat 4.3 gm.
Cholesterol 86 mg.
Sodium 164 mg.

Strawberries in the Sun

This recipe produces whole berries that are almost candied in the syrup. Remember that in a conventional strawberry jam the sugar is almost equal in weight to the strawberries. In this recipe, half as much sugar by weight is used.

For the syrup, sugar and water are cooked together on top of the stove, and then the berries are added. The mixture is neither stirred nor cooked very long on top of the stove, so the berries remain whole. Then the mixture is placed in a roasting pan, covered with a screen (to repel insects), and placed in the sun. It takes about 3 consecutive sunny days to "cook" the berries. The liquid evaporates slowly, and the berries swell in the syrup. *(See photograph, page 429.)*

1½ pounds (3¼ cups) sugar (more if berries are not ripe)
1½ cups water
3 pounds (1½ quarts) small, ripe strawberries, hulled and washed
Toast or cookies (optional)

1. Combine the sugar and water in a large stainless steel saucepan. Bring the mixture to a boil, and boil for 6 to 8 minutes, until the mixture reaches the soft-ball stage (240 degrees). Add the berries, cover, and cook in the syrup for about 2 minutes. Shake the pan gently (instead of stirring), and set the pan aside, covered, off the heat for about 10 minutes. At this point, the berries will have rendered their liquid and be very limp.
2. Transfer the mixture to a roasting pan. (The berry mixture should be about ¾ to 1 inch thick in the pan.) Cover the pan with a window screen, and place it in direct sun for 2 to 3 days, until the syrup is reduced to the desired thickness. If sun is not available, place the pan in a 175- to 180-degree oven for 15 to 20 hours, until the syrup is of the desired thickness. Pour the mixture into jars, and refrigerate until ready to use.
3. To serve, spoon 3 to 4 tablespoons of the preserves per serving into small dessert dishes, and serve as is or with a piece of toast or a cookie, if desired.

CLOUDY-DAY ALTERNATIVE

You also may cook the berries in a 175- to 180-degree oven, which will take up to 20 hours, depending on how much liquid you want around the berries and how thick you like it to be. Remember that the liquid will thicken substantially as it cools. If you intend to serve the berries as a sauce or topping, you will want syrup of a slightly thinner consistency than if you intend to eat the berries as a jam on bread.

Yield: 6 to 8 Servings (Three 12-Ounce Jars)

NUTRITIONAL ANALYSIS PER SERVING:

Calories 376
Protein 1 gm.
Carbohydrates 96 gm.
Fat 0.6 gm.
Saturated fat 0.03 gm.
Cholesterol 0 mg.
Sodium 2 mg.

Glazed Strawberries

This stunningly beautiful recipe is best made when large, ripe, full-flavored berries—preferably with stems—are available. The berries are dipped in warm currant jelly, which hardens around them as it cools. If the glazed berries are to stand for a long time on a buffet table, you might want to add a little unflavored gelatin to the jelly to make it even more binding and resistant to melting.

12 large strawberries, preferably with stems
1 jar (10 ounces) currant jelly
A few sprigs basil or another herb, or edible flowers, for garnish
4 or 8 cookies (optional)

1. Chill a plate in the refrigerator.
2. Wash the berries, and dry them thoroughly with paper towels.
3. Place the currant jelly in a saucepan, and warm it over low heat until it has melted and is smooth.
4. Holding the berries by their stems, dip them, one at a time, in the currant jelly. When they are thoroughly coated with the jelly, lift the berries out, and drain off any excess jelly by scraping the berries gently against the rim of the pan.
5. Place the glazed berries on the very cold plate, and refrigerate them until serving time.
6. At serving time, arrange three berries on each plate, and decorate with the basil, flowers, or herbs. Serve with cookies, if desired.

YIELD: 4 SERVINGS

NUTRITIONAL ANALYSIS PER SERVING:

Calories 113
Protein 0.4 gm.
Carbohydrates 29 gm.
Fat 0.2 gm.
Saturated fat 0.01 gm.
Cholesterol 0 mg.
Sodium 7 mg.

Strawberries are a good source of vitamin C.

GLAZED STRAWBERRIES (ABOVE) AND STRAWBERRIES IN THE SUN (SEE PAGE 427).

Fraises au Soleil

Farina Bavarian Cream Cake with Apricot Sauce

Farina is probably better known in the United States as Cream of Wheat and is sold here under that name, but in France and elsewhere in the world this word means plain white flour, which obviously would not work in this recipe. I cook a small amount of American-style farina in nonfat milk for this lighter version of the classic Bavarian cream cake, traditionally made with whole milk and egg yolks and finished with lots of heavy cream.

Served with apricot preserves flavored with lemon juice and cognac, this is an ideal party dessert. You may decorate the cake, if you wish, with apricot preserves and a little melted chocolate.

Cake

- 2½ cups nonfat milk
- Grated rind of 1 orange (1½ teaspoons)
- Grated rind of 1 lemon (1 teaspoon)
- 1 teaspoon pure vanilla extract
- ¼ cup farina (Cream of Wheat)
- 1 envelope plain gelatin (2 teaspoons)
- ⅓ cup sugar
- ½ cup heavy cream
- ¼ teaspoon canola oil

Apricot Sauce

- ¾ cup (about 8 ounces) apricot preserves
- 2 tablespoons lemon juice
- 2 tablespoons cognac
- 2 teaspoons julienned lemon peel (see How to Julienne Lemon Peel, page 180)
- 1 to 2 tablespoons water (optional)

Decoration (Optional)

- 3 tablespoons apricot preserves, strained
- Red, green, and yellow food coloring
- 1 tablespoon melted bittersweet or semisweet chocolate

For the Cake

1. Combine the milk, orange rind, lemon rind, and vanilla in a large saucepan, and bring the mixture to a boil over medium to high heat. Meanwhile, in a small bowl

(continued)

About Whipped Cream

For this dessert serving six to eight people, I use only ½ cup (8 tablespoons) of cream. Since cream doubles in volume when whipped, this will yield 1 cup of whipped cream. The calories by volume are cut in half as well: whereas 1 tablespoon of heavy cream contains 40 calories, 1 tablespoon of whipped cream has only 20 calories, about as many as a like amount of sour cream.

Chocolate Mint Truffles

Each of these small truffles contains about 30 calories, not as many as you might expect considering their rich flavor. These are especially nice to box and give to friends over the holiday season. They keep well in the refrigerator and can also be frozen.

¼ pound bittersweet chocolate
2 tablespoons milk
1 egg yolk
2 teaspoons finely minced mint
2 teaspoons unsweetened cocoa powder

1. Heat the chocolate and milk together, either in a double boiler over hot water or in a microwave oven set at medium for 30 seconds at a time, until the chocolate has melted. Stir to combine.
2. Add the egg yolk and mint to the chocolate mixture, and mix well. (At this point, the mixture can be heated in a double boiler to 140 degrees and held at that temperature for 3 to 4 minutes to kill any possible salmonella in the egg yolk.)
3. Cool the mixture to room temperature, and then cover and refrigerate it for at least 1 hour until firm.
4. Divide the cold chocolate mixture into twenty small pieces, and press each piece into a roundish ball. (The balls should be uneven so they look more like real truffles.) Sprinkle cocoa over the balls on the plate, and shake the plate so the truffles roll around in the cocoa and become coated.
5. Transfer the truffles to a clean plate, and refrigerate them until serving time.

Yield: 20 Small Truffles

NUTRITIONAL ANALYSIS PER SERVING (TWO TRUFFLES):

Calories 64
Protein 1 gm.
Carbohydrates 7 gm.
Fat 4.6 gm.
Saturated fat 2.3 gm.
Cholesterol 22 mg.
Sodium 2 mg.

CHOCOLATE SOUFFLÉ CAKE WITH RASPBERRY-RUM SAUCE (SEE PAGE 440).
CHOCOLATE AND FRUIT NUT CUPS (SEE PAGE 437).
CHOCOLATE MINT TRUFFLES (ABOVE).
CANDIED ORANGE RIND (SEE PAGE 450).

Brunch & Lunch Dishes

James Beard's Onion Sandwiches

I first tasted this great combination when I went to see James Beard one Sunday morning in the midsixties. Ever since, these onion sandwiches have been a favorite at my house. Rolled on their edges in mayonnaise and then in minced chives, the sandwich is as attractive as it is delicious.

8 thin slices firm-textured white bread (6 to 8 ounces total)
6 tablespoons mayonnaise
4 teaspoons Dijon-style mustard
4 slices red onion, cut ⅛ inch thick from an onion about 3½ inches in diameter
4 tablespoons finely minced fresh chives

1. Arrange the bread slices next to one another on a flat work surface, and, using a glass or a round cutter, cut circles as large as possible out of the slices.
2. Spread each bread circle with 1 teaspoon of the mayonnaise and then with ½ teaspoon of the mustard. Place an onion slice on four of the bread disks (it should cover to the edge). Top with the remaining bread circles. Press lightly to make them adhere.
3. Spread the remaining mayonnaise on the outside edges of each sandwich (about 2 teaspoons per sandwich), and then roll the edges in the chives until coated. Press lightly to make them adhere. Serve.

Yield: 4 Servings

NUTRITIONAL ANALYSIS PER SERVING:

Calories 292
Protein 5 gm.
Carbohydrates 27 gm.
Fat 18.2 gm.
Saturated fat 2.8 gm.
Cholesterol 13 mg.
Sodium 506 mg.

Olive and Tomato Toasts (see page 457).
James Beard's Onion Sandwiches (above).
Smoked Salmon and Cucumber Sandwiches (see page 461).

DRIED TOMATOES IN OIL

YOU CAN RECONSTITUTE DRIED TOMATOES YOURSELF QUITE INEXPENSIVELY (AS OPPOSED TO BUYING THE COSTLY COMMERCIALLY RECONSTITUTED TOMATOES IN OIL). AFTER SOAKING THE TOMATOES IN BOILING WATER, TRANSFER THEM TO A JAR, AND MIX IN A LITTLE OLIVE OIL PLUS WHATEVER GARNISHES YOU LIKE—FROM SLICED GARLIC TO SPRIGS OF ROSEMARY, PIECES OF WALNUTS OR HAZELNUTS, OR HOT PEPPERS. USE THIS MIXTURE ON PASTA AS WELL AS ON SANDWICHES.

Roasted Eggplant Sandwiches

These eggplant sandwiches are different and delicious. They feature thin slices of sautéed eggplant layered with dried tomatoes, fresh basil, and mozzarella cheese on a crusty roll.

- 1½ cups water
- 1 cup dried (not reconstituted) tomatoes (about 1½ ounces)
- 1 tablespoon virgin olive oil
- ¼ cup canola oil
- 1 eggplant (about 1 pound), cut into 16 slices, each about ⅜ inch thick
- Salt and freshly ground pepper to taste
- 4 crusty oval-shaped rolls
- 4 ounces mozzarella cheese, sliced into 12 thin pieces or grated
- 12 large basil leaves

1. Preheat the oven to 400 degrees.
2. In a saucepan, bring the water to a boil. Add the tomatoes, and soak for about 10 minutes. Drain (reserving the liquid for stock), and mix the tomatoes with the olive oil.
3. Heat 1 tablespoon of the canola oil in each of two nonstick skillets. When hot, place four slices of eggplant in each skillet. Sprinkle with salt and pepper, and cook 5 minutes on each side over medium heat. Remove to a dish, and repeat with the remaining canola oil and eggplant.
4. Split the rolls in half, and place them, cut side up, on a work surface. Place two slices of eggplant on the bottom half of each roll. Divide the reconstituted tomato halves on top of the eggplant, and arrange three basil leaves on top. Cover with three thin slices (or grated equivalent) of cheese. Sprinkle, if desired, with a little salt and pepper, and add the remaining eggplant slices, two per roll. Put the tops of the rolls in place, and arrange the assembled sandwiches on a cookie sheet.
5. Bake at 400 degrees for 10 to 12 minutes, until the cheese inside is completely melted. Cut into halves, and serve.

YIELD: 4 SERVINGS

NUTRITIONAL ANALYSIS PER SERVING:

Calories 449
Protein 13 gm.
Carbohydrates 44 gm.
Fat 25.6 gm.
Saturated fat 5.7 gm.
Cholesterol 22 mg.
Sodium 456 mg.

Smoked Salmon and Cucumber Sandwiches

Made with smoked salmon and a delicious cucumber relish, this sandwich can be assembled in just a few minutes. *(See photograph, page 459.)*

Cucumber Relish

- ⅔ cup hot water
- ⅓ cup white distilled vinegar
- ½ teaspoon salt
- ½ teaspoon sugar
- 1 cucumber (12 ounces), peeled, seeded, and very thinly sliced crosswise
- 1 shallot, peeled and very thinly sliced (2 tablespoons)
- 1½ teaspoons finely minced jalapeño pepper
- 2 tablespoons chopped cilantro (coriander or Chinese parsley) leaves

- 8 slices white bread (8 ounces)
- 6 slices smoked salmon (about 8 ounces total)

1. In a bowl, combine the water, vinegar, salt, and sugar. Stir in the cucumber, shallot, jalapeño, and cilantro. Allow the mixture to macerate for at least 1 hour before using, or cover and keep for up to 2 weeks in the refrigerator.
2. At serving time, toast the bread. Drain the cucumbers, and arrange half of them on four slices of toasted bread. Place the salmon slices on top of the cucumbers; top with the remaining cucumbers.
3. Arrange the remaining pieces of toast on top, and trim off the crusts. Cut each sandwich in half to create two rectangles. Serve immediately.

CUCUMBER RELISH

THIS SIMPLE, FRESH-TASTING RELISH HAS BECOME A STAPLE AT MY HOUSE. IT KEEPS FOR WEEKS IN THE REFRIGERATOR AND IS DELICIOUS ON ANY SANDWICH AND AS AN ACCOMPANIMENT TO GRILLED MEAT OR FISH. THE USE OF THE RELISH HERE ELIMINATES THE NEED FOR BUTTER OR MAYONNAISE, MAKING FOR A LIGHTER, MORE SAVORY SANDWICH.

Yield: 4 Servings

NUTRITIONAL ANALYSIS PER SERVING:

Calories 236
Protein 16 gm.
Carbohydrates 33 gm.
Fat 4.6 gm.
Saturated fat 1.0 gm.
Cholesterol 14 mg.
Sodium 1,028 mg.

Salmon is rich in healthful omega-3 fatty acids.

Croque-Monsieur (Grilled Ham and Cheese Sandwich)

The croque-monsieur *is a classic toasted ham and cheese sandwich. I make it here with Gruyère cheese, as is traditional in France. Cut into little squares as it emerges from the oven, it makes a terrific hot hors d'oeuvre. You can vary it—for a* croque-madame, *for example, replace the ham with a slice of chicken.*

YIELD: 4 SERVINGS

NUTRITIONAL ANALYSIS PER SERVING:

Calories 360
Protein 18 gm.
Carbohydrates 29 gm.
Fat 19.1 gm.
Saturated fat 6.7 gm.
Cholesterol 45 mg.
Sodium 742 mg.

Gruyère cheese has slightly more calcium than Swiss cheese.

- 2 **tablespoons canola oil**
- 8 **slices white bread (8 ounces total)**
- 8 **slices Gruyère cheese (about 4 ounces total)**
- 4 **slices honey-cured ham (4 ounces total)**

1. Preheat the oven to 400 degrees.
2. Spread the oil on a cookie sheet. Dip the bread slices (on one side only) in the oil, and arrange them, oiled side up, on a work surface.
3. Place a slice of cheese on top of each slice of bread. Arrange a slice of ham on four of the cheese-covered bread slices, invert the remaining cheese-covered bread slices on top, and press together.
4. Dip both sides of the sandwiches in the remaining oil on the cookie sheet, arrange the sandwiches on the sheet, and place the sheet in the 400-degree oven for 10 minutes.
5. To serve, trim the crusts from the bread, and cut the sandwiches diagonally into triangles. Serve hot.

Pan Bagna

This light, healthy picnic sandwich is especially good when made ahead—preferably the day before—on a large round bread loaf.

- ½ cucumber (about 7 ounces)
- 1 round crusty country-style loaf bread (about 1 pound)
- 18 black oil-cured olives, pitted and chopped
- 3 cloves garlic, peeled, crushed, and finely chopped (about 2 teaspoons)
- 10 small anchovy fillets (2 ounce can), coarsely chopped
- 2 tablespoons virgin olive oil
- 4 or 5 thin slices red onion
- ⅓ green bell pepper (2 ounces), seeded and thinly sliced
- 1 ripe tomato, thinly sliced
- ¼ teaspoon salt
- ¼ teaspoon freshly ground black pepper
- 12 large basil leaves

1. Peel the cucumber, and slice it lengthwise with a vegetable peeler into long thin strips, discarding the seedy center.
2. Cut the loaf of bread in half horizontally.
3. In a bowl, mix together the olives, garlic, anchovies (with their oil), and olive oil. Spread the mixture on the cut surface of both bread halves, and then arrange the slices of onion, green pepper, and tomato on the bottom half of the loaf. Sprinkle with salt and pepper, and arrange the basil leaves and then the cucumber slices on top.
4. Invert the top half of the bread to reform the loaf, and wrap it tightly in plastic wrap. Refrigerate for 2 to 3 hours with a 5-pound weight on top (canned goods or a milk carton). This enables the juices in the filling to flow through the bread.
5. At serving time, unwrap the loaf, and cut it into wedges to serve.

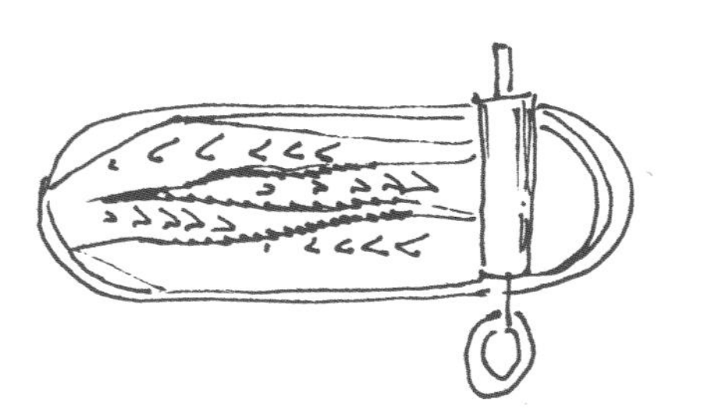

BATHED BREAD

PAN BAGNA LITERALLY MEANS "BATHED BREAD." IT ORIGINALLY CONSISTED OF A VEGETABLE SALAD MIXED WITH PIECES OF LEFTOVER BREAD SO THAT THE BREAD WAS SOAKED WITH VEGETABLE JUICES. IN THE MODERN VERSION, SALAD INGREDIENTS AND, SOMETIMES, ANCHOVIES ARE USED AS A FILLING IN A SPLIT LOAF OF BREAD. THE LOAF IS THEN WRAPPED AND WEIGHTED DOWN. JUICES FROM THE FILLING FLOW THROUGH THE BREAD, AND THE LOAF BECOMES COMPACT ENOUGH SO THAT IT CAN BE CUT INTO PIECES.

YIELD: 4 SERVINGS

NUTRITIONAL ANALYSIS PER SERVING:

Calories 476
Protein 14 gm.
Carbohydrates 63 gm.
Fat 18.8 gm.
Saturated fat 2.9 gm.
Cholesterol 6 mg.
Sodium 1,572 mg.

Breads & Basics

BONY PARTS FOR STOCK

CHICKEN BACKS AND NECKS ARE NOW AVAILABLE PACKAGED AT MOST SUPERMARKETS. IF YOU DON'T SEE THEM, ASK A BUTCHER THERE TO PACKAGE SOME FOR YOU, OR BUY TURKEY BACKS, NECKS, AND GIZZARDS INSTEAD.

Basic Chicken Stock

Stock is used throughout this book in soups, sauces, stews, and other recipes. It takes very little work to make your own stock; mostly it is a matter of staying home for the several hours it takes to cook. From a health standpoint, it is well worth making your own stock, since it will be practically fat-free and salt-free. A flavorful money saver, it can be frozen in small quantities and used as needed.

- 3 **pounds chicken bones (necks, backs, and gizzards, skinless or with as little skin as possible)**
- 6 **quarts lukewarm tap water**
- 1 **tablespoon *herbes de Provence* (see page 467)**
- 1 **large onion (about 8 ounces), peeled and quartered**
- 12 **cloves**
- 4 **bay leaves**
- 1 **tablespoon dark soy sauce**

1. Place the bones and water in a large stockpot, and bring to a boil over high heat. Reduce the heat, and boil gently for 30 minutes. Most of the fat and impurities will rise to the surface during this time; skim off as much of them as you can, and discard them.
2. Add the remainder of the ingredients, return the liquid to a boil, and boil gently for 2½ hours. Strain the stock through a fine-mesh strainer or a colander lined with a dampened kitchen towel or paper towels.
3. Allow the stock to cool. Then remove the surface fat, and freeze the stock in plastic containers with tight lids.

YIELD: 3 QUARTS (12 CUPS)

NUTRITIONAL ANALYSIS PER 1-CUP SERVING:

Calories 30
Protein 3 gm.
Carbohydrates 3 gm.
Fat 2.5 gm.
Saturated fat 0.8 gm.
Cholesterol 0 mg.
Sodium 201 mg.

Herbes de Provence

In response to numerous requests from Today's Gourmet *viewers who have been unable to find* herbes de Provence *in their area, I have devised a recipe for a homemade version of this aromatic herb blend made with fresh herbs that you dry yourself. If fresh herbs aren't available at all, or if only some of those listed here are available, you can make your* herbes de Provence *mixture by combining commercially produced dried herbs in the proportions indicated below.*

Required Herbs
Thyme
Savory
Marjoram
Oregano

Optional Herbs
Sage
Rosemary
Lavender flowers
Fennel seeds

For the Required Herbs

1. Preheat the oven to 180 degrees.
2. Dry the leaves of fresh thyme, savory, marjoram, and oregano by arranging them (one herb variety at a time) in one layer on one or more cookie sheets and placing them in a low oven (180 degrees) until dry (12 to 20 minutes, depending on the herbs), or air dry them outdoors in the summer shade. Mix together equal amounts of these dried herbs.

For the Optional Herbs

3. Dry the sage and rosemary leaves and the lavender flowers as indicated in step 1. Mix together equal proportions of these herbs with a like amount of fennel seeds.
4. Following a 2-to-1 formula, mix a whole portion of the required herbs mixture with a half portion of the optional herbs mixture. Enclose in plastic bags, sealing them tightly to preserve the freshness of the herbs. Use in recipes as needed.

About Herbes de Provence

Herbes de Provence is a blend of dried herbs that is used frequently in the cooking of southern France. This blend always contains thyme, savory, marjoram, and oregano in equal proportions, but lesser amounts of other herbs can also be included. *Herbes de Provence* is, of course, readily available commercially in Provence and elsewhere in the Mediterranean basin, and it can be purchased in many specialty food stores here.

Nutritional analysis per tablespoon:

Calories 3
Protein 0 gm.
Carbohydrates 1 gm.
Fat 0 gm.
Saturated fat 0 gm.
Cholesterol 0 mg.
Sodium 0 mg.

ABOUT BOUQUET GARNI

A French bouquet garni is a mixture of aromatic fresh herbs used as a flavoring for stocks, stews, and casseroles. Traditionally, these herbs are tied together in a small bunch with kitchen twine and submerged in the cooking vessel. At the end of the cooking period—or when the herbs have imparted sufficient flavor to the dish—they are easily removed and discarded.

Bouquet Garni

The classic bouquet garni is made of parsley stems (the leaves are chopped for other uses), sprigs of thyme, and bay laurel leaves. Often, however, greens of leek, a rib of celery, a carrot, and sprigs of available herbs such as tarragon, rosemary, and savory are added.

Required Herbs

15 to 20 parsley stems
A few sprigs thyme
2 or 3 bay laurel leaves

Optional Herbs and Vegetables

A few sprigs tarragon, rosemary, and/or savory
Greens from 2 leeks
1 rib celery
1 carrot

1. Bundle the herbs and vegetables together. Tie them securely, or, if you are using thyme leaves or pieces of bay leaves too small to secure with twine, wrap the mixture in a cheesecloth package before adding it to the pot.

Cilantro Oil

I use cilantro to flavor this oil, but if the assertive flavor of this herb is not to your liking, you can substitute parsley, chives, or your own favorite mixture of fresh green herbs. Shaken well before each use, the flavored oil can be used as is, or you can strain out and discard the herbs and then remove and reserve the oil that rises to the top of the remaining liquid. Either variation is good; combined with vinegar and seasonings, the unstrained version makes an especially appealing vinaigrette dressing. The strained oil adds a decorative element to Skate with Beets and Flavored Oil (page 128). (See About Homemade Flavored Oils for a health warning. This warning does not apply to commercially prepared infused oils, which are specially processed to eliminate the likelihood of contamination.)

- 1 **bunch (4 ounces) fresh cilantro (coriander or Chinese parsley) with stems**
- ⅓ **cup water**
- ½ **cup corn, peanut, or canola oil**

1. Process the cilantro with the water in a mini-chop until pureed. Transfer the puree to a saucepan, bring it to a boil, and immediately set the pan off the heat. When the puree has cooled, pour it into a jar with a tight lid, add the oil, cover, and shake well. Refrigerate for at least 2 hours to develop flavor. Use as is within a few days, refrigerating between uses.
2. For a more refined variation, after the 2-hour macerating period, pour the mixture into a bowl lined with a clean kitchen towel, and press it through the towel into the bowl. Set the liquid aside for 30 to 45 minutes, and then skim off the green oily residue from the top of the mixture and discard it. Pour out and reserve the green oil in the middle, but discard the watery liquid in the bottom of the bowl. Refrigerate the green oil, and use as needed within a few days.

ABOUT HOMEMADE FLAVORED OILS

BECAUSE THE INGREDIENTS INFUSED IN OILS TO FLAVOR THEM—HERBS AND SPICES, FOR EXAMPLE—ARE NOT IN CONTACT WITH OXYGEN, BOTULISM TOXINS CAN DEVELOP IN THE OILS UNLESS PRECAUTIONS ARE TAKEN. TO AVOID ANY HAZARD, MAKE THE OILS ONLY IN SMALL BATCHES, KEEP THEM REFRIGERATED OR FROZEN, AND USE THEM WITHIN A COUPLE OF DAYS.

YIELD: ABOUT ½ CUP STRAINED

NUTRITIONAL ANALYSIS PER 1-TABLESPOON SERVING:

Calories 122
Protein 0.2 gm.
Carbohydrates 0.2 gm.
Fat 13.7 gm.
Saturated fat 1.7 gm.
Cholesterol 0 mg.
Sodium 2 mg.

Curried Oil

Adding ingredients to oils to flavor them is a new technique that young restaurant chefs use widely today. This curry-flavored oil adds a beautiful color and wonderful flavor to vinaigrettes, soups, stews, and sauces (see Skate with Beets and Flavored Oil, page 128). It is also good for sautéing fish. (See About Homemade Flavored Oils, page 469.)

½ cup corn oil

1 teaspoon curry powder

1. Place the oil and curry powder in a jar, cover with a tight lid, and shake well. Refrigerate for 12 hours, shaking the jar a few times during this period.
2. At the end of the maceration period, pour the clear oil into another receptacle, and discard the curry powder mixture that remains in the bottom of the jar. Refrigerate the oil, and use as needed within a few days.

YIELD:
½ CUP

NUTRITIONAL ANALYSIS PER 1-TABLESPOON SERVING:

Calories 121
Protein 0.03 gm.
Carbohydrates 0.2 gm.
Fat 13.7 gm.
Saturated fat 1.7 gm.
Cholesterol 0 mg.
Sodium 0.1 mg.

Tarragon Oil

Herb-flavored oils have added a new dimension to salads and stews, and they are delicious brushed on grilled meat, fish, or poultry (see the alternative for finishing Grilled Chicken with Tarragon Butter on page 215). It is important that the tarragon leaves used in this preparation retain their bright green color. To achieve this, blanch them first, which wilts them and locks in their color. Chop the tarragon by hand for a few seconds to break it down a little, then puree it in a mini-chop or blender, which works much better than a food processor for this purpose. (See About Homemade Flavored Oils, page 469.)

1 cup water, for blanching
½ cup (lightly packed) fresh tarragon leaves
¼ teaspoon salt
½ cup corn, canola, or peanut oil

1. Bring the water to a boil in a saucepan. Add the tarragon leaves, stir, and cook for about 30 seconds, or just until the water returns to a boil again.
2. Drain the leaves in a strainer, and rinse them under cool tap water. Chop them coarsely with a sharp knife, and then place them in the bowl of a mini-chop or blender with the salt and ¼ cup of the oil. Process until thoroughly blended, and transfer to a mixing bowl. Stir in the remaining oil, refrigerate, and use within a few days.

YIELD: ½ CUP

NUTRITIONAL ANALYSIS PER 1-TABLESPOON SERVING:

Calories 124
Protein 0.3 gm.
Carbohydrates 0.6 gm.
Fat 13.7 gm.
Saturated fat 1.7 gm.
Cholesterol 0 mg.
Sodium 69 mg.

Canola oil has the lowest saturated fat among oils.

DO-AHEAD TECHNIQUES

YOU CAN RECRISP LOAVES YOU HAVE MADE AHEAD BY RUNNING THEM UNDER COLD WATER BRIEFLY AND THEN RETURNING THEM TO A 425-DEGREE OVEN FOR ABOUT 10 MINUTES. YOU CAN ALSO PARTIALLY COOK THE LOAVES INITIALLY, BAKING THEM FOR ONLY ABOUT 10 MINUTES—UNTIL THEY REACH THEIR MAXIMUM SIZE BUT ARE STILL PALE IN COLOR AND NOT YET CRISP. IN THIS FORM, THEY CAN BE REFRIGERATED OR FROZEN. WHEN YOU ARE READY TO COMPLETE THE BAKING AND BROWNING OF THE THAWED OR FROZEN LOAVES, PLACE THEM IN A PREHEATED 425-DEGREE OVEN FOR 12 TO 15 MINUTES.

Ficelles ("String" Breads)

Ficelles, or "string" breads, are traditional in French cooking. My recipe includes wheat bran and coarse bulgur wheat, which give the loaves an earthy, chewy texture. As its name implies, the bread is shaped into very thin stringlike or ropelike strips. It cooks much faster in this form and has a wonderfully crunchy crust.

- 1 **cup tepid water**
- 1 **envelope (2 teaspoons) granulated yeast**
- ¼ **teaspoon sugar**
- 2½ **cups all-purpose flour** (about 13 ounces)
- ⅓ **cup wheat bran**
- 2 **tablespoons bulgur wheat** (preferably the coarse variety available in health food stores)
- ¾ **teaspoon salt**
- ½ **teaspoon canola oil**
- 2 **tablespoons coarse cornmeal**
- 2 **to 3 ice cubes**

1. Place the tepid water in the bowl of a food processor, and sprinkle the yeast and sugar over it. Mix a few seconds, just long enough to combine the ingredients, and then let the mixture sit to "proof" for 5 minutes. It should be foamy and have a yeasty smell.
2. Add the flour, bran, bulgur, and salt, and process for about 45 seconds. The mixture will form a soft ball.
3. Grease a mixing bowl with the oil, and place the ball of dough in the bowl, turning it once to coat it on both sides with the oil. Cover the bowl with plastic wrap, and let the dough rise in a warm, draft-free place for about 45 minutes, until it is puffy and about triple in size. "Break" the proofed dough by gently pulling it from the sides of the bowl and pushing it down into the center.
4. Transfer the dough to a cookie sheet, and extend it by alternately rolling and squeezing it until you form it into a cylinder about 16 inches long. Cut the cylinder lengthwise into four equal very thin strips of dough, or *ficelles*.
5. Sprinkle the cornmeal on the cookie sheet, and roll the *ficelles* in it. Then arrange them on the sheet with enough space between so they have room to rise. Cover with plastic wrap, and let rise for about 30 minutes.
6. After about 20 minutes, place a small cake pan on the bottom shelf of the oven, and preheat the oven to 425 degrees.

7. When the *ficelles* have risen, cut several gashes about ¼ inch deep in the tops of them, or snip them on top with scissors, creating a design to your liking.
8. Place the *ficelles* on the middle shelf of the oven, and throw a few ice cubes in the hot cake pan underneath to create steam (which helps make the exterior of the bread crustier). Bake for about 20 minutes, until the loaves are brown and crisp. Cool on a rack, and serve lukewarm or at room temperature.

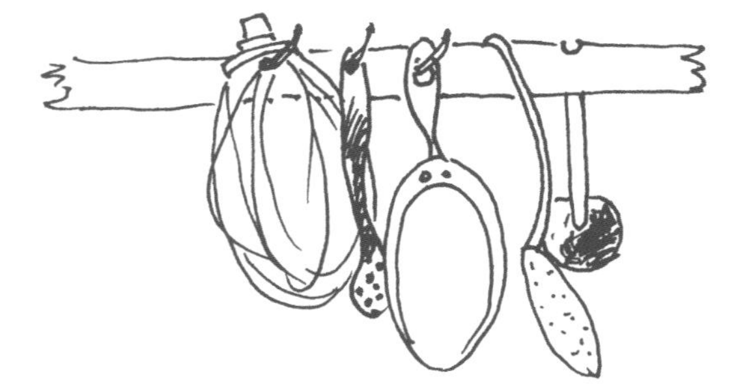

ABOUT BREAD DOUGH

DEPENDING ON WHERE IN THE COUNTRY YOU LIVE AND ON THE TEMPERATURE AND HUMIDITY WHEN YOU BAKE THE BREAD, YOU MAY NEED TO ADJUST THE QUANTITY OF YEAST. IF THE WEATHER IS PARTICULARLY HUMID, FOR EXAMPLE, ¾ ENVELOPE OF YEAST MAY BE SUFFICIENT FOR 2½ CUPS OF FLOUR. BE SURE TO DIP YOUR MEASURING CUP DIRECTLY INTO THE FLOUR AND THEN LEVEL IT OFF TO GET THE PROPER AMOUNT OF FLOUR (2½ CUPS, OR ABOUT 13 OUNCES).

YIELD: 4 SERVINGS

NUTRITIONAL ANALYSIS PER SERVING:

Calories 388
Protein 12 gm.
Carbohydrates 81 gm.
Fat 1.8 gm.
Saturated fat 0.2 gm.
Cholesterol 0 mg.
Sodium 416 mg.

Buttermilk Bread

This bread is very dense and freezes well; it will also keep a few days without freezing. Cut into very thin slices, it is ideal for breakfast with the Smoked Whitefish Molds (see page 134). It also goes well with caviar, smoked salmon, or the like.

- **1 envelope yeast**
- **½ cup tepid tap water (about 110 degrees)**
- **1 tablespoon sugar**
- **½ stick (2 ounces) unsalted butter**
- **2 cups whole wheat flour (about 10 ounces)**
- **2 cups bread flour (about 10 ounces)**
- **1 cup buttermilk, plus 1 tablespoon for brushing on the loaf before baking**
- **1 teaspoon salt**
- **½ teaspoon canola oil**

1. Place the yeast, water, and sugar in the bowl of a food processor, and allow the mixture to proof for 10 minutes. Add the butter, the whole wheat flour, the bread flour, 1 cup of the buttermilk, and the salt, and process for 1 minute. Use the oil to coat a large bowl, and place the dough in the bowl. Set aside to rise, covered, for 2 hours.
2. Punch the dough down into the bowl, and shape it into a ball about 6 inches in diameter. Place the ball of dough on a cookie sheet, and cover with the overturned proofing bowl. Allow to proof for 1 hour more.
3. Near the end of the proofing period, preheat the oven to 400 degrees.
4. Brush the proofed dough with the additional buttermilk. Using a razor blade, make a crisscross slash on the top of the round loaf. Bake at 400 degrees for 45 to 50 minutes, until the bread sounds hollow when tapped. Cool to room temperature, slice, and serve.

YIELD: 8 TO 10 SERVINGS

NUTRITIONAL ANALYSIS PER SERVING:

Calories 287
Protein 9 gm.
Carbohydrates 49 gm.
Fat 6.7 gm.
Saturated fat 3.5 gm.
Cholesterol 15 mg.
Sodium 278 mg.

Buttermilk is rich in calcium and protein and naturally low in fat.

Comments on Long-Proofed Breads

In the recipes that follow, I present five different breads made with variations on the basic dough used traditionally for standard French breads. Included are a Large Country Bread (see page 477), which contains wheat bran; a Farmer Bread (see page 478), made with both wheat bran and rye flour; a Farmer Bread with Mixed Leavening (see page 479), made with leftover dough instead of yeast; a *Gros Pain* (see page 480), which means "big bread" in French and is a version of the standard large loaves made there with plain white flour; and Long-Proofed Baguettes (see page 481), which contain wheat bran, bulgur wheat, and a limited amount of yeast, so they are proofed (allowed to rise) longer.

By definition, the longer bread is proofed, the longer it will keep. When I was a child growing up in France during the Second World War, older farmers made bread without any leavening agents at all. There are some wild yeast cells in flour, although the quantities are relatively minute: while one gram (1/28 ounce) of fresh yeast is composed of several billion live yeast cells, one pound of flour contains only about ten thousand wild yeast cells. Granted, this represents an enormous difference, but if you keep "feeding" a flour-and-water "starter" with more flour, as was done by farmers years ago, the wild yeast cells develop, multiply, and, eventually, create a dough.

Commercial yeast has been available in France since the seventeenth century and has been used by professional bakers since then. Yet some country bakers still make bread with a *levain,* using only wild yeast. When creating the recipes for this book, I found I liked the results I got when I used a minimum of packaged yeast and let the dough proof a long time. The resulting loaves have a thick, crusty exterior and will stay fresh—at least the larger loaves—for up to a week if stored in plastic bags.

For conventional French loaves, the dough is always composed of flour, water, yeast, and a little salt. In addition to these basic ingredients, to some of my doughs I have added light, healthful wheat bran, which is the covering of the wheat grain. Bulgur wheat—cooked wheat berries—also is used in one of the recipes, and rye flour appears in the two farmer breads, which are characteristically darker in France. I use granulated yeast, available in envelopes at supermarkets.

Traditionally, *boulangeries* (French bakery shops) make a "sponge" with yeast, a little flour, and some water, proof it for a few hours, and then add flour to create the final dough for the bread. This "sponge" method enables the baker to produce a great quantity of bread in a relatively small space.

PROOFING AND GLUTEN

THE QUALITY OF BREAD IS DETERMINED BY SEVERAL FACTORS, AMONG THEM THE AMOUNT OF TIME THE DOUGH IS PROOFED AND THE TEMPERATURE AT WHICH IT IS PROOFED. AFTER MIXING, BREAD DOUGH SHOULD NOT EXCEED 70 TO 75 DEGREES AND SHOULD BE PROOFED AT A ROOM TEMPERATURE OF 68 TO 70 DEGREES. THE AMOUNT OF GLUTEN (PROTEIN) IN THE FLOUR ALSO HAS A BEARING ON THE OUTCOME. IN THE RECIPES THAT FOLLOW, I USE UNBLEACHED ALL-PURPOSE FLOUR, WHICH CONTAINS BETWEEN 9 AND 12 PERCENT GLUTEN.

MIXER OR FOOD PROCESSOR

THE BREAD INGREDIENTS CAN BE COMBINED AND "KNEADED" IN A HEAVY-DUTY MIXER WITH A DOUGH HOOK, IF YOU HAVE ONE. OTHERWISE, PREPARE THE DOUGH IN A FOOD PROCESSOR, WHICH WORKS ESPECIALLY WELL IF YOURS, LIKE MINE, HAS VARIABLE SPEEDS, BUT WILL DO AN ADEQUATE JOB EVEN IF IT DOESN'T. THE FOOD PROCESSOR I USE IS A LARGE ONE; IF YOURS IS SMALL, DIVIDE THE INGREDIENTS IN HALF, AND MIX THE BREAD IN TWO BATCHES.

Here, I use the direct method—mixing everything together at once—because the goal is to create a single batch of bread. For one of the loaves, the Farmer Bread with Mixed Leavening (see page 479), I use a piece of dough reserved from a batch of bread made previously. The reserved dough, which will keep for 4 to 5 days in the refrigerator, serves as a leavening agent in this recipe, eliminating the need for any yeast if the dough is proofed, as it is here, for a long time—as long as 24 hours.

The remaining recipes, containing granulated yeast, are proofed for at least 4 hours, although they can proof longer, as the Farmer Bread does (see page 478). It works very well to let the dough proof slowly at room temperature overnight, then shape it in the morning, and let it rise an additional 1½ hours before baking it. It takes 1½ hours to bake the large single loaves at a high temperature. For best results, let the large loaves rest for at least 3 hours before slicing them.

Although the bread dough can be proofed in any large, deep container, I use large plastic buckets with lids that I obtained from my fishmonger. These are large enough so I can shape a loaf in the bucket, place the loaf on a tray for final proofing, and invert the bucket over it to serve as a kind of "hothouse" in which the dough proofs.

I like to line the cookie sheets or baking trays with parchment paper and then sprinkle them with a little semolina, farina, oatmeal, or cornmeal to add a light coating to the bottom of the bread. The advantages of the paper are that it keeps the pans clean and provides a surface from which the baked bread slides off easily. In addition, if you bake bread on a bread or pizza stone (which I often do since I have a stone on a rack in my oven at home), you can slide the paper with the proofed loaf directly onto the stone for baking.

Professional ovens used for bread baking have the capacity to inject steam as the bread bakes. This helps proof the bread, enabling it to "push up" in a sense at the beginning and cook quickly. I attempt to duplicate these conditions and create the same effect by throwing a little water on the floor of my oven at the beginning of the cooking process.

At first I cook the bread at a very high temperature; then I reduce the temperature in most instances and continue cooking the loaves for a long time. When properly cooked, bread reaches an internal temperature of approximately 210 degrees.

It's fun to make homemade bread. Delicious as is for the first few days after baking, it makes great toast when it begins to dry out a little.

Large Country Bread

(See photograph, page 241.)

- **4½ cups unbleached all-purpose flour (1½ pounds), plus 2 tablespoons for sprinkling on the work surface and the loaves**
- **½ cup wheat bran (½ ounce)**
- **1½ teaspoons granulated yeast**
- **2 teaspoons salt**
- **2 cups cool bottled water or spring water (approximately 70 degrees)**
- **1 tablespoon yellow cornmeal**
- **1 tablespoon tap water**

1. Place the 4½ cups flour, the wheat bran, yeast, salt, and the bottled water in a mixer or food processor bowl fitted with a blade. Mix at low speed for about 45 seconds; the dough should be satiny and elastic and no warmer than about 75 degrees. (It will weigh about 2 pounds 10 ounces.)
2. Place the dough in a plastic bucket, cover it, and set it aside to proof at room temperature (68 to 70 degrees) for 4 hours.
3. After rising for 4 hours, the dough should have tripled in volume. Break it down by bringing its outer edges into the center of the bowl and pressing down on the dough to release the air inside. Cover the dough again, and allow it to proof for another 2 hours. Then break it down again the same way.
4. Sprinkle 1 tablespoon of the remaining flour on your work surface. Place the dough on the floured surface, and form it into a large ball, stretching and tucking the sides underneath, to make the top smooth and taut. Press on the top of the ball lightly with the palm of one hand to push the air out.
5. Line a large cookie sheet with parchment paper, sprinkle it with the cornmeal, and place the ball of dough seam side down on the sheet. Cover it with the inverted bucket, and let it proof at room temperature for 1¼ to 1½ hours.
6. After 1 to 1¼ hours, preheat the oven to 425 degrees.
7. Sprinkle the top of the proofed loaf with the remaining tablespoon of flour, and cut several slits across the top of the loaf with a serrated knife. Place the loaf in the oven and throw the 1 tablespoon of tap water on the floor of the oven (to create steam) immediately before closing the door. Bake for 15 minutes, then reduce the oven heat to 400 degrees, and cook the loaf for 1 hour longer, until it is nicely browned and makes a hollow sound when you tap it.
8. Cool the loaf on a rack at room temperature for about 3 hours before cutting it into slices for serving. Wrapped in plastic wrap, the bread will keep for 4 to 5 days. It can also be frozen.

YIELD:
1 LOAF
(ABOUT
2 POUNDS
BAKED)

NUTRITIONAL ANALYSIS PER LOAF:

Calories 2,616
Protein 77 gm.
Carbohydrates 550 gm.
Fat 7.8 gm.
Saturated fat 1.2 gm.
Cholesterol 0 mg.
Sodium 4,419 mg.

Wheat bran provides additional fiber, magnesium, and zinc.

Farmer Bread

(See photograph, page 241.)

- 4 cups unbleached all-purpose flour (1 pound, 5 ounces), plus 1 teaspoon for sprinkling on the loaves
- ½ cup rye flour (about 3 ounces)
- ½ cup wheat bran (½ ounce)
- 2½ teaspoons salt
- 1 teaspoon granulated yeast
- 2⅓ cups cool tap water or bottled water (approximately 70 degrees), plus 1 tablespoon to throw on the oven floor
- 2 tablespoons cornmeal

1. Place the 4 cups unbleached flour, the rye flour, bran, salt, yeast, and 2⅓ cups water in a mixer bowl, and mix at low speed for 3 to 4 minutes to create a smooth dough. Alternatively, place the ingredients in the bowl of a food processor, and process for about 45 seconds. (The dough will weigh about 2 pounds 10 ounces.)
2. Transfer the dough to a deep glass or ceramic bowl or a plastic bucket, cover tightly with a lid or plastic wrap, and let rise at room temperature (about 65 degrees) overnight (12 to 14 hours).
3. Bring the sides of the risen dough into the center of the bowl, folding it in on itself, and press down on the dough to release the air inside. Form the dough into a ball. Line a cookie sheet with parchment paper, sprinkle it with the cornmeal, and place the ball of dough seam side down in the center. Invert the bowl or bucket over the dough. (The bowl or bucket should be deep and wide enough so that the dough does not touch and stick to it as it rises.) Let the dough rise at room temperature for 1½ hours.
4. Near the end of the proofing period, preheat the oven to 425 degrees.
5. Sprinkle the risen loaf with the teaspoon of flour and, using a serrated knife, cut several decorative slits across the top of the loaf. Place the loaf in the oven, and throw the 1 tablespoon of water on the floor of the oven (to create steam) immediately before closing the door. Bake the loaf for 15 minutes, then reduce the heat to 400 degrees, and cook the loaf for 1 hour longer.
6. Remove the bread from the cookie sheet, place it on a wire rack, and cool it at room temperature for about 3 hours before cutting it into slices for serving. Wrapped in plastic wrap, the bread will keep for 4 to 5 days. It can also be frozen.

Yield: 1 Large Loaf (About 2 Pounds Baked)

NUTRITIONAL ANALYSIS PER LOAF:

Calories 2,615
Protein 77 gm.
Carbohydrates 556 gm.
Fat 9.1 gm.
Saturated fat 1.4 gm.
Cholesterol 0 mg.
Sodium 5,513 mg.

Farmer Bread with Mixed Leavening

(See photograph, page 241.)

- **10 ounces leftover dough from a previous batch of bread (see Comments on Long-Proofed Breads, page 475)**
- **4½ cups unbleached all-purpose flour (1½ pounds), plus 1 teaspoon for sprinkling on the loaf**
- **1 cup wheat bran (1 ounce)**
- **½ cup rye flour (about 3 ounces)**
- **2½ teaspoons salt**
- **2 cups cool water (approximately 70 degrees), plus 2 tablespoons to throw on the oven floor**
- **2 tablespoons oatmeal flakes or cornmeal**

1. Mix the leftover dough, 4½ cups flour, wheat bran, rye flour, salt, and 2 cups cool water at low speed in a mixer fitted with a bread hook for 4 to 5 minutes. Alternatively, place the ingredients in the bowl of a large food processor, and process them at low to medium speed (if your processor has variable speeds) for 45 seconds. (The dough will weigh about 3 pounds 5 ounces.)
2. Transfer the dough to a plastic bucket, cover it with the lid, and proof it at room temperature (65 to 70 degrees) for at least 12 hours and as long as 24 hours (remember, there is no yeast in the recipe).
3. Break down the risen dough by bringing its outer edges into the center of the bowl and pressing down on the dough to release the air inside. Form the dough into a large round or oval loaf, tucking the sides underneath and seaming them so the loaf is smooth and taut on top.
4. Sprinkle the oatmeal evenly in the center of a cookie sheet, and place the bread loaf seam side down in the middle of the sheet. Invert the plastic bucket over the loaf, and let it rise at room temperature for 2 hours.
5. After about 1¾ hours, preheat the oven to 425 degrees.
6. Sprinkle the proofed loaf with the remaining teaspoon of flour, and cut several decorative slits across the top of the loaf with a serrated knife or razor blade.
7. Place the loaf in the oven, and throw 1 tablespoon of water on the floor of the oven (to create steam) immediately before closing the door. Bake the bread for 5 minutes, then throw another tablespoon of water on the floor of the oven, and bake for 15 minutes longer. Reduce the oven temperature to 400 degrees, and continue baking the loaf for 1 hour, until it is brown and sounds hollow when tapped.
8. Cool the bread on a rack for at least 3 hours before cutting it into slices and serving. The loaf will keep for at least 5 days if wrapped tightly in a cloth bag (an old pillow case, perhaps) or longer if enclosed in a plastic bag. It can also be frozen.

Yield: 1 Large Loaf (About 2½ Pounds Baked)

Nutritional Analysis per Loaf:

Calories 3,517
Protein 103 gm.
Carbohydrates 745 gm.
Fat 11.9 gm.
Saturated fat 1.8 gm.
Cholesterol 0 mg.
Sodium 6,573 mg.

Rye flour contains more protein, phosphorus, iron, and potassium than whole wheat flour.

Gros Pain

(See photograph, page 241.)

4½ **cups unbleached all-purpose flour (1½ pounds), plus 3 tablespoons for kneading purposes and for sprinkling on the loaves**
2½ **teaspoons salt**
1 **envelope granulated yeast (about 2 teaspoons)**
2 **cups cool water (approximately 70 degrees), plus 2 tablespoons to throw on the oven floor**
1 **tablespoon cornmeal or farina**

1. Place the 4½ cups flour, salt, yeast, and 2 cups water in the bowl of a large food processor. Process the mixture for about 45 seconds on low speed if your processor has variable speeds, or about 30 seconds if your processor has only one speed. (The temperature of the dough should not exceed 75 degrees.) (The dough will weigh about 2½ pounds.)
2. Transfer the dough to a large, deep ceramic or stainless steel bowl or a plastic bucket (preferable), cover tightly with a lid or plastic wrap, and set aside to rise at room temperature (65 to 70 degrees) for 5 hours.
3. Break down the dough by bringing its outer edges into the center of the bowl and pressing down to release the air inside. Then lift the dough from the bucket with one hand, and sprinkle 2 tablespoons of the flour into the bucket with the other. Return the ball of dough to the bucket, and knead it until the flour is incorporated and the dough has elasticity, about 1 minute. Form the dough into a ball, stretching and seaming it underneath so it is nicely rounded and taut on top.
4. Line a large cookie sheet with parchment paper, and sprinkle the cornmeal on top. Place the dough seam side down on the sheet, and cover it with the overturned bowl or bucket. Set the loaf aside to rise at room temperature for 2 hours.
5. After about 1¾ hours, preheat the oven to 425 degrees.
6. Sprinkle the top of the proofed loaf with the remaining tablespoon of flour, and cut several slits across the top of the loaf with a serrated knife. Place the loaf in the oven, and throw 1 tablespoon of water on the floor of the oven (to create steam) immediately before closing the door. After 5 minutes, throw another tablespoon of water on the oven floor. Bake the loaf for 15 minutes more at 425 degrees, then reduce the oven temperature to 400 degrees, and bake for 1 hour longer.
7. Cool the bread on a rack for at least 3 hours, then slice and serve it.

YIELD: 1 LARGE LOAF (ABOUT 2 POUNDS BAKED)

NUTRITIONAL ANALYSIS PER LOAF:

Calories 2,616
Protein 76 gm.
Carbohydrates 547 gm.
Fat 7.2 gm.
Saturated fat 1.1 gm.
Cholesterol 0 mg.
Sodium 5,513 mg.

Long-Proofed Baguettes

(See photograph, page 241.)

- **4½ cups unbleached all-purpose flour (1½ pounds), plus 2½ tablespoons for sprinkling on the work surface and the loaves**
- **½ cup wheat bran (½ ounce)**
- **½ cup bulgur wheat (2½ ounces)**
- **2 teaspoons granulated yeast**
- **2½ teaspoons salt**
- **2¼ cups cool water (approximately 70 degrees), plus 1 tablespoon to throw on the oven floor**
- **2 tablespoons cornmeal**

1. Place the 4½ cups of flour, wheat bran, bulgur wheat, yeast, salt, and 2¼ cups water in a mixer bowl, and mix with a bread hook at low speed for 3 to 5 minutes. Alternatively, place the ingredients in the bowl of a large food processor, and process at medium speed (if your processor has variable speeds) for 45 seconds. (The dough will weigh about 2 pounds 12 ounces.)
2. Transfer the dough to a large, deep ceramic or stainless steel bowl or a plastic bucket, cover, and let rise at room temperature (65 to 70 degrees) for at least 4½ hours.
3. Break down the dough by bringing its outer edges into the center of the bowl and pressing down to release the air inside. Form the dough into a ball. Sprinkle your work surface with 2 tablespoons of the remaining flour, place the ball of dough on top, and press down to form it into a rough rectangular shape. Cut the rectangle lengthwise into 4 equal strips, and roll each strip into an 18-inch length.
4. Sprinkle four metal baguette molds with the cornmeal, dividing it as evenly as possible among the molds, and place a dough strip in each mold. Cover the molds with plastic wrap, and let the bread rise for 1 hour at room temperature.
5. After about 50 minutes, preheat the oven to 425 degrees.
6. Sprinkle the tops of the risen loaves with the remaining ½ tablespoon of flour, and cut four diagonal slits on the top surface of each loaf with a serrated knife or razor blade.
7. Arrange the molds on a cookie sheet or tray, place them in the oven, and throw 1 tablespoon of water on the floor of the oven (to create steam) immediately before closing the door. Bake the baguettes for 35 minutes.
8. Remove the baguettes from the molds, and cool them on a rack for at least 45 minutes before slicing and serving. Wrapped in plastic wrap, the loaves will keep for about 48 hours.

BROWN-AND-SERVE TECHNIQUE

You can partially bake baguettes for about 25 minutes, until they have achieved maximum size but are not yet brown. Let the loaves cool until lukewarm, wrap tightly, and freeze. When needed, unwrap the frozen bread, and bake it on the center rack of a preheated 400-degree oven for 15 minutes, until brown and crusty.

Yield: 4 Baguettes (About 8 Ounces Each Baked)

Nutritional Analysis per Baguette:

Calories 727
Protein 22 gm.
Carbohydrates 153 gm.
Fat 2.2 gm.
Saturated fat 0.3 gm.
Cholesterol 0 mg.
Sodium 1,382 mg.

Bulgur wheat is high in magnesium and fiber.

HEALTH NOTES

of these dishes are: Breast of Veal *Cocotte* (page 274), Fillet of Pork *Charcutière* (page 247), *Garbure* Soup Farmer-Style (page 240), and Chicken *Ballottine* Stuffed with Red Rice (page 224).

I have suggested several dessert recipes that are quite low in calories, too. While a typical portion of dessert often contains as many as 500 calories per serving, the following desserts are much lighter and contain under 140 calories: Meringue Chocolate Mousse (page 442), Grapefruit in Nectar (page 398), Raspberry Velvet (page 422), and Russian Cranberry *Kissel* (page 372).

On special occasions, we tend to consume a few more calories than we would during the rest of the year. I have suggested a holiday menu (page 10) that is delicious but contains approximately half the calories of a typical feast. It features Sautéed Scallops with Snow Peas (page 151), Roasted Turkey with Mushroom Stuffing (page 228), Puree of Carrot and Ginger (page 307), Chocolate Mint Truffles (page 438), and Candied Orange Rind (page 450).

Cholesterol

The American Heart Association recommends that we consume no more than 300 mg. of cholesterol per day. In most instances, I use oils instead of butter to cut down on cholesterol. In addition, my recipes minimize the number of egg yolks per serving, since yolks are high in cholesterol.

Fats and Low-Fat Alternatives

Experts believe that a healthy diet is one in which no more than 30 percent of the daily calories consumed are derived from the intake of fat. To achieve this percentage, I sometimes substitute low-fat alternatives in my recipes. For example, I may use nonfat or low-fat yogurt instead of sour cream.

Some fats have proved beneficial to health. Salmon, although it is a fatty fish, contains what are now described by experts as "heart-healthy fats" or omega-3 fatty acids. These omega-3s help keep blood from getting "sticky" and forming clots that lead to heart attacks. Eating fatty fishes has also been correlated with lower blood levels of certain fats called triglycerides. Because of these benefits, health experts are urging us to eat more fish, up to 15 pounds per year. Fish is featured prominently in many of my menus.

Oils

Today's supermarket offers a vast selection of oils. It is important to understand the nature of oils to know which one to choose. For instance, some oils are lower in saturated fat than others, some are more strongly flavored, and some may burn at a relatively low temperature, giving off bad odors and flavor.

At room temperature, all oils are liquid fat. Some oils, such as palm and coconut oil, are very high in saturated fat and therefore can boost the level of blood cholesterol. In much of my cooking, I use the oil that is lowest in saturated fat—canola oil.

Virgin olive oil is usually dark, with a rich olive flavor. The color and flavor are the result of olive solids present in the oil. Virgin olive oil is so named because it has been removed from the olives by mechanical pressing, from the sheer weight of the olives. No heat or chemical processes are used to extract this oil. The olive solids, which impart flavor and color, burn at fairly low temperatures, so virgin olive oil is best used for salads and marinades.

The best oils to use in sautéing are flavorless safflower and canola oils, or, for mild flavor, peanut oil. They are ideal for sautéing because they can withstand high temperatures without burning.

Sugars

It is important to use moderation when consuming refined sugar. Refined sugar can lead to tooth decay and, when combined with fat, can be tremendously caloric. But who can resist sweet treats on special occasions? For this reason, I have included recipes for White Peach and Walnut Tart (page 364), Ice-Cream Phyllo Napoleons (page 449), Farina Bavarian Cream Cake with Apricot Sauce (page 433), and Chocolate and Fruit Nut Cups (page 437). A small bit of a rich dessert can help you to feel satisfied without overdoing it.

Salt

I have some special tips for cutting down on salt. Because I like highly seasoned foods, I use a variety of seasonings as salt substitutes. Plenty of fresh herbs and strong-flavored spices are excellent substitutes.

The key to reducing the amount of salt used in cooking is to bring out the natural flavor in the food itself. For example, if you crystallize the juices on the outside of meat by browning it well first, as I do in my Fricassee of Veal recipe (page 265), you can bring up the flavor without adding an excess of salt. Another way to enhance flavor, featured in my Osso Buco (page 272), is to use citrus fruit, such as lemon or orange, or the numerous fresh herbs and spices available today. And don't forget about flavor-enhancing cooking techniques such as grilling, steaming, and broiling.

Vegetables

Vegetables are the most important kind of food to emphasize in our diets. They are naturally low in calories and high in fiber, vitamins, and minerals.

Producer's Acknowledgments

The seventy-eight programs of *Today's Gourmet* are the public evidence of a personally rewarding collaboration with Jacques Pépin, one that started (in a manner that I now see as typical of Jacques's flair for teaching) on the very first day we met at his home in Connecticut in 1990. It was a humid summer morning, and after a few hours of brainstorming about our new series, we adjourned to the kitchen while he made a quick lunch. Good manners suggested I ought to help . . . while common sense told me, who was I kidding? I feebly offered my assistance, and Jacques tossed me a few peaches to peel for dessert. While I'm a passable cook, manual dexterity is my downfall. After watching me mangle one too many beautiful summer peaches, Jacques patiently demonstrated to me the proper technique for holding the knife and turning the fruit (even adopting my left-handed approach). Something clicked—and suddenly I knew what *Today's Gourmet* was going to be.

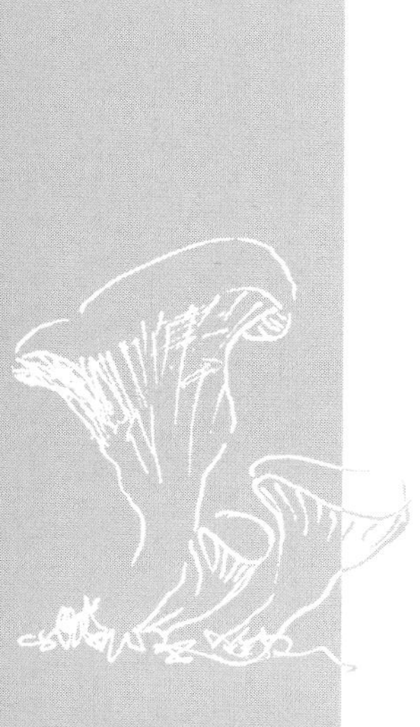

That was the first of my many cooking lessons from Jacques, most of them learned just as his viewers and readers have learned, by watching and listening to his clear approach, not only to food but also to a philosophy of simple, joyful living. In return, I am happy to have given Jacques a home-away-from-home at KQED in San Francisco, as well as a platform for sharing his ideas with the public. It is an effort participated in by many—too many to list entirely—but I would like to acknowledge some key contributors now:

Our funders: Sun-Maid Raisins, Wish-Bone Dressings, Blue Ribbon Figs, Braun Inc., Cambria Winery & Vineyard, and Russell Range, Inc., whose sponsorship over the years has been the *sine qua non* of our series.

Peggy Lee Scott, producer of our second and third seasons; Katherine Russell, our director for the whole series; talented associate producers Linda Brandt, Susie Heller, June Ouellette, and Tina Salter, who are the organizational geniuses in the studio; the kitchen staffs who work tirelessly, headed by Carl Abbott and Dan Bowe; Marjorie Poore, who got it all started at KQED; Joanne Sutro, whose marketing efforts have sustained the series; the design and styling achievements of Bernie Schimbke, Ron Haake, Greg King, Ken Short, Merilee Hague, and Heidi Gintner; Jolee Hoyt, Greg Swartz, and Larry Reid, who always make the production smooth; Gloria and Claudine Pépin for their patience and understanding; Norma Galehouse, Jacques's indispensable assistant, for her always clear thinking; and the creative crew at KQED who shoot, record, and edit our work. To all, many thanks.

—Peter L. Stein, *Executive Producer*

Production of the public television series *Today's Gourmet with Jacques Pépin* is made possible by generous grants from

BLUE RIBBON FIGS

BRAUN INC.

CAMBRIA WINERY & VINEYARD

RUSSELL RANGE, INC.

SUN-MAID RAISINS

WISH-BONE DRESSINGS

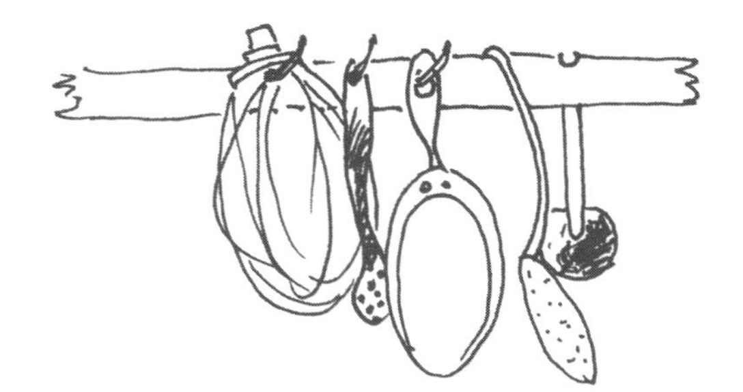

Today's Gourmet with Jacques Pépin thanks the following companies for their generous support of the three seasons' programs.

WINES PROVIDED BY:
Associated Wine Distributors
Boisset Wines USA
Bordeaux Wine Bureau
Buena Vista Winery
Cliquot, Inc.
Dreyfus-Ashby & Co.
Fetzer Vineyards
The Hess Collection
Kendall-Jackson Winery
Kermit Lynch Wine Merchant
Kobrand Corporation
Merryvale Vineyards
Le Monjea Distingué Wine Importers
Murphy-Goode Estate Winery
Paterno Imports
Platinum Sales Promotion
Seagram Chateau & Estate Wines Company
Seagram Classic Wine Company
Shaw-Ross International Importers
William Grant & Sons, Inc.
Val d'Orbieu Wines

FOOD PROVIDED BY:
Allied SYSCO
BiRite Foodservice Distributors
California Crayfish, Inc.
East Coast Exotics, Inc.
Greenleaf Produce
Marin County Farmers' Market
Modesto Food Distributors
C. J. Olson Cherries
Rapelli of California
United Meat Company, Inc.

SPECIAL THANKS TO:
Campton Place Hotel, Kempinski San Francisco
Ritz-Carlton, San Francisco
Levi Strauss & Co.
All-Clad Metalcrafters
Ames Gallery
Angray Flowers
Berkeley Farmers' Market
Bernardaud
Biordi Art Imports
Bourgeat USA
Champagne Wines Information Bureau
Chantal Cookware
Chantry/Charlotte Clark Ltd.
Chappellet Vineyard
Chef'sChoice® by EdgeCraft
Corning, Inc.
Cost Plus, Inc.
Crate & Barrel
Le Creuset of America
Cuisinart Corp.
JB Cumberland & Associates
Dacor Ovens
Dandelion
Domestications Catalog
Dvorson's Food Service Equipment Co.
(Distributors of Wolf Ranges)
Farberware, Inc.
Forrest Jones, Inc.
General Electric Appliances
George V Collection
Hartford Court Winery
Harvey Antiques
Isgro & Co.
Iwatani International Corp.
Krups North America
Macy's California
Nicolazzo & Associates
Norton Company
Oscartielle Equipment, California
Pak-Sher Quicksheets
La Parisienne Posters
Peoples Woods
Pier 1 Imports
Pierre Deux
D. Porthault & Co.
Pottery Barn
Rent-A-Computer, San Francisco/Santa Clara
Republic Uniform Sales
Rowoco
Safeway, Inc.
Saint-Louis Cristal—Hermès Art de la Table
Sakura, Inc.
Signature China
Terra Firma Farms
Thermador
Trade Associates Group Ltd.
Westside Farms
Williams-Sonoma
Wüsthof-Trident
Zen Center at Green Gulch

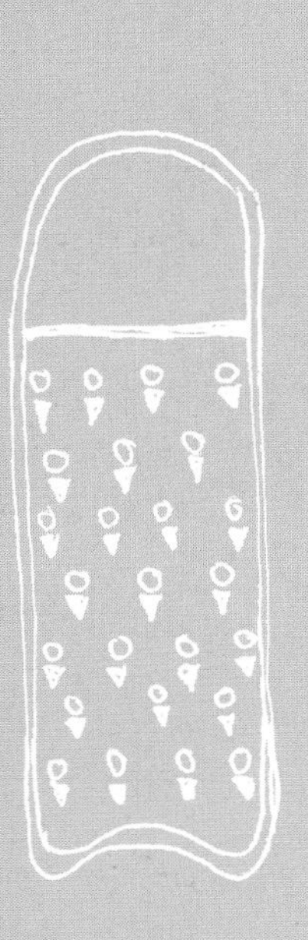

Index

Numbers in *italic* indicate photographs,
and those in **boldface** indicate the menu that includes the dish.

Numbers in *italic* indicate photographs,
and those in **boldface** indicate the menu that includes the dish.

Numbers in *italic* indicate photographs,
and those in **boldface** indicate the menu that includes the dish.

Numbers in *italic* indicate photographs,
and those in **boldface** indicate the menu that includes the dish.

Numbers in *italic* indicate photographs,
and those in **boldface** indicate the menu that includes the dish.

Numbers in *italic* indicate photographs,
and those in **boldface** indicate the menu that includes the dish.

Numbers in *italic* indicate photographs,
and those in **boldface** indicate the menu that includes the dish.

Numbers in *italic* indicate photographs,
and those in **boldface** indicate the menu that includes the dish.

Numbers in *italic* indicate photographs,
and those in **boldface** indicate the menu that includes the dish.

Numbers in *italic* indicate photographs,
and those in **boldface** indicate the menu that includes the dish.

Numbers in *italic* indicate photographs,
and those in **boldface** indicate the menu that includes the dish.

Numbers in *italic* indicate photographs,
and those in **boldface** indicate the menu that includes the dish.

Numbers in *italic* indicate photographs,
and those in **boldface** indicate the menu that includes the dish.

Numbers in *italic* indicate photographs,
and those in **boldface** indicate the menu that includes the dish.

Numbers in *italic* indicate photographs,
and those in **boldface** indicate the menu that includes the dish.

Numbers in *italic* indicate photographs,
and those in **boldface** indicate the menu that includes the dish.

Numbers in *italic* indicate photographs,
and those in **boldface** indicate the menu that includes the dish.

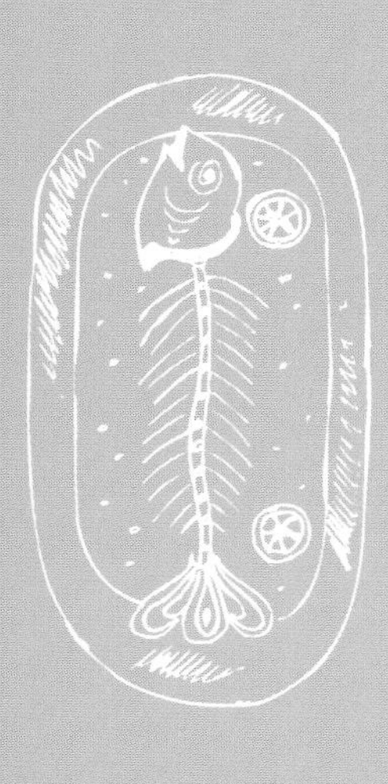

Numbers in *italic* indicate photographs,
and those in **boldface** indicate the menu that includes the dish.

Numbers in *italic* indicate photographs,
and those in **boldface** indicate the menu that includes the dish.

Numbers in *italic* indicate photographs,
and those in **boldface** indicate the menu that includes the dish.

Numbers in *italic* indicate photographs,
and those in **boldface** indicate the menu that includes the dish.

Numbers in *italic* indicate photographs,
and those in **boldface** indicate the menu that includes the dish.

Y

Z

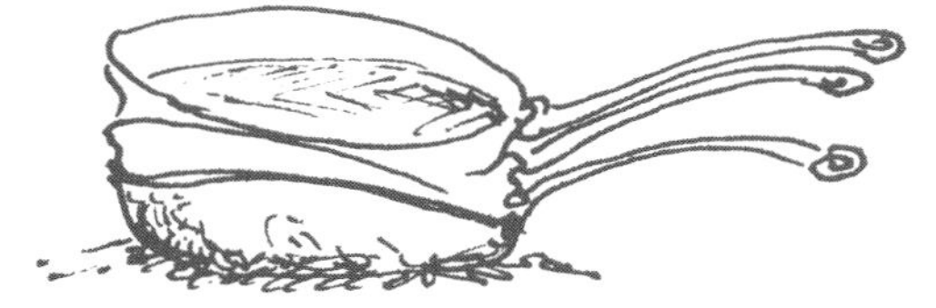

Numbers in *italic* indicate photographs,
and those in **boldface** indicate the menu that includes the dish.

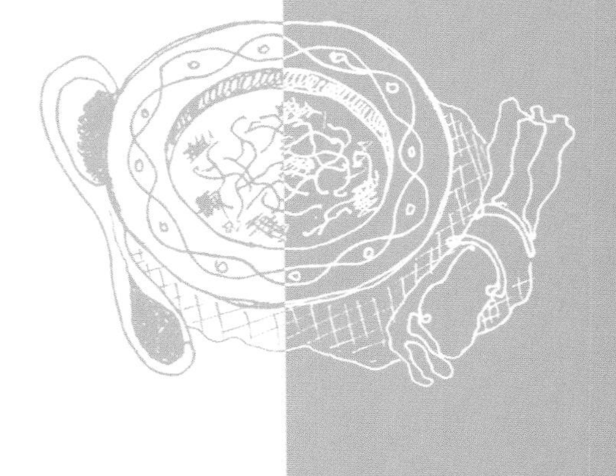

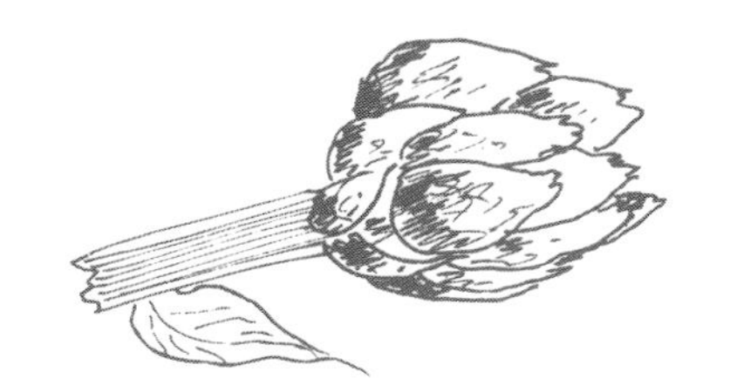